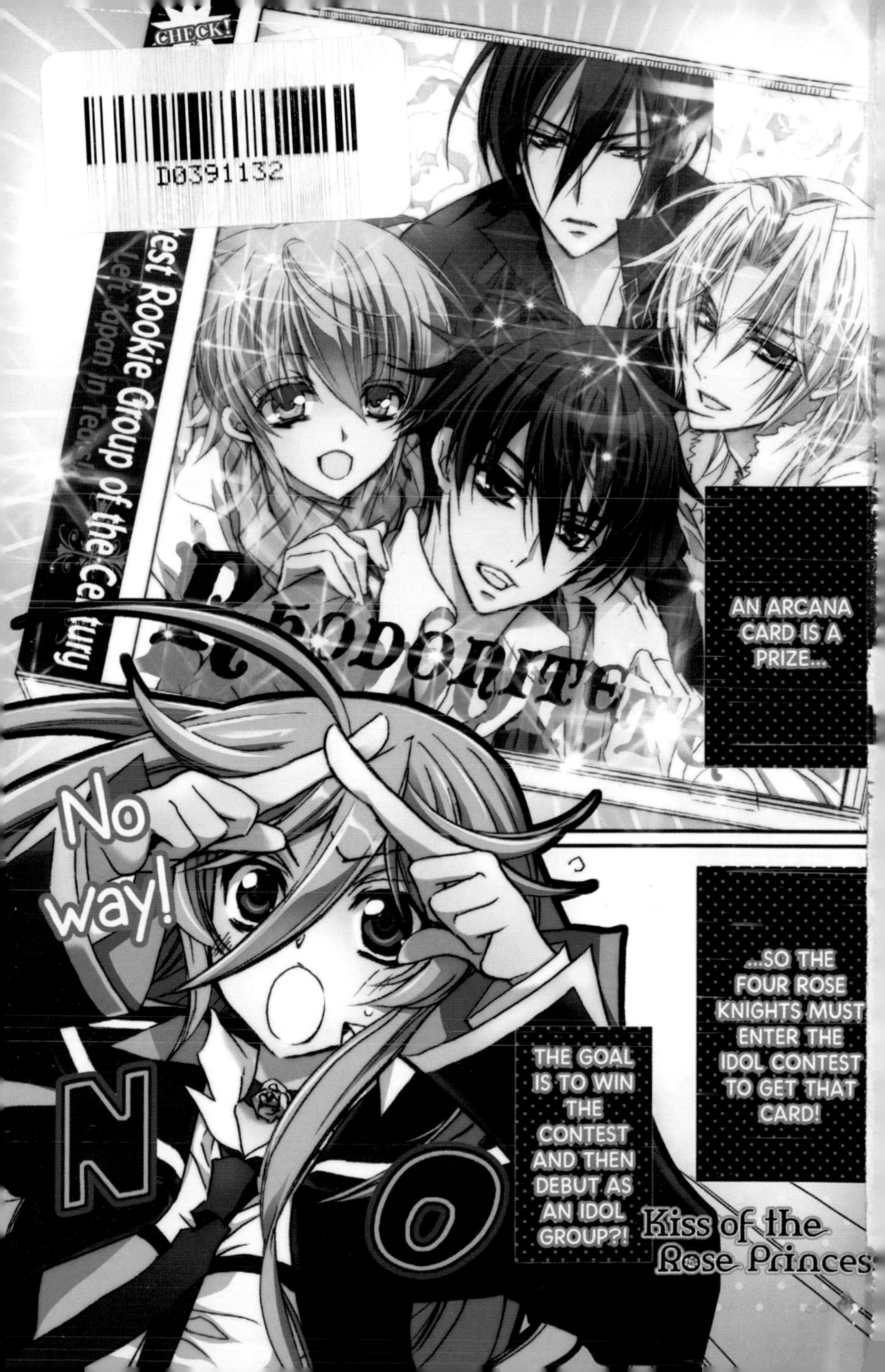
CHECK!
test Rookie Group of the Century
AN ARCANA CARD IS A PRIZE...
...SO THE FOUR ROSE KNIGHTS MUST ENTER THE IDOL CONTEST TO GET THAT CARD!
THE GOAL IS TO WIN THE CONTEST AND THEN DEBUT AS AN IDOL GROUP?!
No way!
NO
Kiss of the Rose Princess

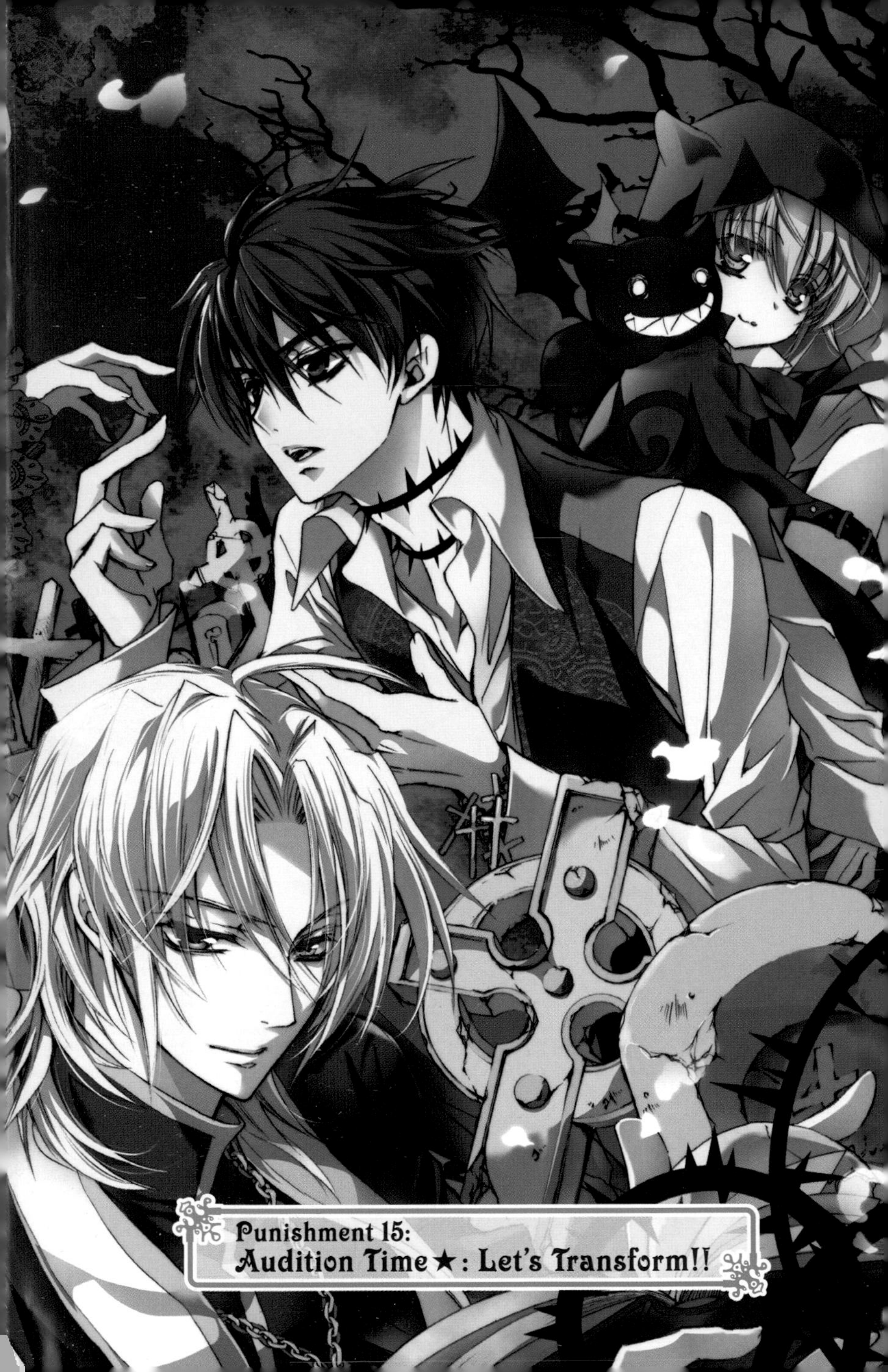
Punishment 15:
Audition Time★: Let's Transform!!

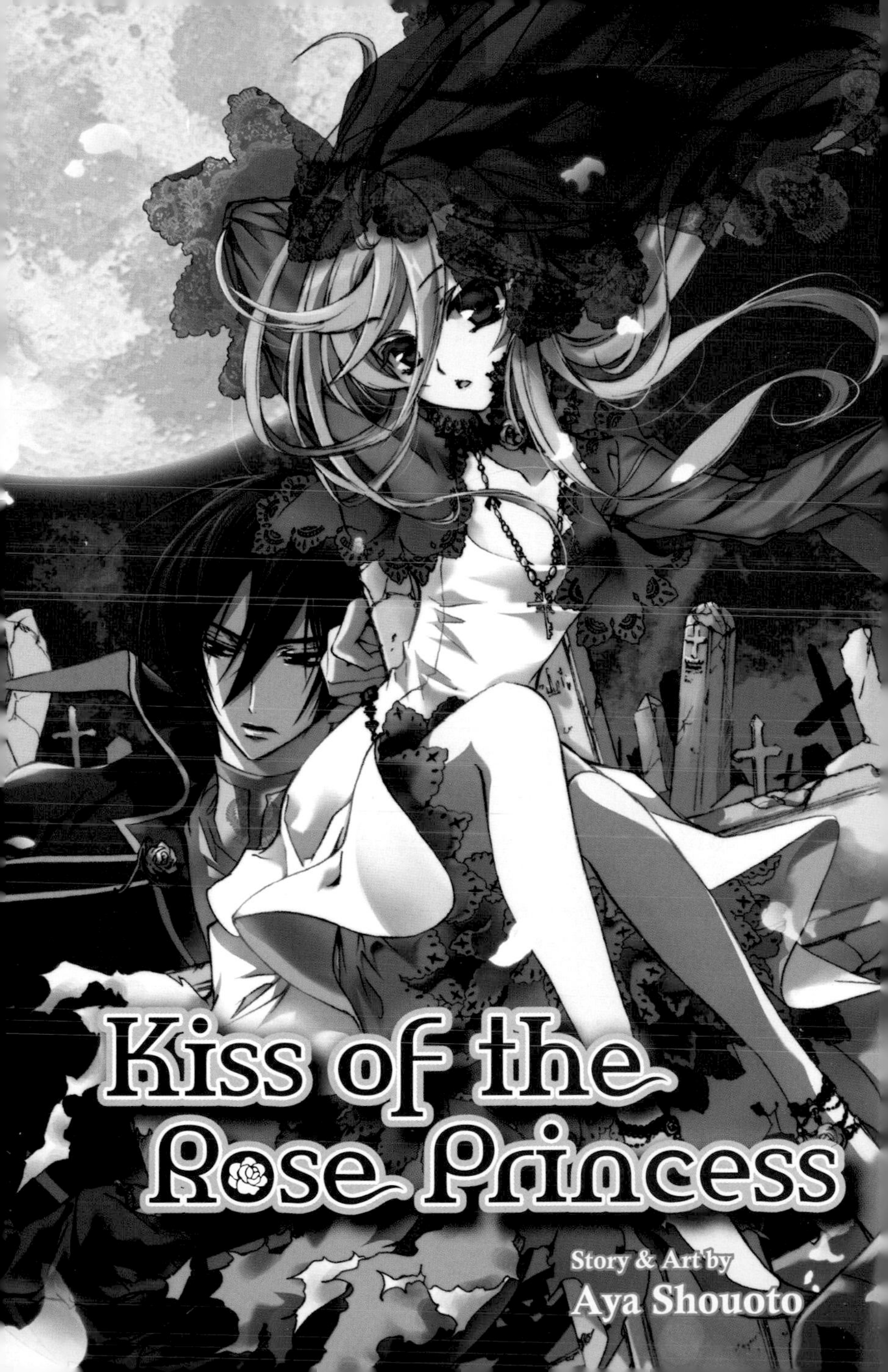
Kiss of the Rose Princess
Story & Art by
Aya Shouoto

Kiss of the Rose Princess

Contents

Characters

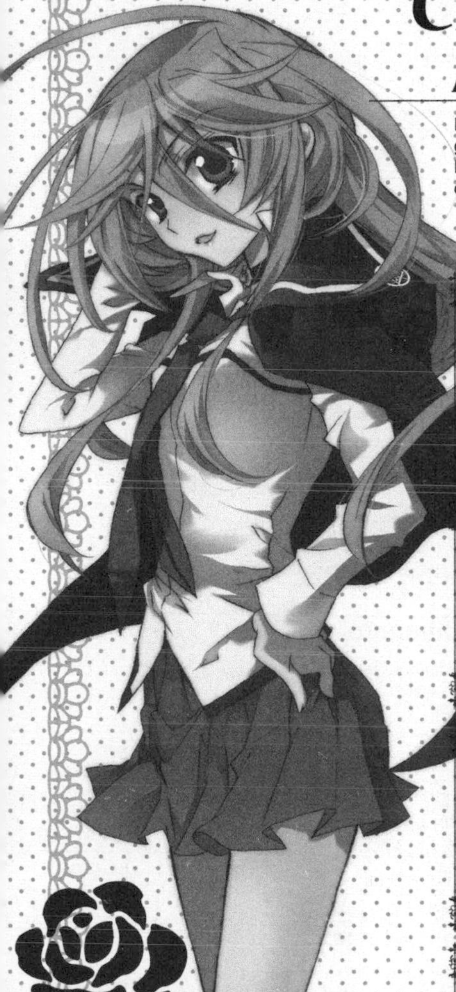

Anise Yamamoto

First-year at Shobi Academy. She's a strong-willed girl who dreams of one day finding and dating her Prince Charming.♥ She dislikes being the center of attention.

Rose Knights

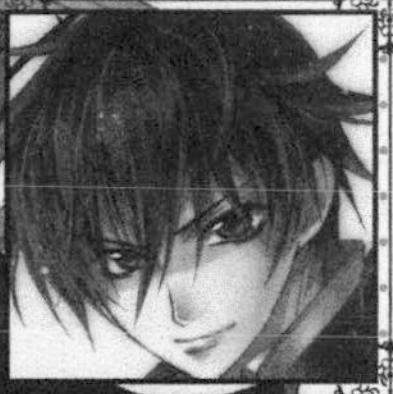

Kaede Higa (Red Rose)

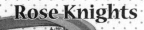

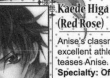

Anise's classmate. He's an excellent athlete who often teases Anise.
Specialty: Offence

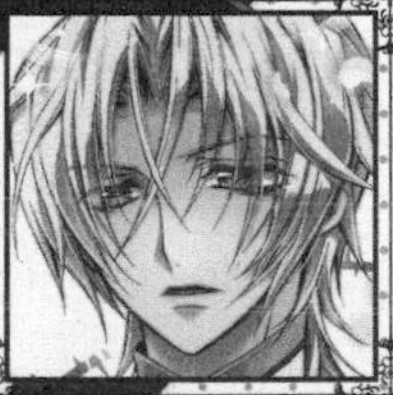

Mitsuru Tenjo (White Rose)

Third-year and Student Council President. He is revered by both male and female students. Super-rich.
Specialty: Healing, Defense

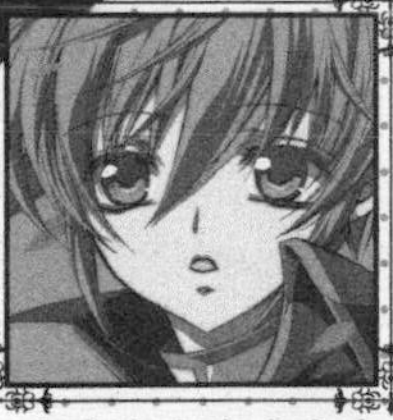

Seiran Asagi (Blue Rose)

First-year. This boy is cuter than any girl at school, and he doesn't know he's the school idol. He's well-versed in a wide range of topics.
Specialty: Alchemy, Science

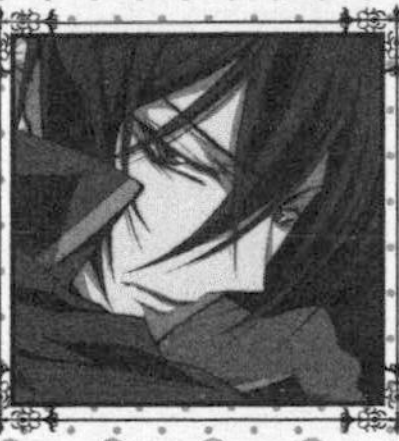

Mutsuki Kurama (Black Rose)

Second-year. There are many frightening rumors about this mysterious student. Apparently he lives in the basement of Tenjo's house.
Specialty: Discovery, Capture

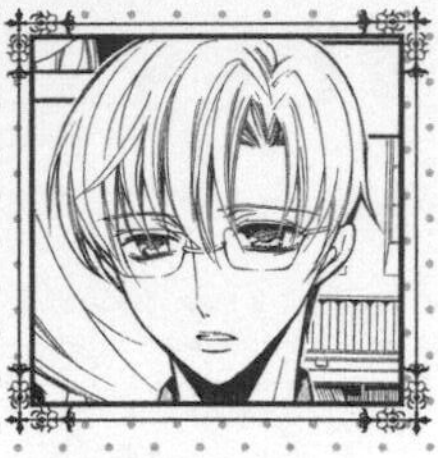

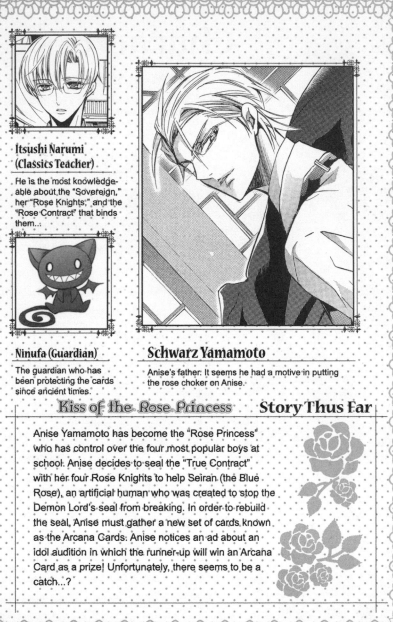

Itsushi Narumi (Classics Teacher)

He is the most knowledgeable about the "Sovereign," her "Rose Knights," and the "Rose Contract" that binds them...

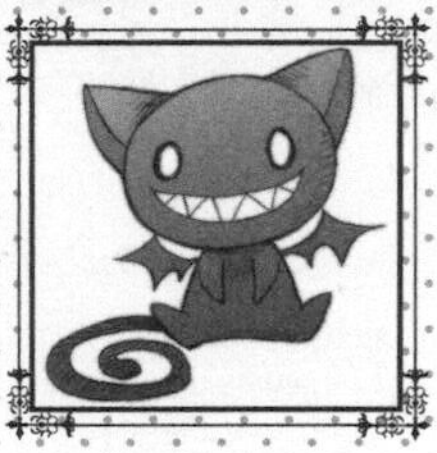

Ninufa (Guardian)

The guardian who has been protecting the cards since ancient times.

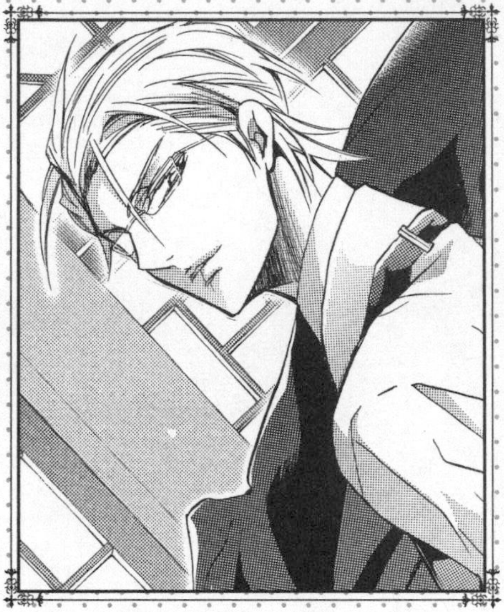

Schwarz Yamamoto

Anise's father. It seems he had a motive in putting the rose choker on Anise.

Kiss of the Rose Princess Story Thus Far

Anise Yamamoto has become the "Rose Princess" who has control over the four most popular boys at school. Anise decides to seal the "True Contract" with her four Rose Knights to help Seiran (the Blue Rose), an artificial human who was created to stop the Demon Lord's seal from breaking. In order to rebuild the seal, Anise must gather a new set of cards known as the Arcana Cards. Anise notices an ad about an idol audition in which the runner-up will win an Arcana Card as a prize! Unfortunately, there seems to be a catch...?

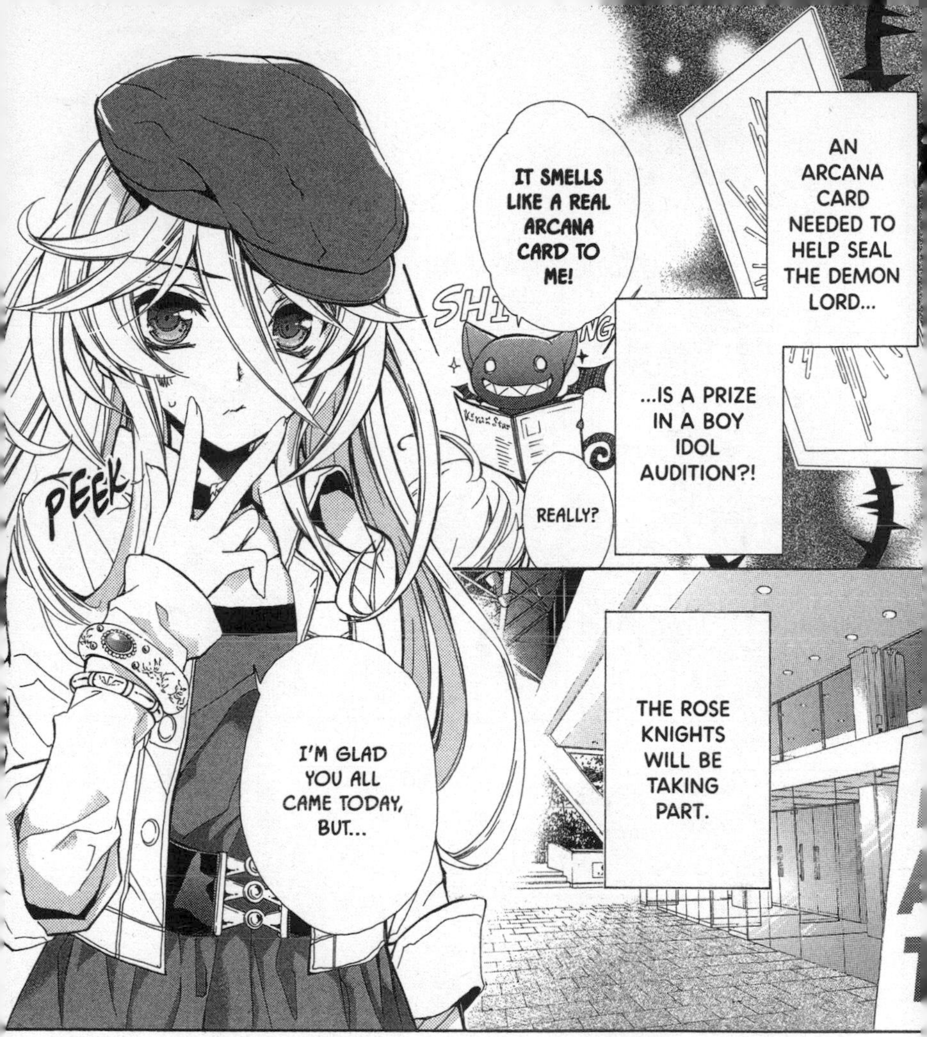
AN ARCANA CARD NEEDED TO HELP SEAL THE DEMON LORD...
...IS A PRIZE IN A BOY IDOL AUDITION?!
IT SMELLS LIKE A REAL ARCANA CARD TO ME!
REALLY?
THE ROSE KNIGHTS WILL BE TAKING PART.
PEEK
I'M GLAD YOU ALL CAME TODAY, BUT...

Rose Kiss Poem Corner

"Private Life" Haiku

Now before bedtime

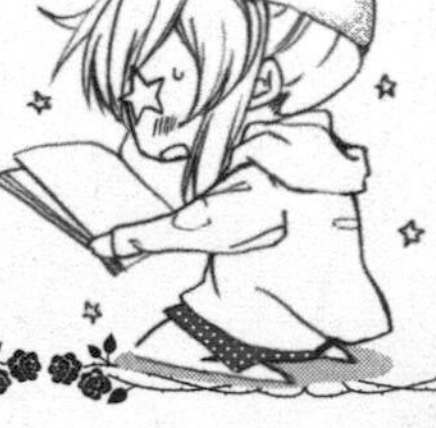

I read about male idols

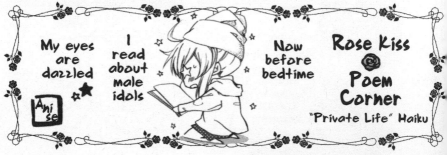

My eyes are dazzled ★

Anise

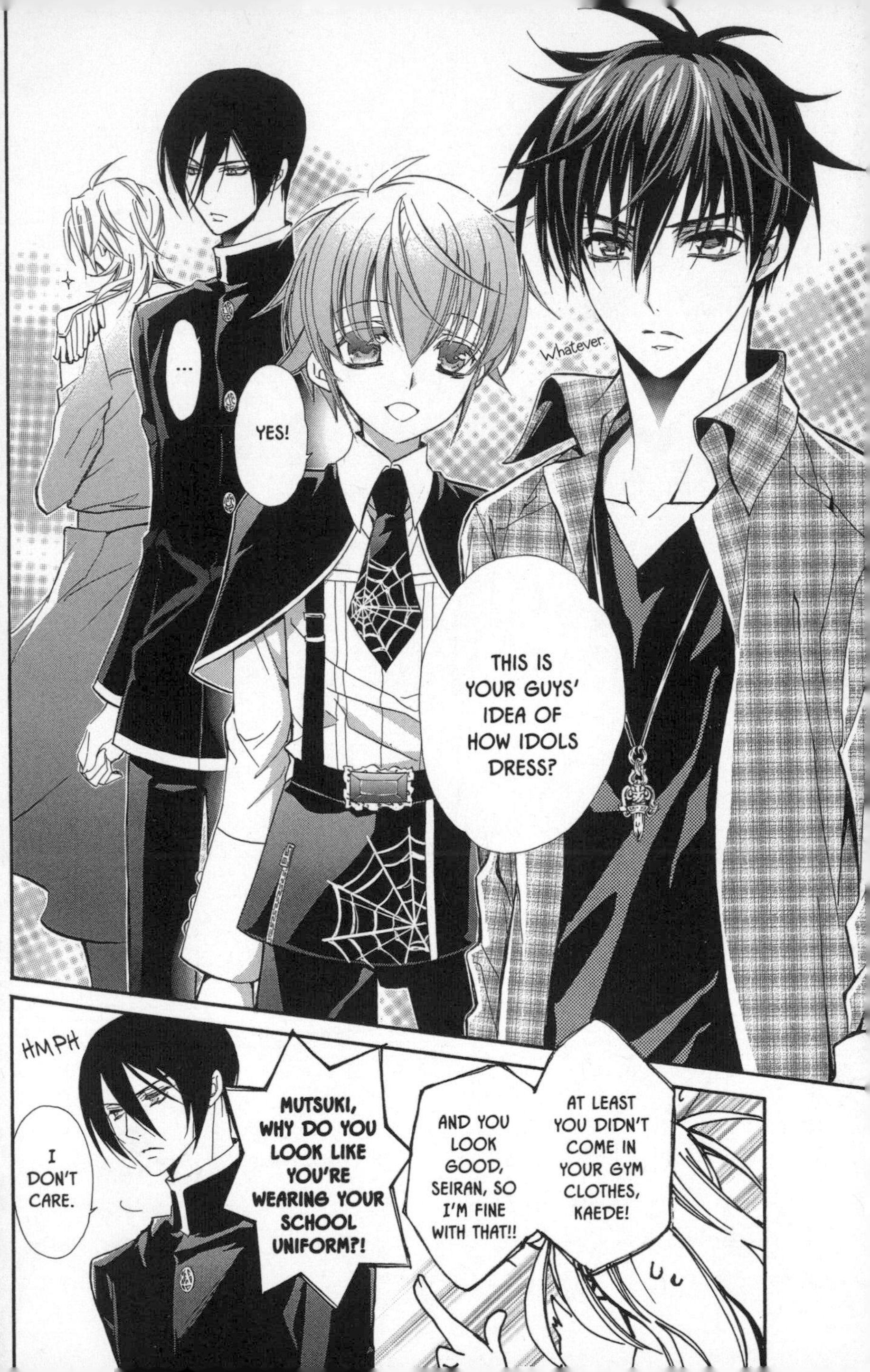
Whatever.
THIS IS YOUR GUYS' IDEA OF HOW IDOLS DRESS?
YES!
...
AT LEAST YOU DIDN'T COME IN YOUR GYM CLOTHES, KAEDE!
AND YOU LOOK GOOD, SEIRAN, SO I'M FINE WITH THAT!!
MUTSUKI, WHY DO YOU LOOK LIKE YOU'RE WEARING YOUR SCHOOL UNIFORM?!
HMPH
I DON'T CARE.

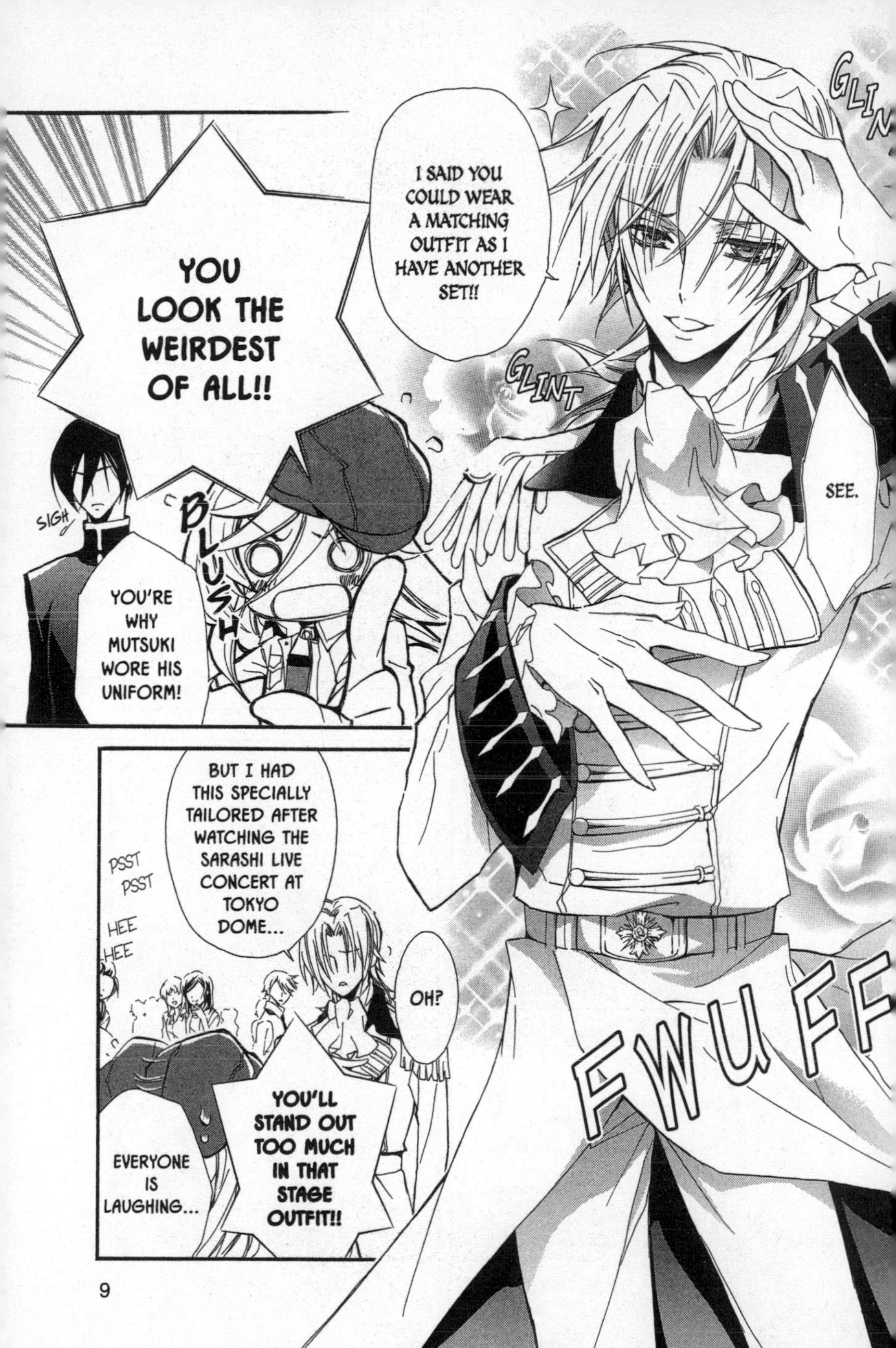
GLIN
I SAID YOU COULD WEAR A MATCHING OUTFIT AS I HAVE ANOTHER SET!!
GLINT
SEE.
FWUFF
YOU LOOK THE WEIRDEST OF ALL!!
SIGH
BLUSH
YOU'RE WHY MUTSUKI WORE HIS UNIFORM!
BUT I HAD THIS SPECIALLY TAILORED AFTER WATCHING THE SARASHI LIVE CONCERT AT TOKYO DOME...
PSST PSST
HEE HEE
OH?
YOU'LL STAND OUT TOO MUCH IN THAT STAGE OUTFIT!!
EVERYONE IS LAUGHING...

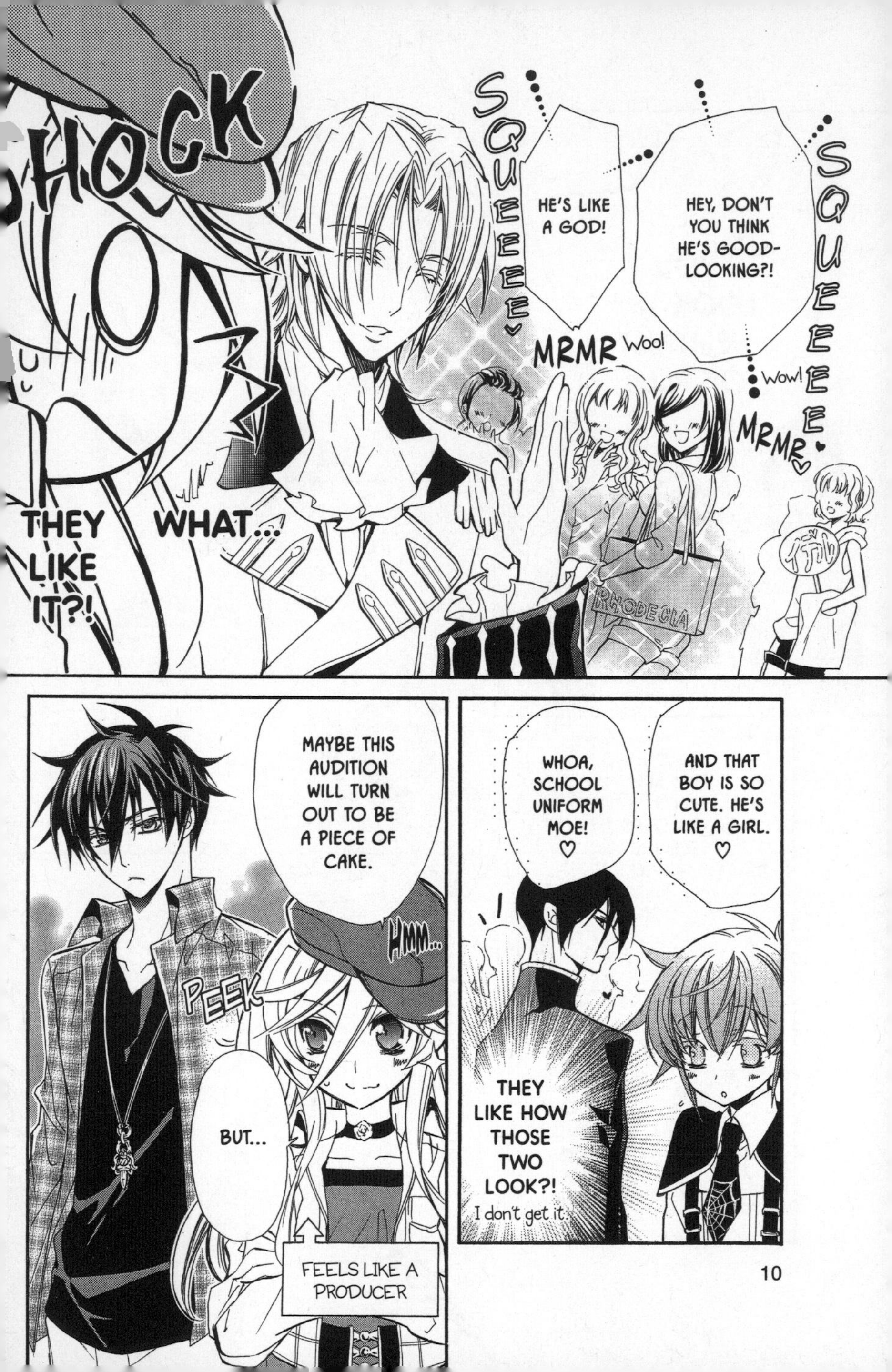
SQUEEE
HEY, DON'T YOU THINK HE'S GOOD-LOOKING?!
Wow!
MRMR
HE'S LIKE A GOD!
SQUEEE
MRMR Woo!
RHODECIA
WHAT...
SHOCK
THEY LIKE IT?!
AND THAT BOY IS SO CUTE. HE'S LIKE A GIRL. ♡
WHOA, SCHOOL UNIFORM MOE! ♡
THEY LIKE HOW THOSE TWO LOOK?!
I don't get it.
MAYBE THIS AUDITION WILL TURN OUT TO BE A PIECE OF CAKE.
HMM...
PEEK
BUT...
FEELS LIKE A PRODUCER

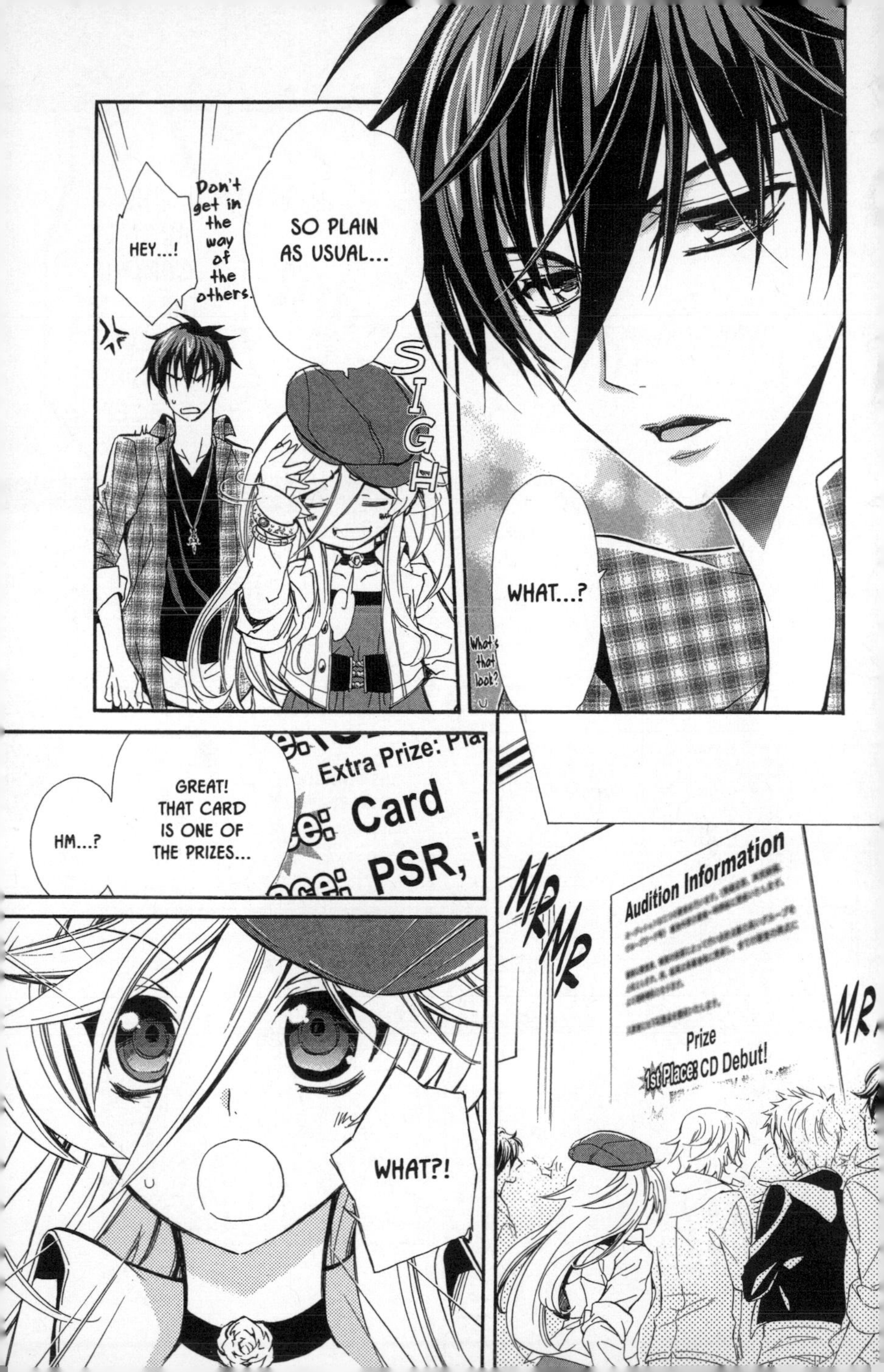
WHAT...?
What's that look?
SO PLAIN AS USUAL...
SIGH
HEY...!
Don't get in the way of the others.
MR MR
Audition Information
Prize
1st Place: CD Debut!
MR
Extra Prize:
Card
PSR,
GREAT! THAT CARD IS ONE OF THE PRIZES...
HM...?
WHAT?!

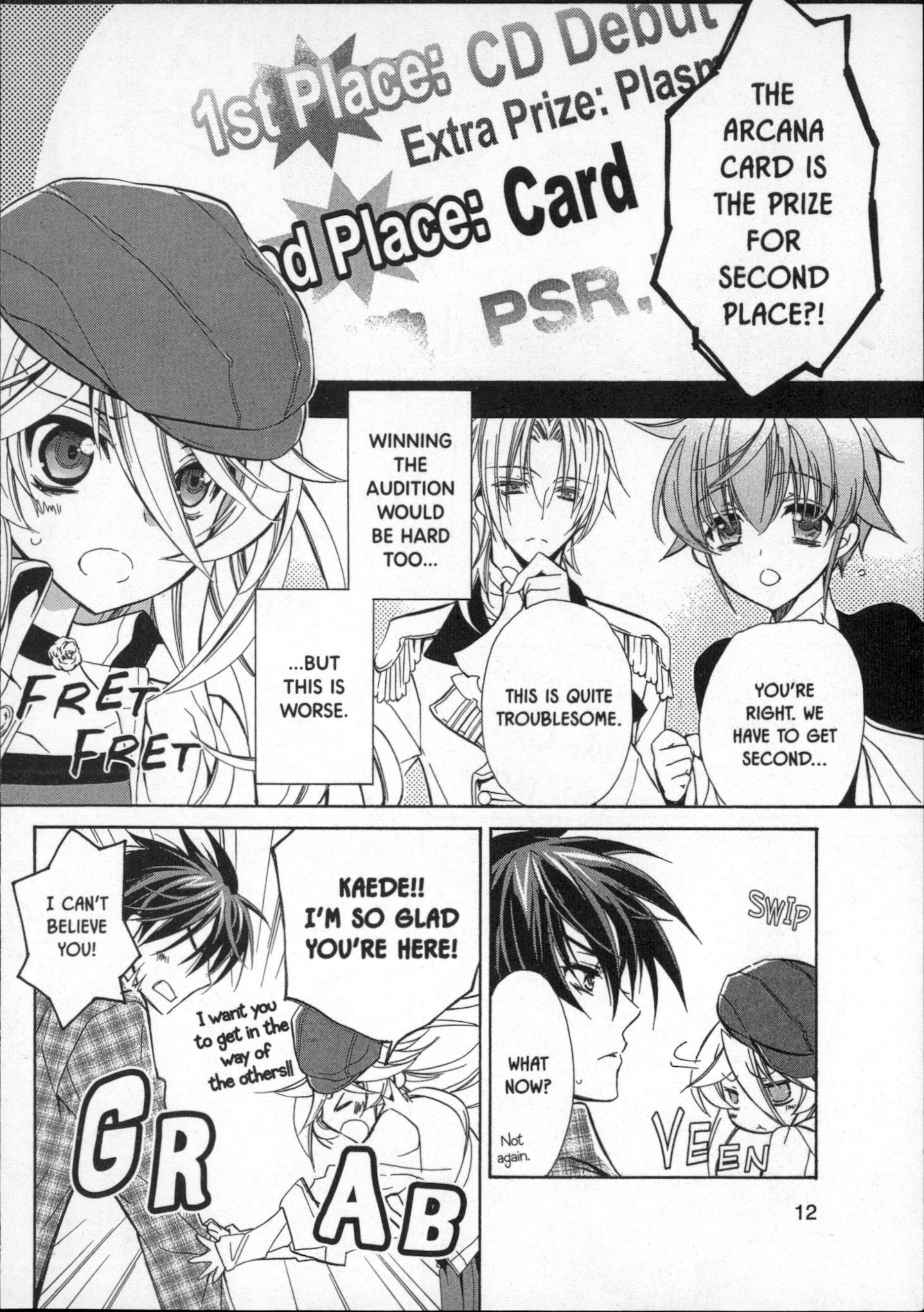
1st Place: CD Debut
Extra Prize: Plasm
nd Place: Card
PSR.
THE ARCANA CARD IS THE PRIZE FOR SECOND PLACE?!
YOU'RE RIGHT. WE HAVE TO GET SECOND...
THIS IS QUITE TROUBLESOME.
WINNING THE AUDITION WOULD BE HARD TOO...
...BUT THIS IS WORSE.
FRET FRET
SWIP
WHAT NOW?
Not again.
VEEEN
KAEDE!! I'M SO GLAD YOU'RE HERE!
I CAN'T BELIEVE YOU!
I want you to get in the way of the others!!
GRAB

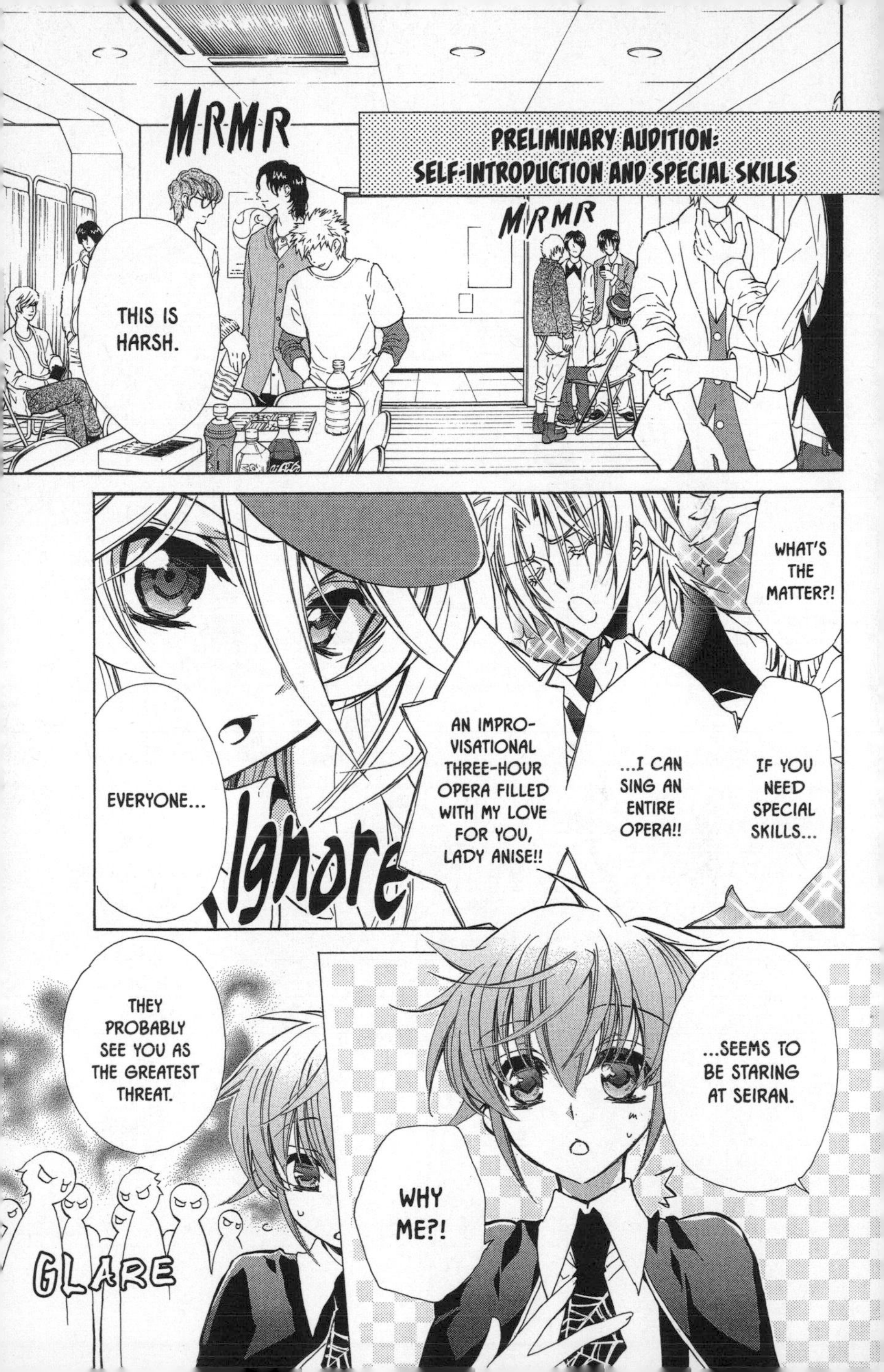
PRELIMINARY AUDITION: SELF-INTRODUCTION AND SPECIAL SKILLS
MRMR
MRMR
THIS IS HARSH.
WHAT'S THE MATTER?!
IF YOU NEED SPECIAL SKILLS...
...I CAN SING AN ENTIRE OPERA!!
AN IMPROVISATIONAL THREE-HOUR OPERA FILLED WITH MY LOVE FOR YOU, LADY ANISE!!
Ignore
EVERYONE...
...SEEMS TO BE STARING AT SEIRAN.
WHY ME?!
THEY PROBABLY SEE YOU AS THE GREATEST THREAT.
GLARE

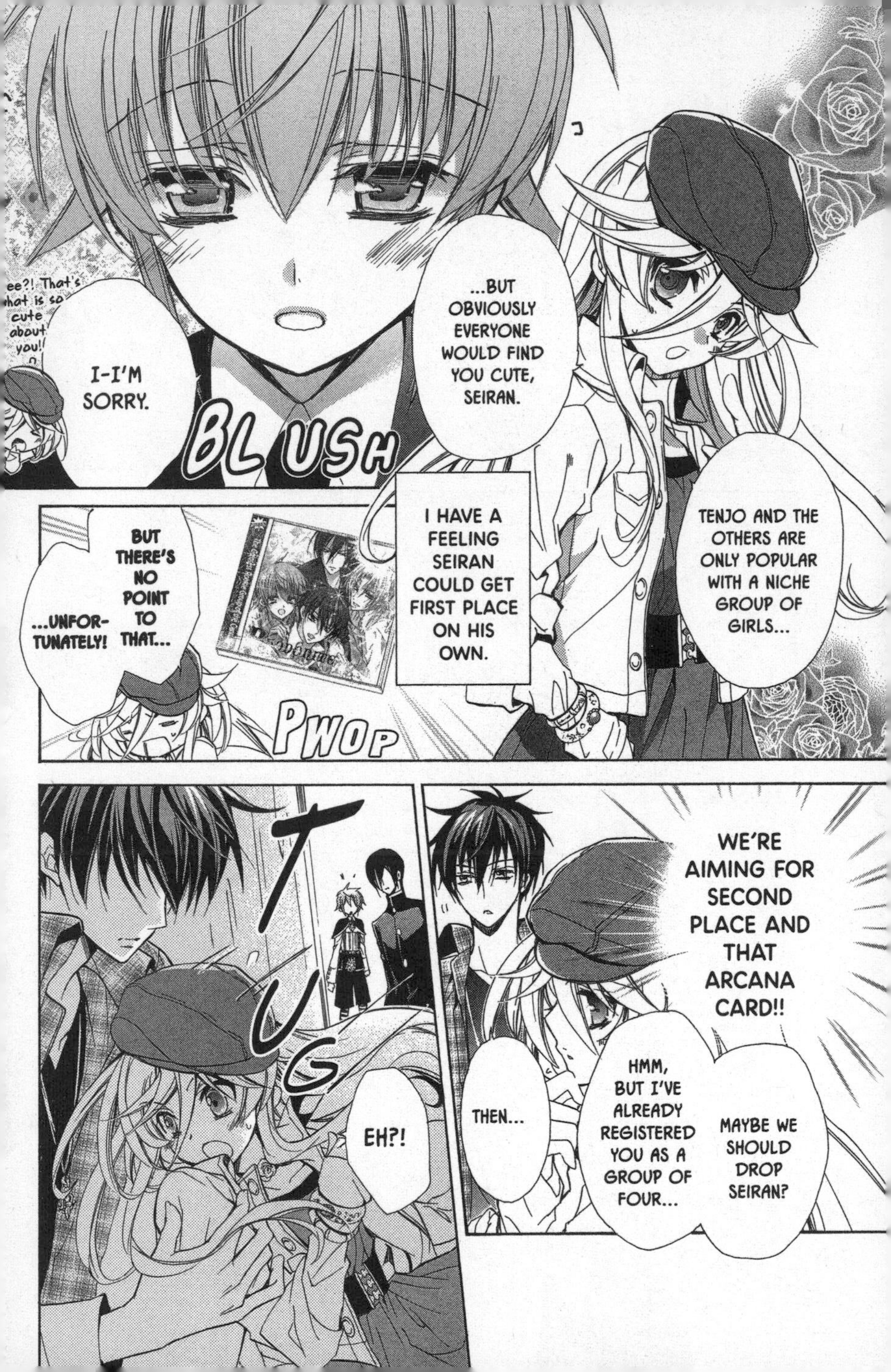
...BUT OBVIOUSLY EVERYONE WOULD FIND YOU CUTE, SEIRAN.
I-I'M SORRY.
BLUSH
TENJO AND THE OTHERS ARE ONLY POPULAR WITH A NICHE GROUP OF GIRLS...
I HAVE A FEELING SEIRAN COULD GET FIRST PLACE ON HIS OWN.
BUT THERE'S NO POINT TO THAT...
...UNFOR-TUNATELY!
PWOP
WE'RE AIMING FOR SECOND PLACE AND THAT ARCANA CARD!!
MAYBE WE SHOULD DROP SEIRAN?
HMM, BUT I'VE ALREADY REGISTERED YOU AS A GROUP OF FOUR...
THEN...
TUG
EH?!

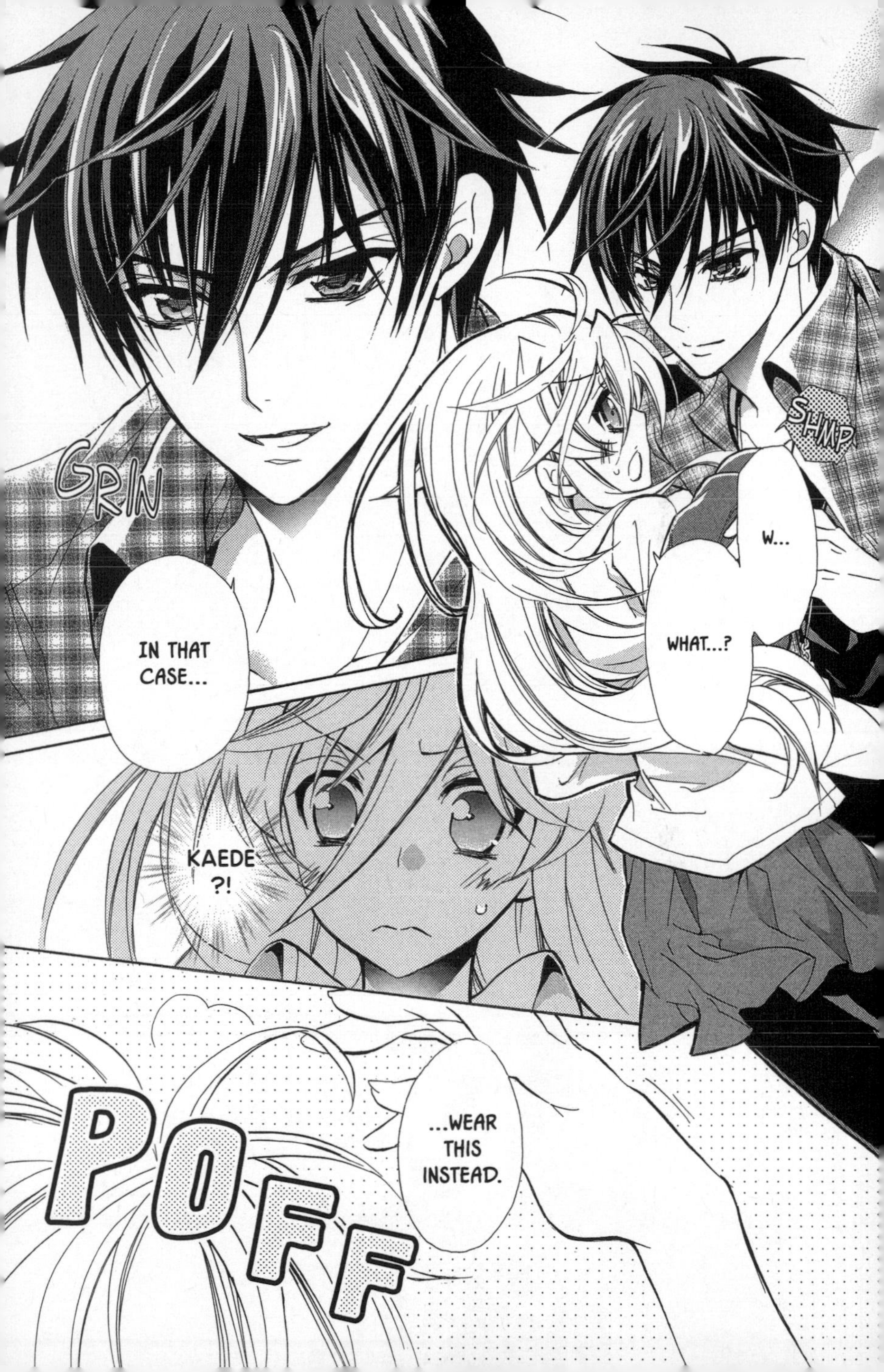
GRIN
IN THAT CASE...
SHMP
W...
WHAT...?
KAEDE ?!
...WEAR THIS INSTEAD.
POFF

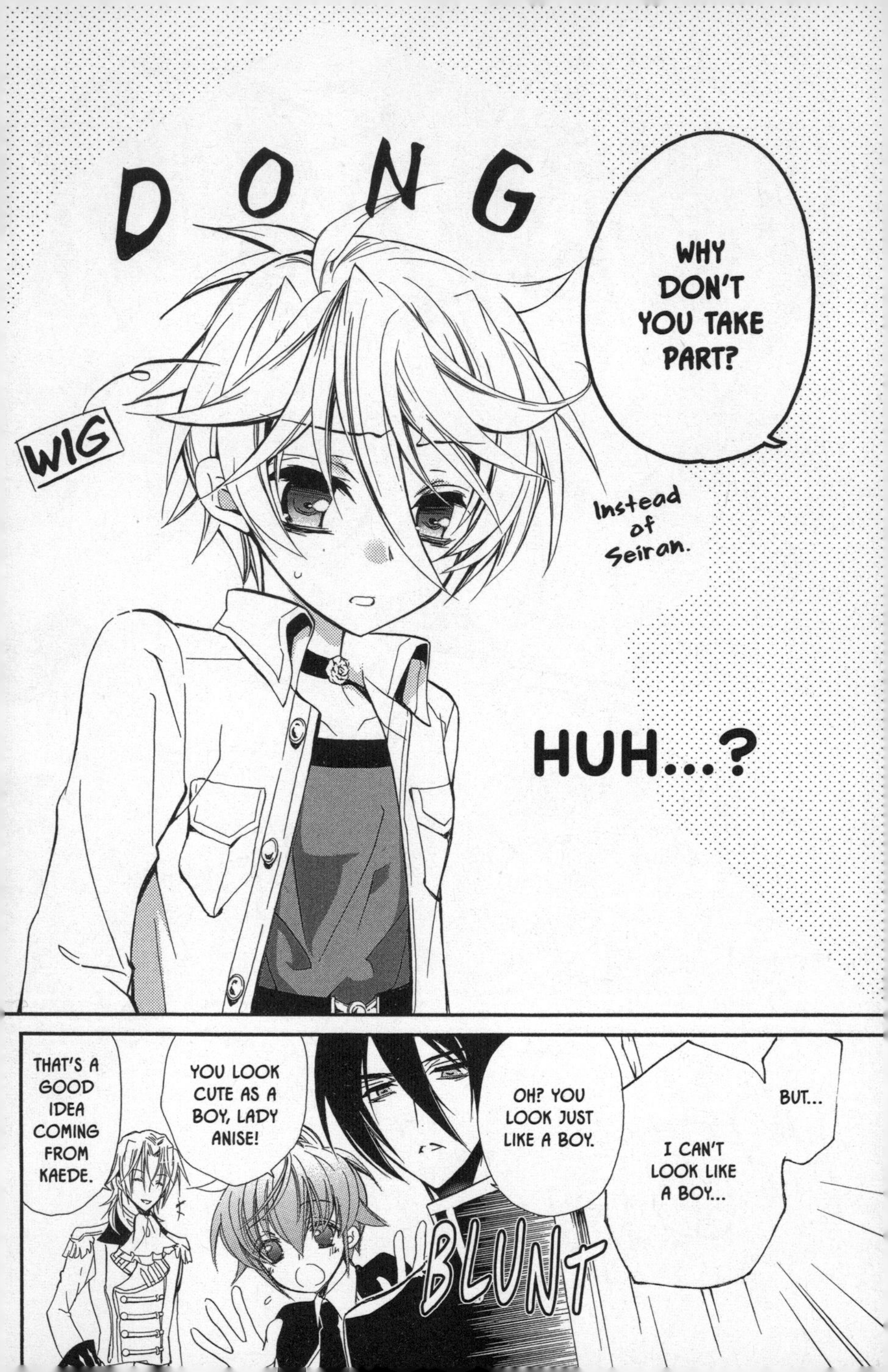
WHY DON'T YOU TAKE PART?
DONG
Instead of Seiran.
WIG
HUH...?
BUT...
I CAN'T LOOK LIKE A BOY...
OH? YOU LOOK JUST LIKE A BOY.
BLUNT
YOU LOOK CUTE AS A BOY, LADY ANISE!
THAT'S A GOOD IDEA COMING FROM KAEDE.

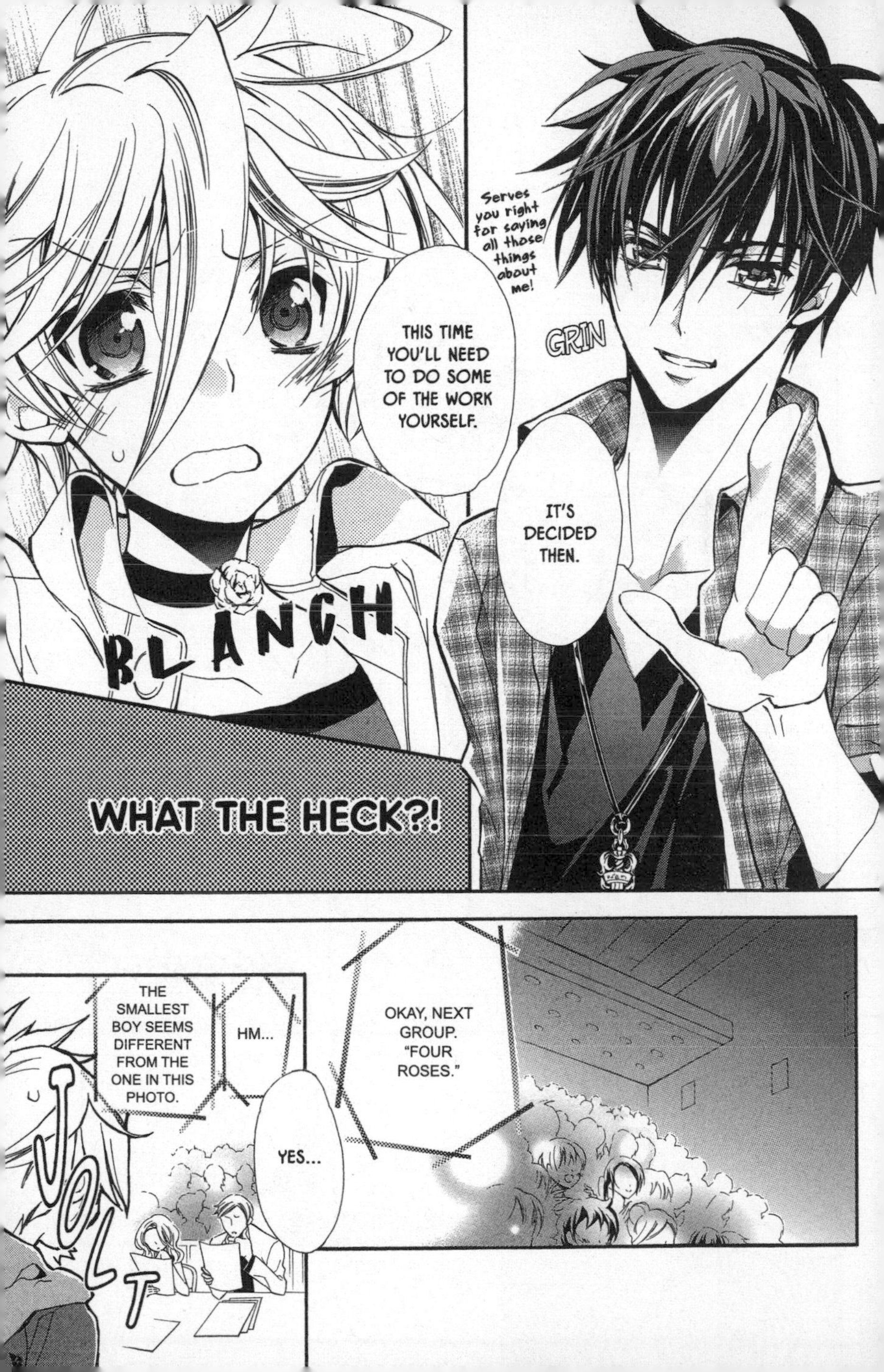
Serves you right for saying all those things about me!
GRIN
THIS TIME YOU'LL NEED TO DO SOME OF THE WORK YOURSELF.
IT'S DECIDED THEN.
BLANCH
WHAT THE HECK?!
OKAY, NEXT GROUP. "FOUR ROSES."
YES...
HM...
THE SMALLEST BOY SEEMS DIFFERENT FROM THE ONE IN THIS PHOTO.
JOLT

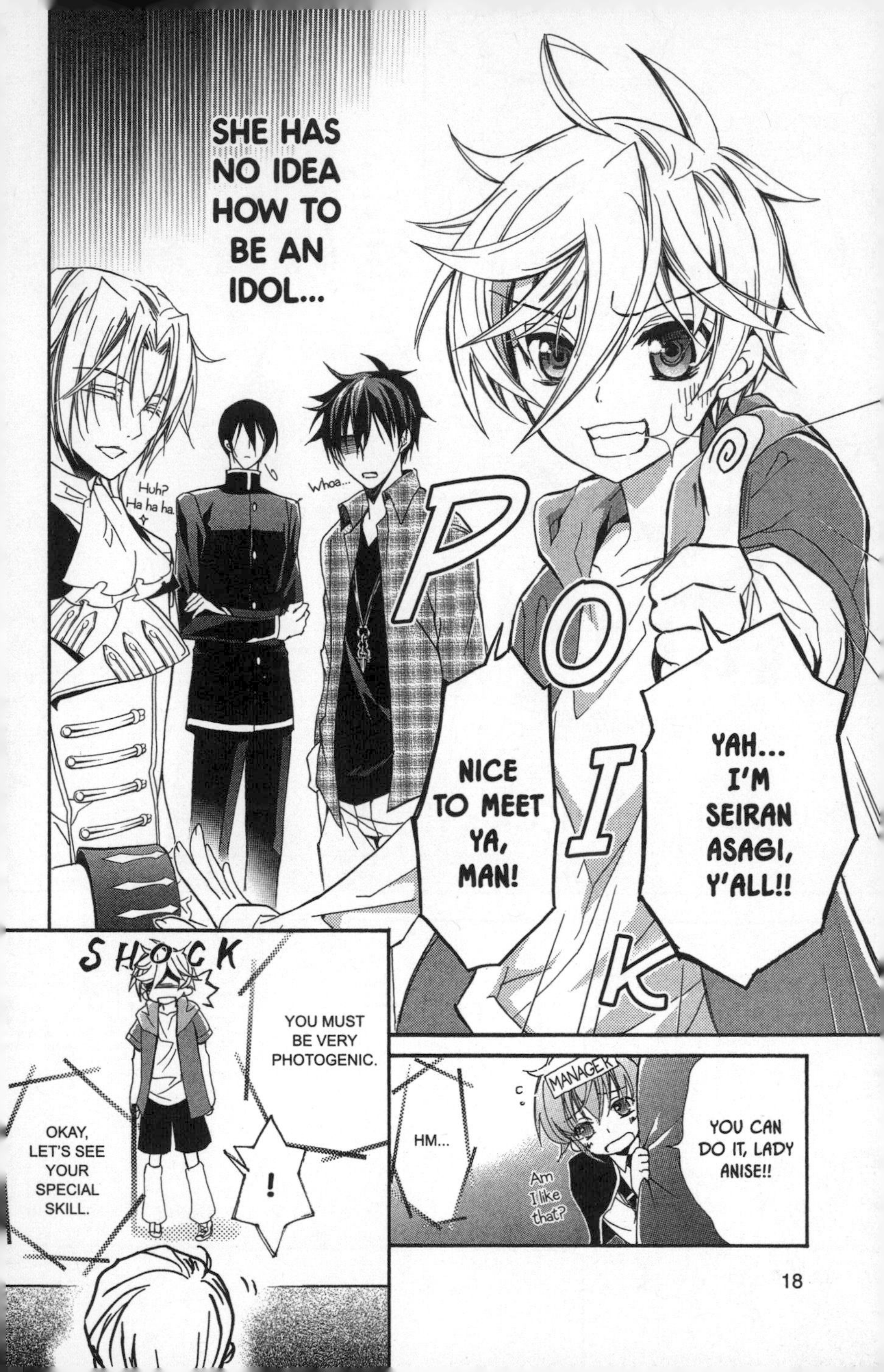
YAH... I'M SEIRAN ASAGI, Y'ALL!!
NICE TO MEET YA, MAN!
POK
SHE HAS NO IDEA HOW TO BE AN IDOL...
Whoa...
Huh? Ha ha ha.
MANAGER
YOU CAN DO IT, LADY ANISE!!
Am I like that?
HM...
SHOCK
YOU MUST BE VERY PHOTOGENIC.
!
OKAY, LET'S SEE YOUR SPECIAL SKILL.

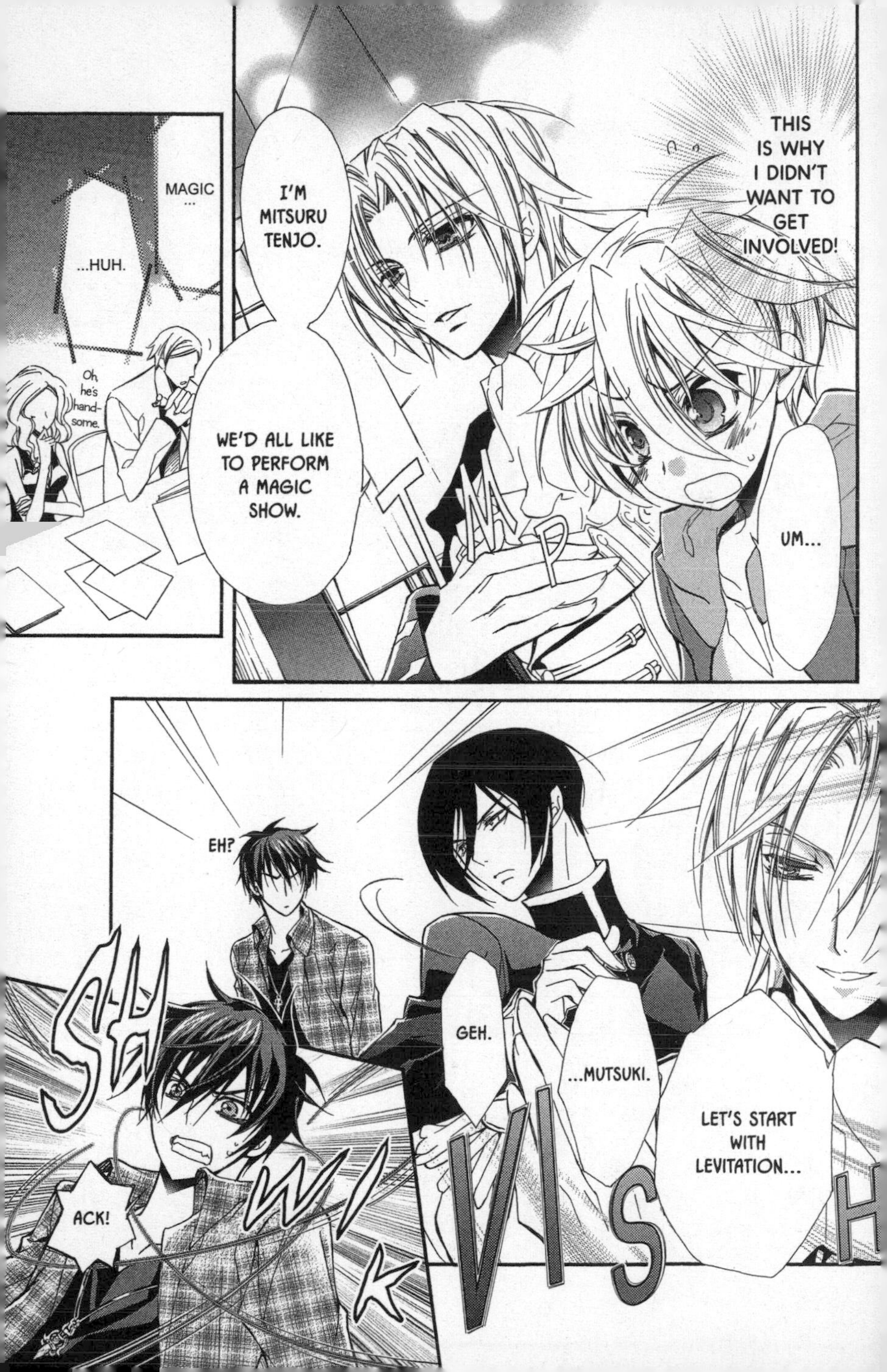
THIS IS WHY I DIDN'T WANT TO GET INVOLVED!
UM...
I'M MITSURU TENJO.
WE'D ALL LIKE TO PERFORM A MAGIC SHOW.
TMP
MAGIC ...
...HUH.
Oh, he's hand-some.
LET'S START WITH LEVITATION...
...MUTSUKI.
GEH.
VISH
EH?
SHWIK
ACK!

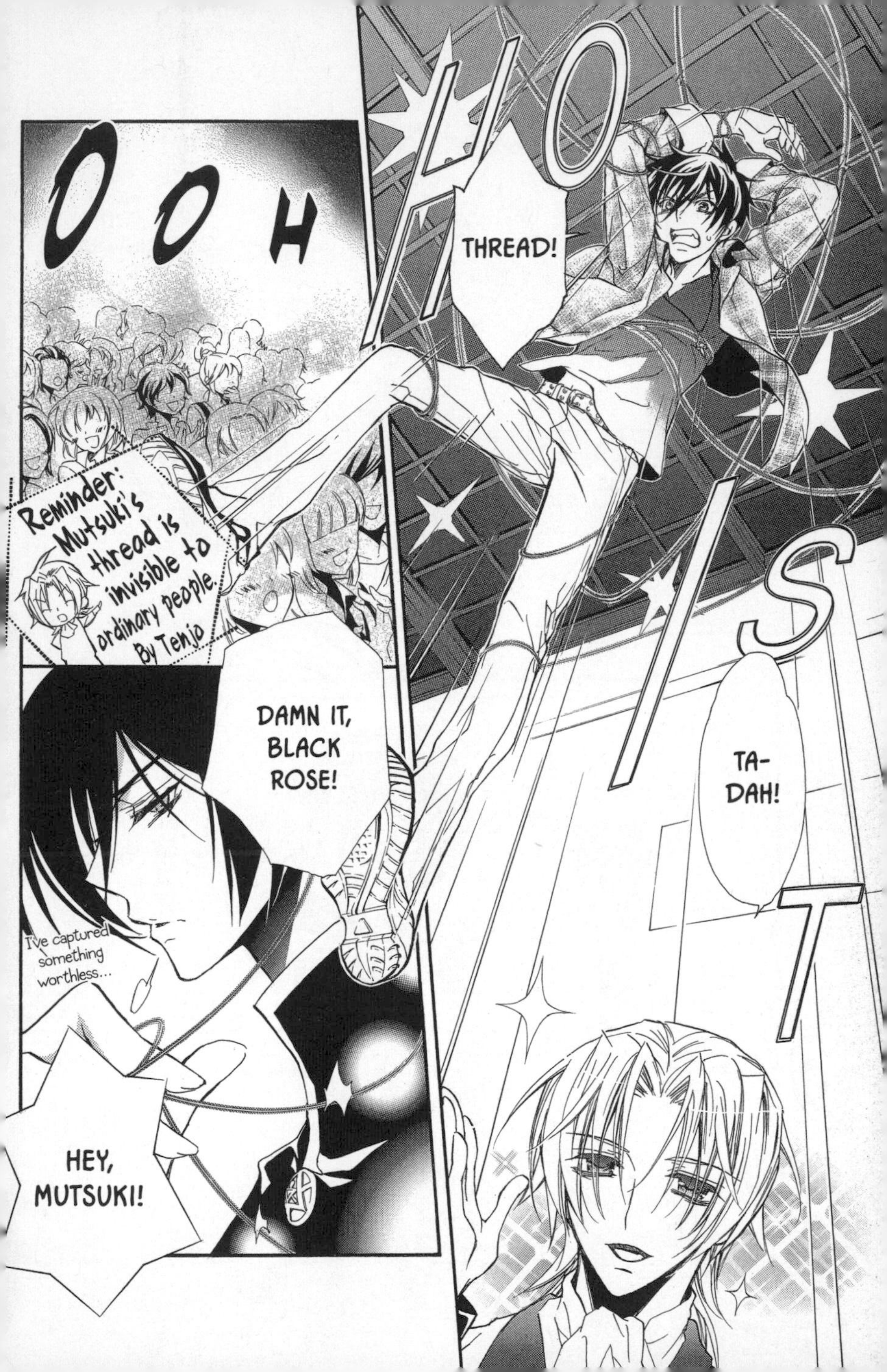
HOIST
THREAD!
TA-DAH!
OOOH
Reminder: Mutsuki's thread is invisible to ordinary people. By Tenjo
DAMN IT, BLACK ROSE!
I've captured something worthless...
HEY, MUTSUKI!

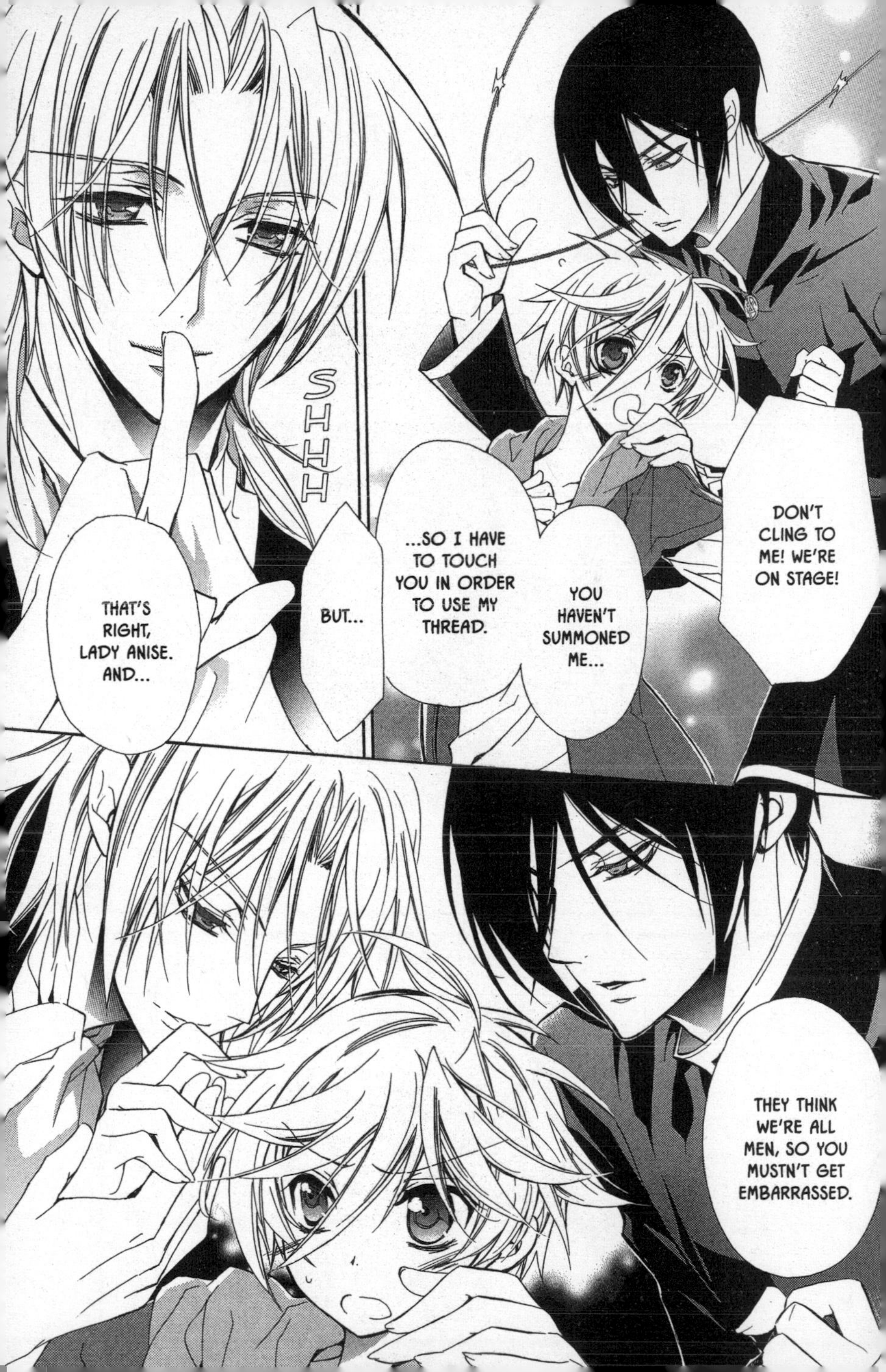
DON'T CLING TO ME! WE'RE ON STAGE!
YOU HAVEN'T SUMMONED ME...
...SO I HAVE TO TOUCH YOU IN ORDER TO USE MY THREAD.
SHHH
BUT...
THAT'S RIGHT, LADY ANISE. AND...
THEY THINK WE'RE ALL MEN, SO YOU MUSTN'T GET EMBARRASSED.

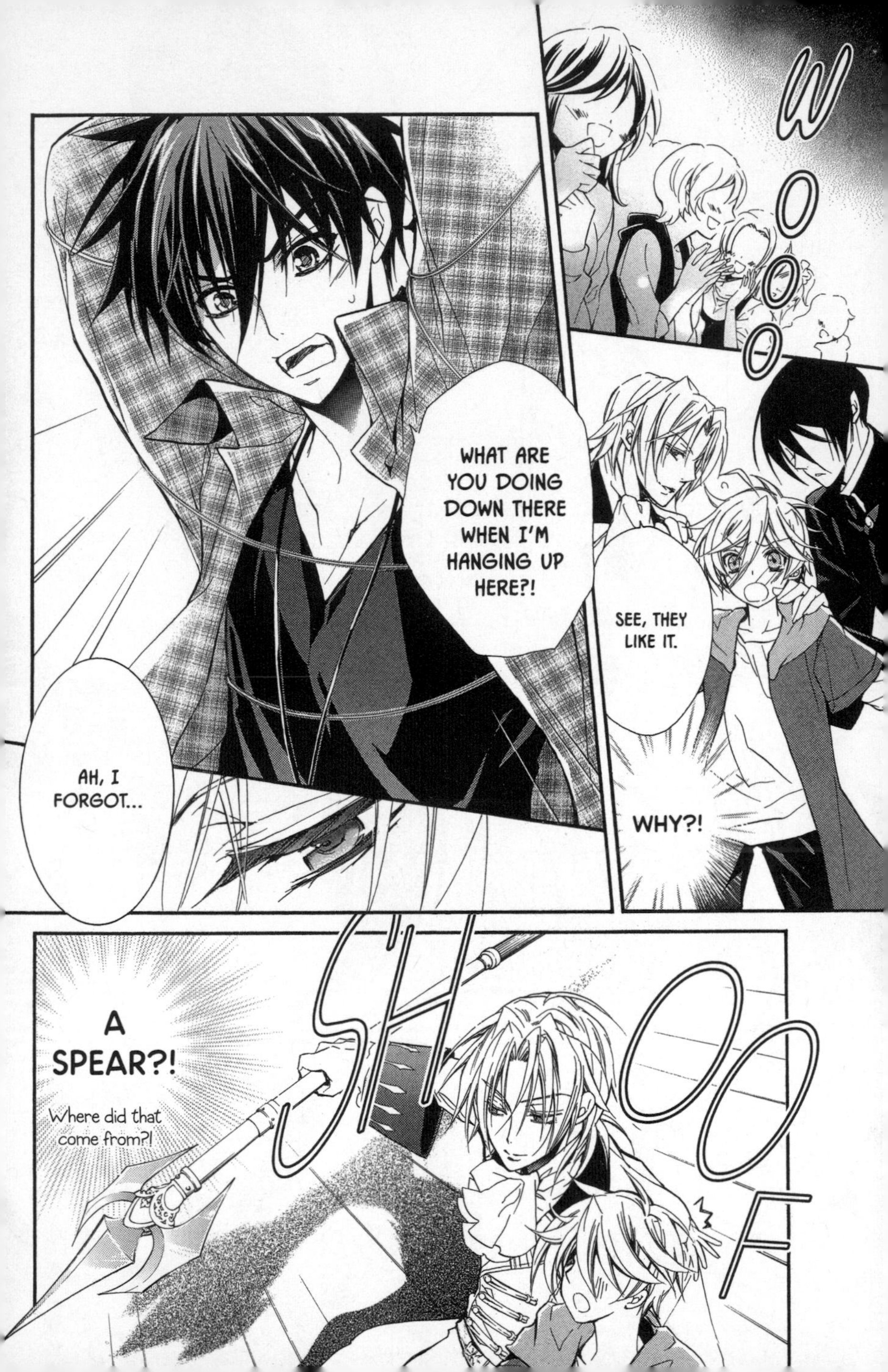
WOOOO
SEE, THEY LIKE IT.
WHY?!
WHAT ARE YOU DOING DOWN THERE WHEN I'M HANGING UP HERE?!
AH, I FORGOT...
SHOOF
A SPEAR?!
Where did that come from?!

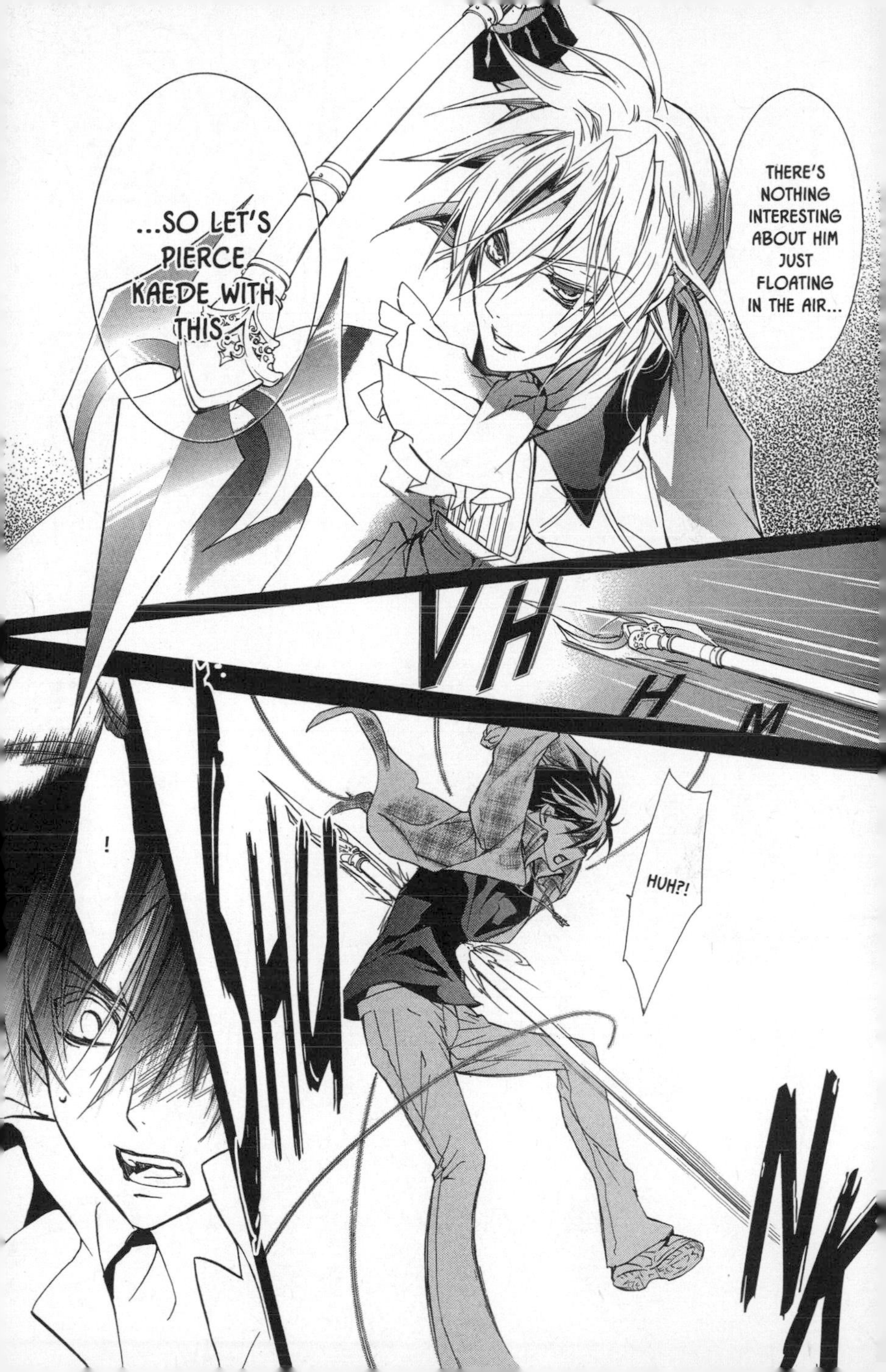
THERE'S NOTHING INTERESTING ABOUT HIM JUST FLOATING IN THE AIR...
...SO LET'S PIERCE KAEDE WITH THIS.
VHHM
HUH?!
!
THUNK

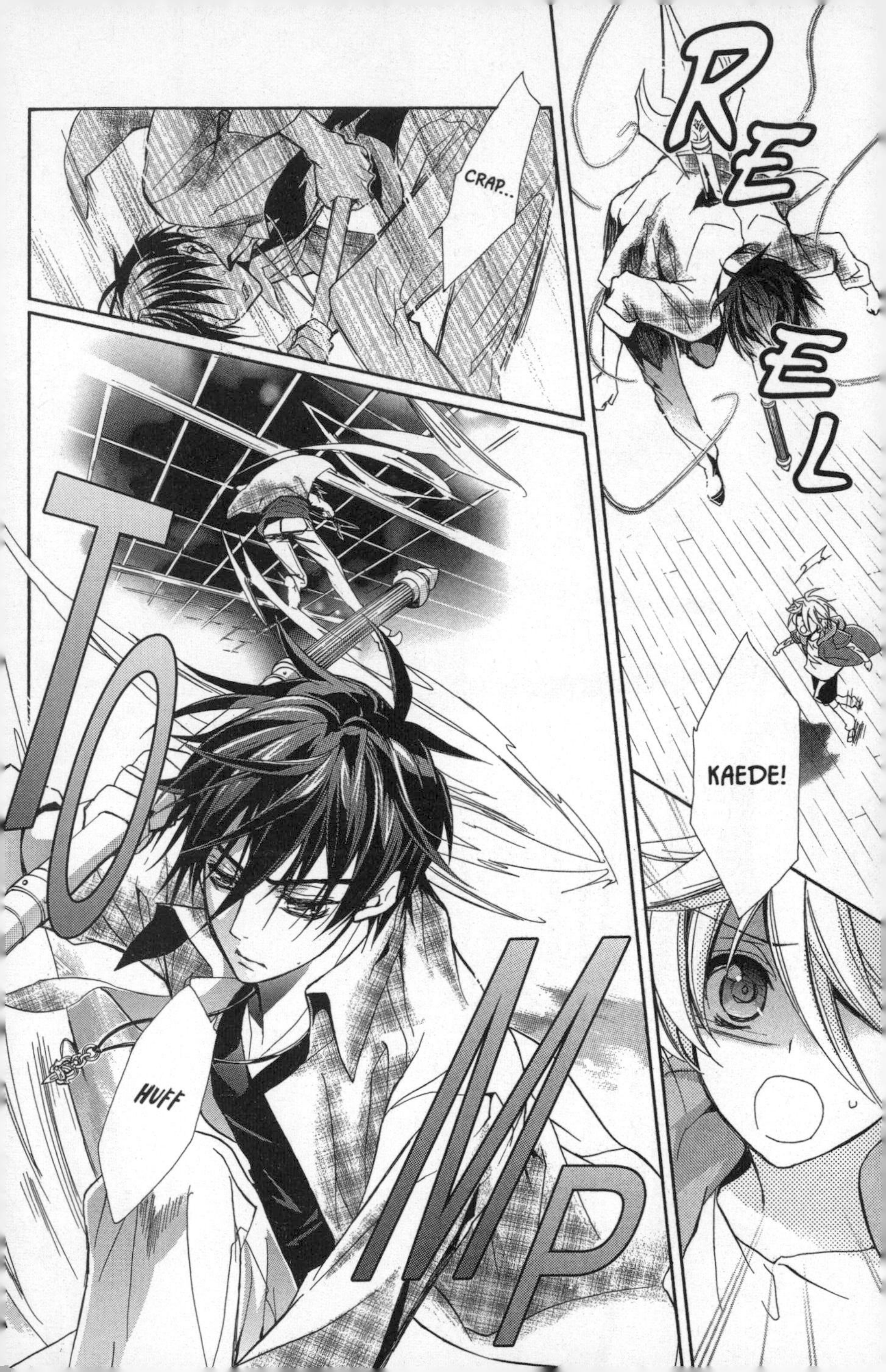
REEL
KAEDE!
CRAP...
TOMP
HUFF

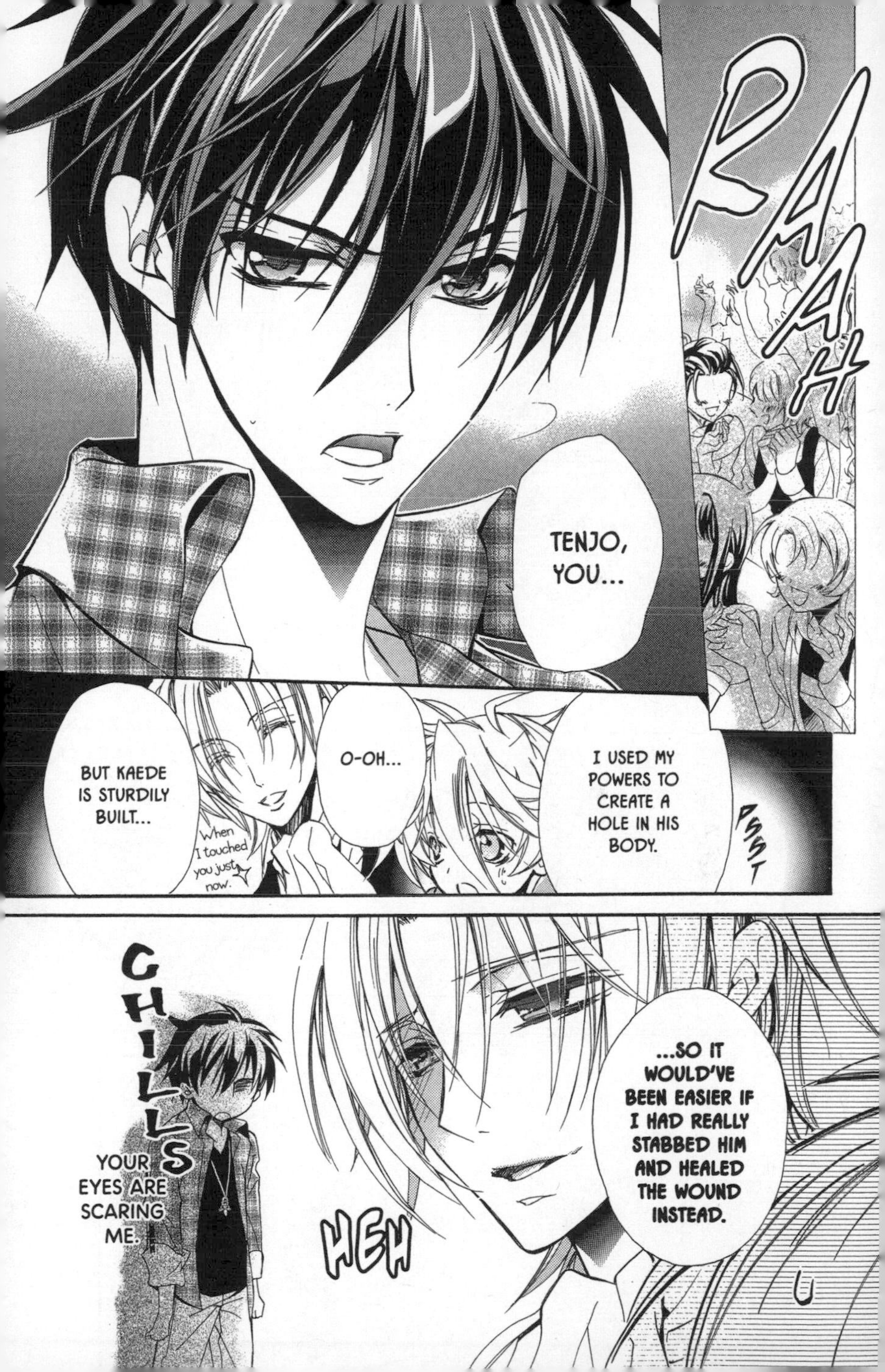
RAAH
TENJO, YOU...
PSST
I USED MY POWERS TO CREATE A HOLE IN HIS BODY.
O-OH...
BUT KAEDE IS STURDILY BUILT...
When I touched you just now.
...SO IT WOULD'VE BEEN EASIER IF I HAD REALLY STABBED HIM AND HEALED THE WOUND INSTEAD.
HEH
CHILLS
YOUR EYES ARE SCARING ME.

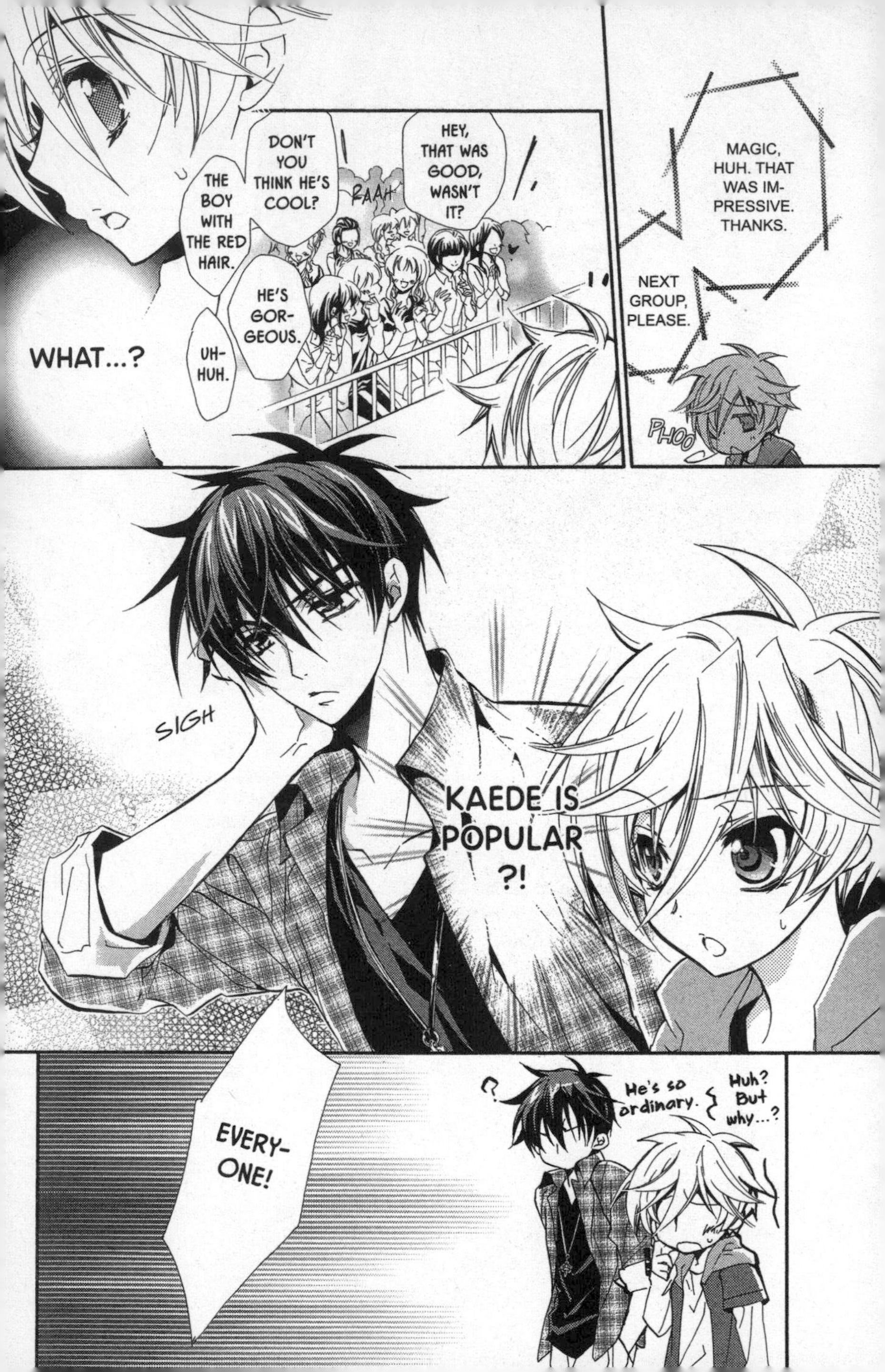
MAGIC, HUH. THAT WAS IMPRESSIVE. THANKS.
NEXT GROUP, PLEASE.
PHOO
HEY, THAT WAS GOOD, WASN'T IT?
RAAH
DON'T YOU THINK HE'S COOL?
THE BOY WITH THE RED HAIR.
HE'S GORGEOUS.
UH-HUH.
WHAT...?
KAEDE IS POPULAR ?!
SIGH
Huh? But why...?
He's so ordinary.
?
EVERY-ONE!

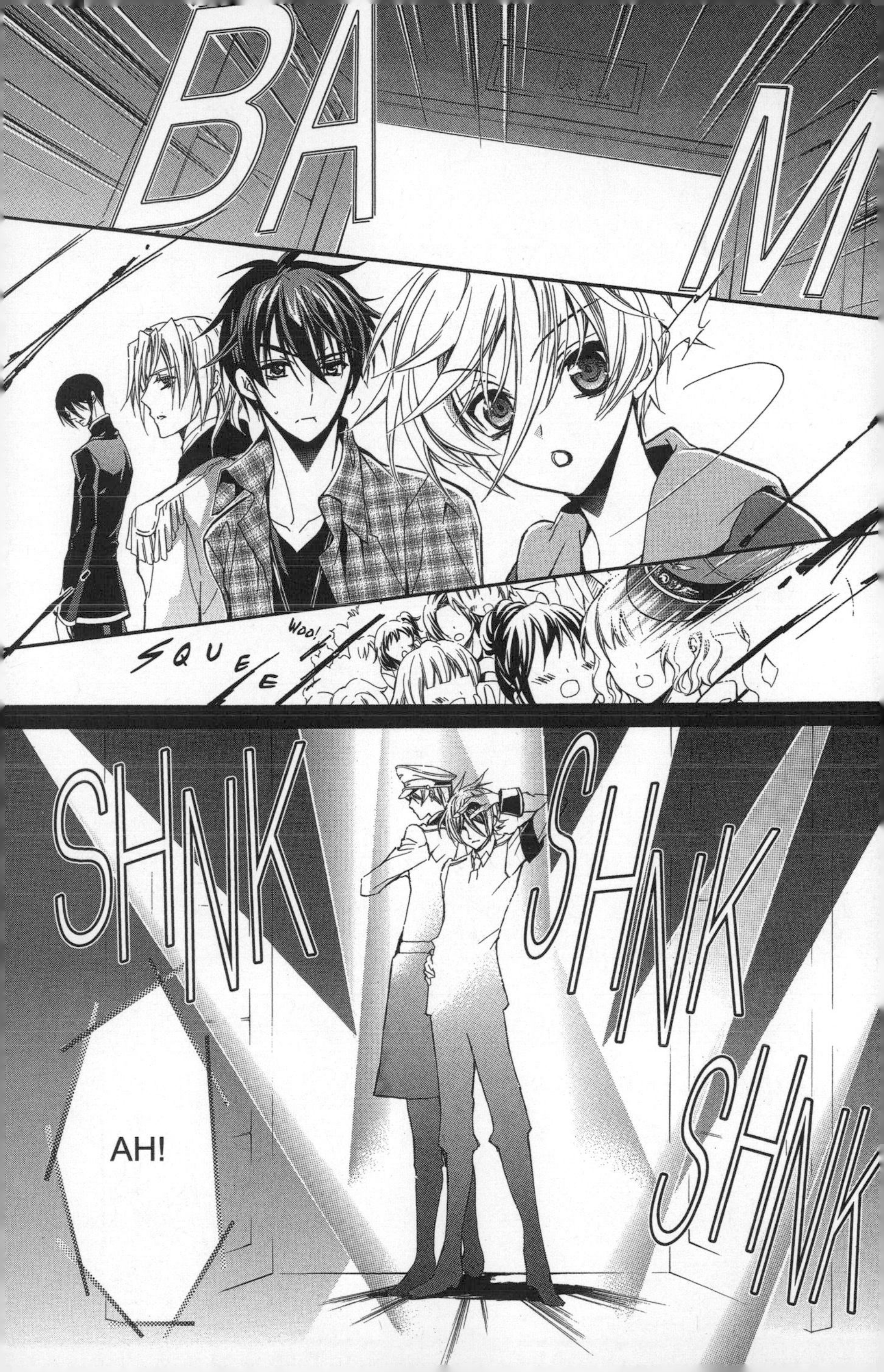
BAM
WOO!
SQUEE
SHNK
SHNK
SHNK
AH!

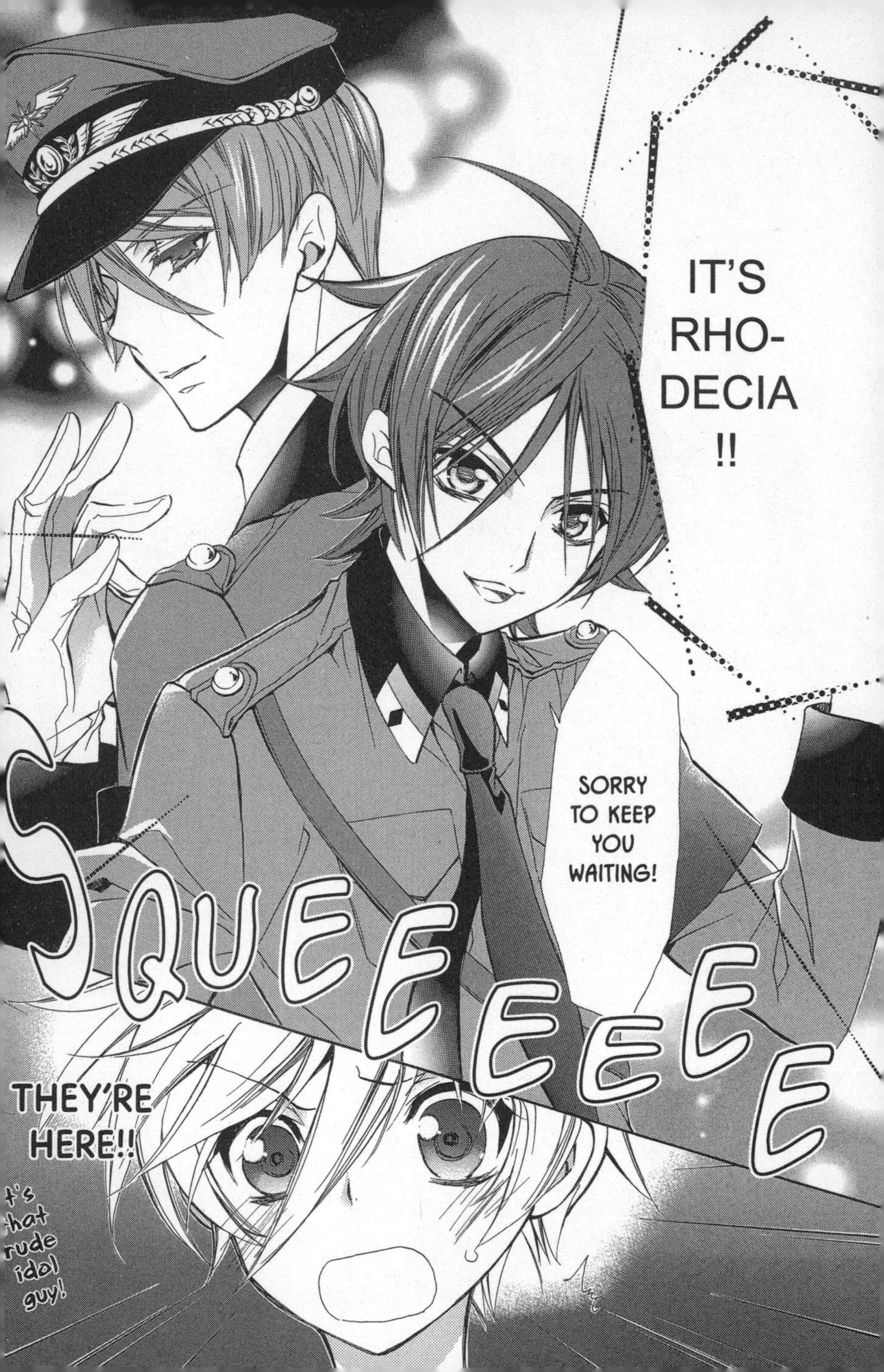
IT'S RHO-DECIA !!
SORRY TO KEEP YOU WAITING!
SQUEEEEEE
THEY'RE HERE!!
rude idol guy!

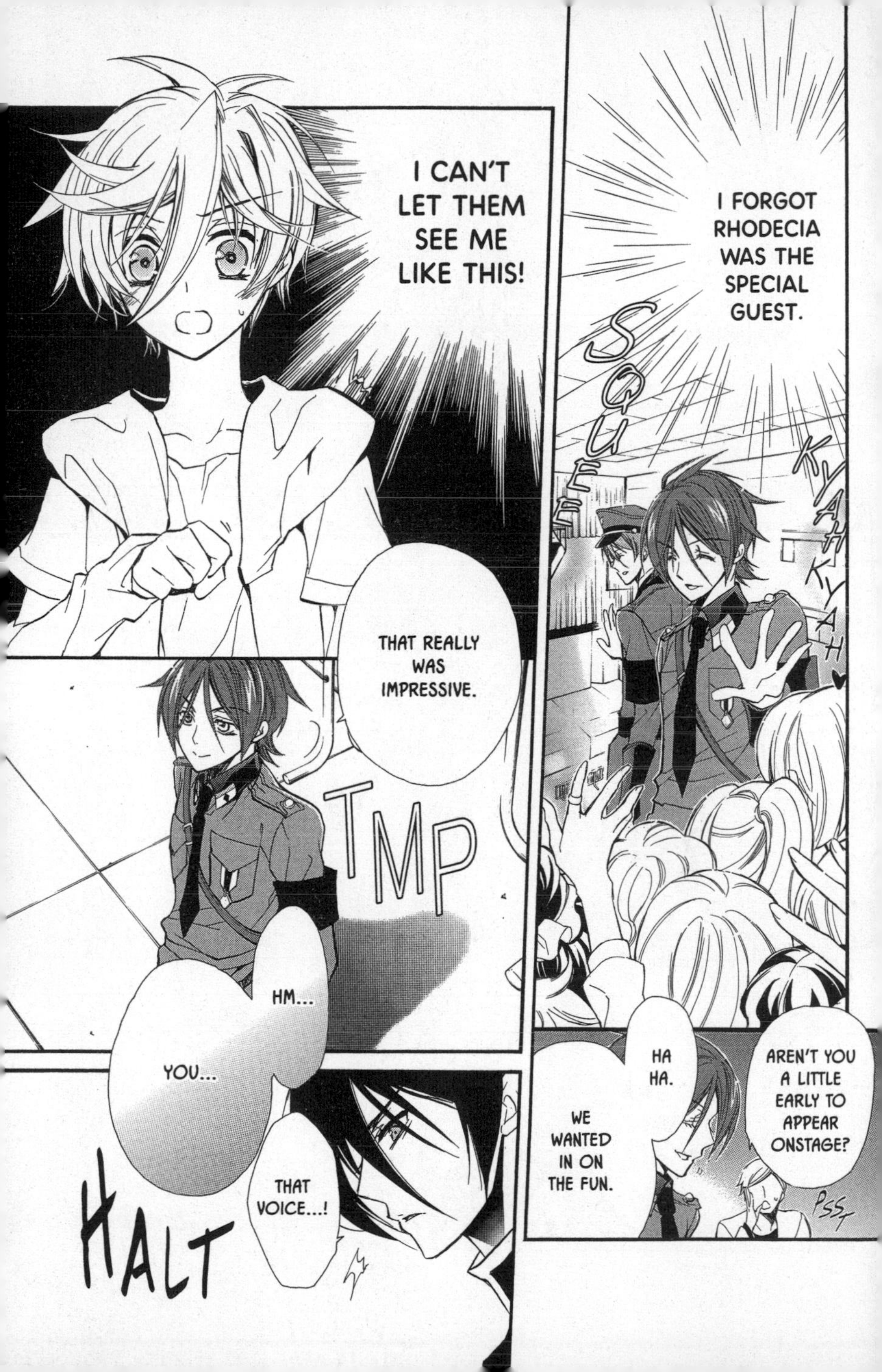
I FORGOT RHODECIA WAS THE SPECIAL GUEST.
SQUEEE
KYAH KYAH
AREN'T YOU A LITTLE EARLY TO APPEAR ONSTAGE?
PSST
HA HA.
WE WANTED IN ON THE FUN.
I CAN'T LET THEM SEE ME LIKE THIS!
THAT REALLY WAS IMPRESSIVE.
TMP
HM...
YOU...
THAT VOICE...!
HALT

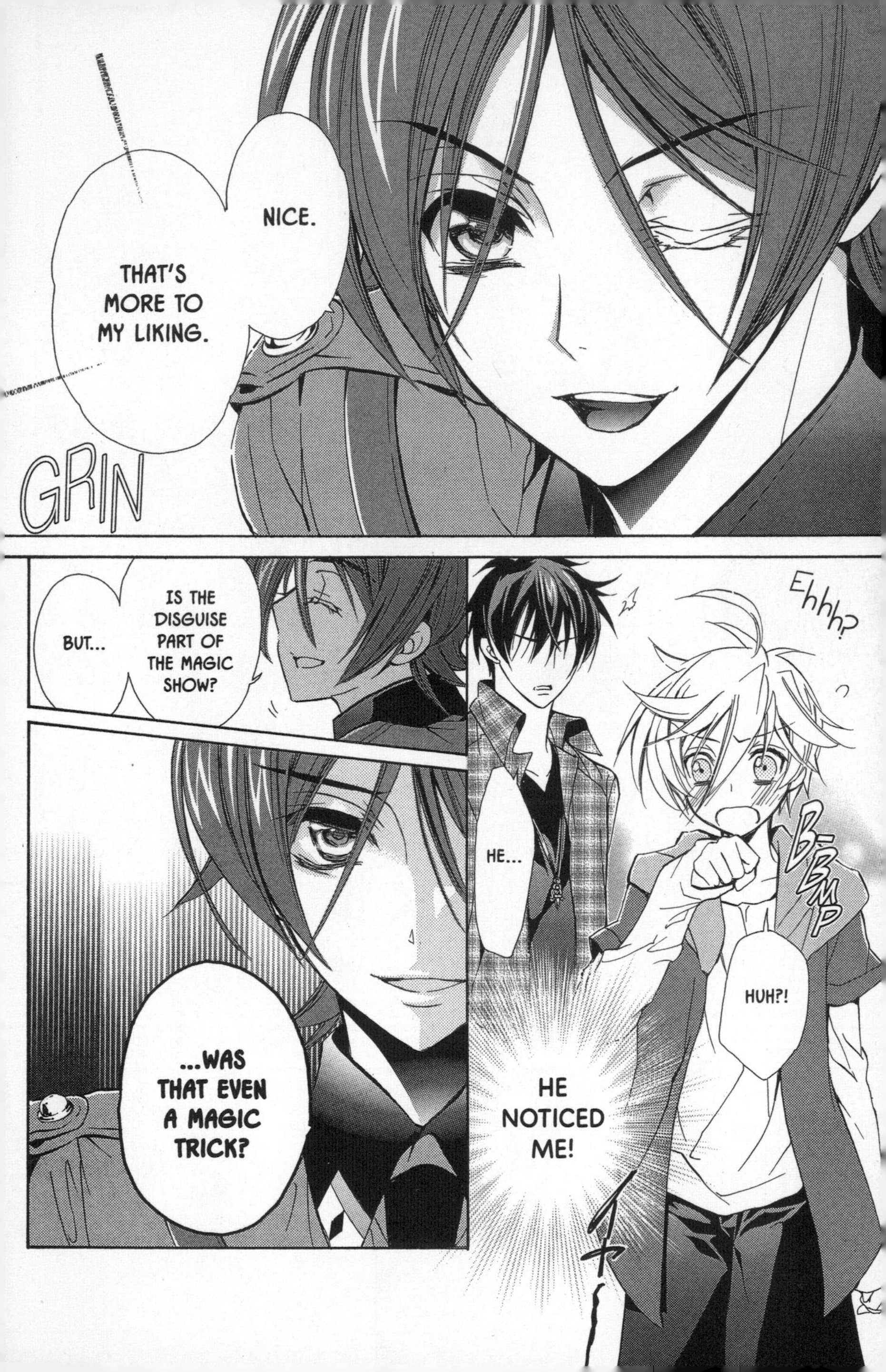
NICE.
THAT'S MORE TO MY LIKING.
GRIN
Ehhh?
HE...
B-BMP
HUH?!
HE NOTICED ME!
BUT... IS THE DISGUISE PART OF THE MAGIC SHOW?
...WAS THAT EVEN A MAGIC TRICK?

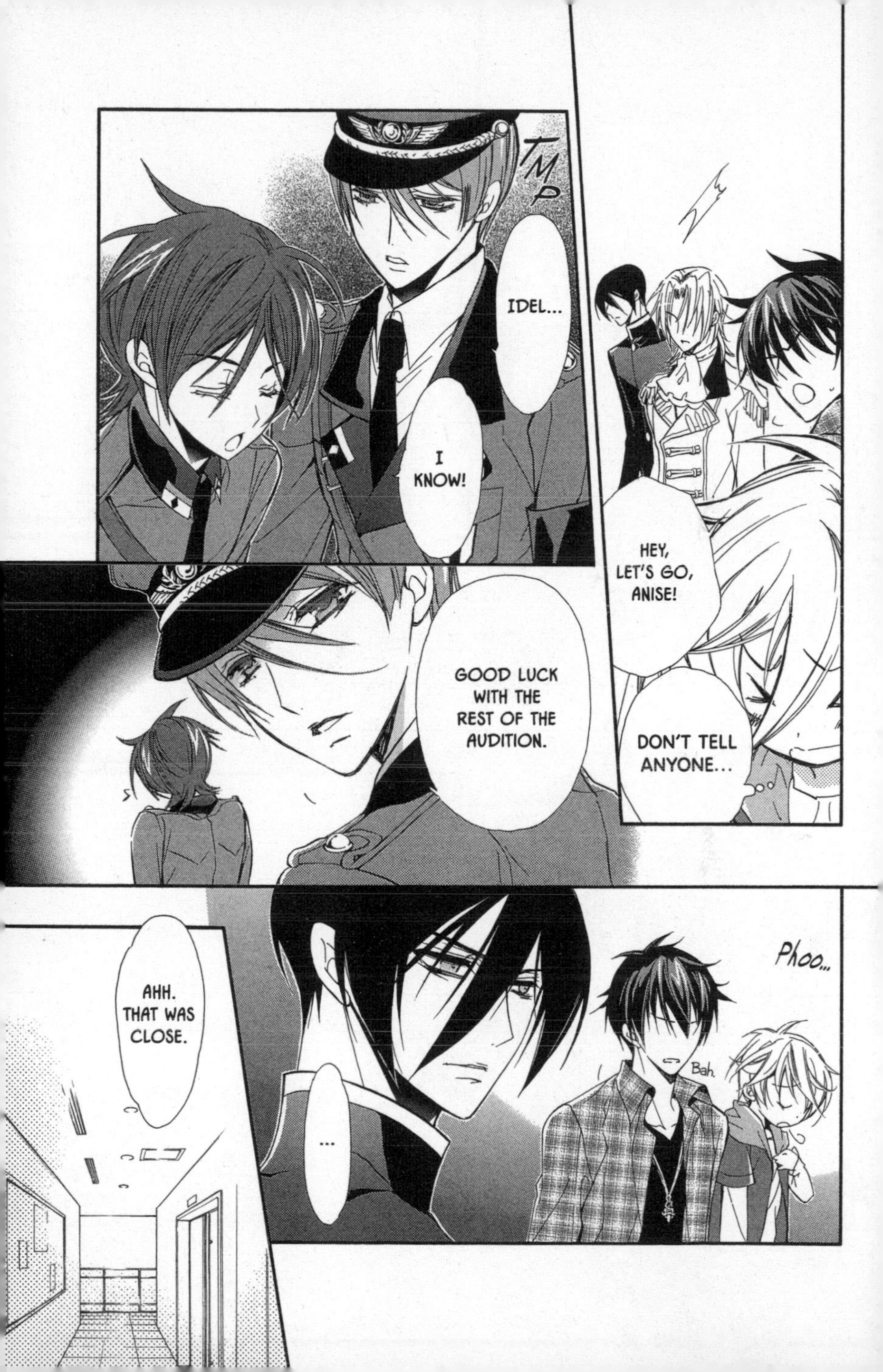
HEY, LET'S GO, ANISE!
DON'T TELL ANYONE...
TMP
IDEL...
I KNOW!
GOOD LUCK WITH THE REST OF THE AUDITION.
Phoo...
Bah.
...
AHH. THAT WAS CLOSE.

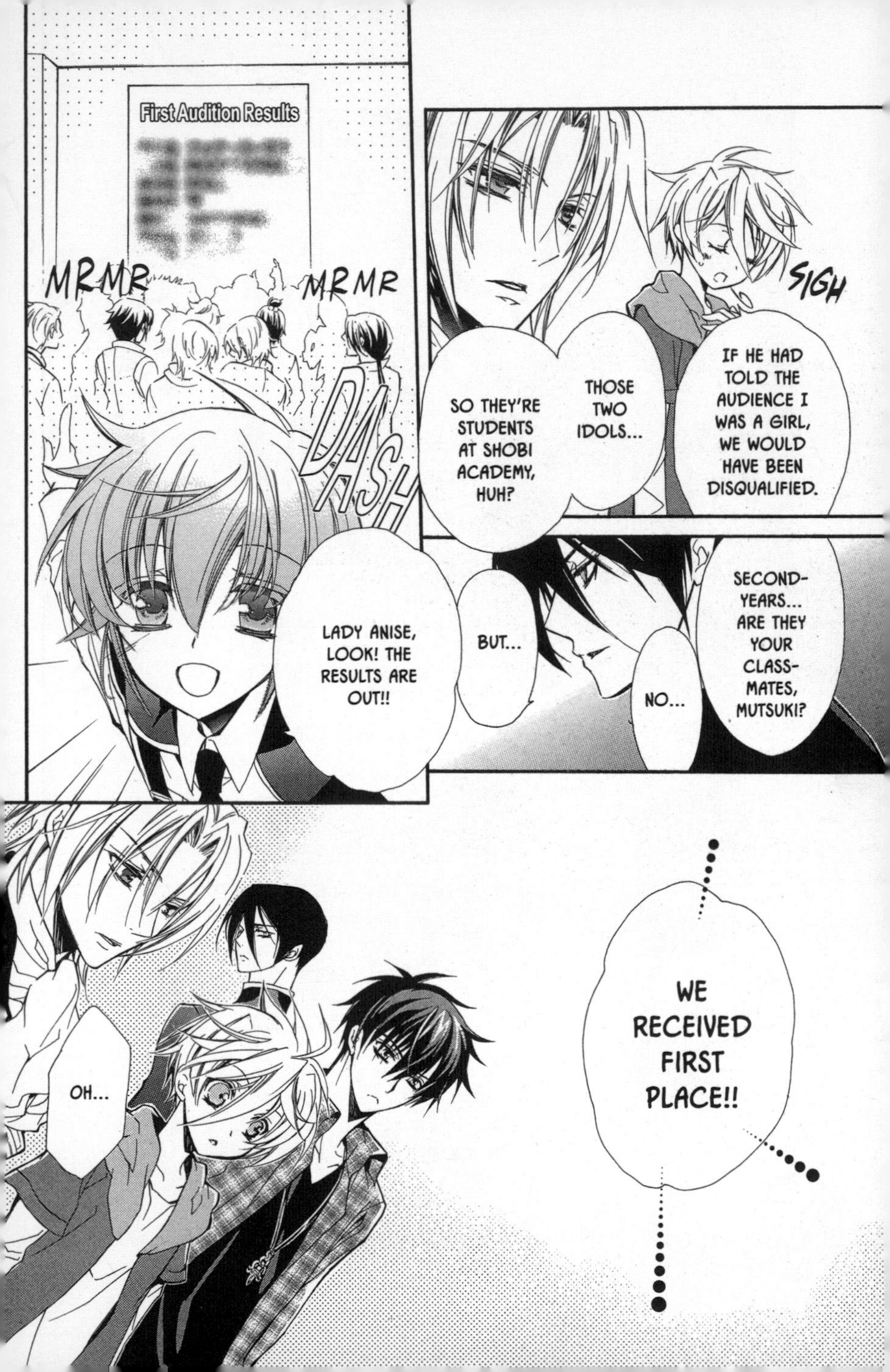
SIGH
IF HE HAD TOLD THE AUDIENCE I WAS A GIRL, WE WOULD HAVE BEEN DISQUALIFIED.
THOSE TWO IDOLS...
SO THEY'RE STUDENTS AT SHOBI ACADEMY, HUH?
SECOND-YEARS... ARE THEY YOUR CLASS-MATES, MUTSUKI?
NO...
BUT...
First Audition Results
MRMR
MRMR
DASH
LADY ANISE, LOOK! THE RESULTS ARE OUT!!
WE RECEIVED FIRST PLACE!!
OH...

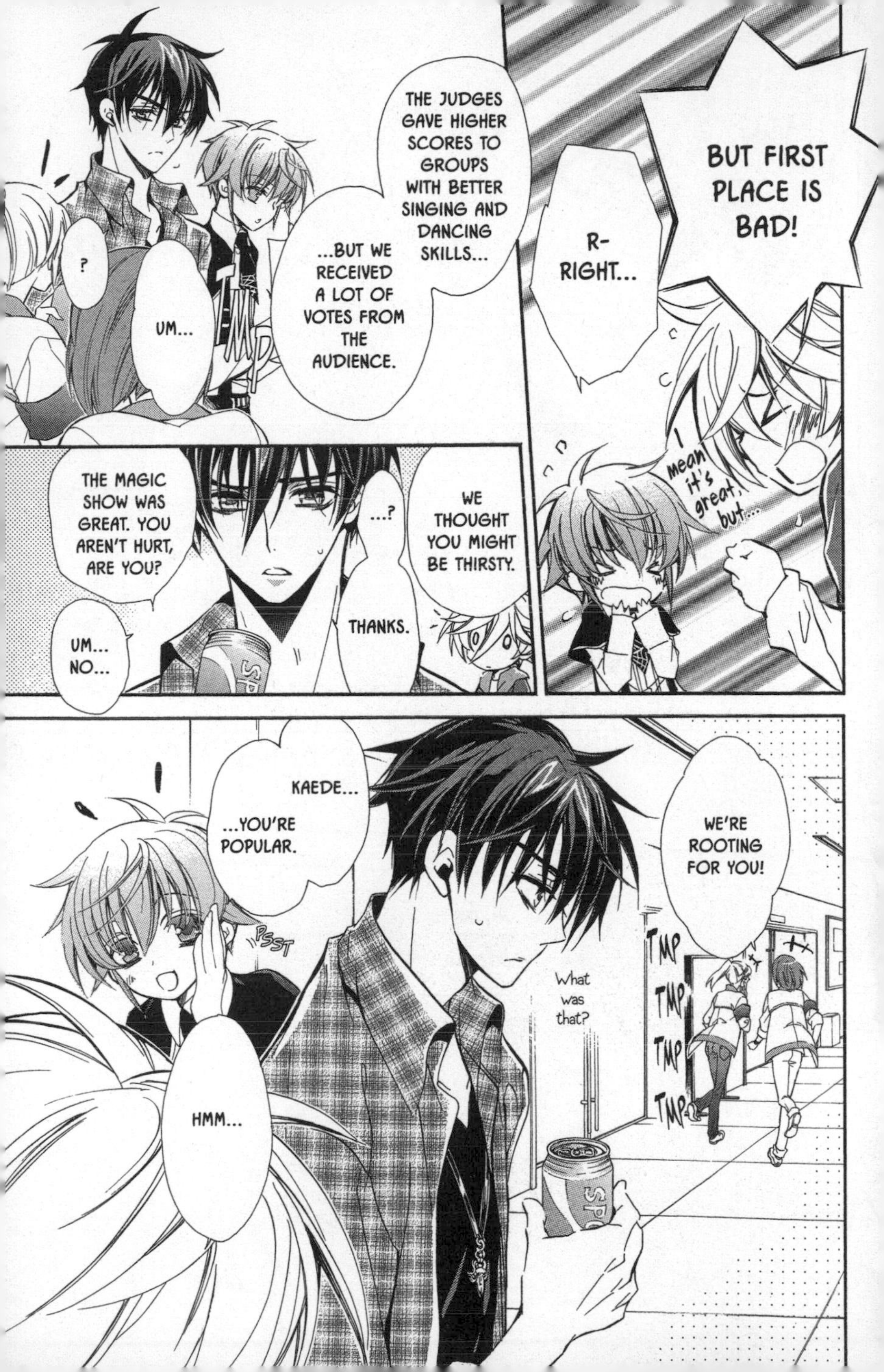
BUT FIRST PLACE IS BAD!
R-RIGHT...
I mean it's great, but...
THE JUDGES GAVE HIGHER SCORES TO GROUPS WITH BETTER SINGING AND DANCING SKILLS...
...BUT WE RECEIVED A LOT OF VOTES FROM THE AUDIENCE.
UM...
?
WE THOUGHT YOU MIGHT BE THIRSTY.
...?
THANKS.
THE MAGIC SHOW WAS GREAT. YOU AREN'T HURT, ARE YOU?
UM... NO...
WE'RE ROOTING FOR YOU!
TMP TMP TMP TMP
What was that?
KAEDE...
...YOU'RE POPULAR.
PSST
HMM...

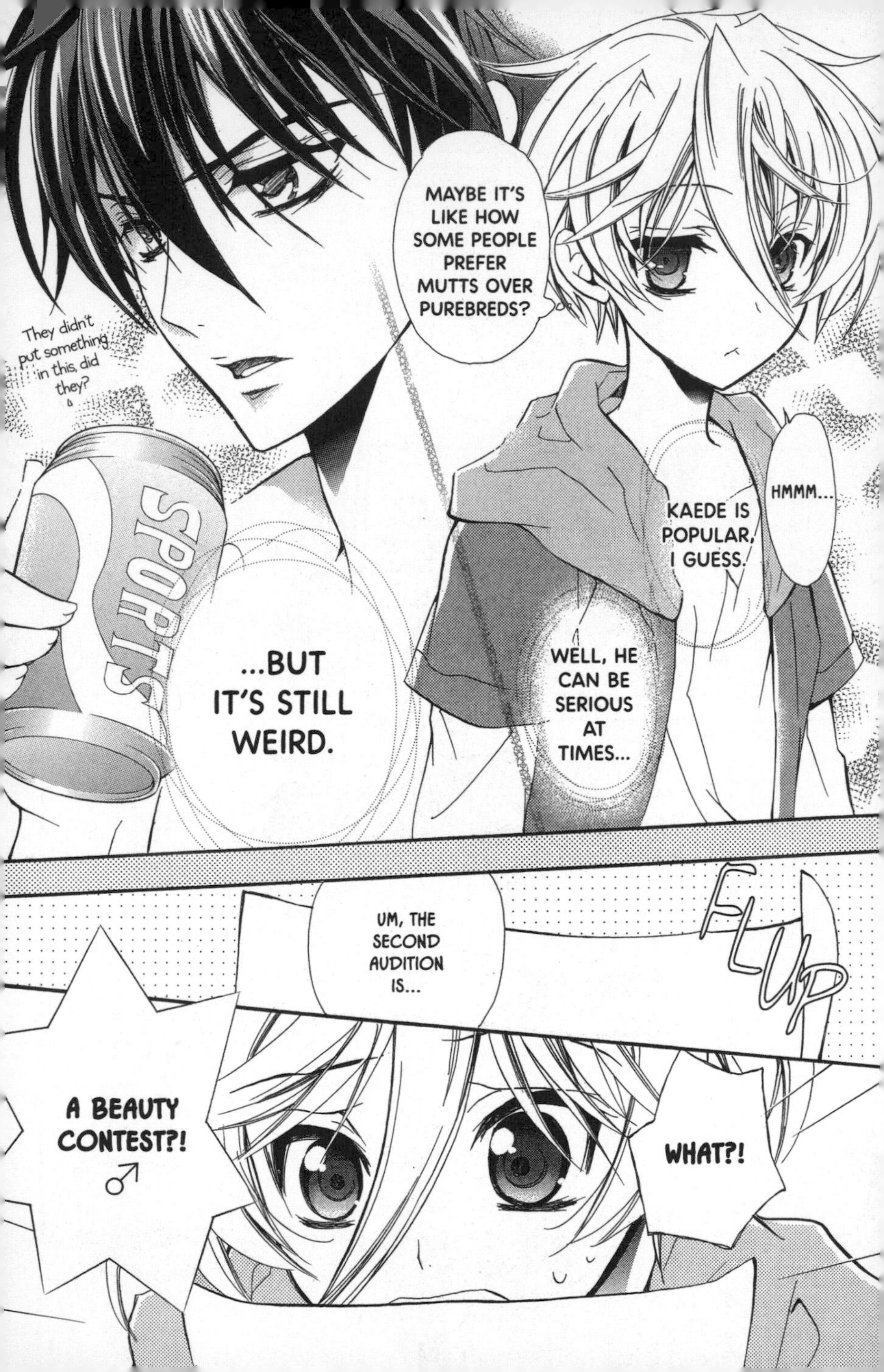
MAYBE IT'S LIKE HOW SOME PEOPLE PREFER MUTTS OVER PUREBREDS?
HMMM...
KAEDE IS POPULAR, I GUESS.
WELL, HE CAN BE SERIOUS AT TIMES...
They didn't put something in this, did they?
SPORTS
...BUT IT'S STILL WEIRD.
FLUP
UM, THE SECOND AUDITION IS...
WHAT?!
A BEAUTY CONTEST?! ♂

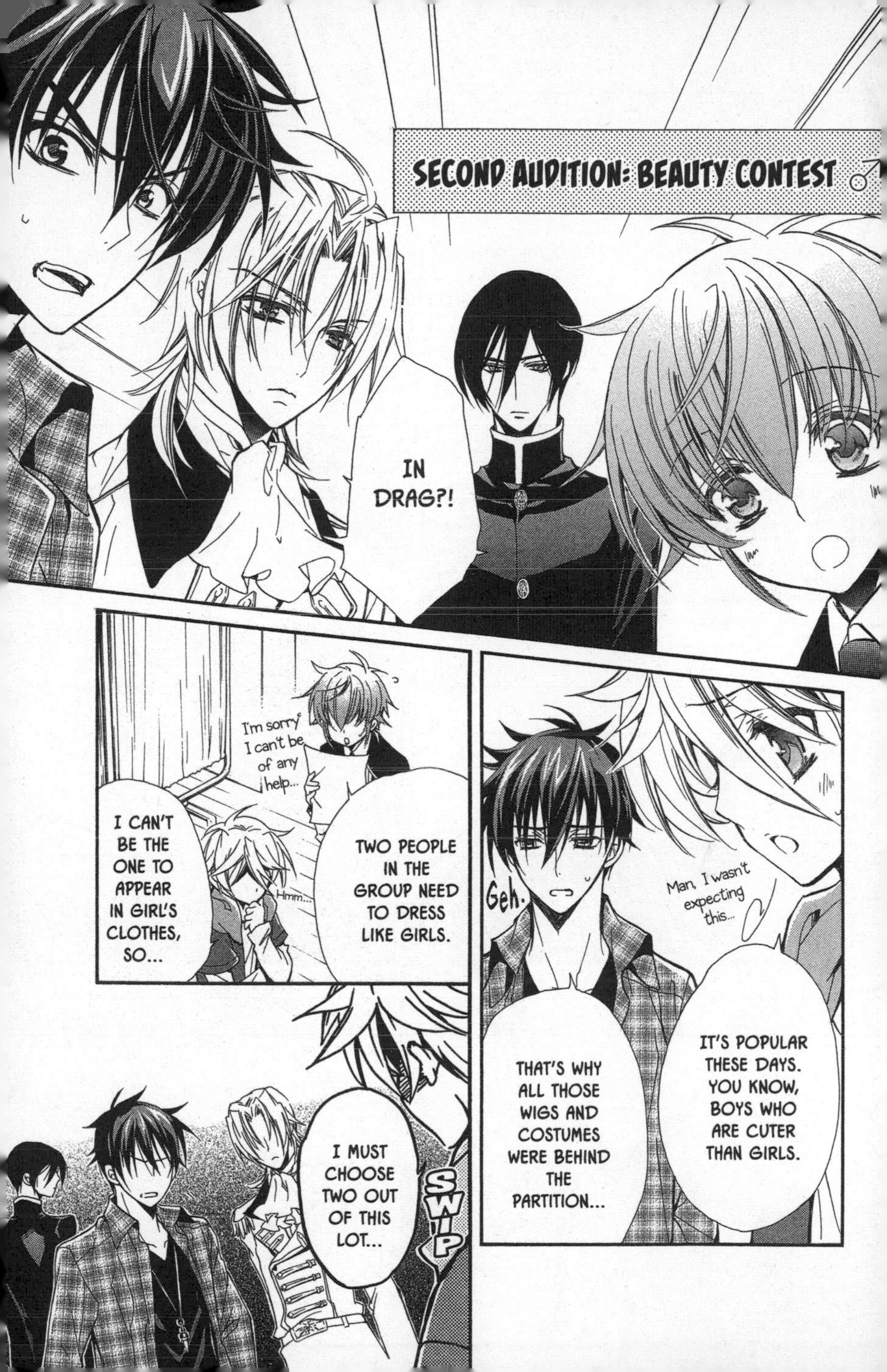
SECOND AUDITION: BEAUTY CONTEST ♂
IN DRAG?!
Man, I wasn't expecting this...
Geh.
IT'S POPULAR THESE DAYS. YOU KNOW, BOYS WHO ARE CUTER THAN GIRLS.
THAT'S WHY ALL THOSE WIGS AND COSTUMES WERE BEHIND THE PARTITION...
TWO PEOPLE IN THE GROUP NEED TO DRESS LIKE GIRLS.
I'm sorry I can't be of any help...
Hmm...
I CAN'T BE THE ONE TO APPEAR IN GIRL'S CLOTHES, SO...
SWIP
I MUST CHOOSE TWO OUT OF THIS LOT...

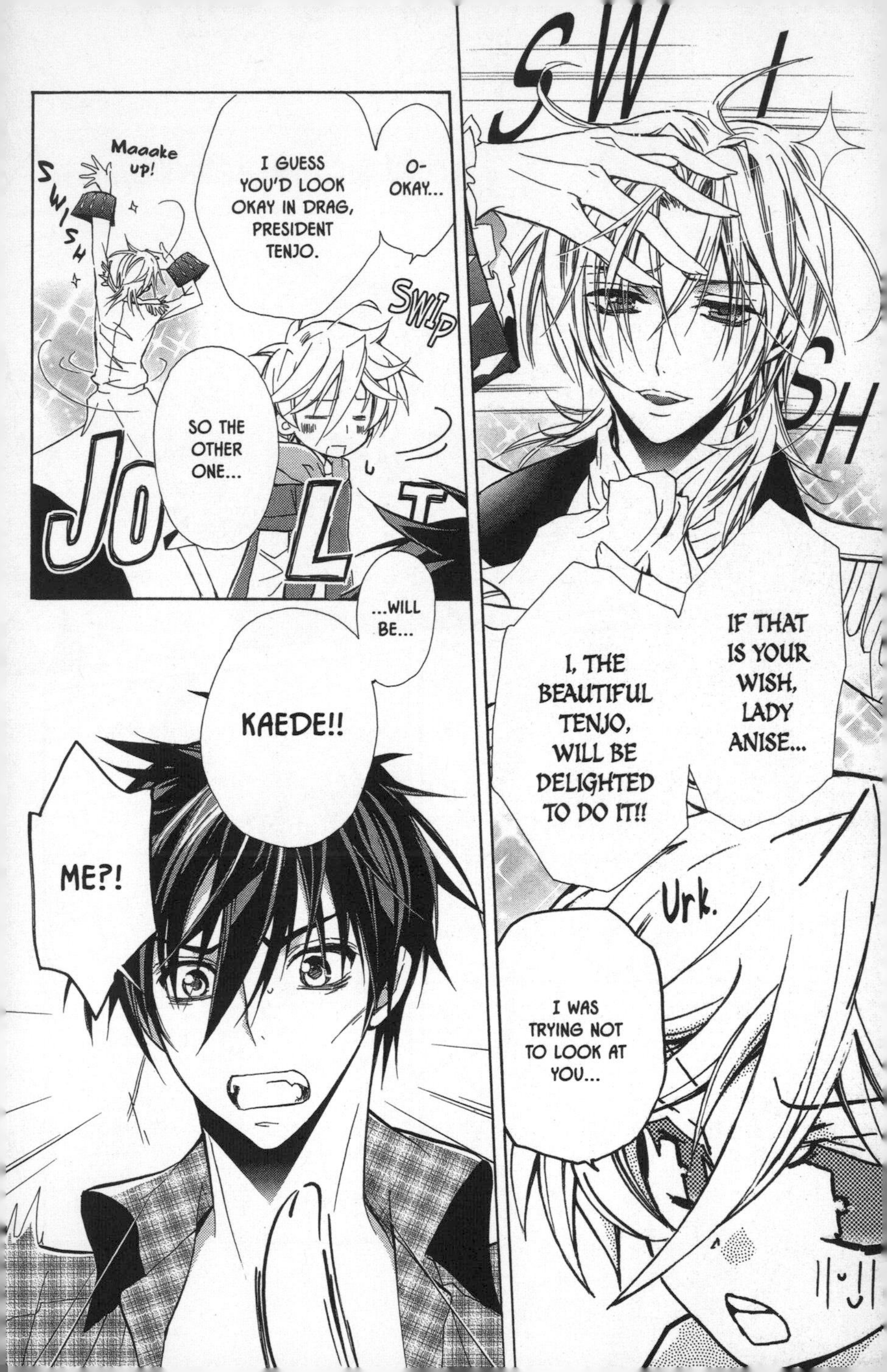
SWISH
IF THAT IS YOUR WISH, LADY ANISE...
I, THE BEAUTIFUL TENJO, WILL BE DELIGHTED TO DO IT!!
Urk.
I WAS TRYING NOT TO LOOK AT YOU...
O-OKAY...
I GUESS YOU'D LOOK OKAY IN DRAG, PRESIDENT TENJO.
Maaake up!
SWISH
SWIP
SO THE OTHER ONE...
JOLT
...WILL BE...
KAEDE!!
ME?!

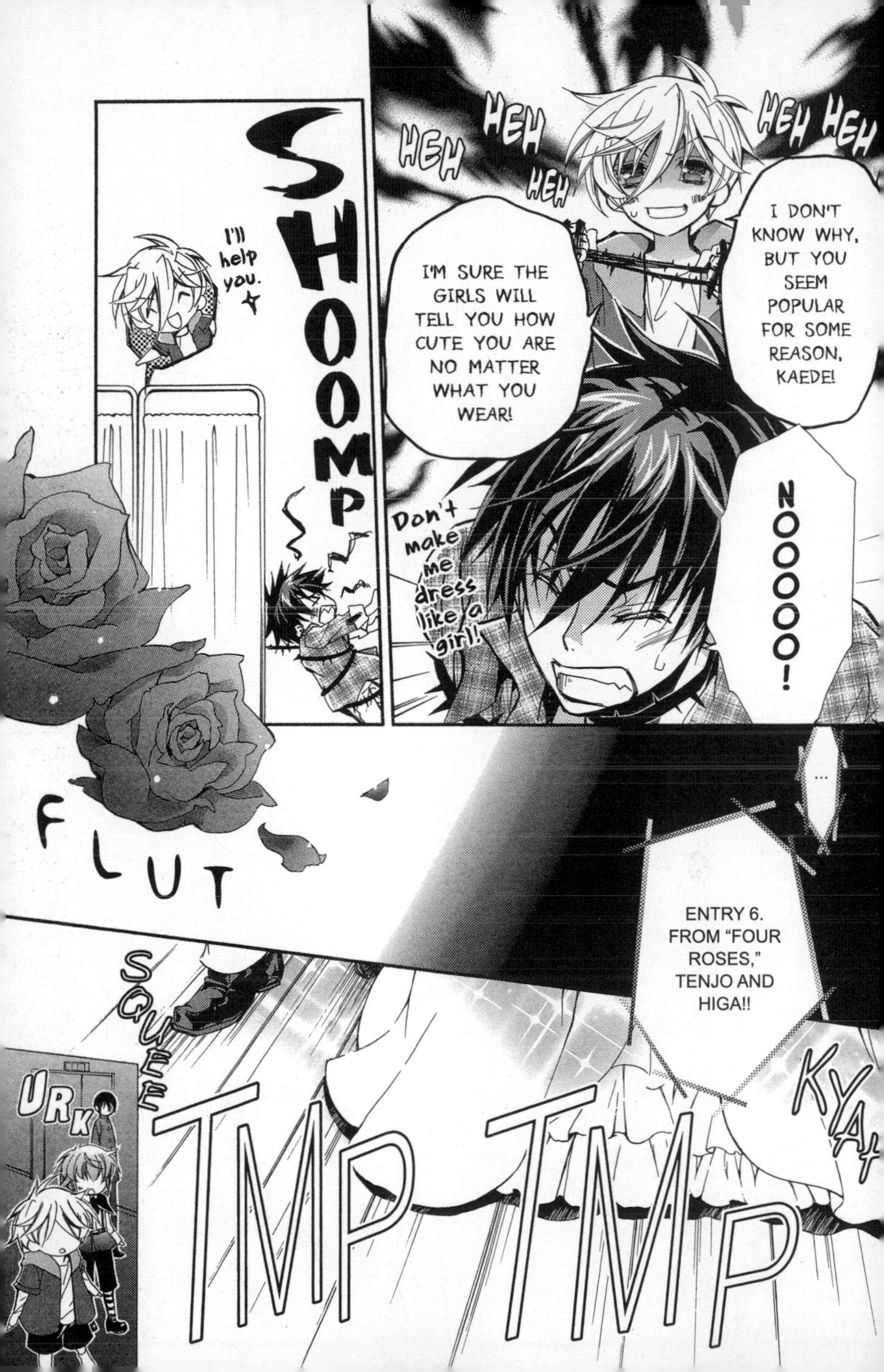
HEH HEH
I DON'T KNOW WHY, BUT YOU SEEM POPULAR FOR SOME REASON, KAEDE!
I'M SURE THE GIRLS WILL TELL YOU HOW CUTE YOU ARE NO MATTER WHAT YOU WEAR!
HEH HEH HEH HEH
NOOOOOO!
Don't make me dress like a girl!
SHOOMP
I'll help you.
...
FLUT
ENTRY 6. FROM "FOUR ROSES," TENJO AND HIGA!!
KYA
TMP TMP
SQUEE
URK

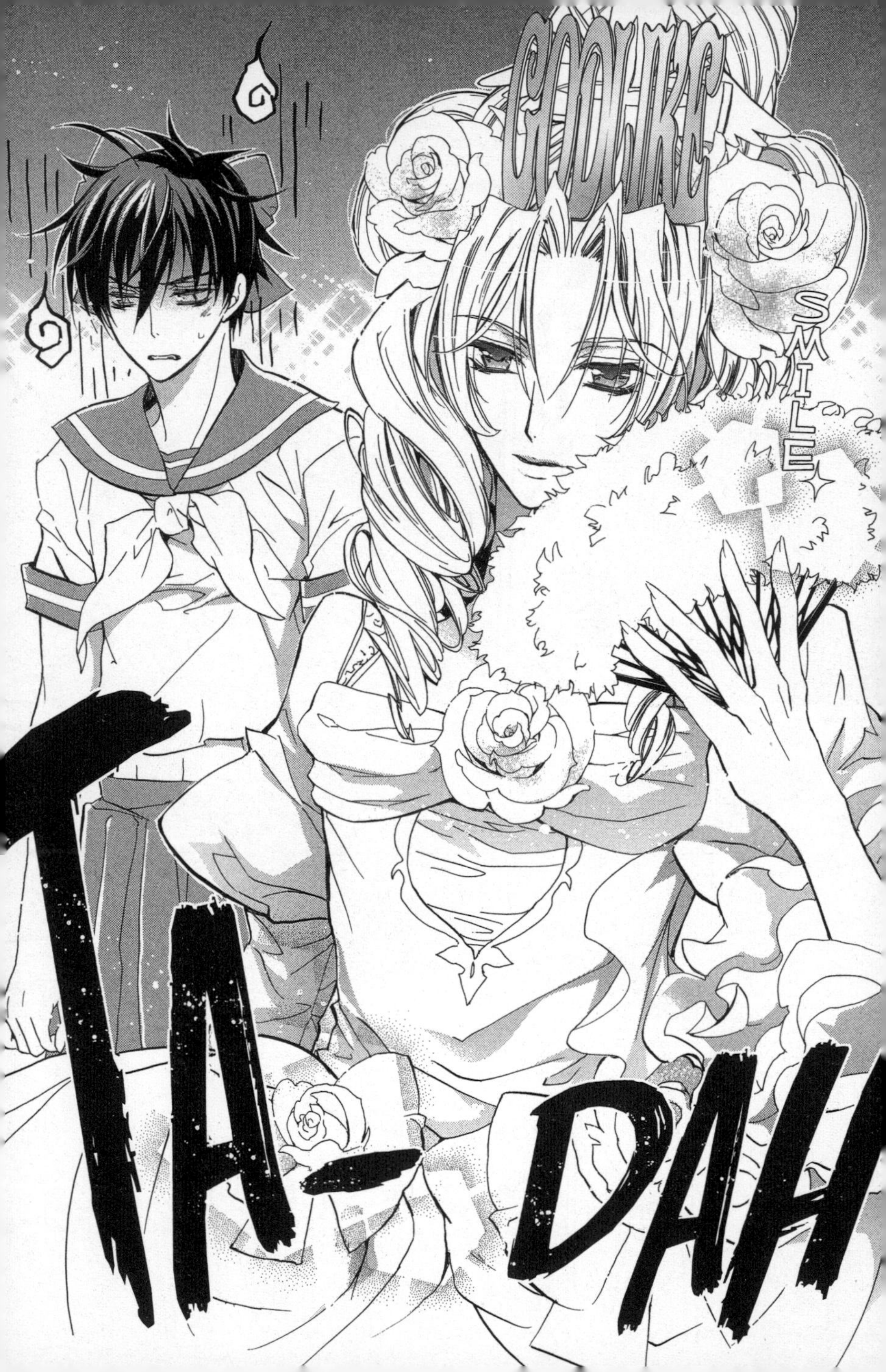
SMILE
TA-DAH

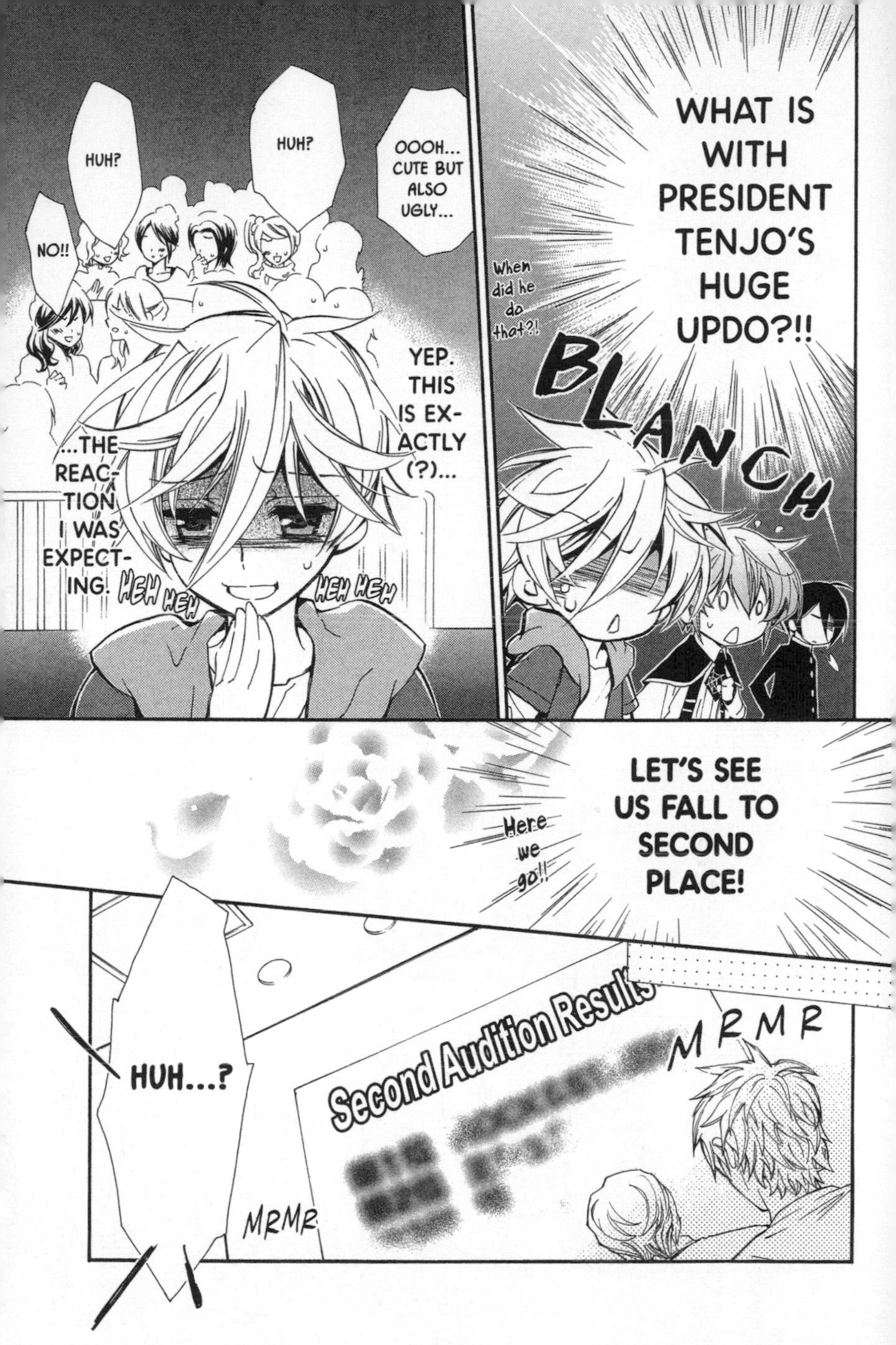
WHAT IS WITH PRESIDENT TENJO'S HUGE UPDO?!!
When did he do that?!
BLANCH
OOOH... CUTE BUT ALSO UGLY...
HUH?
HUH?
NO!!
YEP. THIS IS EX-ACTLY (?)...
...THE REAC-TION I WAS EXPECT-ING.
HEH HEH
HEH HEH
LET'S SEE US FALL TO SECOND PLACE!
Here we go!!
Second Audition Results
MRMR
HUH...?
MRMR

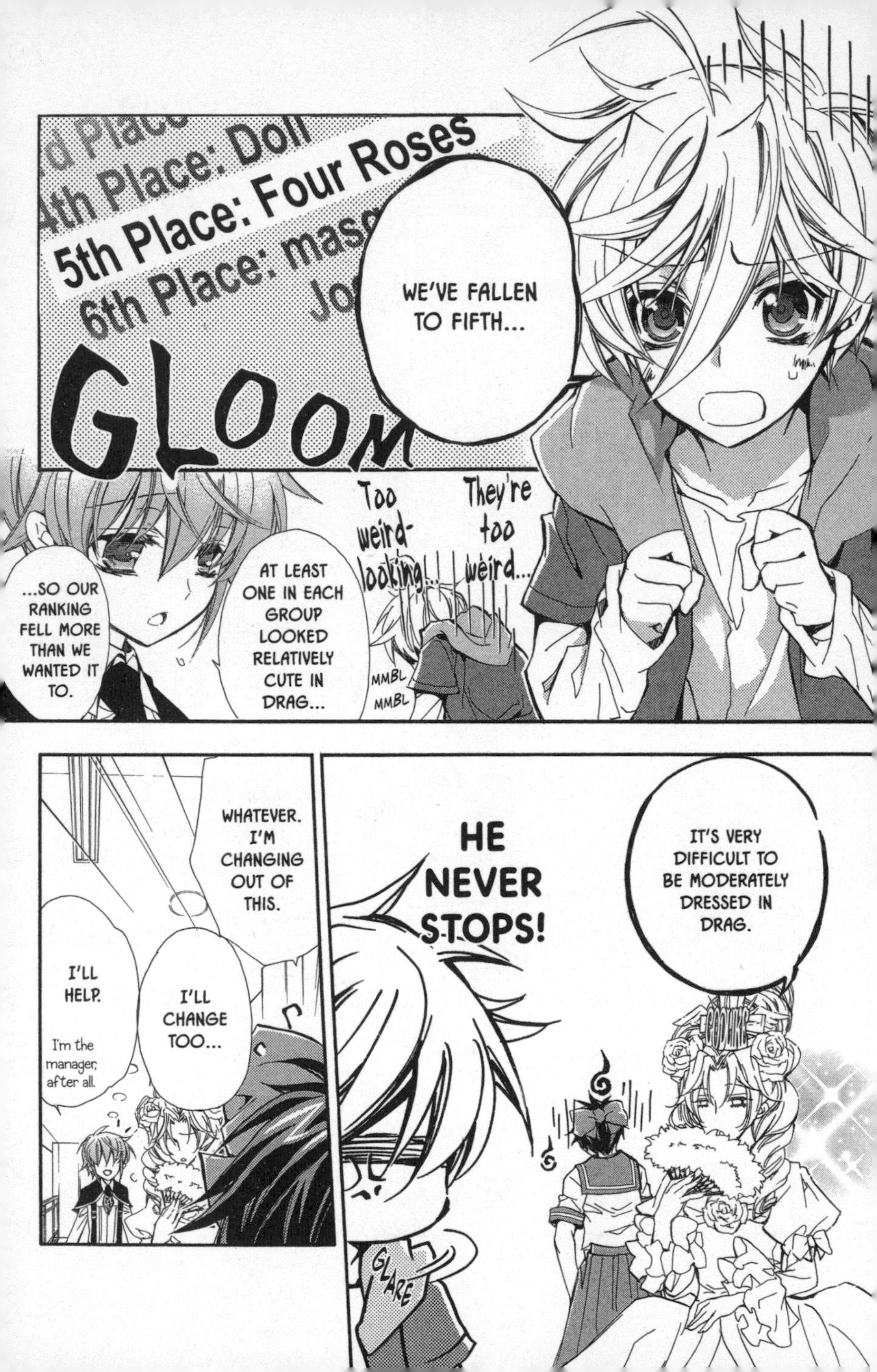
WE'VE FALLEN TO FIFTH...
4th Place: Doll
5th Place: Four Roses
6th Place: mas
GLOOM
They're too weird...
Too weird-looking...
MMBL MMBL
AT LEAST ONE IN EACH GROUP LOOKED RELATIVELY CUTE IN DRAG...
...SO OUR RANKING FELL MORE THAN WE WANTED IT TO.
IT'S VERY DIFFICULT TO BE MODERATELY DRESSED IN DRAG.
HE NEVER STOPS!
GLARE
WHATEVER. I'M CHANGING OUT OF THIS.
I'LL CHANGE TOO...
I'LL HELP.
I'm the manager, after all.

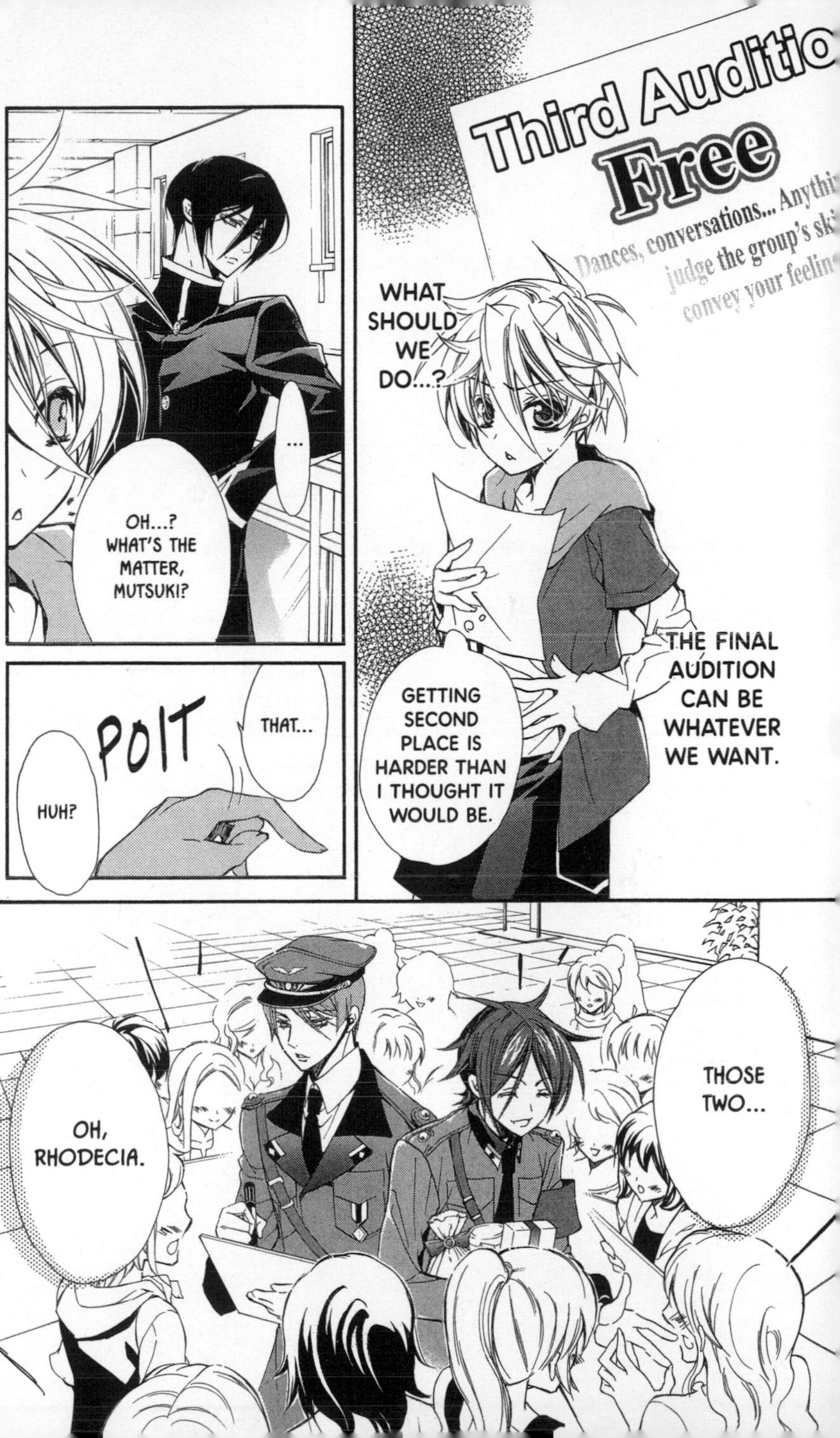
Third Auditio
Free
Dances, conversations... Anythi
judge the group's ski
convey your feelin
WHAT SHOULD WE DO...?
THE FINAL AUDITION CAN BE WHATEVER WE WANT.
GETTING SECOND PLACE IS HARDER THAN I THOUGHT IT WOULD BE.
...
OH...? WHAT'S THE MATTER, MUTSUKI?
THAT...
POIT
HUH?
THOSE TWO...
OH, RHODECIA.

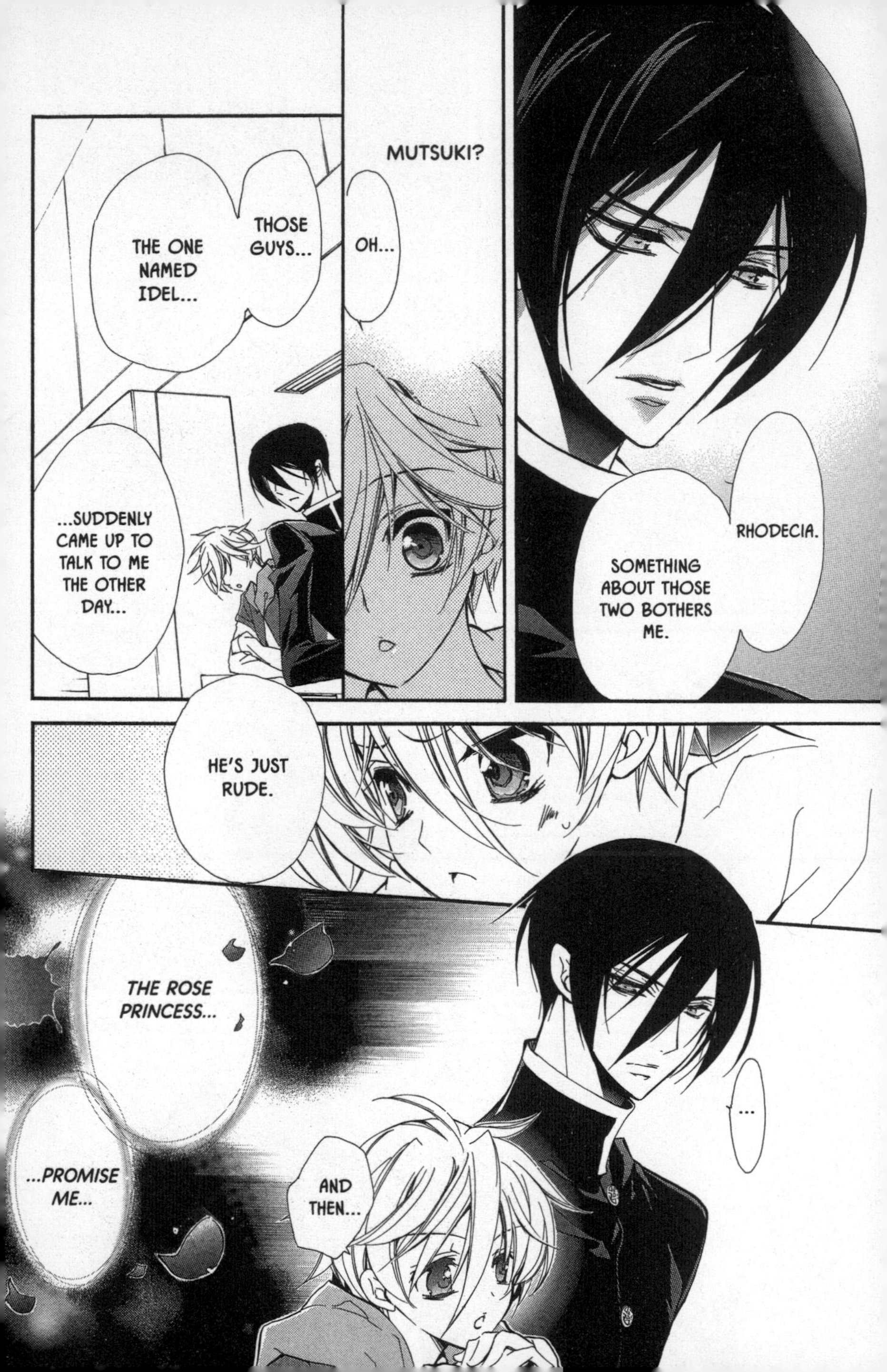
RHODECIA.
SOMETHING ABOUT THOSE TWO BOTHERS ME.
MUTSUKI?
OH...
THOSE GUYS...
THE ONE NAMED IDEL...
...SUDDENLY CAME UP TO TALK TO ME THE OTHER DAY...
HE'S JUST RUDE.
...
AND THEN...
THE ROSE PRINCESS...
...PROMISE ME...

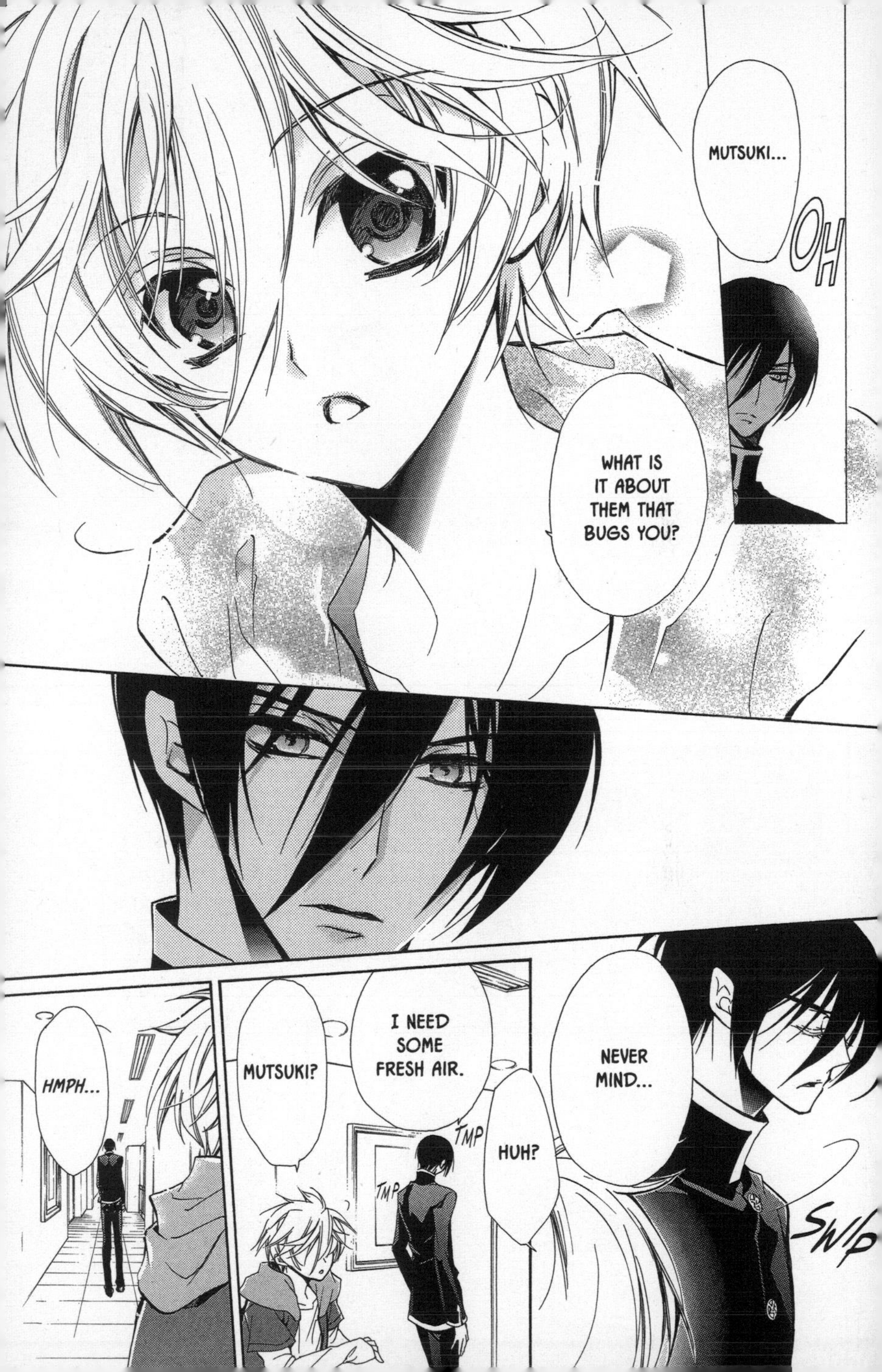
MUTSUKI...
OH
WHAT IS IT ABOUT THEM THAT BUGS YOU?
NEVER MIND...
SWIP
HUH?
I NEED SOME FRESH AIR.
TMP
TMP
MUTSUKI?
HMPH...

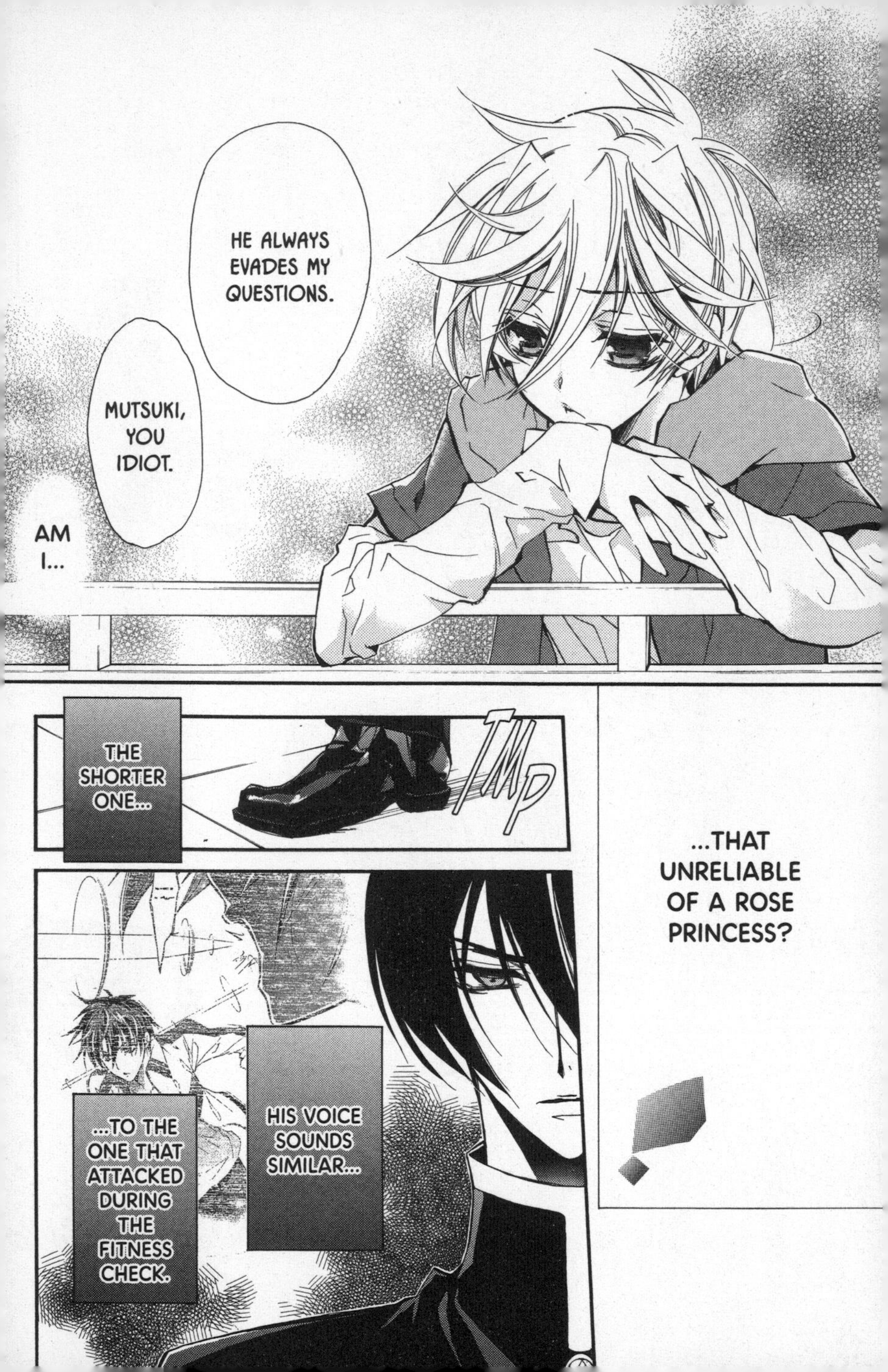
HE ALWAYS EVADES MY QUESTIONS.
MUTSUKI, YOU IDIOT.
AM I...
...THAT UNRELIABLE OF A ROSE PRINCESS?
THE SHORTER ONE...
TMP
HIS VOICE SOUNDS SIMILAR...
...TO THE ONE THAT ATTACKED DURING THE FITNESS CHECK.

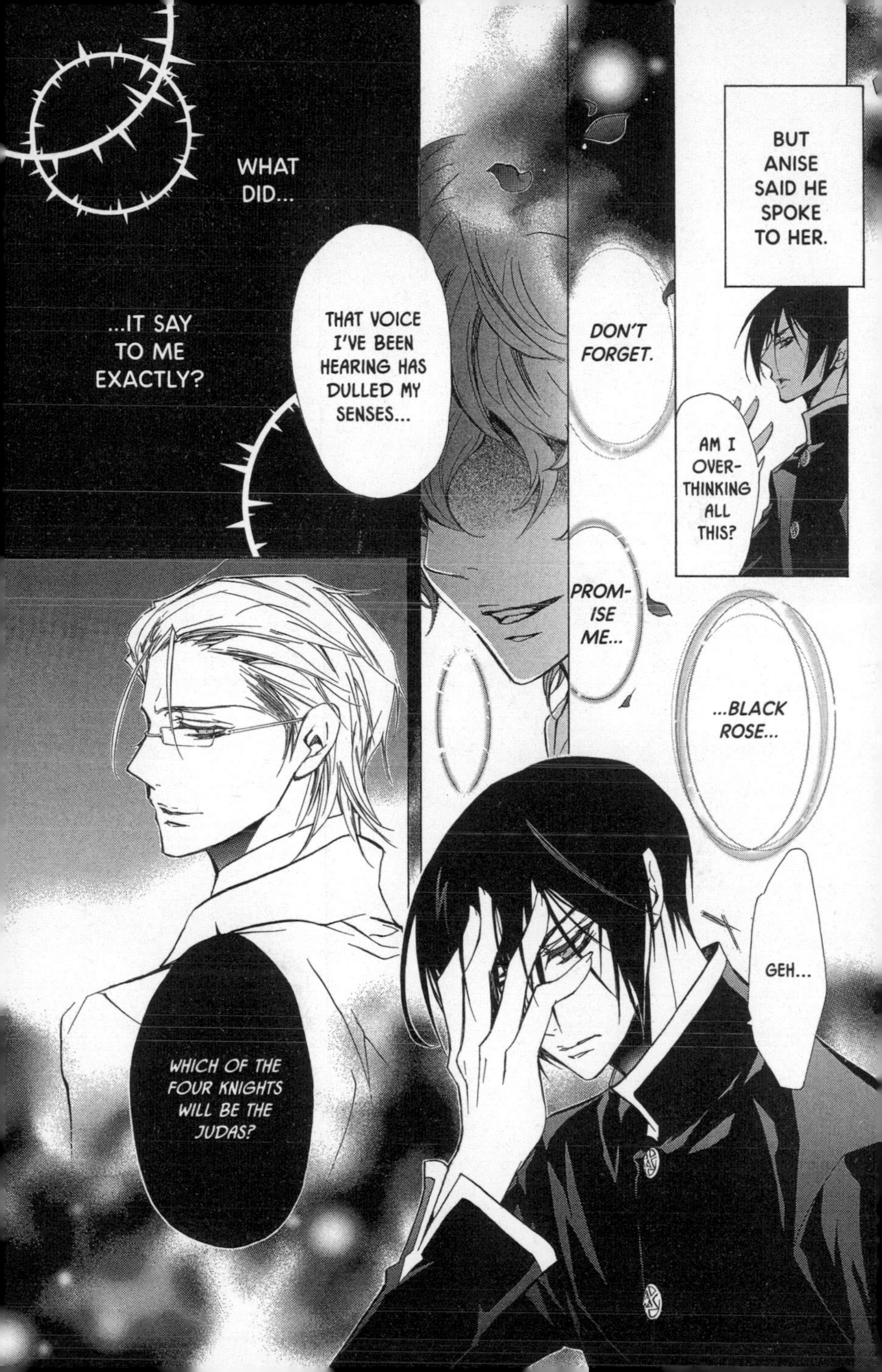
BUT ANISE SAID HE SPOKE TO HER.
AM I OVER-THINKING ALL THIS?
DON'T FORGET.
PROM-ISE ME...
...BLACK ROSE...
THAT VOICE I'VE BEEN HEARING HAS DULLED MY SENSES...
WHAT DID...
...IT SAY TO ME EXACTLY?
GEH...
WHICH OF THE FOUR KNIGHTS WILL BE THE JUDAS?

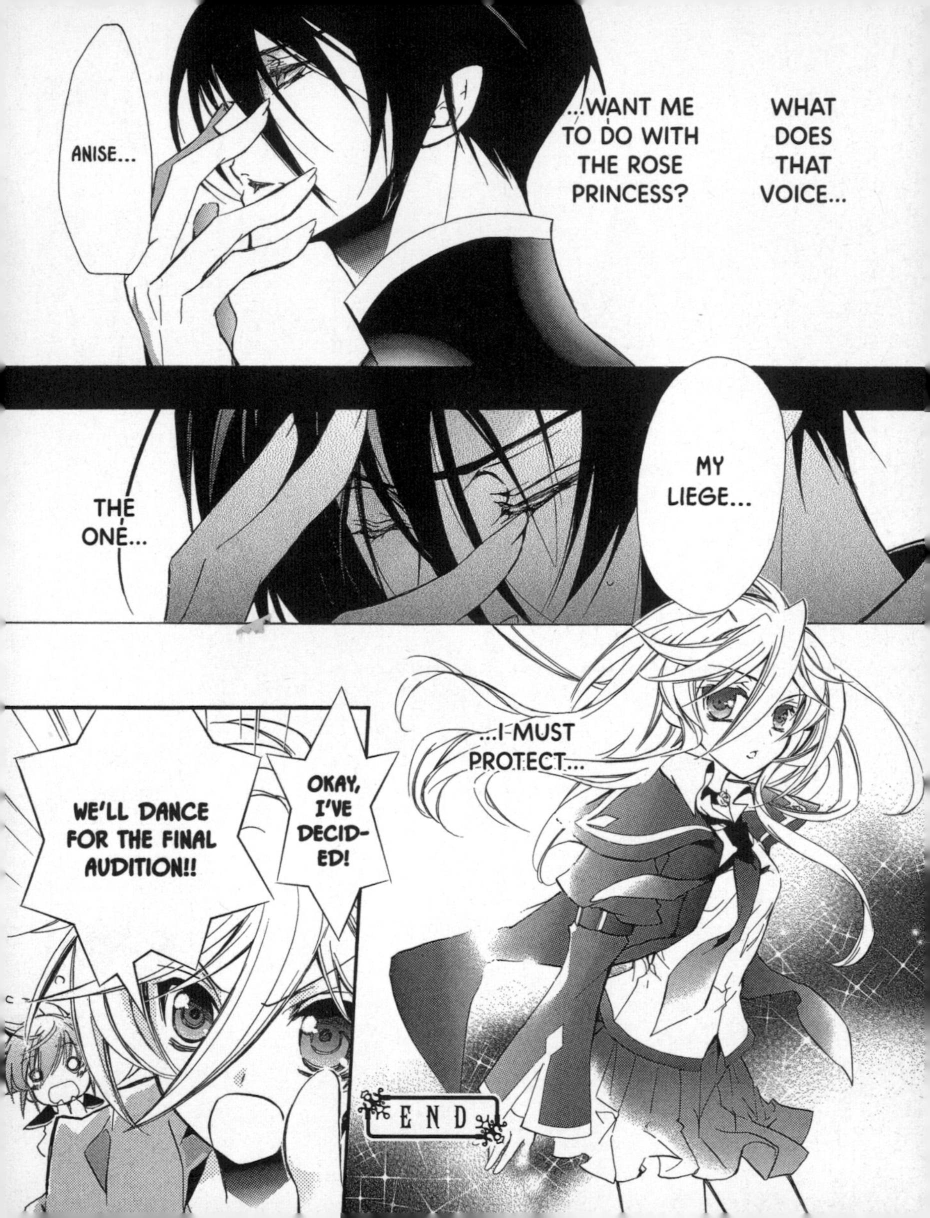
WHAT DOES THAT VOICE...
...WANT ME TO DO WITH THE ROSE PRINCESS?
ANISE...
MY LIEGE...
THE ONE...
...I MUST PROTECT...
OKAY, I'VE DECID-ED!
WE'LL DANCE FOR THE FINAL AUDITION!!
END

Kiss of the Rose
Princess

Kiss of the Rose Princess

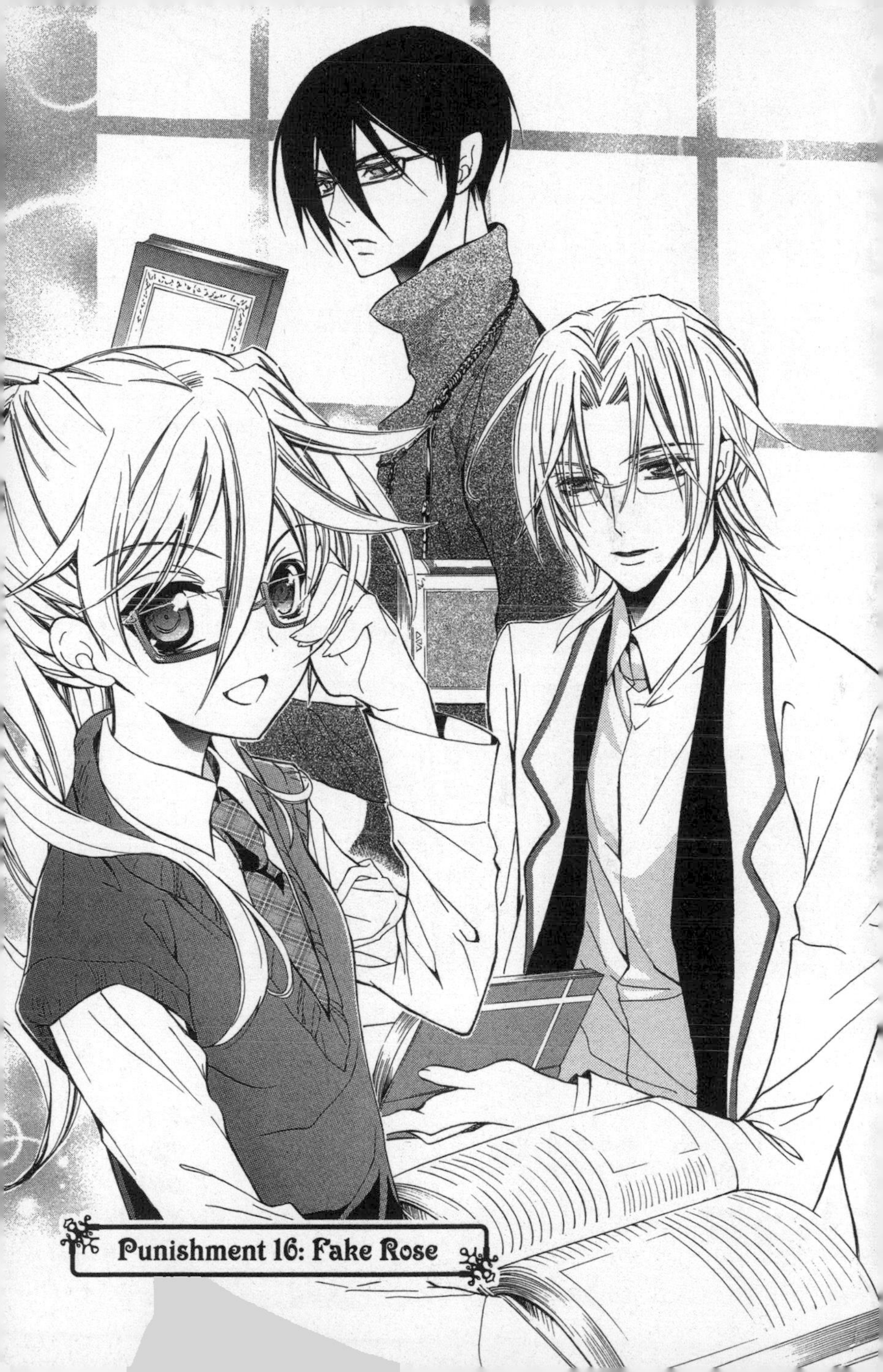
Punishment 16: Fake Rose

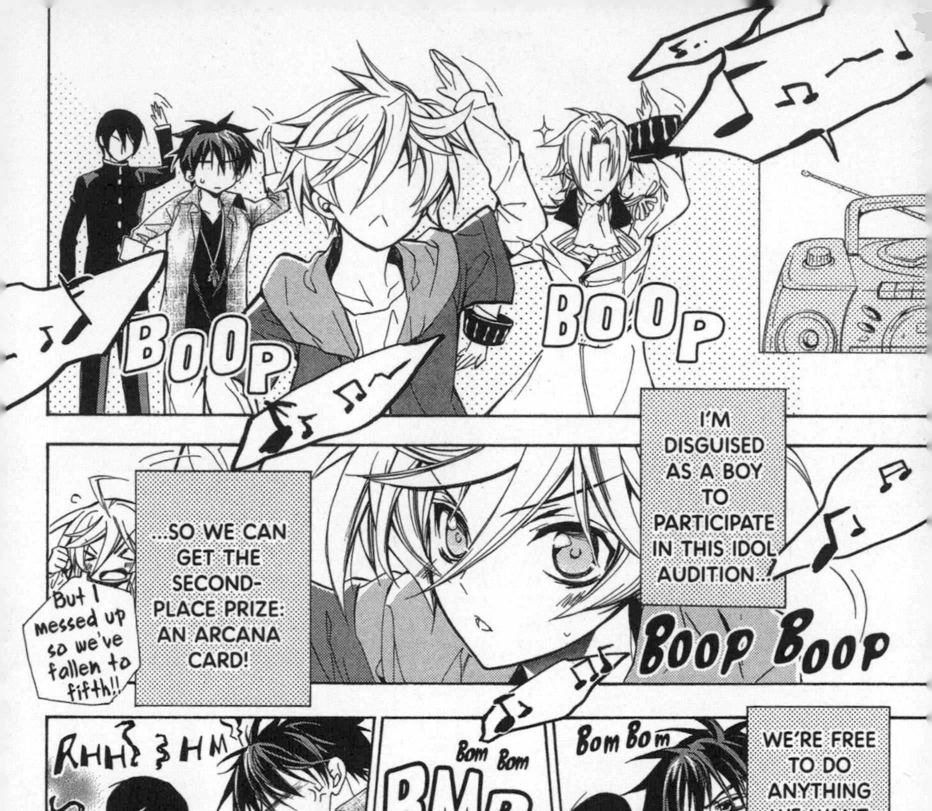
BOOP
BOOP
I'M DISGUISED AS A BOY TO PARTICIPATE IN THIS IDOL AUDITION...
BOOP BOOP
...SO WE CAN GET THE SECOND-PLACE PRIZE: AN ARCANA CARD!
But I messed up so we've fallen to fifth!!
WE'RE FREE TO DO ANYTHING WE WANT TO IN THE FINAL AUDITION...
Bom Bom
BMP
Bom Bom
BMP
RHH HM
BOOP BOOP BOOP

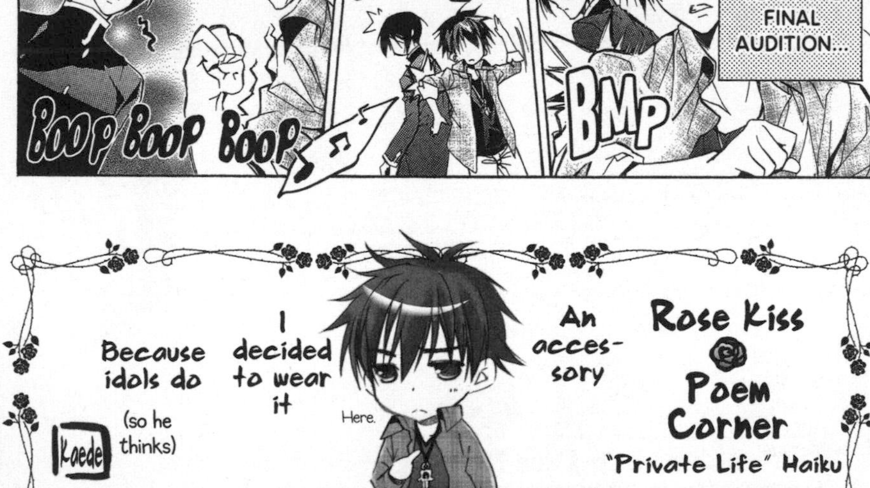
Rose Kiss Poem Corner
"Private Life" Haiku
An acces-sory
I decided to wear it
Because idols do
(so he thinks)
Kaede
Here.

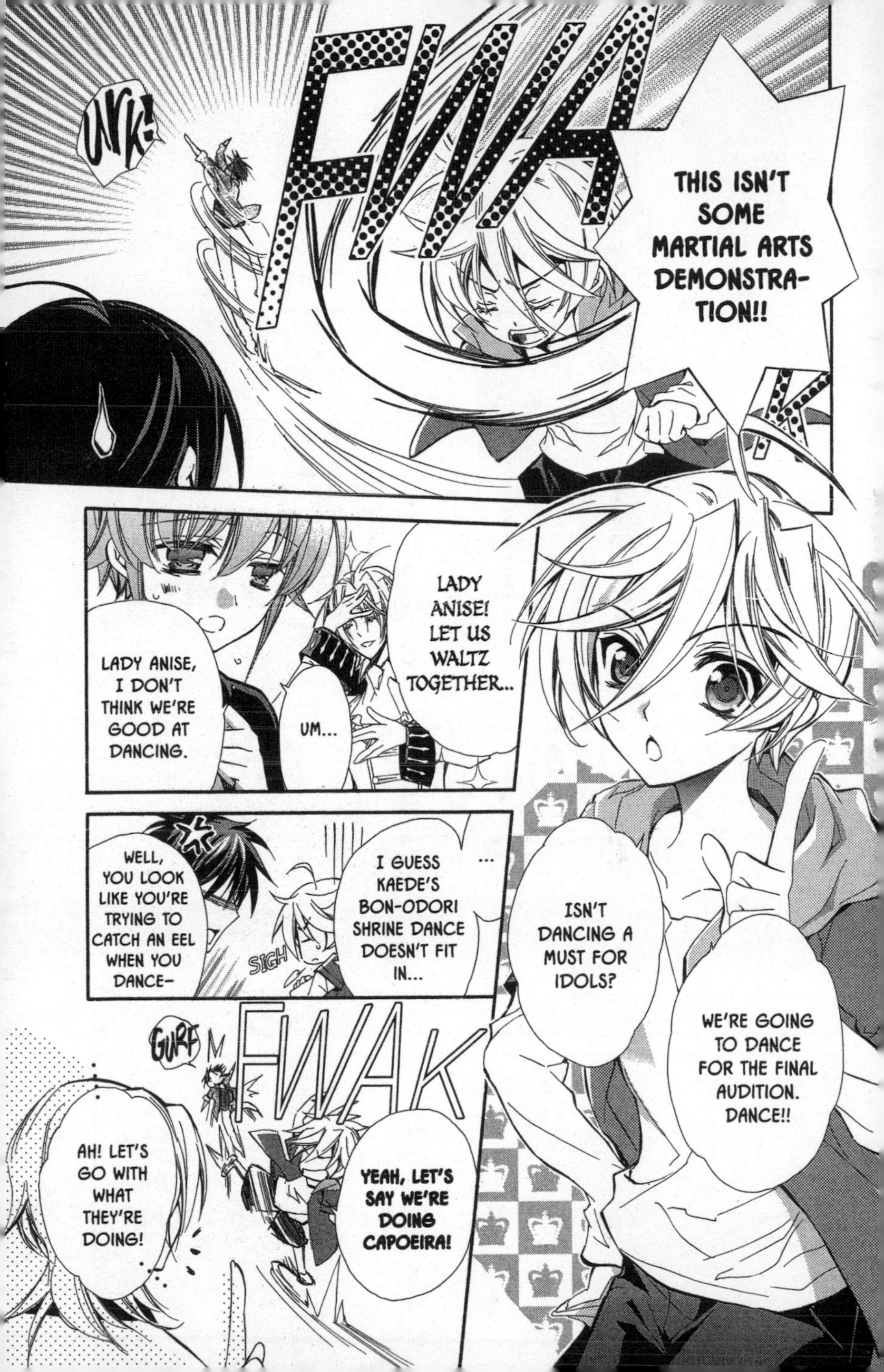
FWA
K
THIS ISN'T SOME MARTIAL ARTS DEMONSTRATION!!
UNK!
ISN'T DANCING A MUST FOR IDOLS?
WE'RE GOING TO DANCE FOR THE FINAL AUDITION. DANCE!!
LADY ANISE! LET US WALTZ TOGETHER...
UM...
LADY ANISE, I DON'T THINK WE'RE GOOD AT DANCING.
...
I GUESS KAEDE'S BON-ODORI SHRINE DANCE DOESN'T FIT IN...
SIGH
WELL, YOU LOOK LIKE YOU'RE TRYING TO CATCH AN EEL WHEN YOU DANCE-
FWAK
GURF M
YEAH, LET'S SAY WE'RE DOING CAPOEIRA!
AH! LET'S GO WITH WHAT THEY'RE DOING!

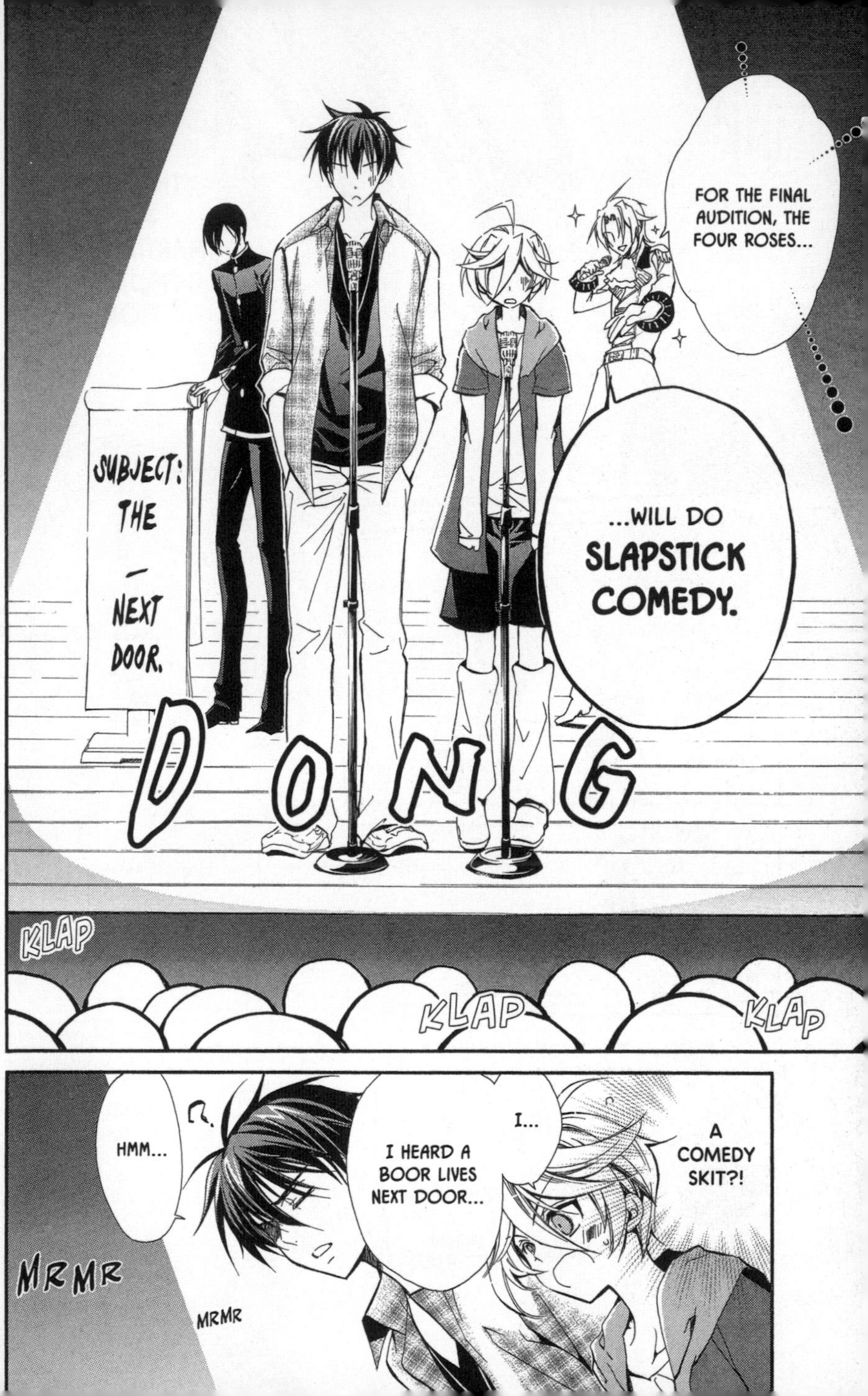
FOR THE FINAL AUDITION, THE FOUR ROSES...
...WILL DO SLAPSTICK COMEDY.
SUBJECT: THE — NEXT DOOR.
DONG
KLAP
KLAP
KLAP
A COMEDY SKIT?!
I...
I HEARD A BOOR LIVES NEXT DOOR...
HMM...
MRMR
MRMR

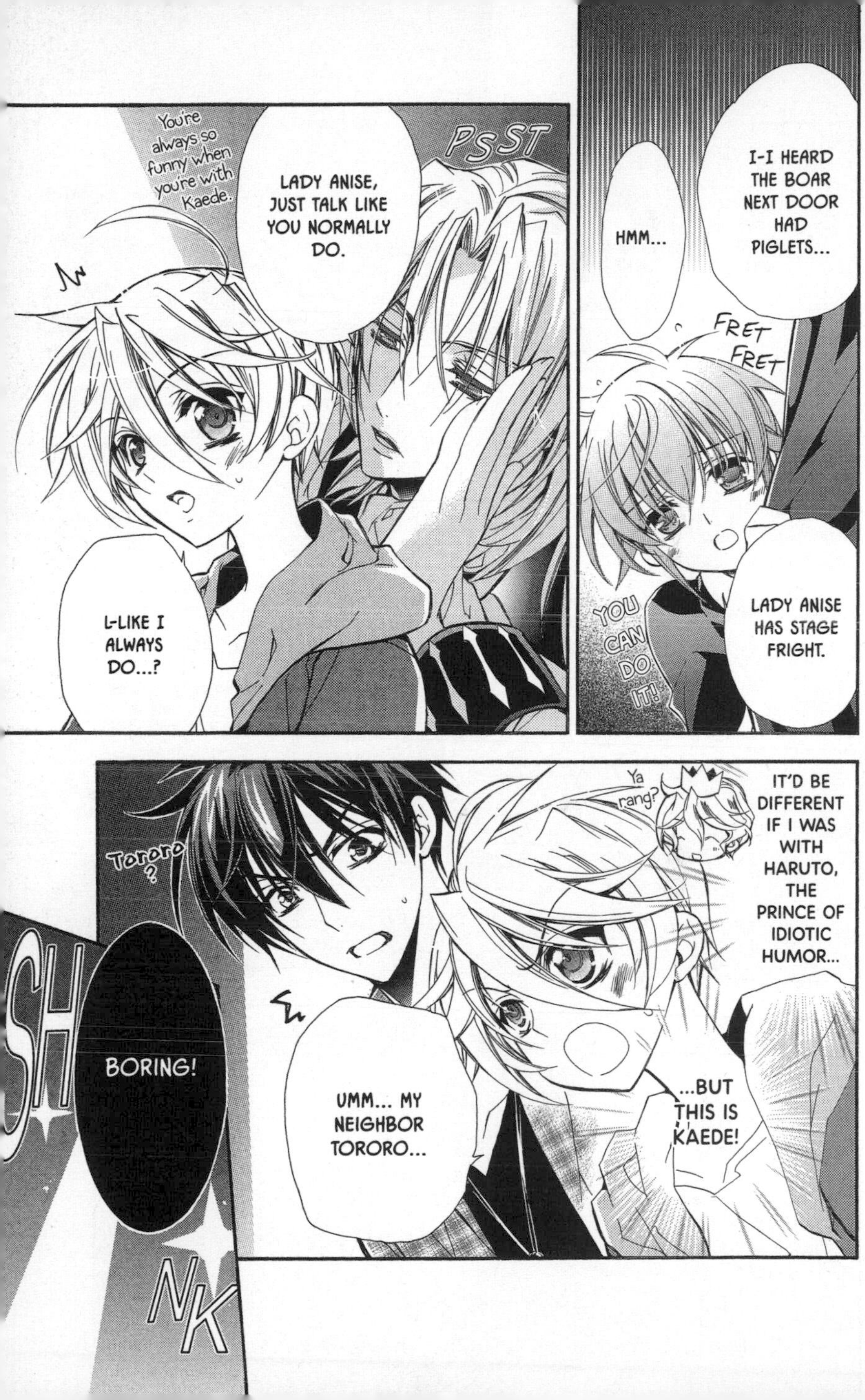
I-I HEARD THE BOAR NEXT DOOR HAD PIGLETS...
HMM...
FRET FRET
LADY ANISE HAS STAGE FRIGHT.
YOU CAN DO IT!
PSST
LADY ANISE, JUST TALK LIKE YOU NORMALLY DO.
You're always so funny when you're with Kaede.
L-LIKE I ALWAYS DO...?
IT'D BE DIFFERENT IF I WAS WITH HARUTO, THE PRINCE OF IDIOTIC HUMOR...
Ya rang?
...BUT THIS IS KAEDE!
Tororo ?
UMM... MY NEIGHBOR TORORO...
BORING!
SHNK

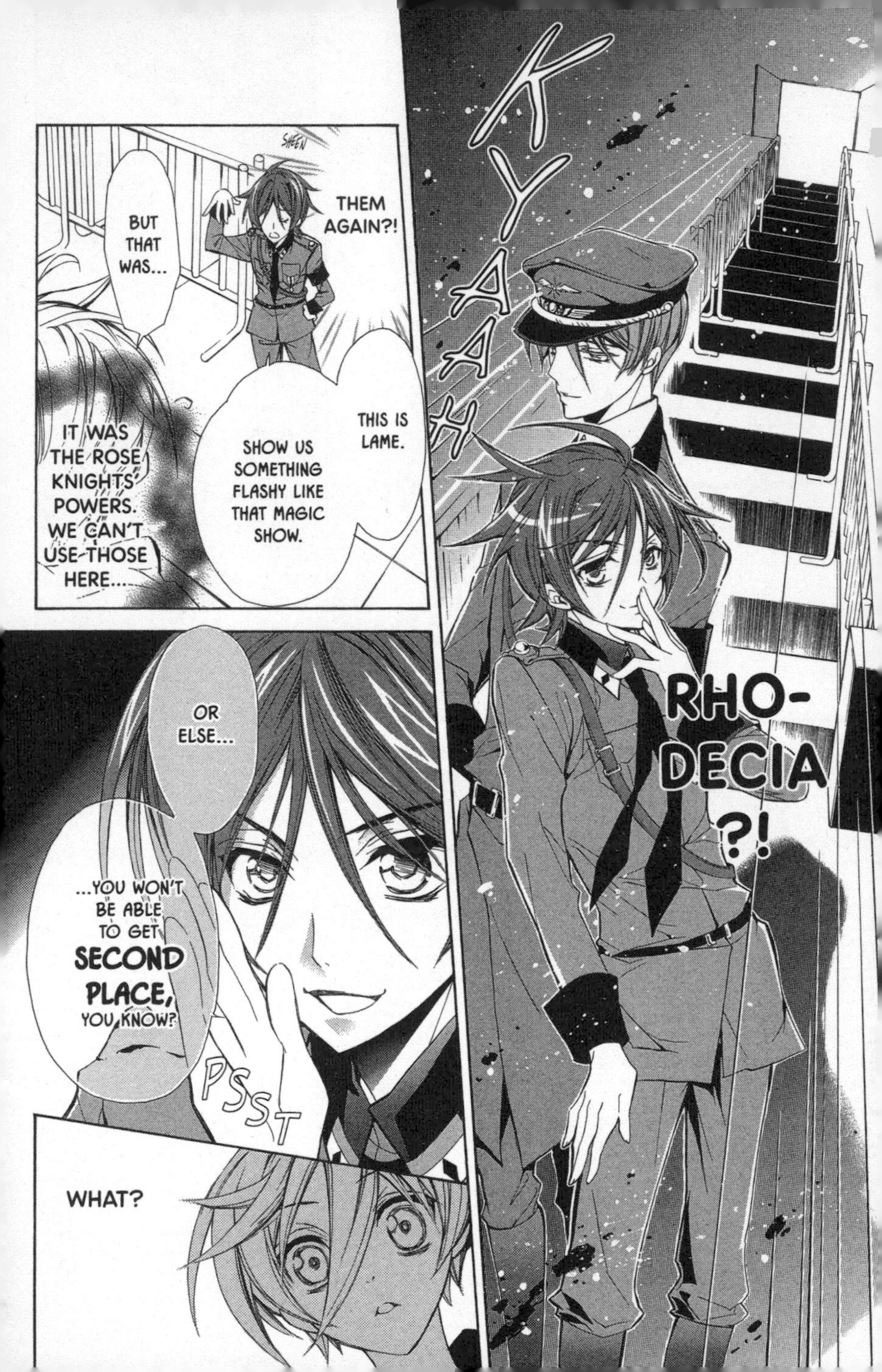
KYAAAH
RHODECIA?!
THEM AGAIN?!
SHEEN
BUT THAT WAS...
THIS IS LAME.
SHOW US SOMETHING FLASHY LIKE THAT MAGIC SHOW.
IT WAS THE ROSE KNIGHTS' POWERS. WE CAN'T USE THOSE HERE...
OR ELSE...
...YOU WON'T BE ABLE TO GET SECOND PLACE, YOU KNOW?
PSST
WHAT?

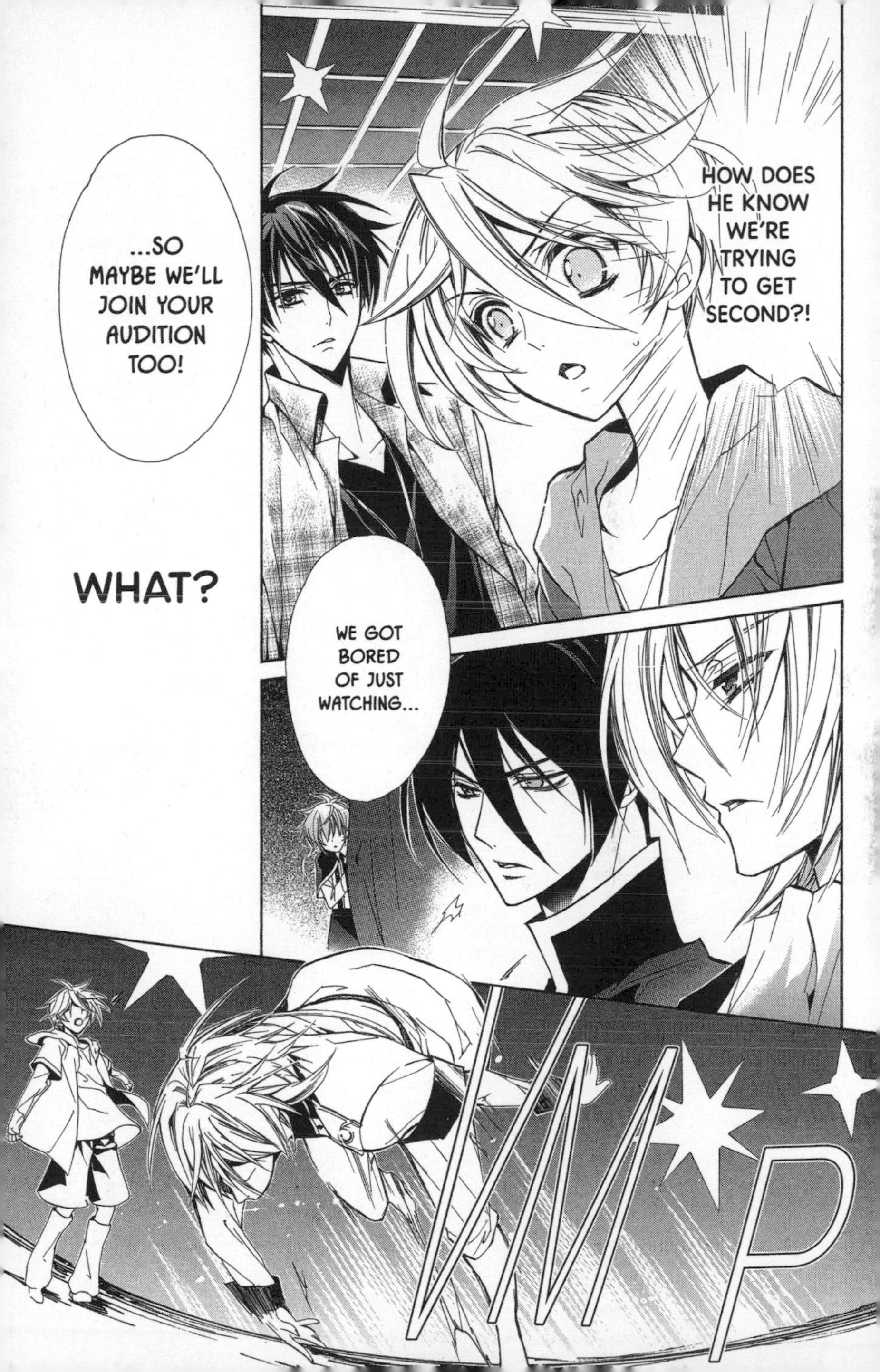
HOW DOES HE KNOW WE'RE TRYING TO GET SECOND?!
WE GOT BORED OF JUST WATCHING...
...SO MAYBE WE'LL JOIN YOUR AUDITION TOO!
WHAT?
WHIP

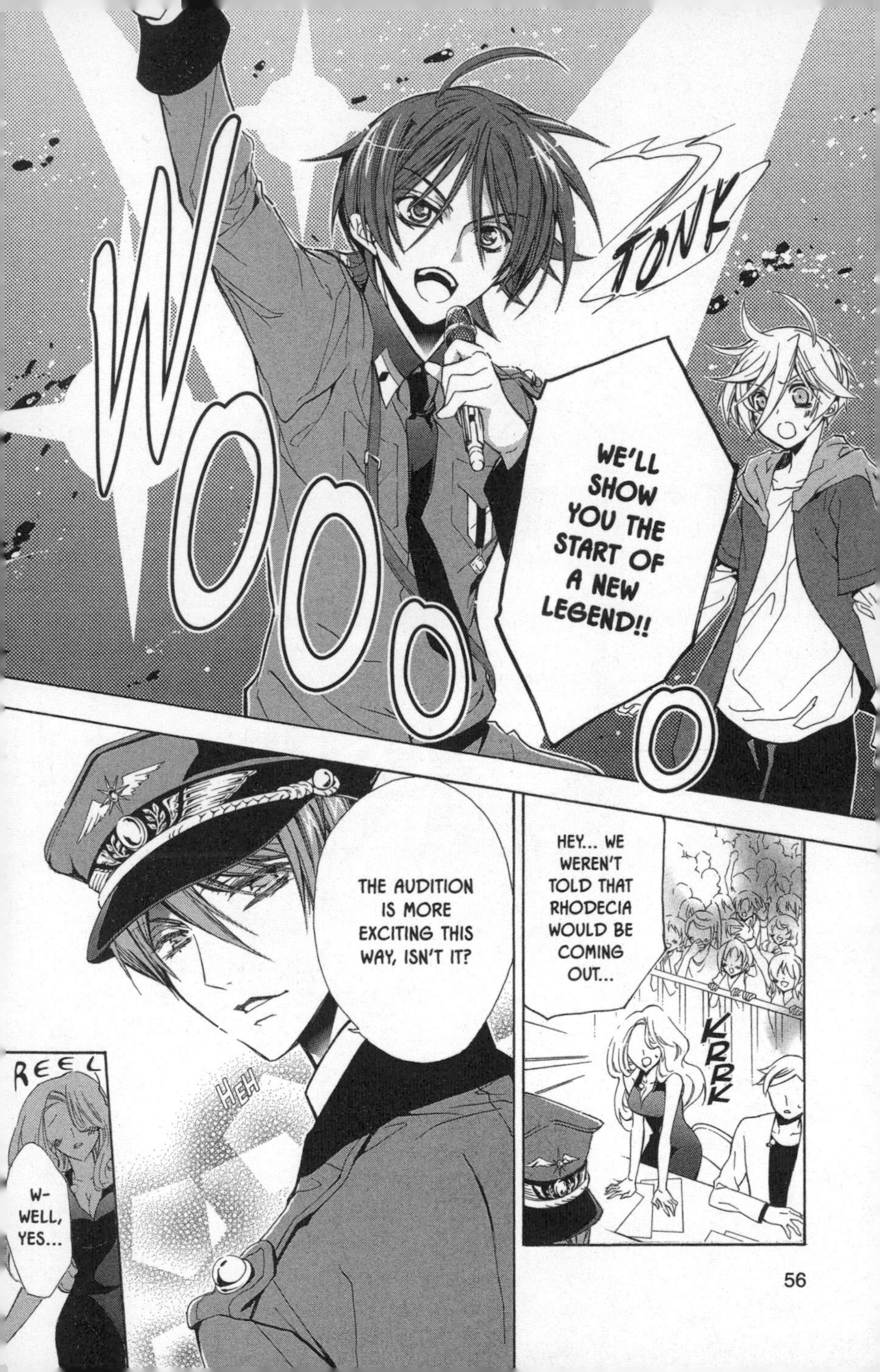
TONK
WOOOOOO
WE'LL SHOW YOU THE START OF A NEW LEGEND!!
HEY... WE WEREN'T TOLD THAT RHODECIA WOULD BE COMING OUT...
KRRK
THE AUDITION IS MORE EXCITING THIS WAY, ISN'T IT?
HEH
REEL
W-WELL, YES...

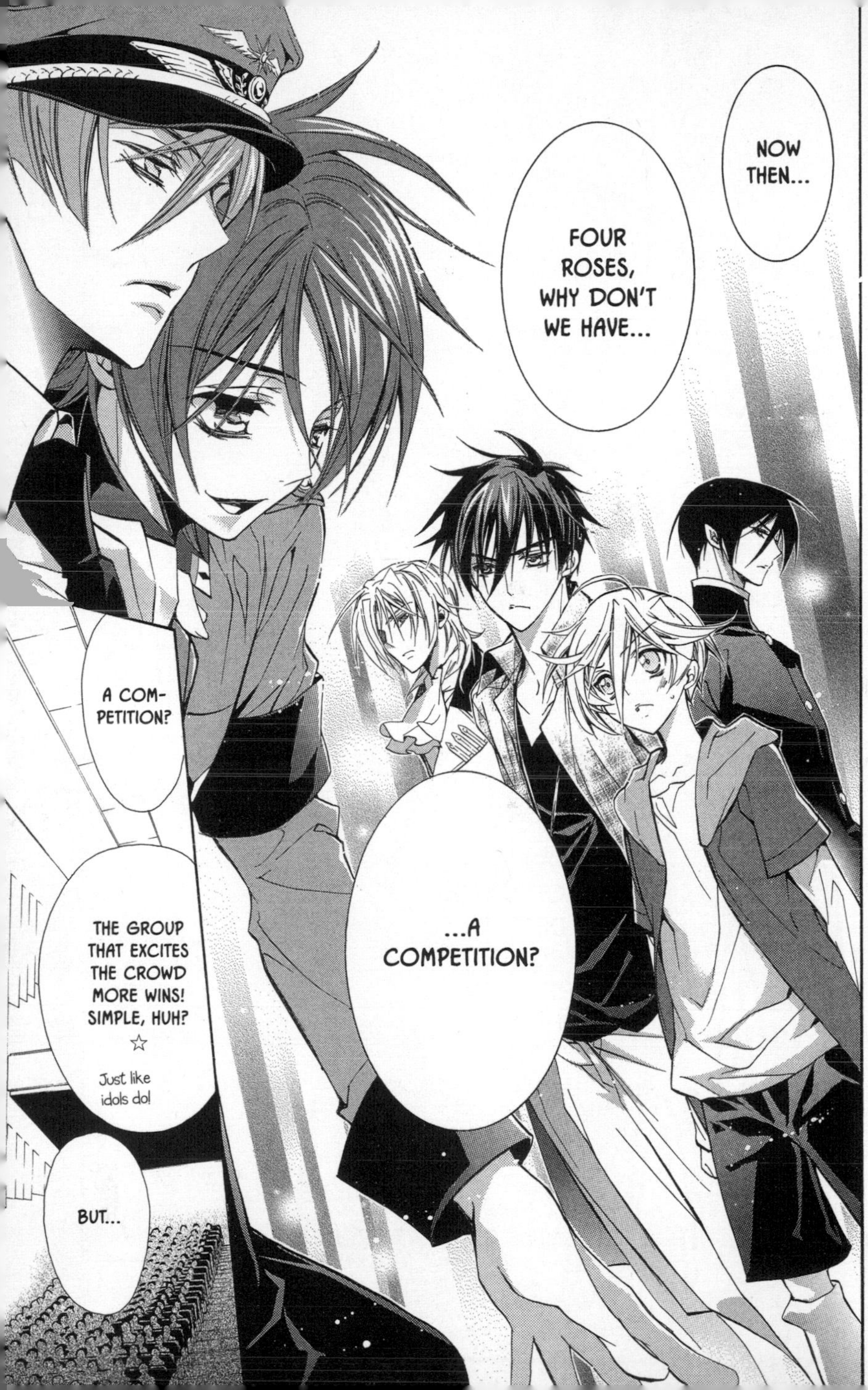
NOW THEN...
FOUR ROSES, WHY DON'T WE HAVE...
...A COMPETITION?
A COMPETITION?
THE GROUP THAT EXCITES THE CROWD MORE WINS! SIMPLE, HUH? ☆
Just like idols do!
BUT...

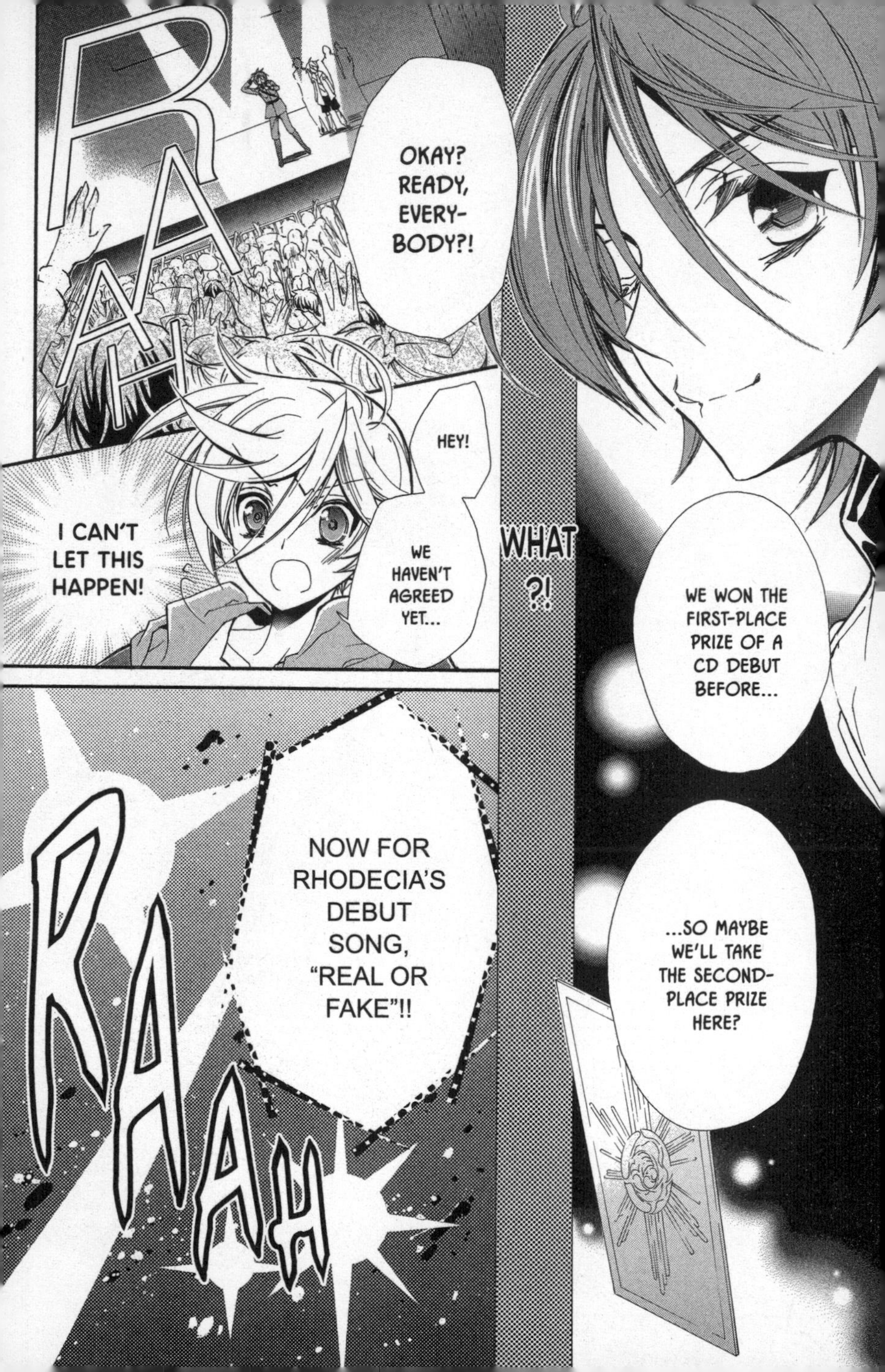

WE WON THE FIRST-PLACE PRIZE OF A CD DEBUT BEFORE...
...SO MAYBE WE'LL TAKE THE SECOND-PLACE PRIZE HERE?
OKAY? READY, EVERY-BODY?!
RAAH
HEY!
WE HAVEN'T AGREED YET...
WHAT?!
I CAN'T LET THIS HAPPEN!
NOW FOR RHODECIA'S DEBUT SONG, "REAL OR FAKE"!!
RAAH

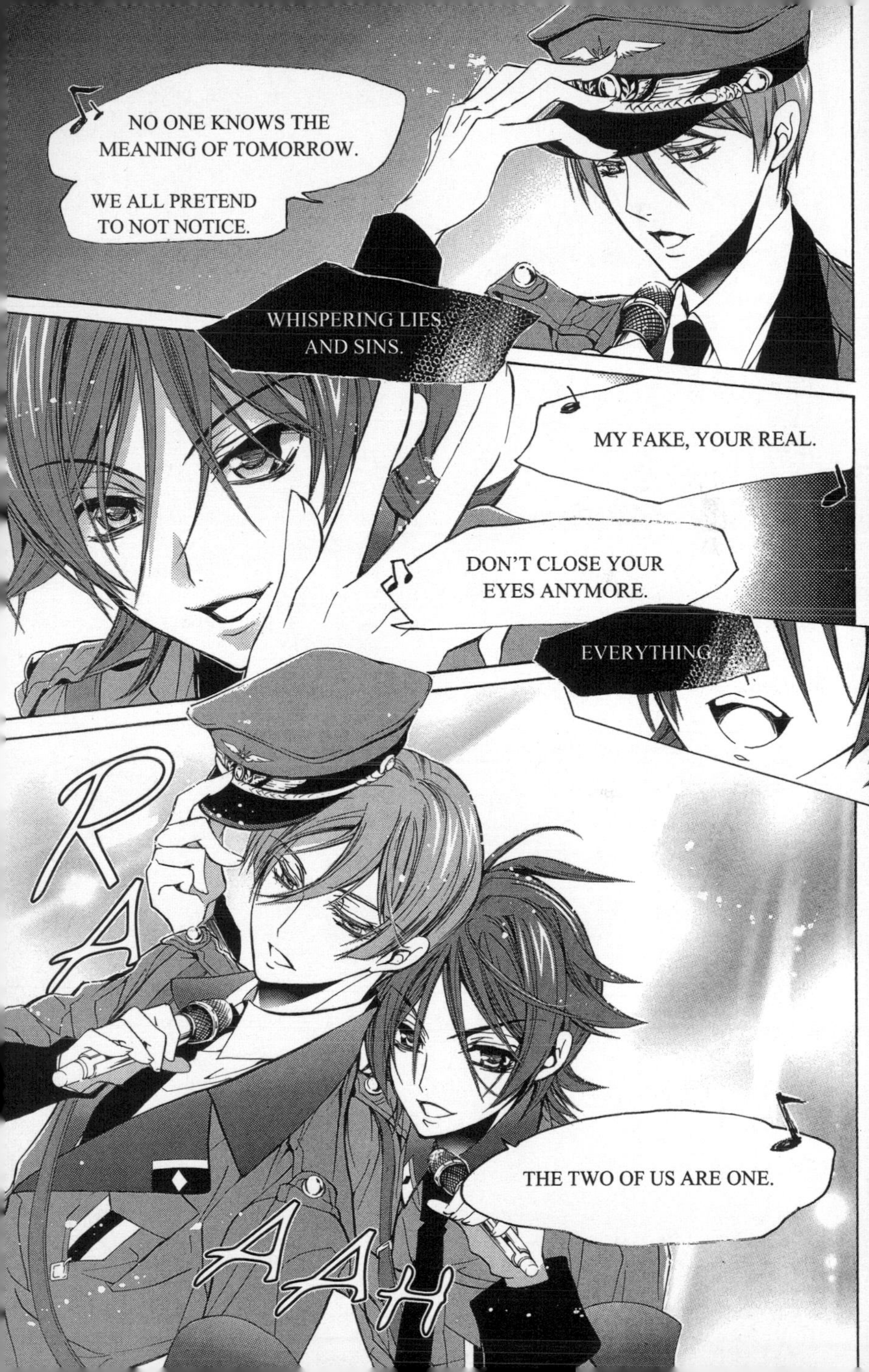
NO ONE KNOWS THE MEANING OF TOMORROW.
WE ALL PRETEND TO NOT NOTICE.
WHISPERING LIES AND SINS.
MY FAKE, YOUR REAL.
DON'T CLOSE YOUR EYES ANYMORE.
EVERYTHING.
THE TWO OF US ARE ONE.
RAAAH

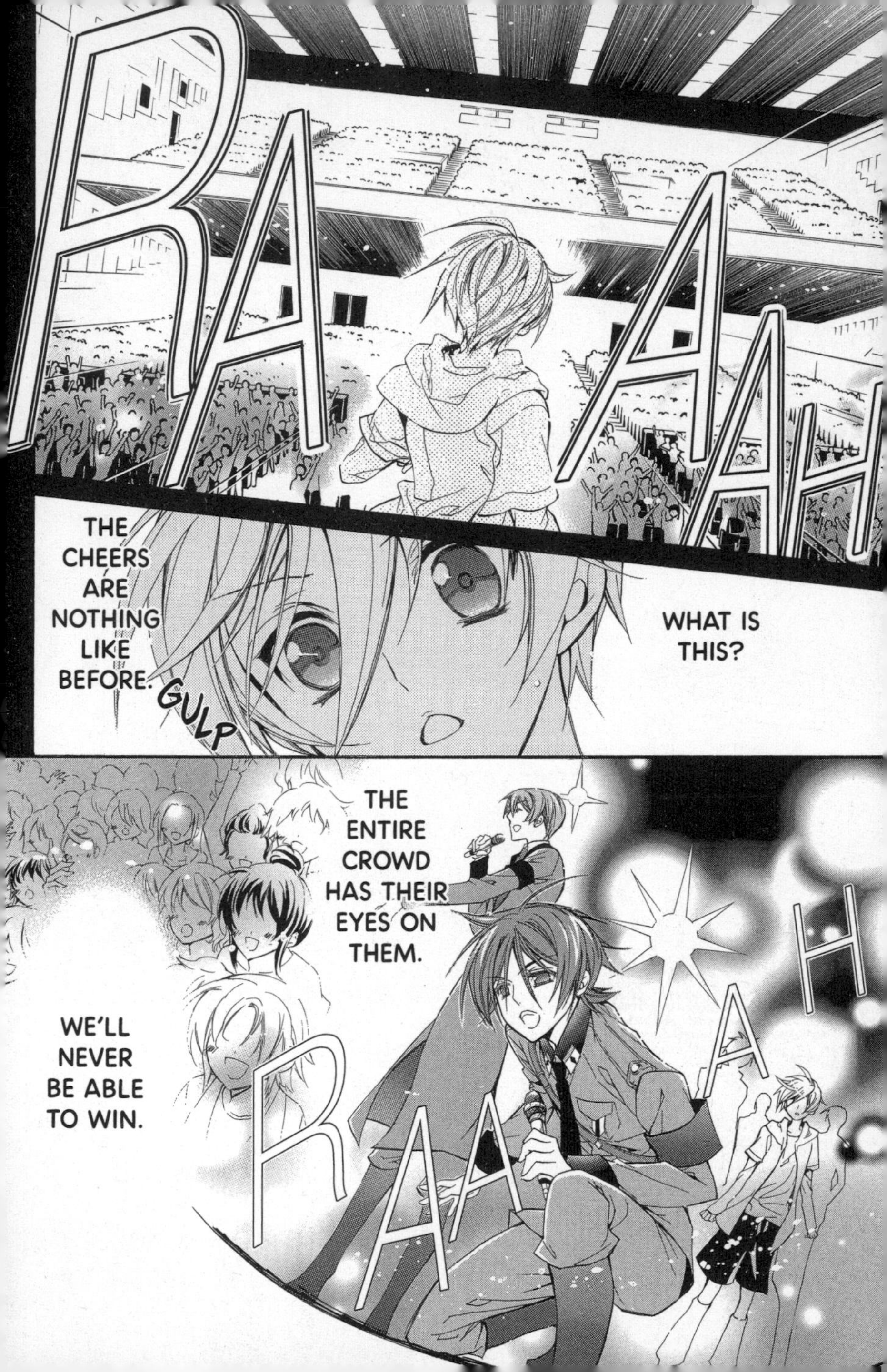
RAAAAH
WHAT IS THIS?
THE CHEERS ARE NOTHING LIKE BEFORE.
GULP
THE ENTIRE CROWD HAS THEIR EYES ON THEM.
RAAAAH
WE'LL NEVER BE ABLE TO WIN.

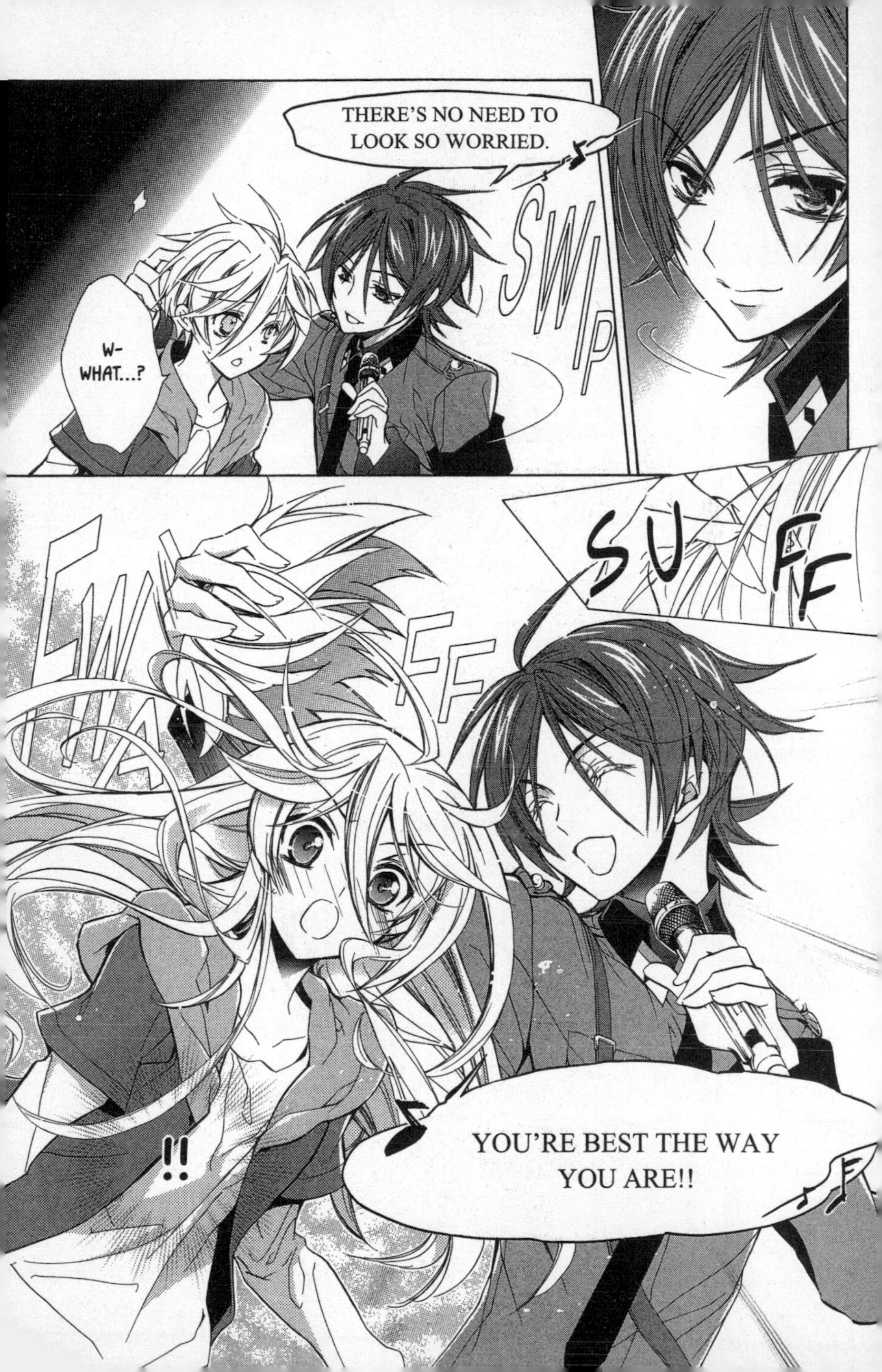

THERE'S NO NEED TO LOOK SO WORRIED.
SWIP
W- WHAT...?
SUFF
FWAFF
YOU'RE BEST THE WAY YOU ARE!!
!!

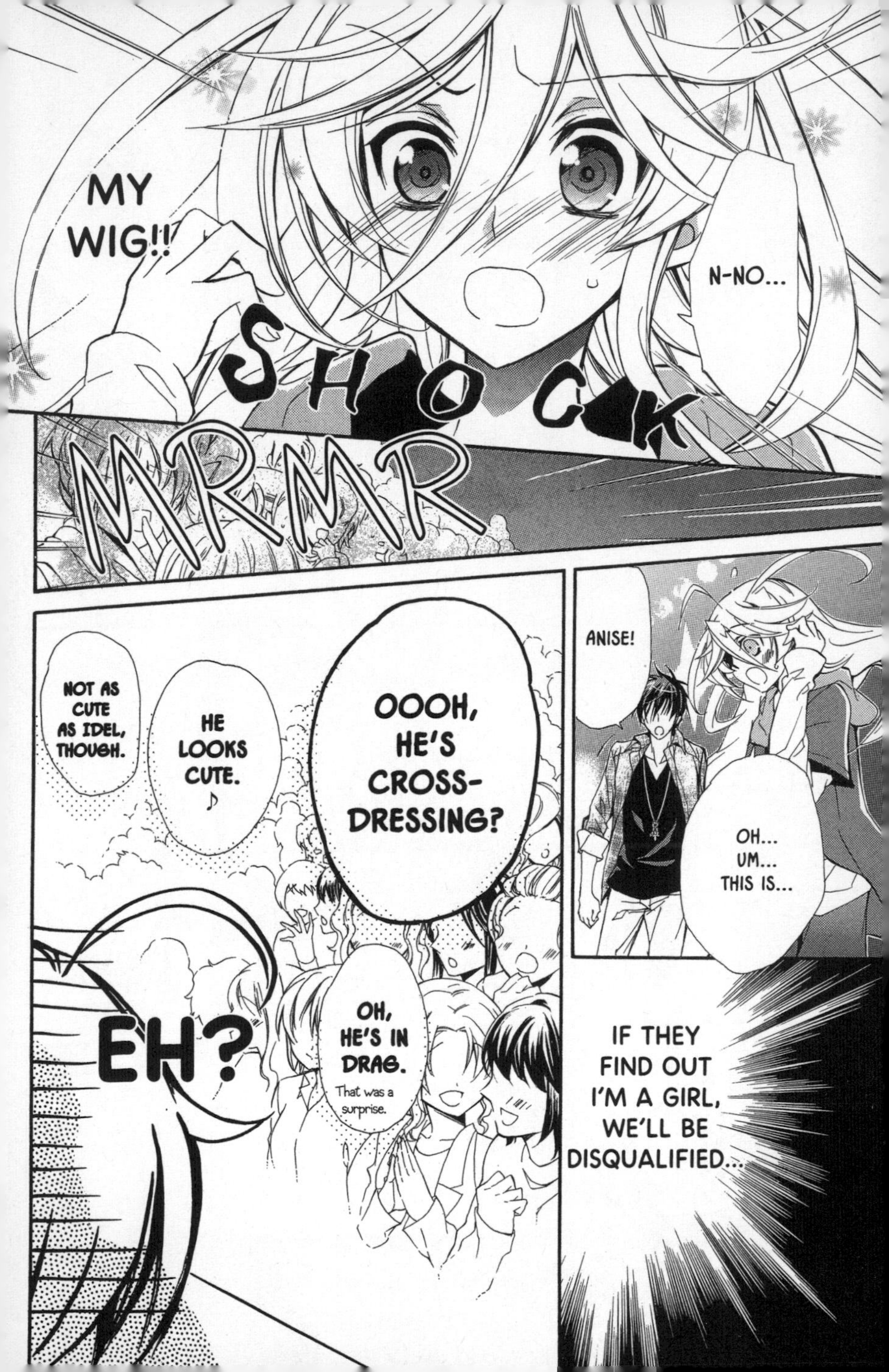
N-NO...
MY WIG!!
SHOCK
MRMR
ANISE!
OH... UM... THIS IS...
IF THEY FIND OUT I'M A GIRL, WE'LL BE DISQUALIFIED...
OOOH, HE'S CROSS-DRESSING?
HE LOOKS CUTE. ♪
NOT AS CUTE AS IDEL, THOUGH.
OH, HE'S IN DRAG.
That was a surprise.
EH?

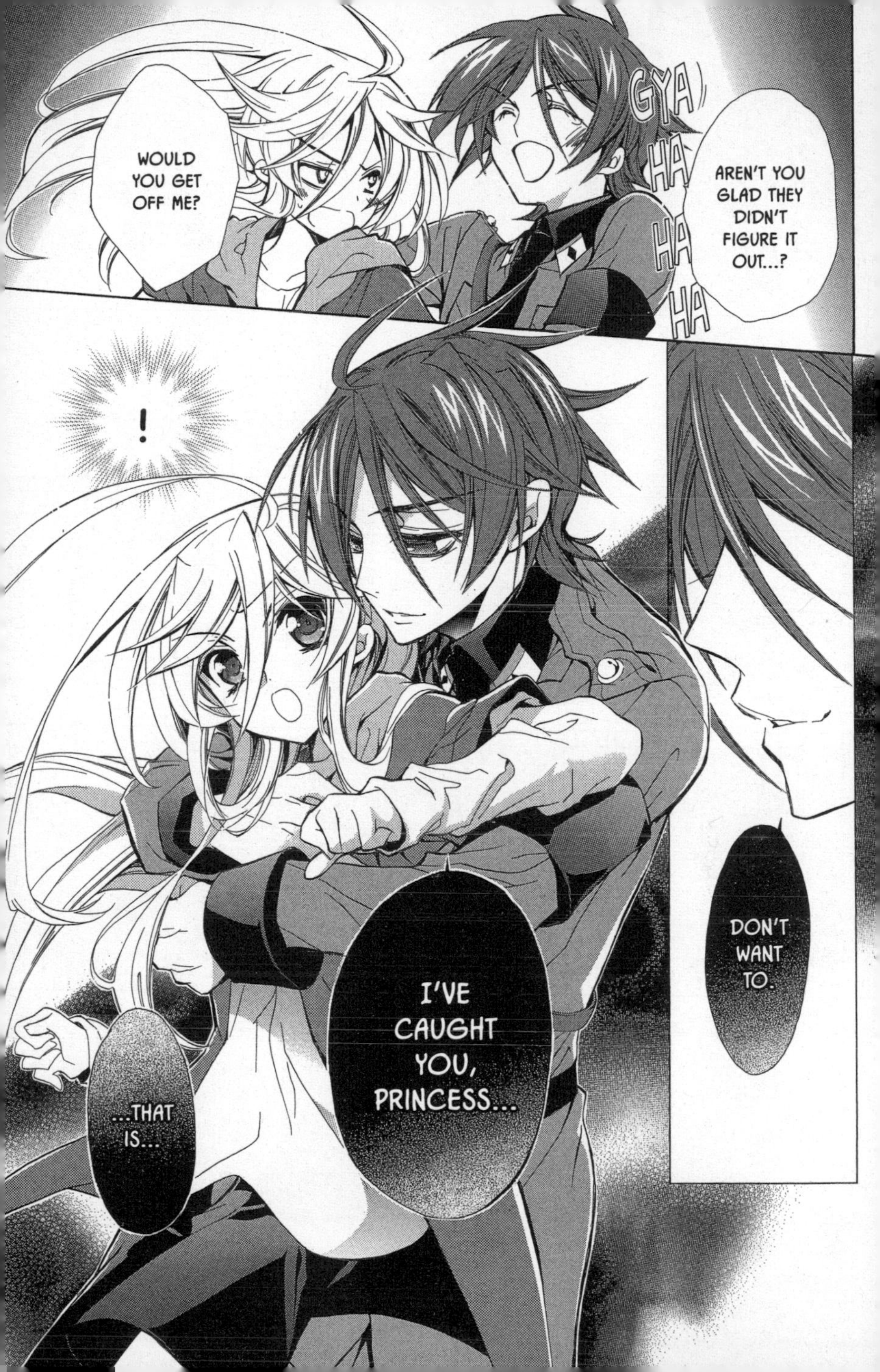
GYA HA HA HA
AREN'T YOU GLAD THEY DIDN'T FIGURE IT OUT...?
WOULD YOU GET OFF ME?
DON'T WANT TO.
!
I'VE CAUGHT YOU, PRINCESS...
...THAT IS...

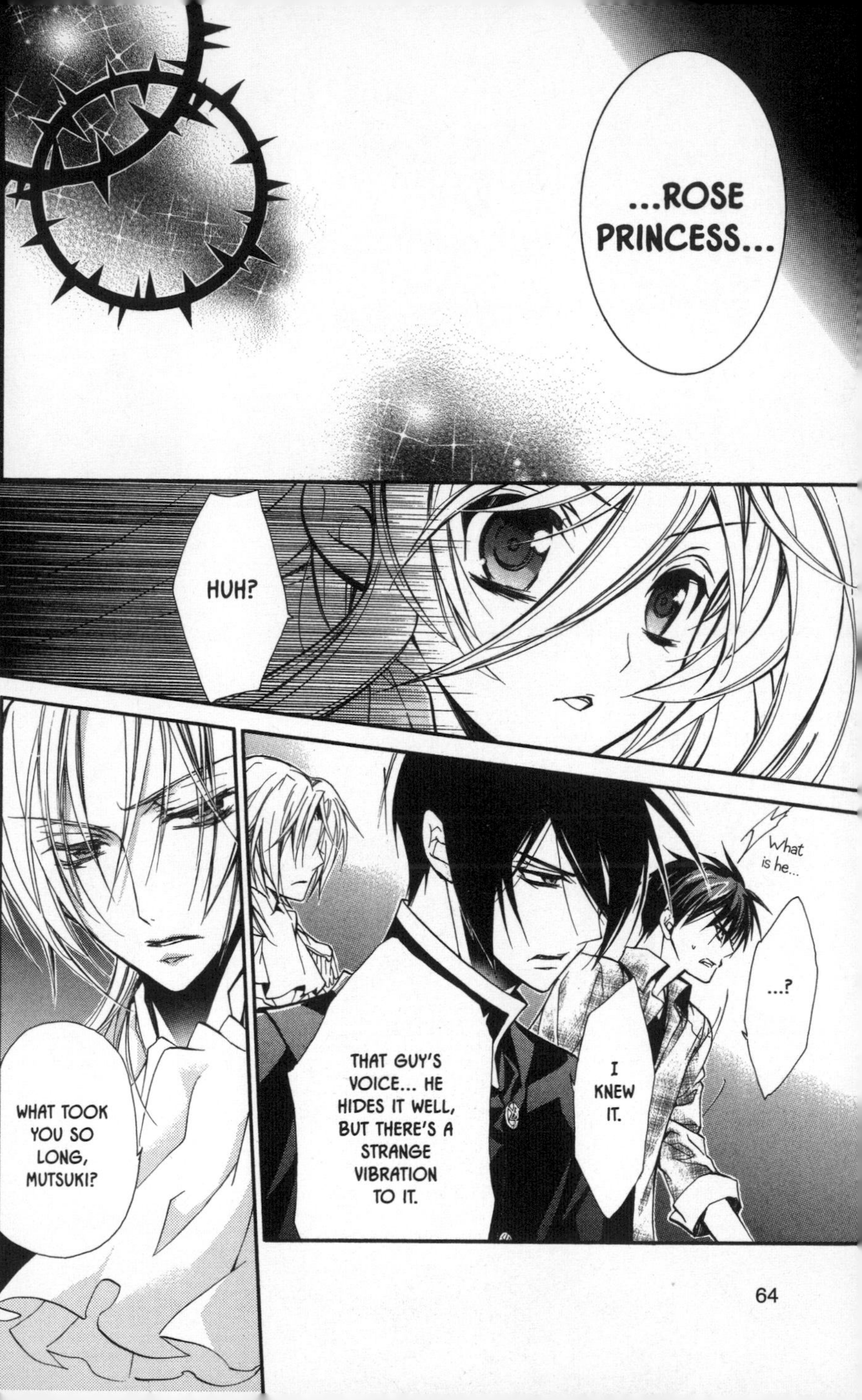
...ROSE PRINCESS...
HUH?
What is he...
...?
I KNEW IT.
THAT GUY'S VOICE... HE HIDES IT WELL, BUT THERE'S A STRANGE VIBRATION TO IT.
WHAT TOOK YOU SO LONG, MUTSUKI?

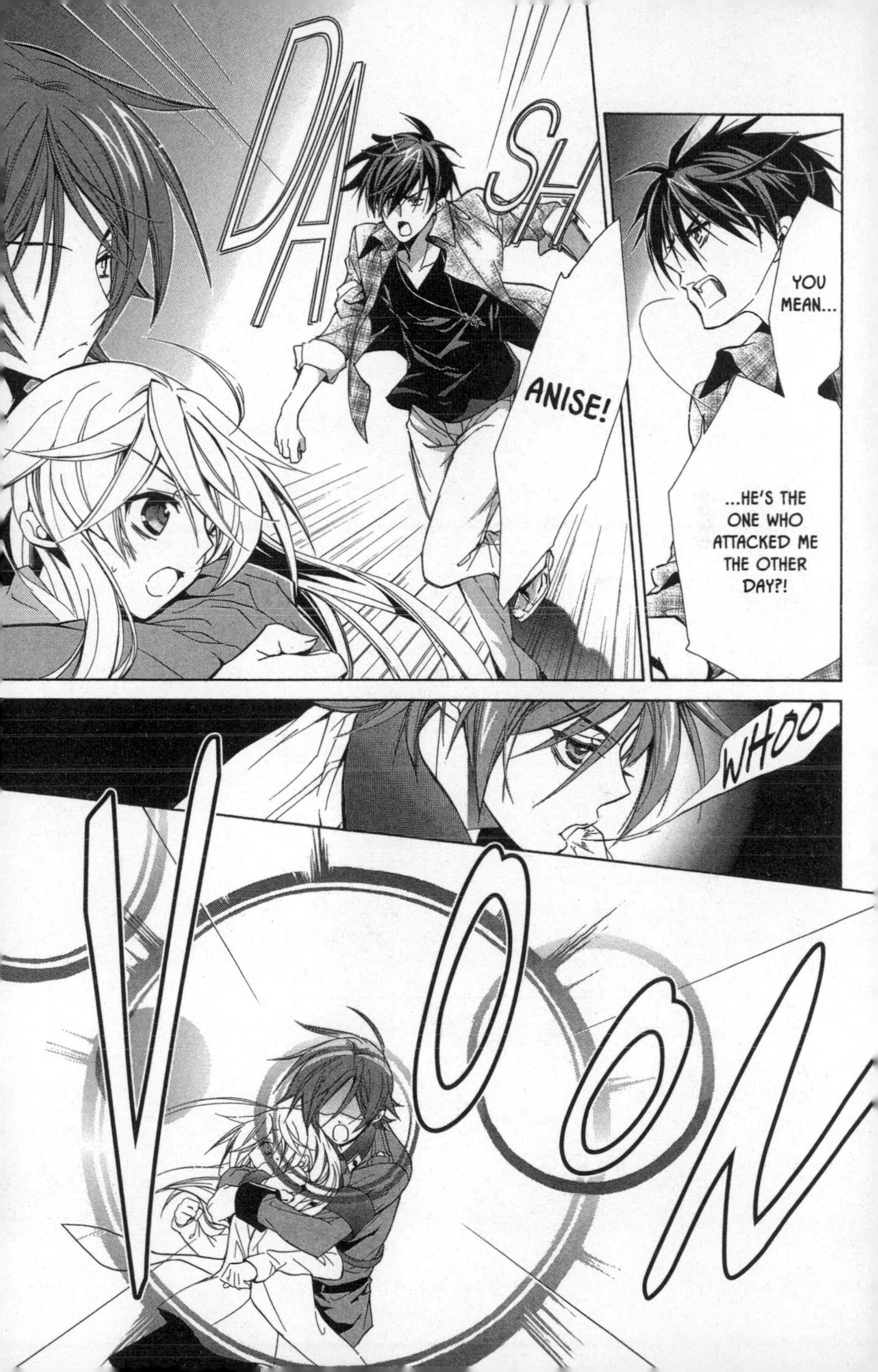
YOU MEAN...
...HE'S THE ONE WHO ATTACKED ME THE OTHER DAY?!
DASH
ANISE!
WHOO
VOOOM

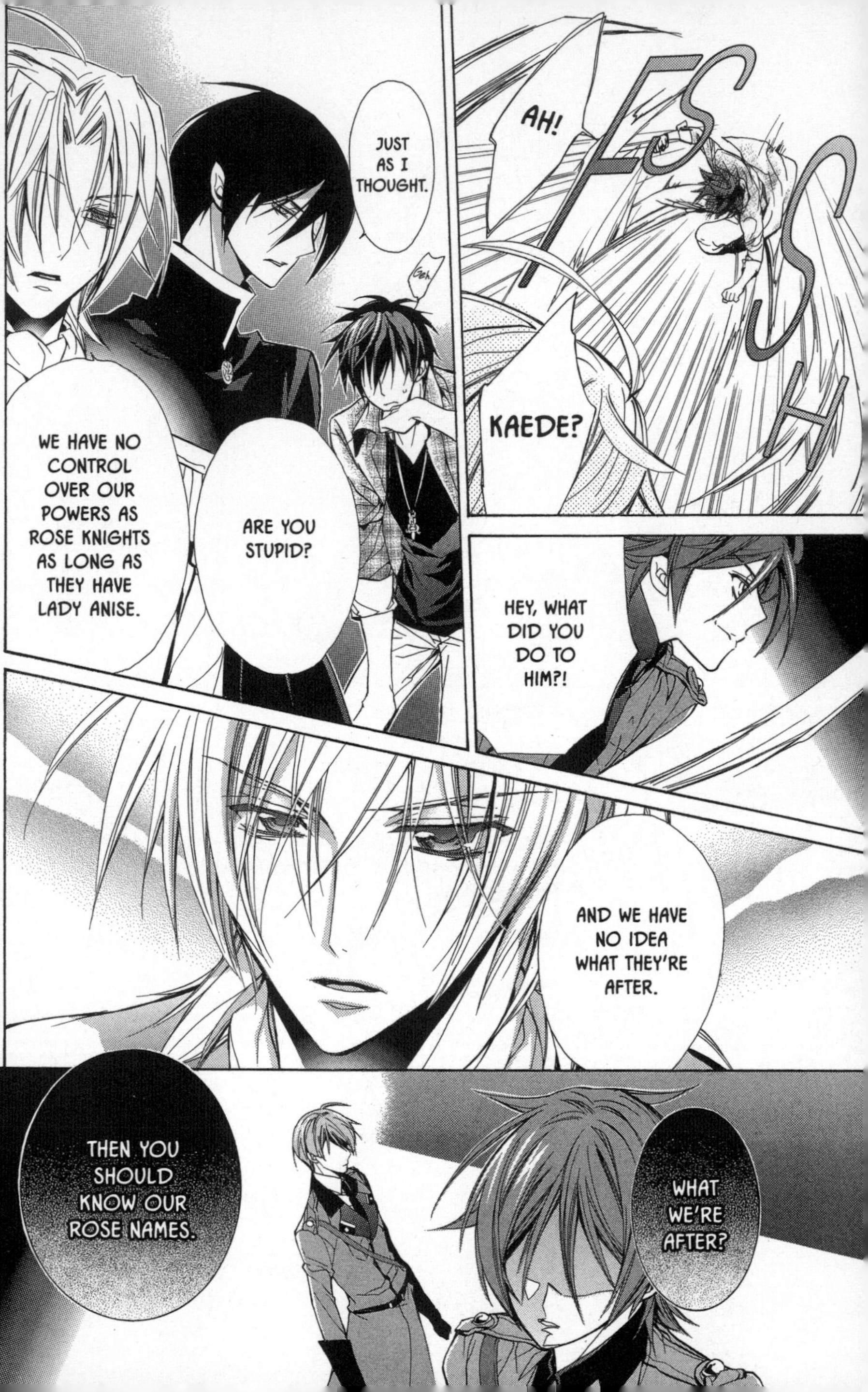
AH!
FESSH
KAEDE?
HEY, WHAT DID YOU DO TO HIM?!
JUST AS I THOUGHT.
Geh.
ARE YOU STUPID?
WE HAVE NO CONTROL OVER OUR POWERS AS ROSE KNIGHTS AS LONG AS THEY HAVE LADY ANISE.
AND WE HAVE NO IDEA WHAT THEY'RE AFTER.
WHAT WE'RE AFTER?
THEN YOU SHOULD KNOW OUR ROSE NAMES.

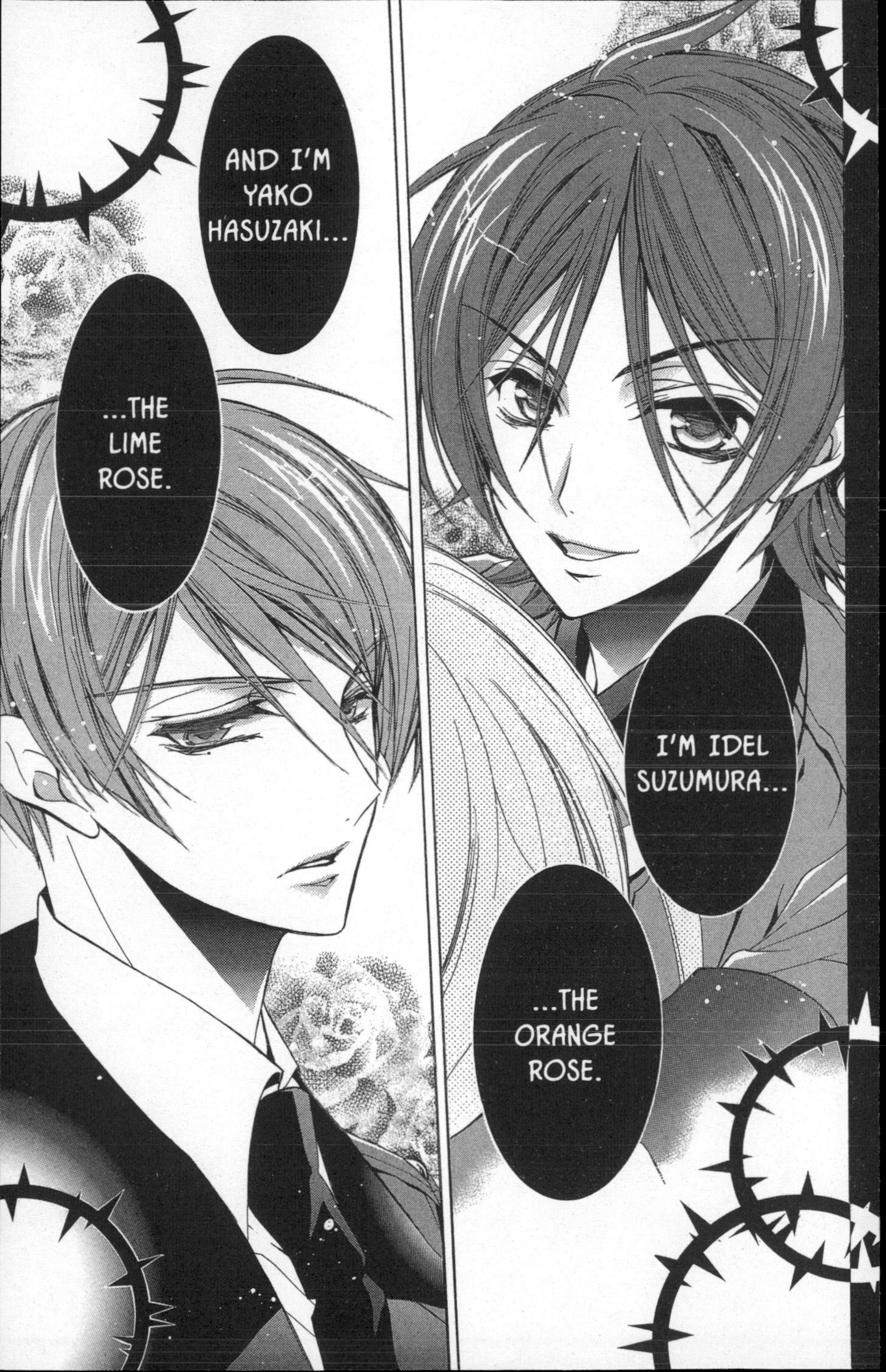
I'M IDEL SUZUMURA...
...THE ORANGE ROSE.
AND I'M YAKO HASUZAKI...
...THE LIME ROSE.

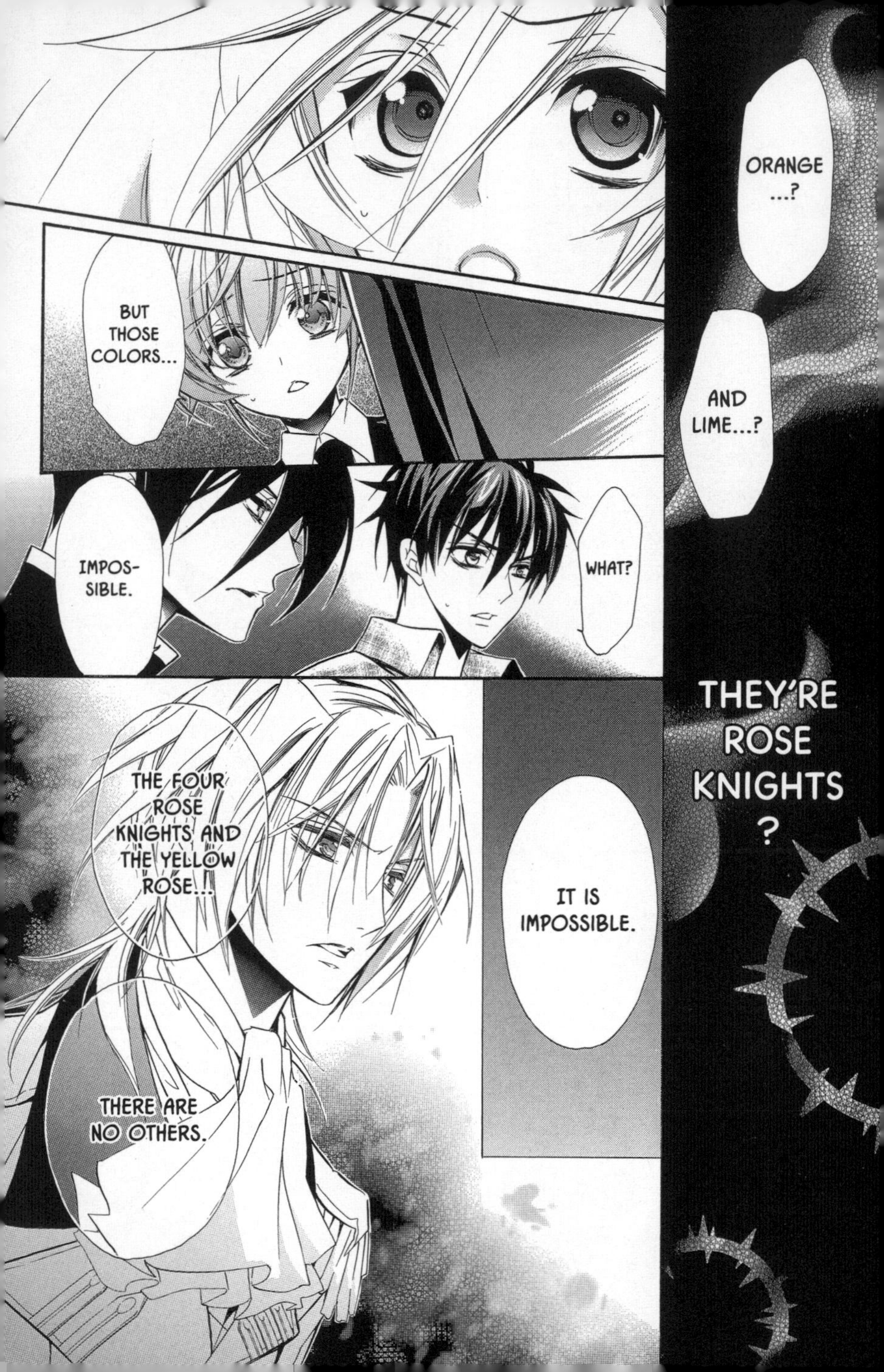
ORANGE ...?
AND LIME...?
THEY'RE ROSE KNIGHTS ?
BUT THOSE COLORS...
WHAT?
IMPOS-SIBLE.
IT IS IMPOSSIBLE.
THE FOUR ROSE KNIGHTS AND THE YELLOW ROSE...
THERE ARE NO OTHERS.

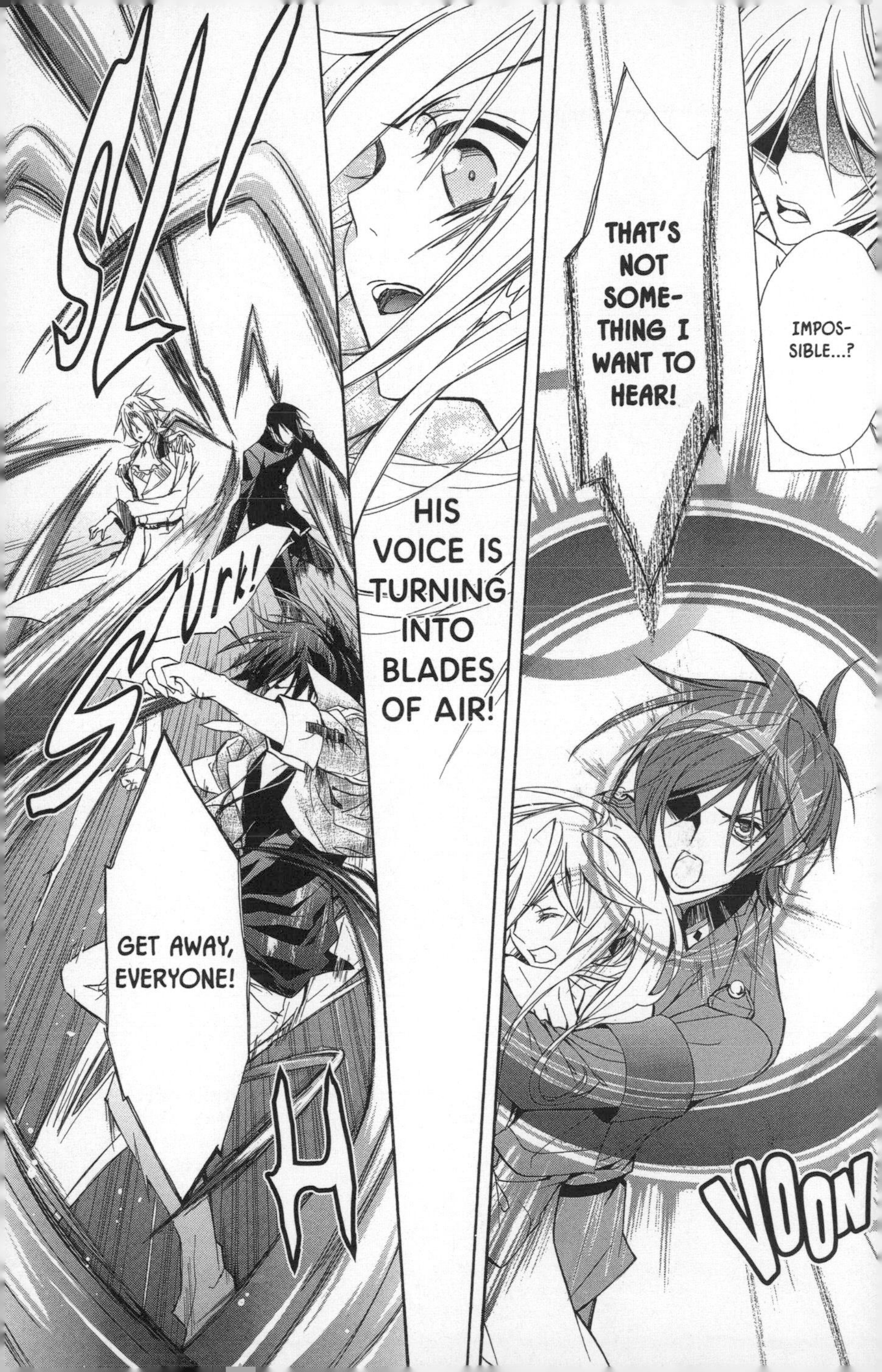
IMPOSSIBLE...?
THAT'S NOT SOMETHING I WANT TO HEAR!
VOON
HIS VOICE IS TURNING INTO BLADES OF AIR!
SHURK!
GET AWAY, EVERYONE!

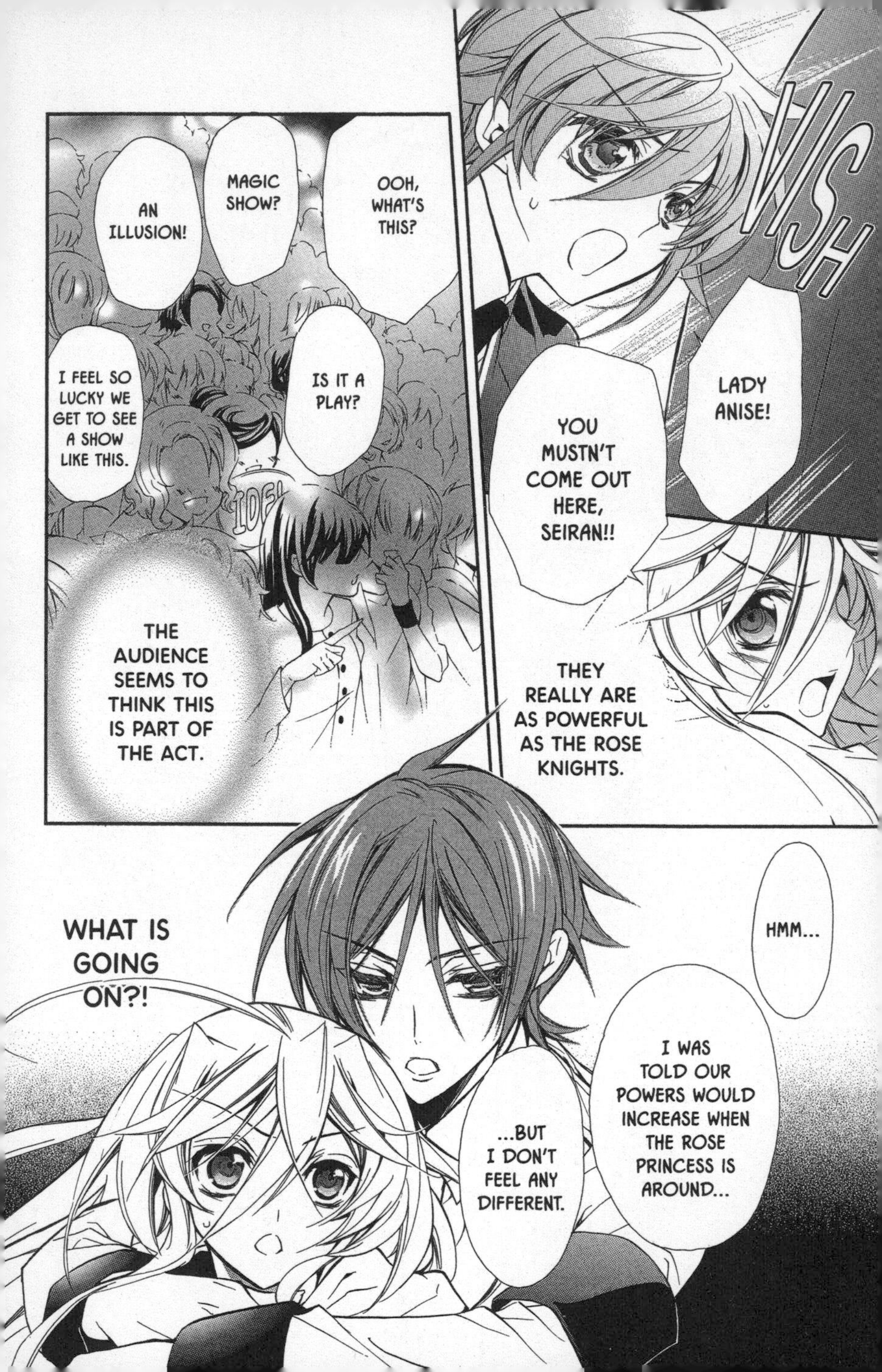
VISH
LADY ANISE!
YOU MUSTN'T COME OUT HERE, SEIRAN!!
THEY REALLY ARE AS POWERFUL AS THE ROSE KNIGHTS.
OOH, WHAT'S THIS?
MAGIC SHOW?
AN ILLUSION!
IS IT A PLAY?
I FEEL SO LUCKY WE GET TO SEE A SHOW LIKE THIS.
THE AUDIENCE SEEMS TO THINK THIS IS PART OF THE ACT.
HMM...
I WAS TOLD OUR POWERS WOULD INCREASE WHEN THE ROSE PRINCESS IS AROUND...
...BUT I DON'T FEEL ANY DIFFERENT.
WHAT IS GOING ON?!

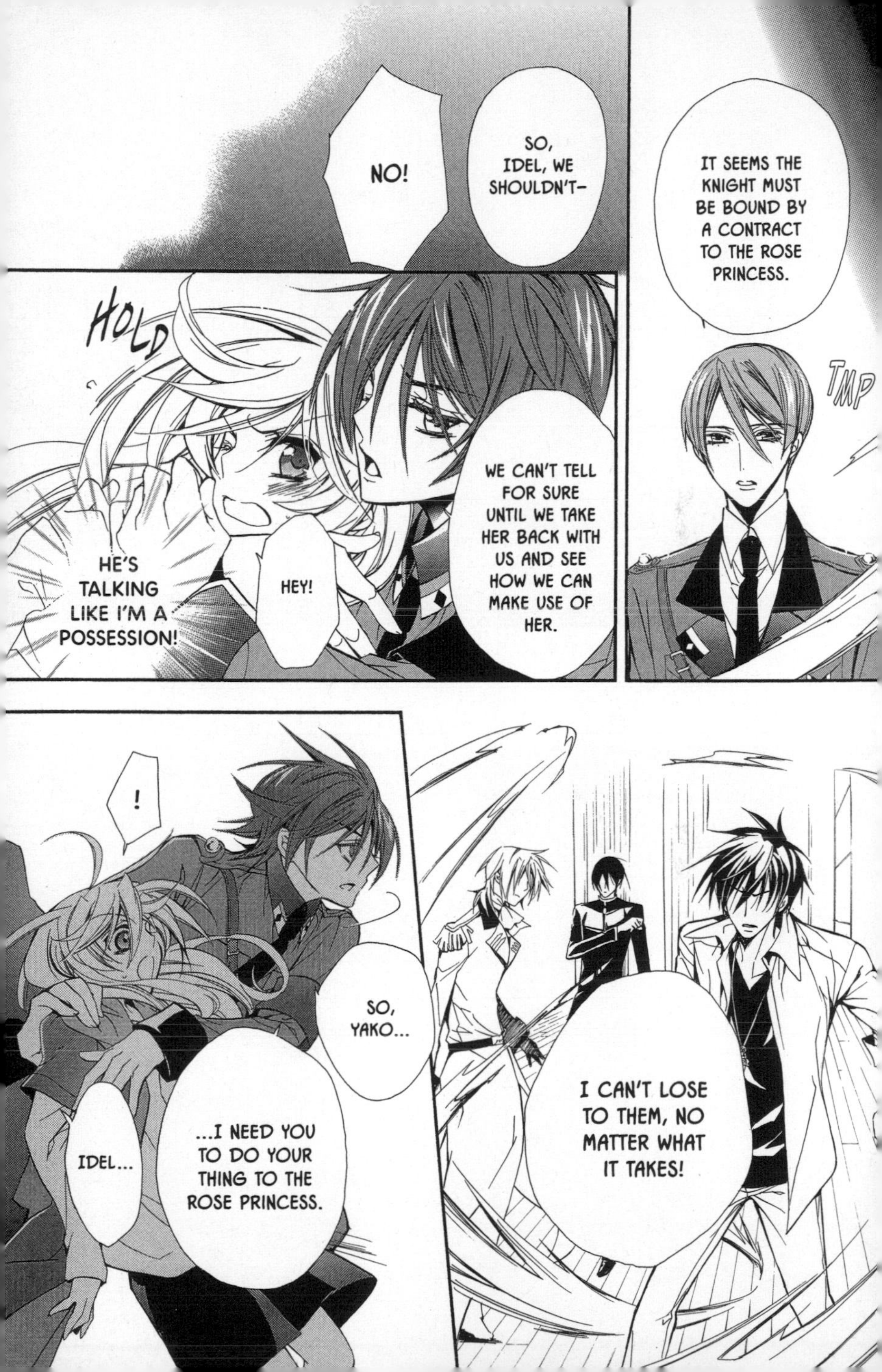
IT SEEMS THE KNIGHT MUST BE BOUND BY A CONTRACT TO THE ROSE PRINCESS.
SO, IDEL, WE SHOULDN'T–
NO!
TMP
HOLD
WE CAN'T TELL FOR SURE UNTIL WE TAKE HER BACK WITH US AND SEE HOW WE CAN MAKE USE OF HER.
HEY!
HE'S TALKING LIKE I'M A POSSESSION!
I CAN'T LOSE TO THEM, NO MATTER WHAT IT TAKES!
!
SO, YAKO...
...I NEED YOU TO DO YOUR THING TO THE ROSE PRINCESS.
IDEL...

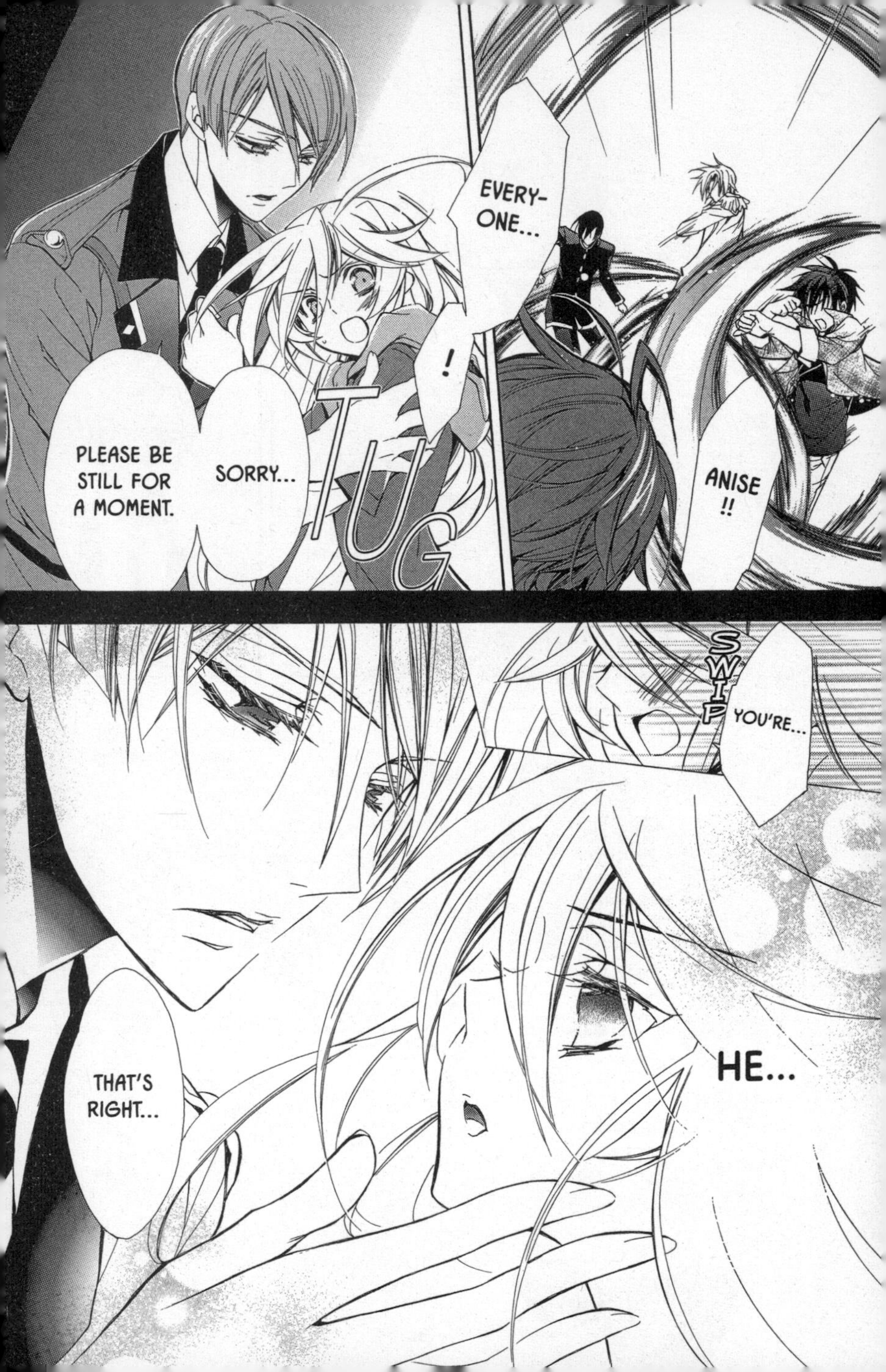
ANISE !!
EVERY-ONE...
!
TUG
SORRY...
PLEASE BE STILL FOR A MOMENT.
SWIP
YOU'RE...
HE...
THAT'S RIGHT...

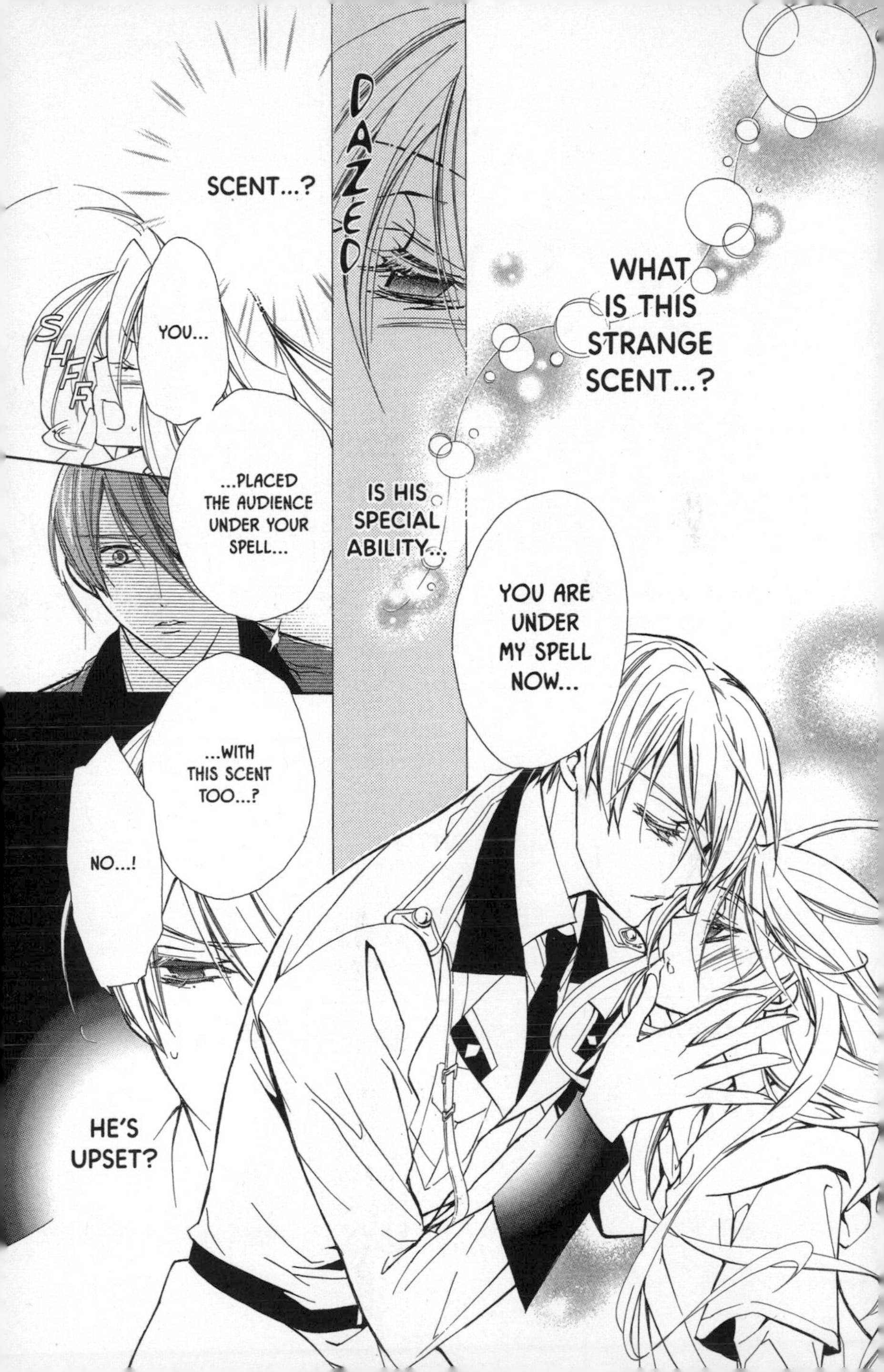
WHAT IS THIS STRANGE SCENT...?
YOU ARE UNDER MY SPELL NOW...
DAZED
IS HIS SPECIAL ABILITY...
SCENT...?
SHFF
YOU...
...PLACED THE AUDIENCE UNDER YOUR SPELL...
...WITH THIS SCENT TOO...?
NO...!
HE'S UPSET?

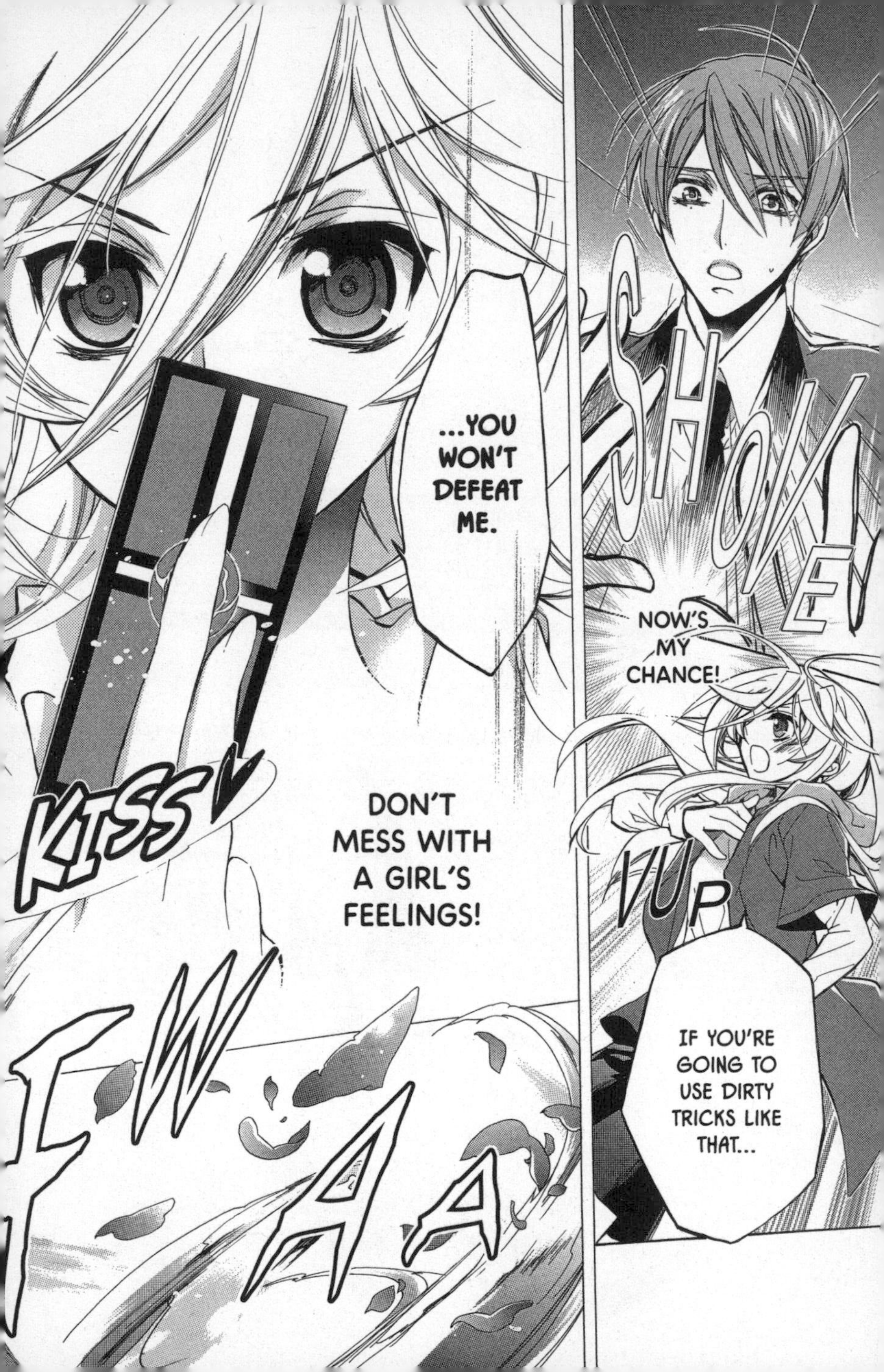
SHOVE
NOW'S MY CHANCE!
VUP
IF YOU'RE GOING TO USE DIRTY TRICKS LIKE THAT...
...YOU WON'T DEFEAT ME.
KISS
DON'T MESS WITH A GIRL'S FEELINGS!
FWAA

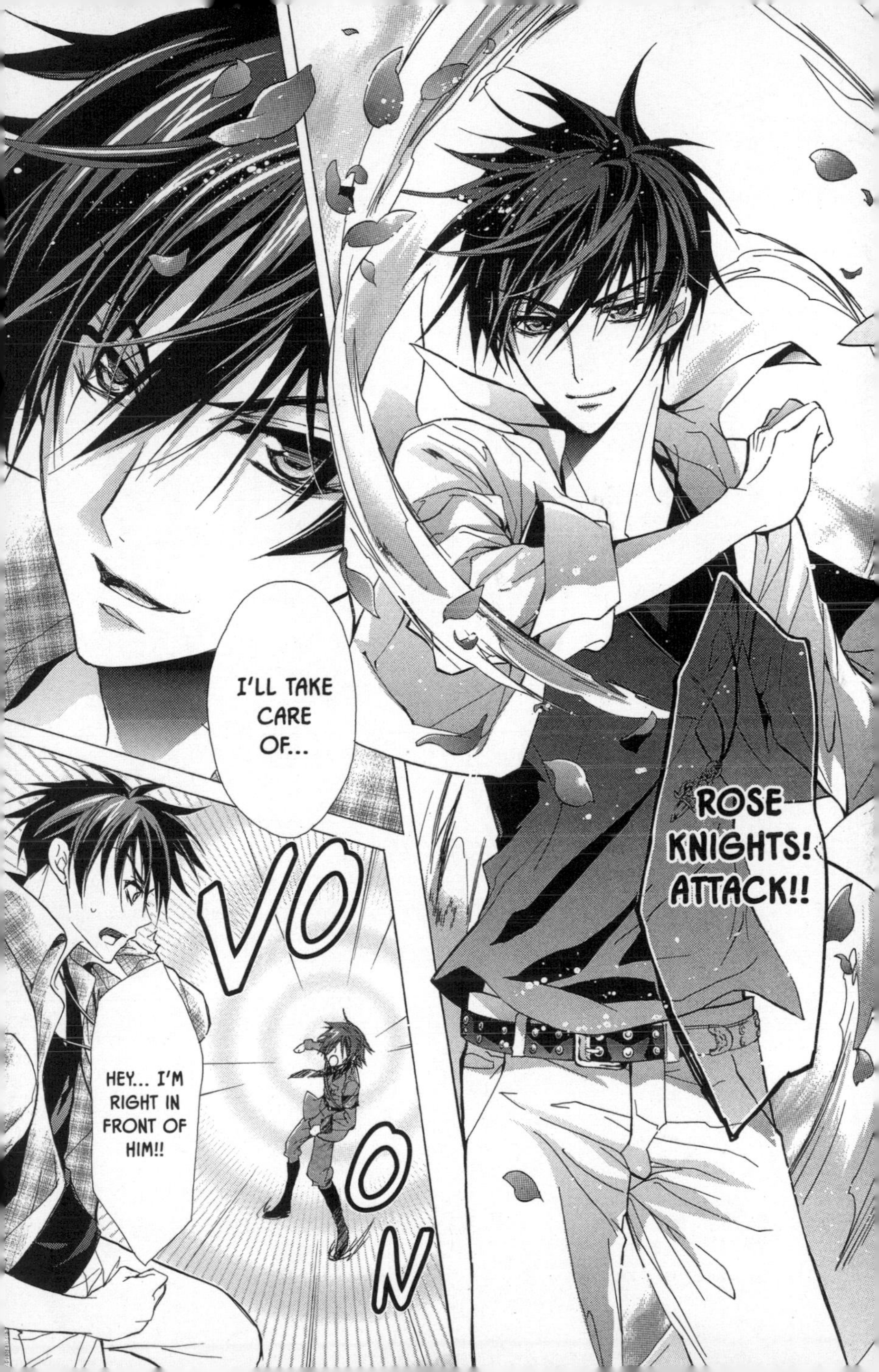
ROSE KNIGHTS! ATTACK!!
I'LL TAKE CARE OF...
VOOON
HEY... I'M RIGHT IN FRONT OF HIM!!

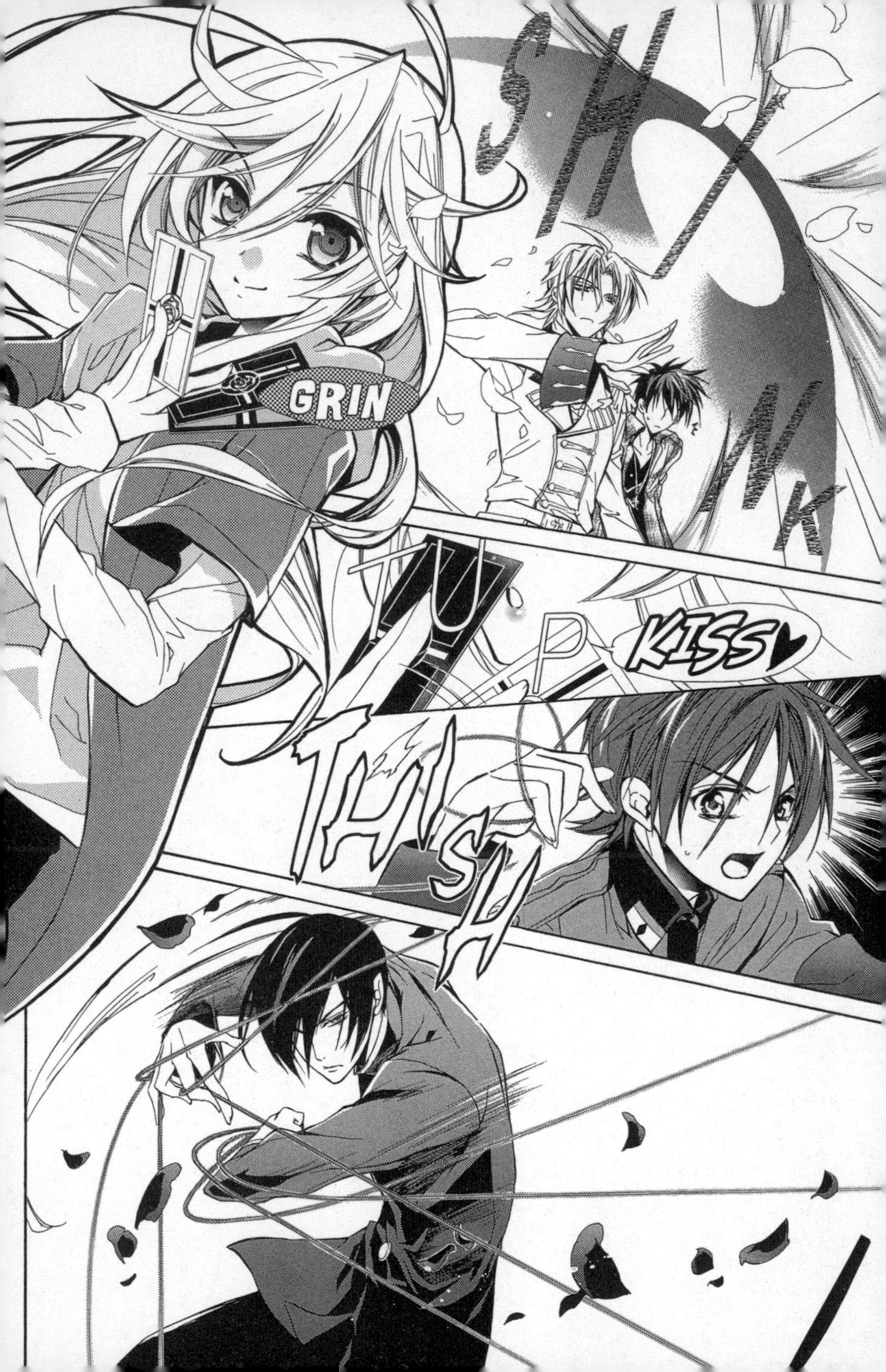
SHINK
GRIN
TUP
KISS♥
THSH

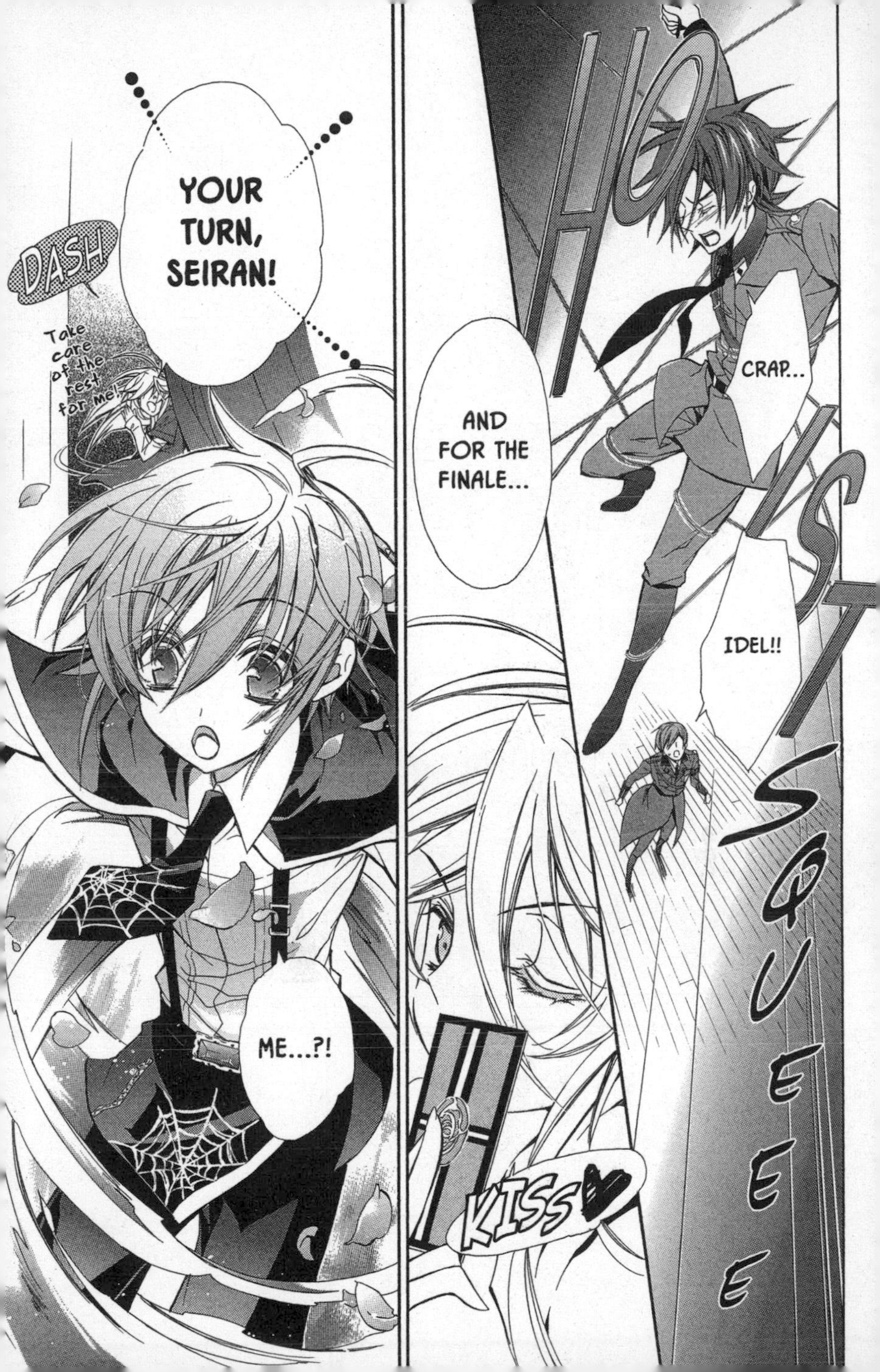
HOIST
CRAP...
AND FOR THE FINALE...
IDEL!!
SQUEEEEE
KISS
YOUR TURN, SEIRAN!
DASH
Take care of the rest for me!
ME...?!

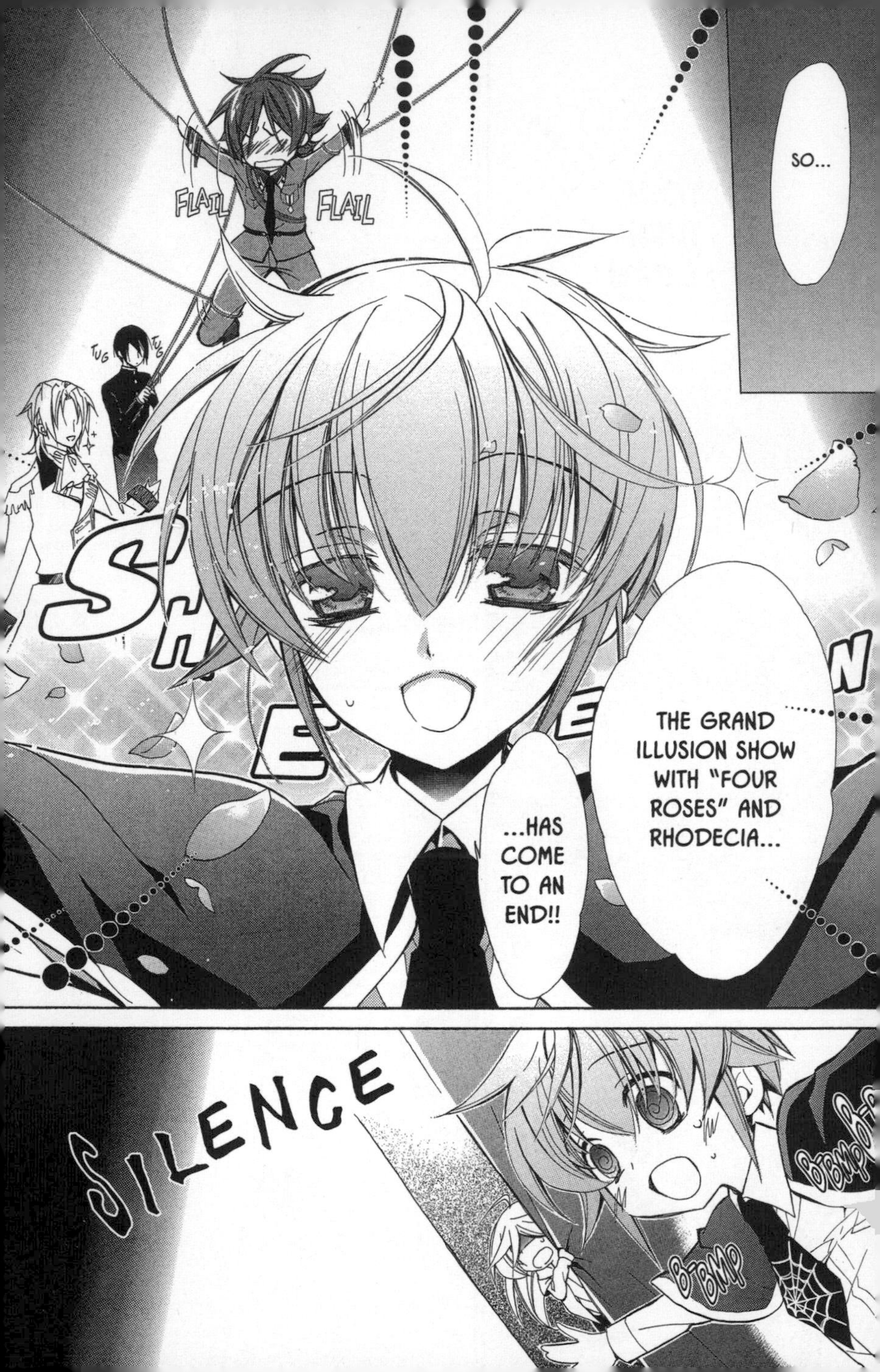
SO...
FLAIL
FLAIL
TUG
TUG
THE GRAND ILLUSION SHOW WITH "FOUR ROSES" AND RHODECIA...
...HAS COME TO AN END!!
B-BMP
B-BMP
B-BMP
SILENCE

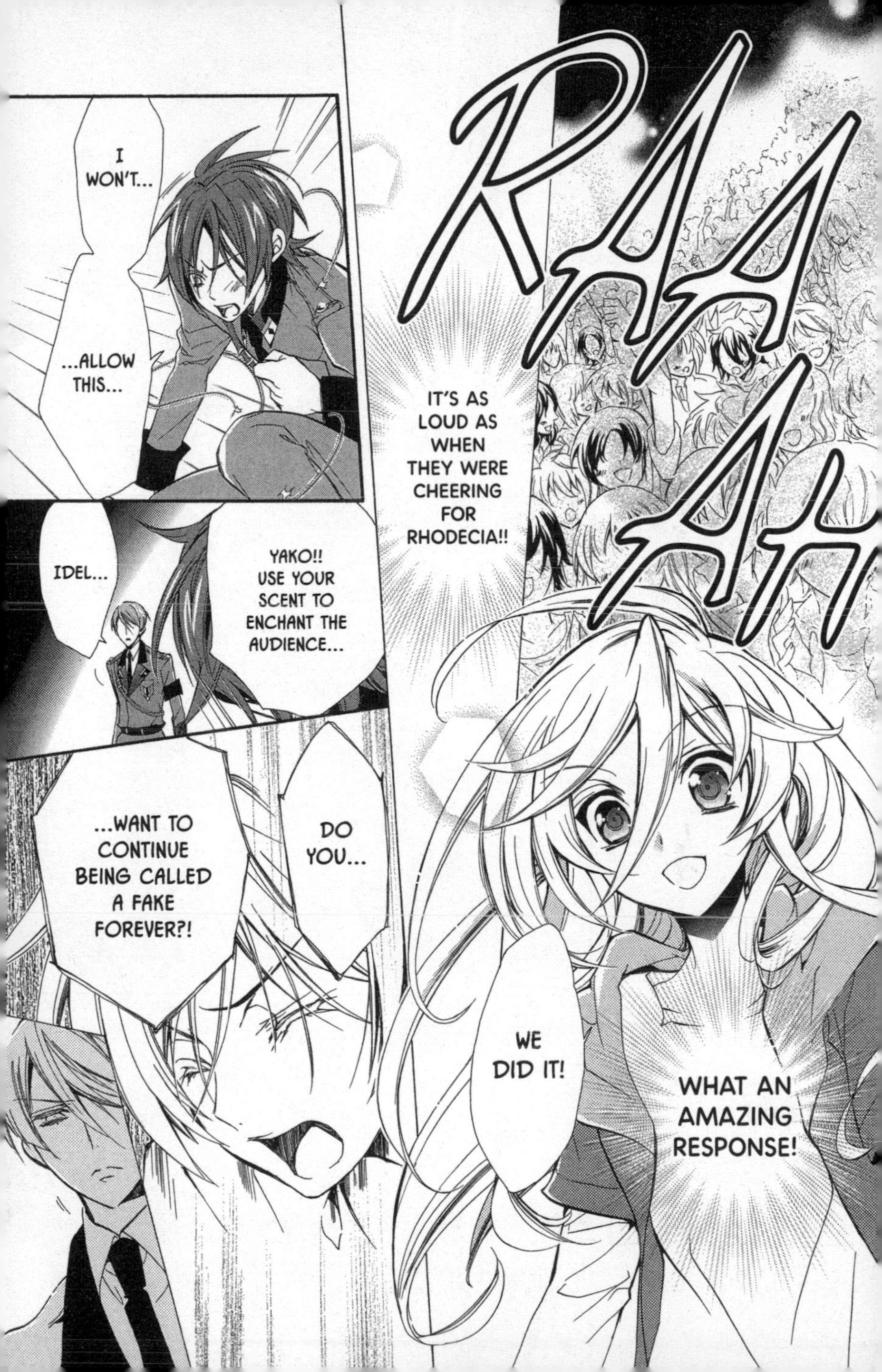
RAAAH
IT'S AS LOUD AS WHEN THEY WERE CHEERING FOR RHODECIA!!
WE DID IT!
WHAT AN AMAZING RESPONSE!
I WON'T...
...ALLOW THIS...
YAKO!! USE YOUR SCENT TO ENCHANT THE AUDIENCE...
IDEL...
DO YOU...
...WANT TO CONTINUE BEING CALLED A FAKE FOREVER?!

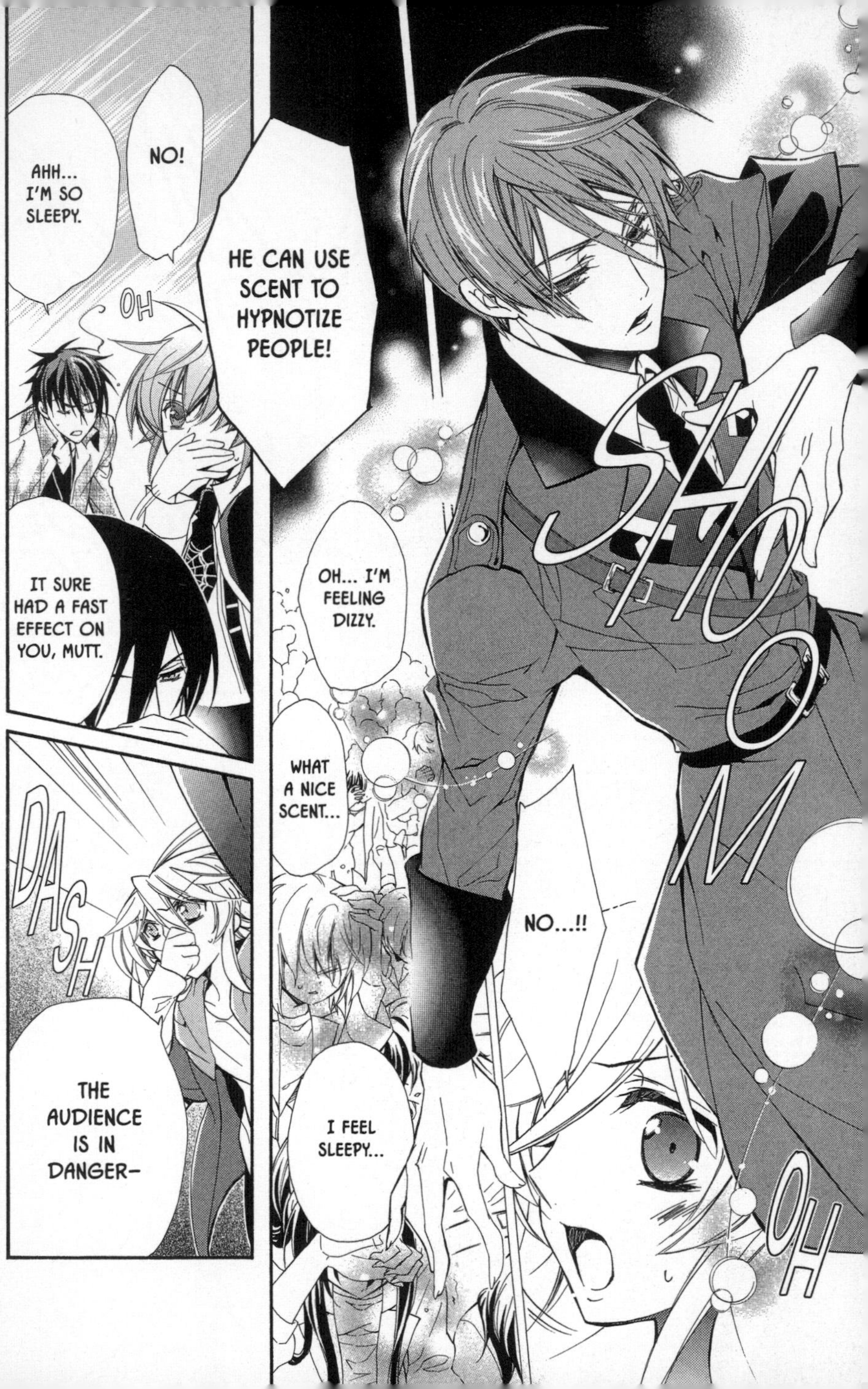
SHOOM
HE CAN USE SCENT TO HYPNOTIZE PEOPLE!
OH... I'M FEELING DIZZY.
NO...!!
WHAT A NICE SCENT...
OH
I FEEL SLEEPY...
NO!
AHH... I'M SO SLEEPY.
OH
IT SURE HAD A FAST EFFECT ON YOU, MUTT.
DASH
THE AUDIENCE IS IN DANGER–

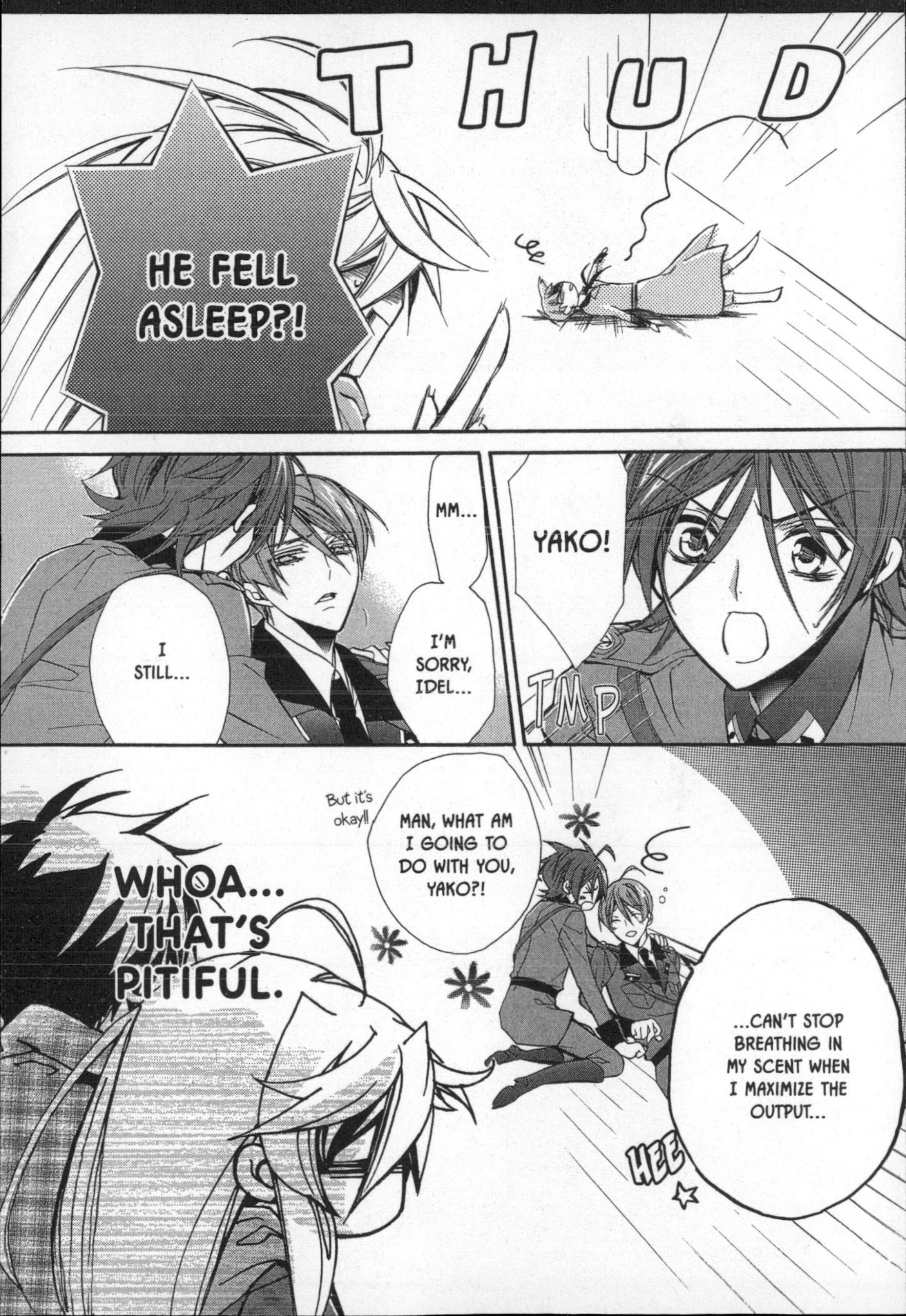
THUD
HE FELL ASLEEP?!
YAKO!
TMP
MM...
I'M SORRY, IDEL...
I STILL...
...CAN'T STOP BREATHING IN MY SCENT WHEN I MAXIMIZE THE OUTPUT...
HEE
MAN, WHAT AM I GOING TO DO WITH YOU, YAKO?!
But it's okay!!
WHOA... THAT'S PITIFUL.

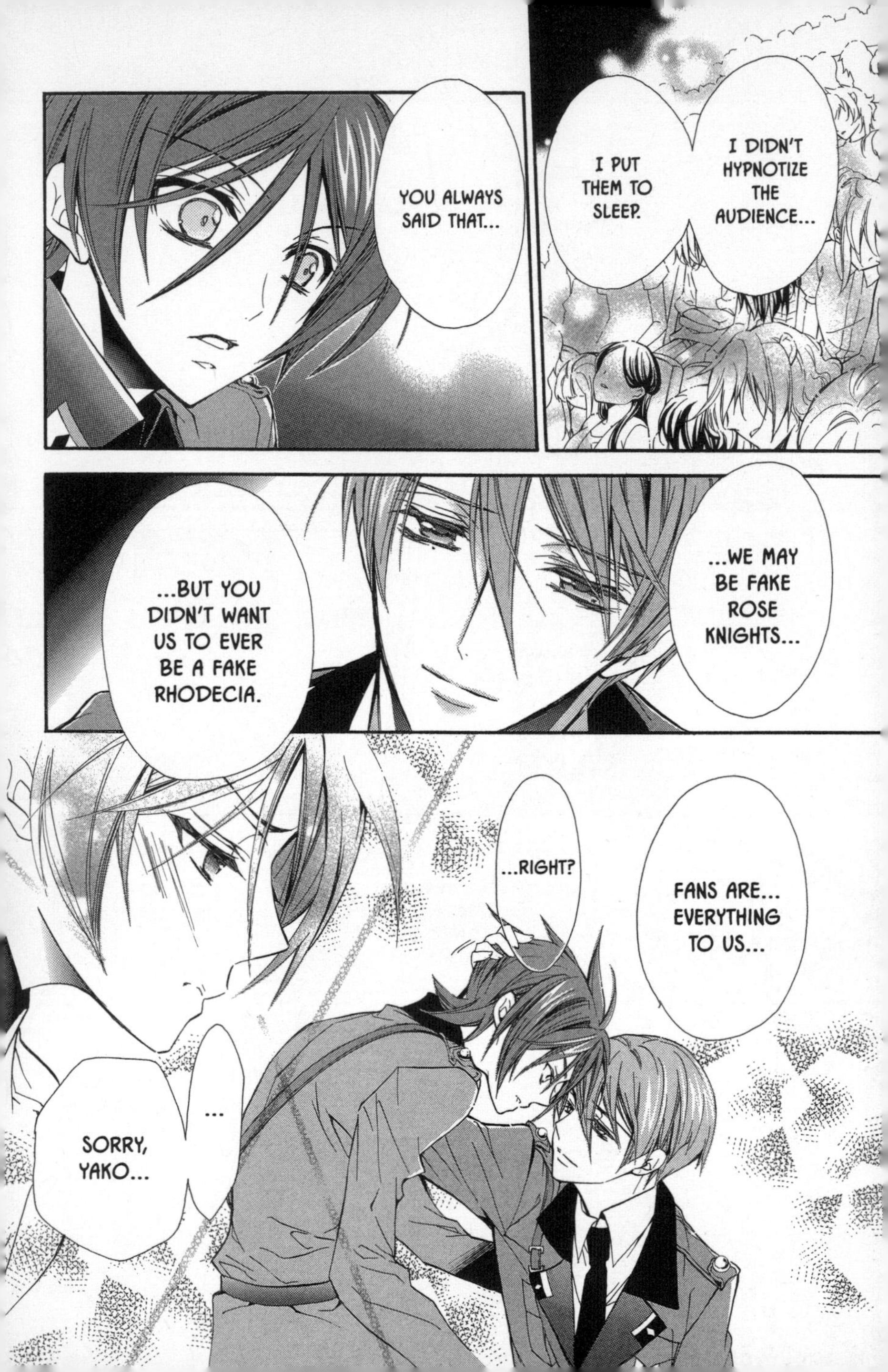

I DIDN'T HYPNOTIZE THE AUDIENCE...
I PUT THEM TO SLEEP.
YOU ALWAYS SAID THAT...
...WE MAY BE FAKE ROSE KNIGHTS...
...BUT YOU DIDN'T WANT US TO EVER BE A FAKE RHODECIA.
FANS ARE... EVERYTHING TO US...
...RIGHT?
...
SORRY, YAKO...

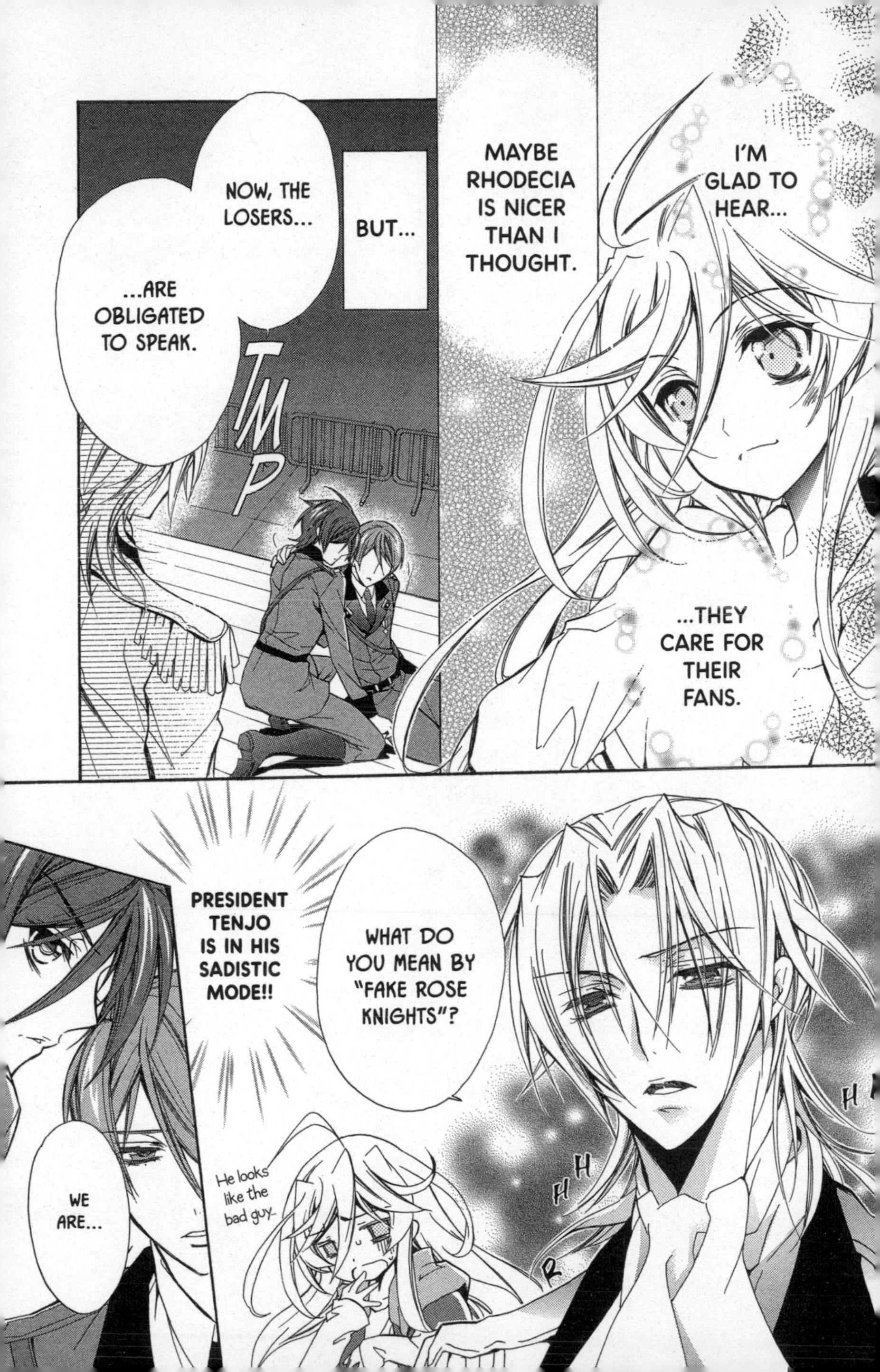
I'M GLAD TO HEAR...
...THEY CARE FOR THEIR FANS.
MAYBE RHODECIA IS NICER THAN I THOUGHT.
BUT...
NOW, THE LOSERS...
...ARE OBLIGATED TO SPEAK.
TMP
WHAT DO YOU MEAN BY "FAKE ROSE KNIGHTS"?
H
HHH
R
PRESIDENT TENJO IS IN HIS SADISTIC MODE!!
He looks like the bad guy..
WE ARE...

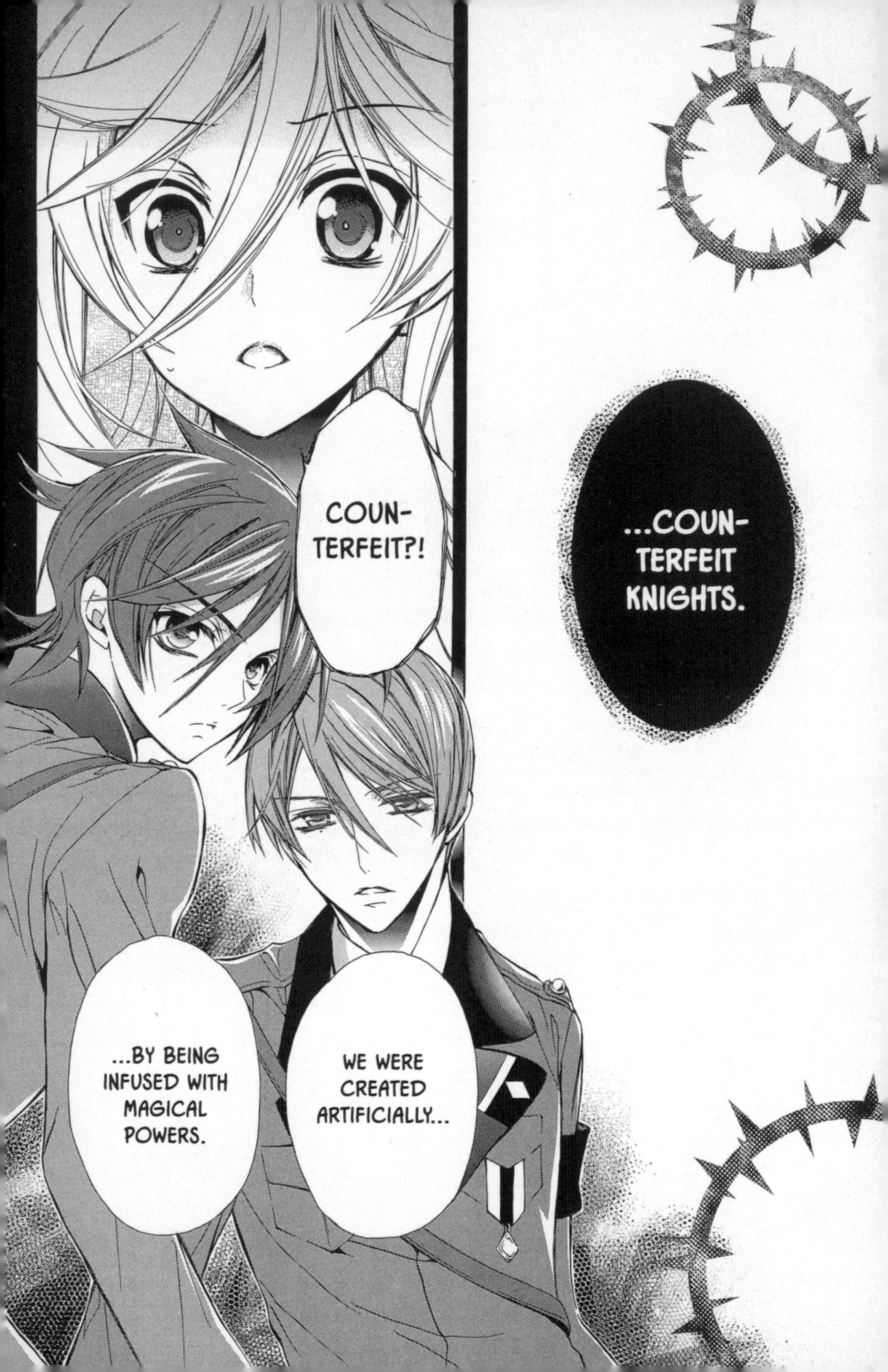
...COUN-
TERFEIT
KNIGHTS.
COUN-
TERFEIT?!
WE WERE
CREATED
ARTIFICIALLY...
...BY BEING
INFUSED WITH
MAGICAL
POWERS.

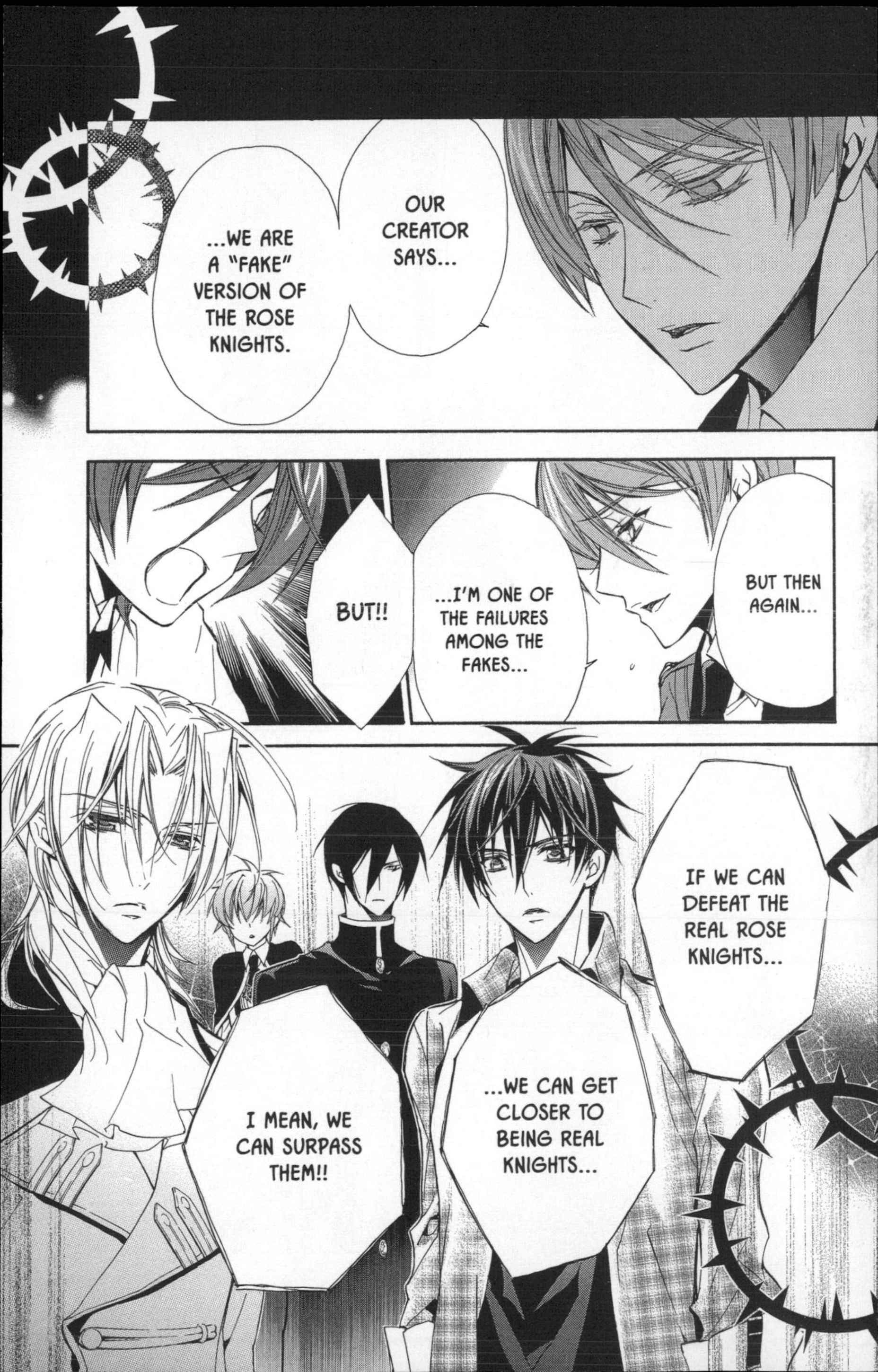
OUR CREATOR SAYS...
...WE ARE A "FAKE" VERSION OF THE ROSE KNIGHTS.
BUT THEN AGAIN...
...I'M ONE OF THE FAILURES AMONG THE FAKES...
BUT!!
IF WE CAN DEFEAT THE REAL ROSE KNIGHTS...
...WE CAN GET CLOSER TO BEING REAL KNIGHTS...
I MEAN, WE CAN SURPASS THEM!!

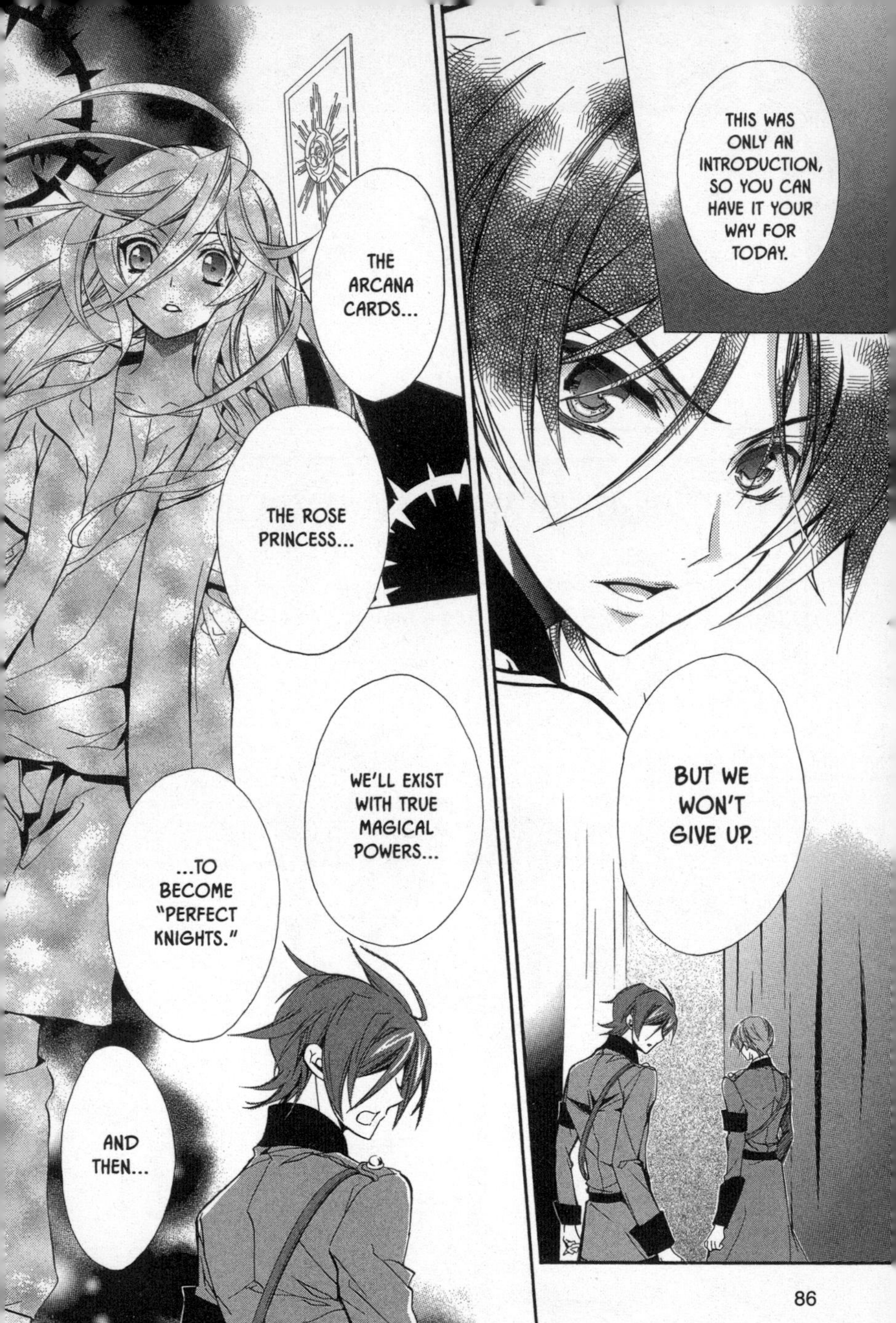
THIS WAS ONLY AN INTRODUCTION, SO YOU CAN HAVE IT YOUR WAY FOR TODAY.
BUT WE WON'T GIVE UP.
THE ARCANA CARDS...
THE ROSE PRINCESS...
WE'LL EXIST WITH TRUE MAGICAL POWERS...
...TO BECOME "PERFECT KNIGHTS."
AND THEN...

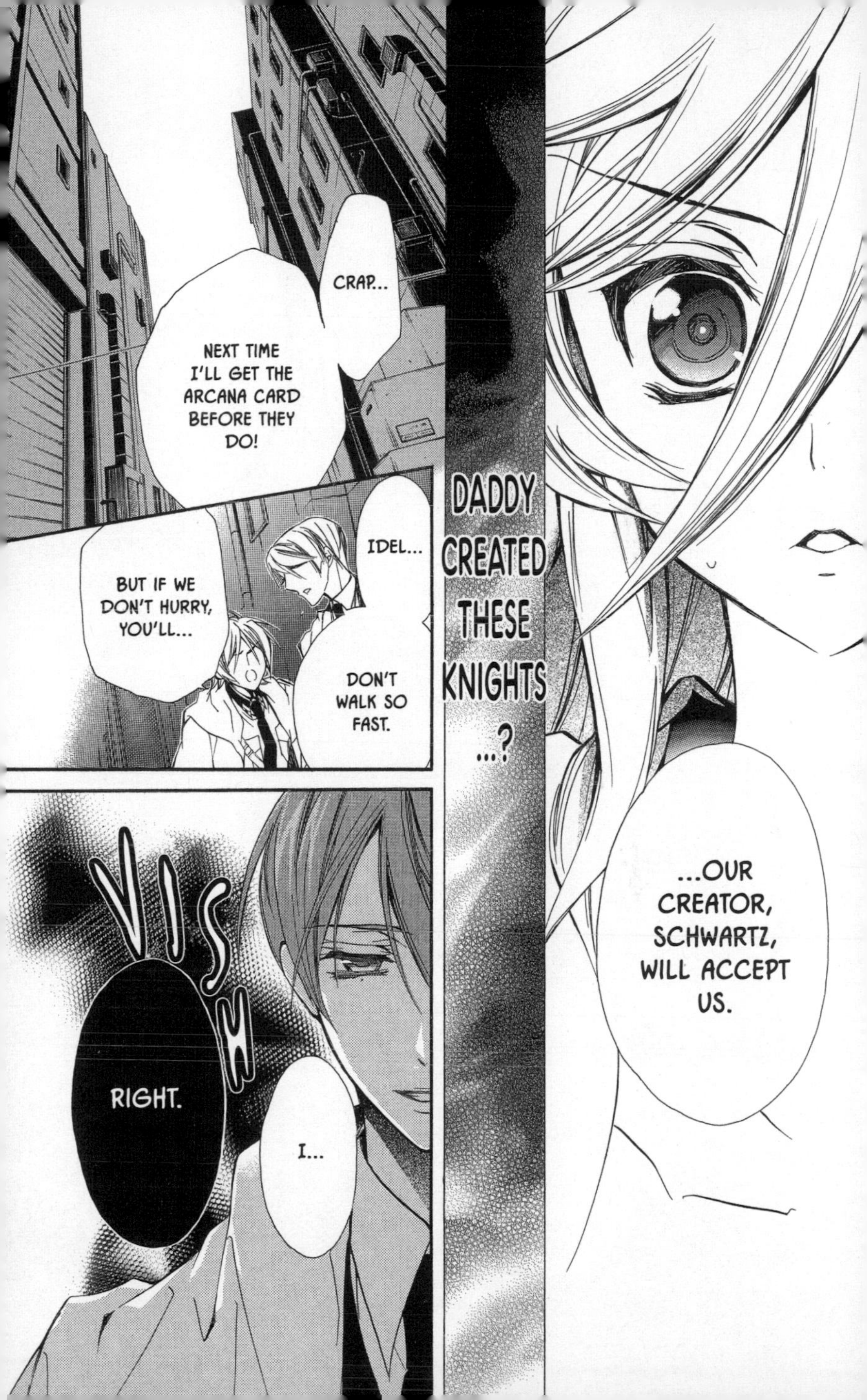
...OUR CREATOR, SCHWARTZ, WILL ACCEPT US.
DADDY CREATED THESE KNIGHTS ...?
CRAP...
NEXT TIME I'LL GET THE ARCANA CARD BEFORE THEY DO!
IDEL...
DON'T WALK SO FAST.
BUT IF WE DON'T HURRY, YOU'LL...
VISH
I...
RIGHT.

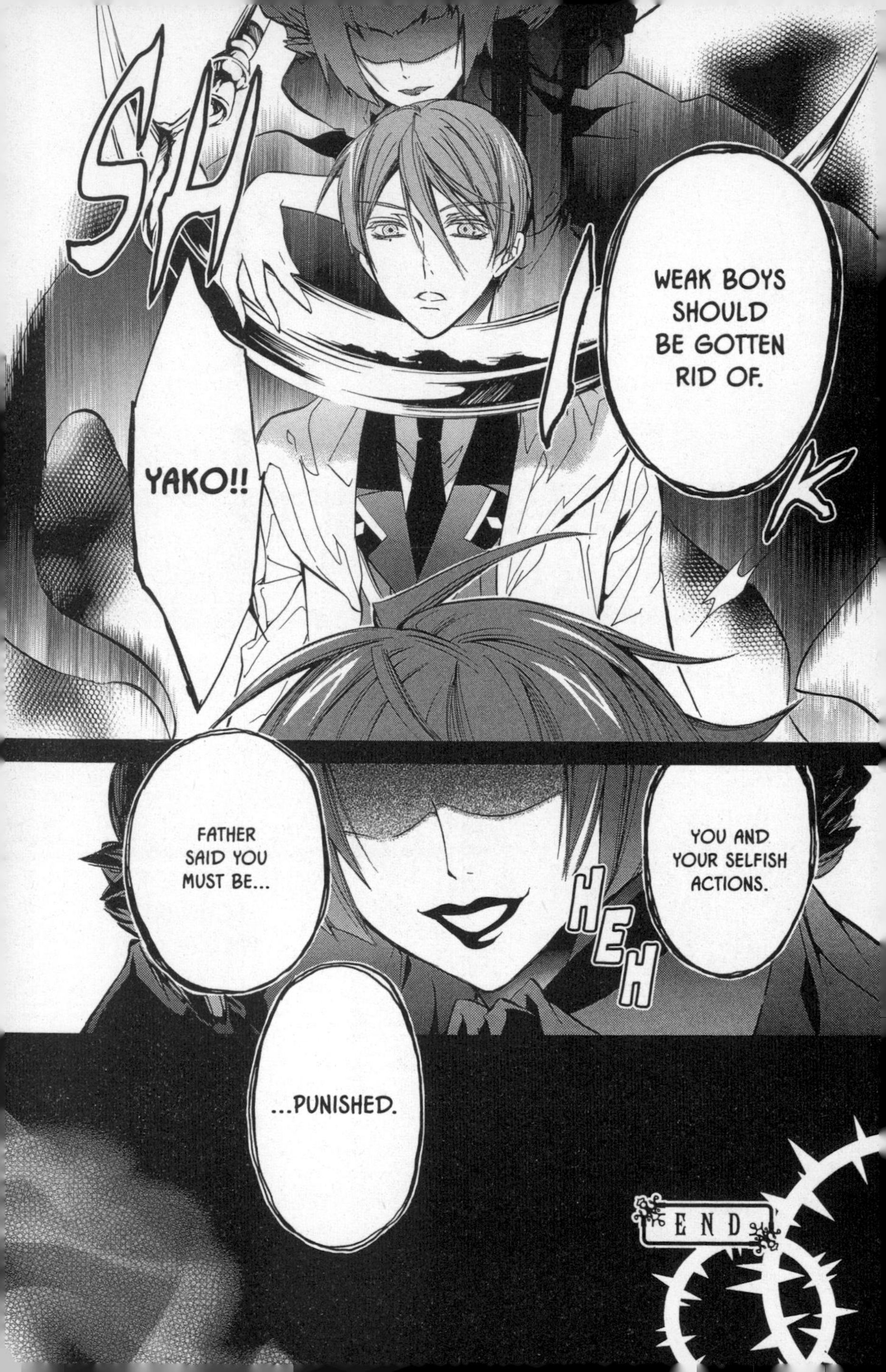
WEAK BOYS SHOULD BE GOTTEN RID OF.
SHK
YAKO!!
YOU AND YOUR SELFISH ACTIONS.
HEH
FATHER SAID YOU MUST BE...
...PUNISHED.
END

Kiss of the Rose
Princess

Kiss of the Rose Princess

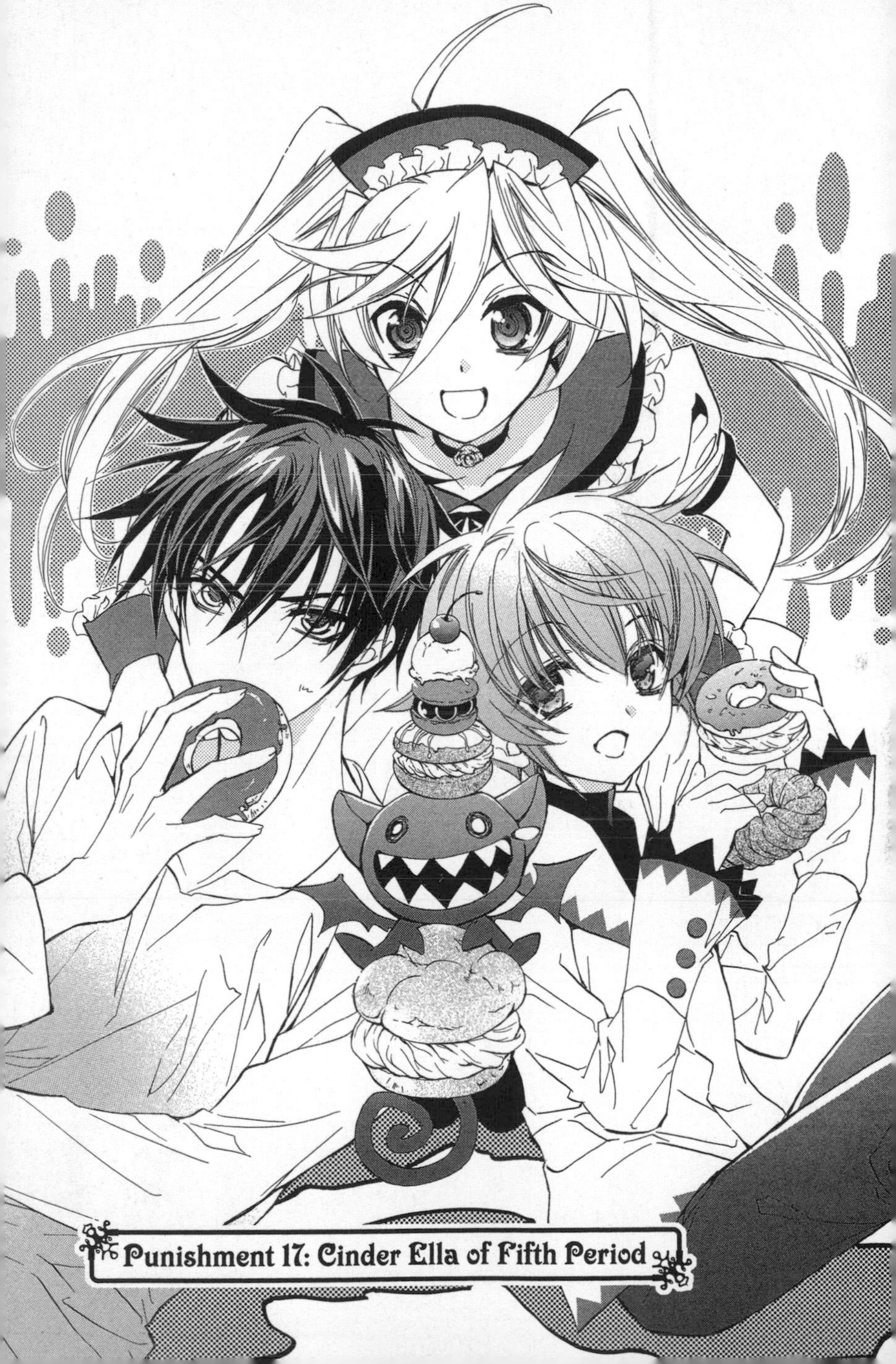

Punishment 17: Cinder Ella of Fifth Period

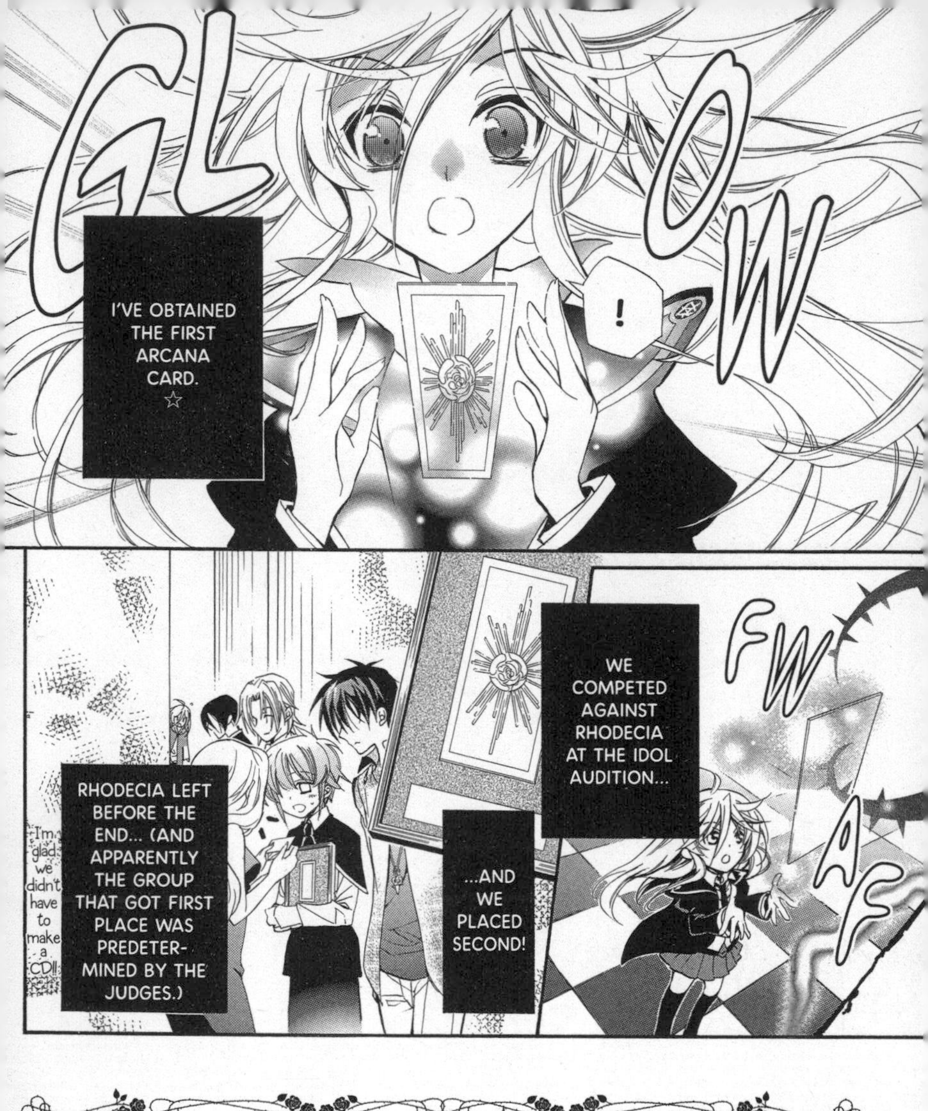
GLOW
I'VE OBTAINED THE FIRST ARCANA CARD. ☆
!
WE COMPETED AGAINST RHODECIA AT THE IDOL AUDITION...
FWAF
...AND WE PLACED SECOND!
RHODECIA LEFT BEFORE THE END... (AND APPARENTLY THE GROUP THAT GOT FIRST PLACE WAS PREDETER-MINED BY THE JUDGES.)
I'm glad we didn't have to make a CD!!

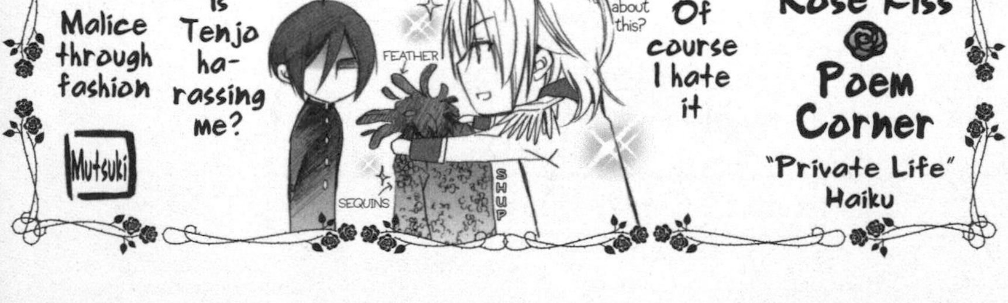
Rose Kiss Poem Corner
"Private Life" Haiku
Of course I hate it
How about this?
FEATHER
SEQUINS
SHUP
Is Tenjo harassing me?
Malice through fashion
Mutsuki

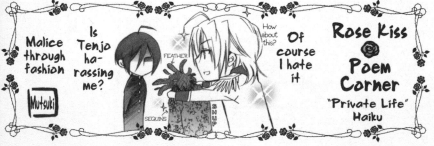

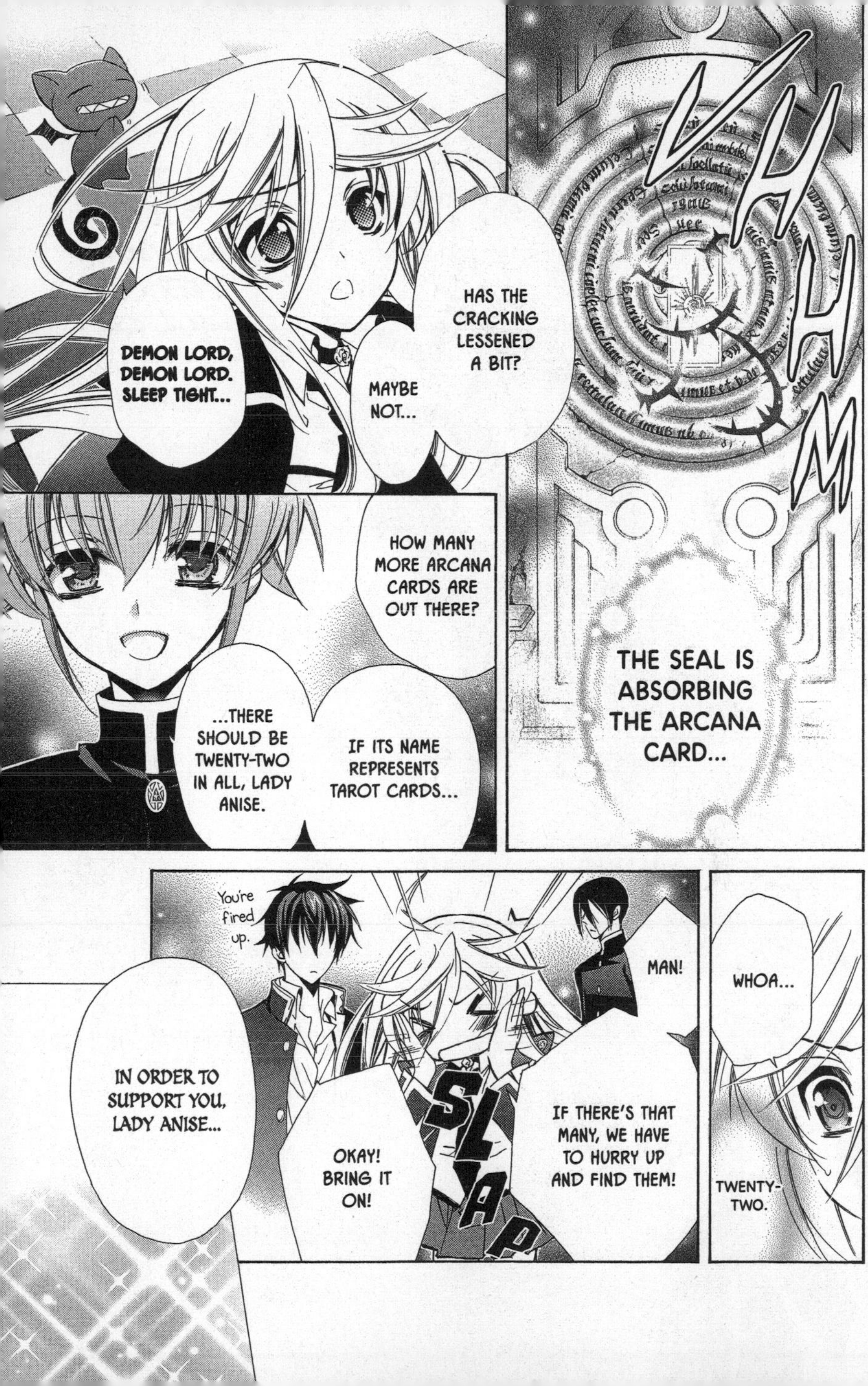
VHHM
THE SEAL IS ABSORBING THE ARCANA CARD...
HAS THE CRACKING LESSENED A BIT?
MAYBE NOT...
DEMON LORD, DEMON LORD. SLEEP TIGHT...
HOW MANY MORE ARCANA CARDS ARE OUT THERE?
IF ITS NAME REPRESENTS TAROT CARDS...
...THERE SHOULD BE TWENTY-TWO IN ALL, LADY ANISE.
WHOA...
TWENTY-TWO.
MAN!
IF THERE'S THAT MANY, WE HAVE TO HURRY UP AND FIND THEM!
OKAY! BRING IT ON!
SLAP
You're fired up.
IN ORDER TO SUPPORT YOU, LADY ANISE...

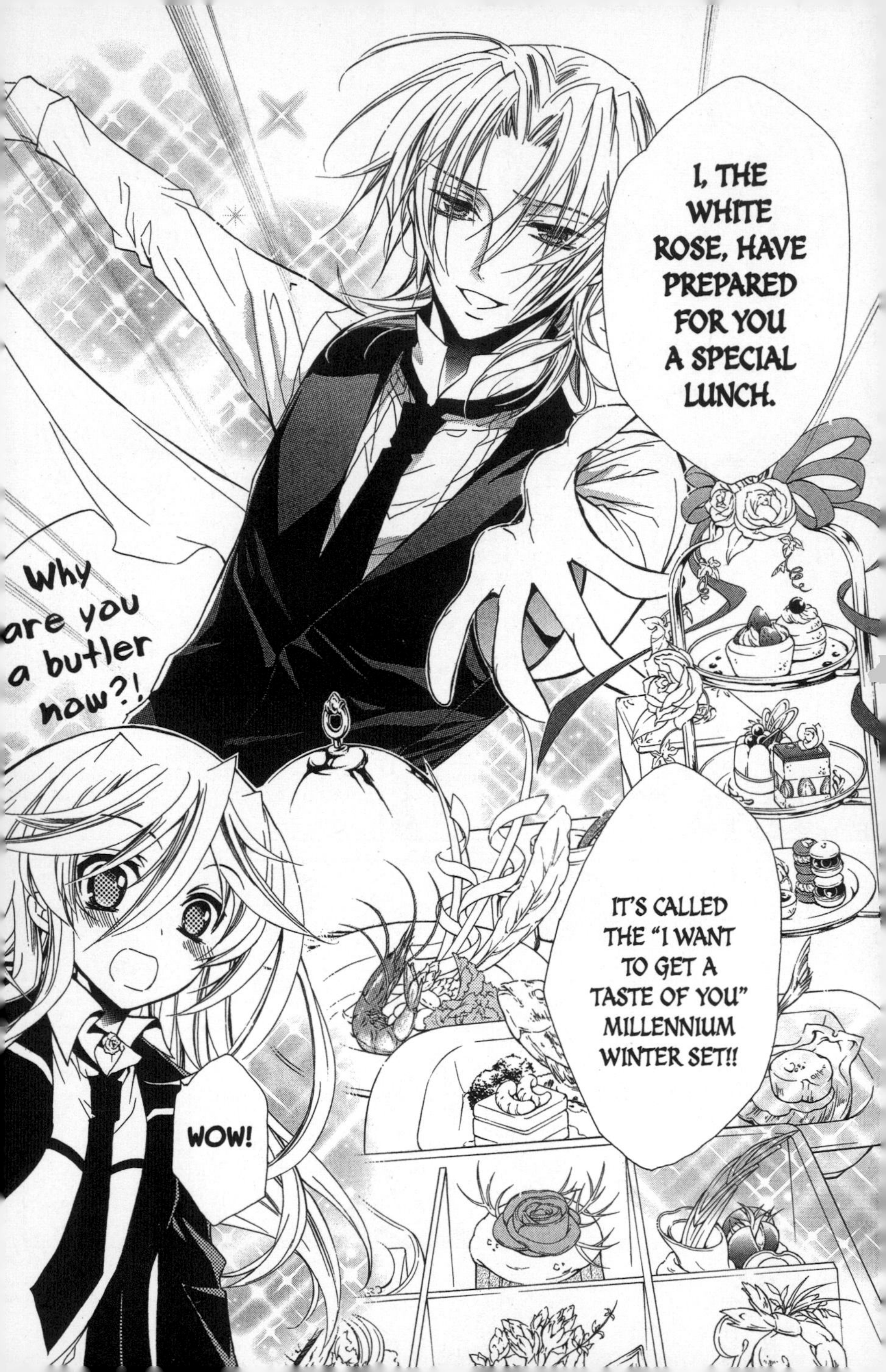
I, THE WHITE ROSE, HAVE PREPARED FOR YOU A SPECIAL LUNCH.
Why are you a butler now?!
IT'S CALLED THE "I WANT TO GET A TASTE OF YOU" MILLENNIUM WINTER SET!!
WOW!

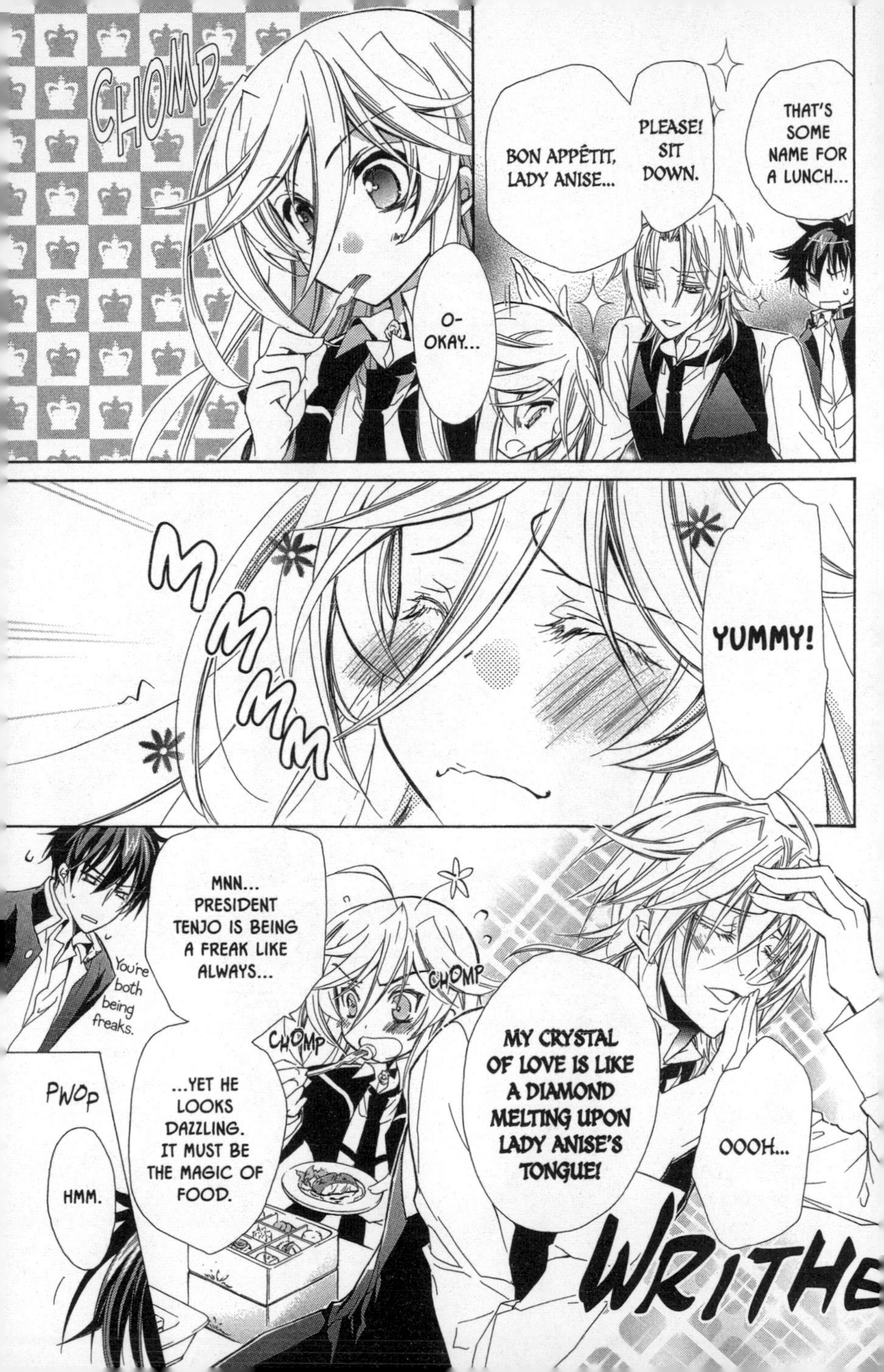
THAT'S SOME NAME FOR A LUNCH...
PLEASE! SIT DOWN.
BON APPÉTIT, LADY ANISE...
CHOMP
O-OKAY...
YUMMY!
MMMMM
OOOH...
MY CRYSTAL OF LOVE IS LIKE A DIAMOND MELTING UPON LADY ANISE'S TONGUE!
CHOMP
MNN... PRESIDENT TENJO IS BEING A FREAK LIKE ALWAYS...
You're both being freaks.
CHOMP
...YET HE LOOKS DAZZLING. IT MUST BE THE MAGIC OF FOOD.
PWOP
HMM.
WRITHE

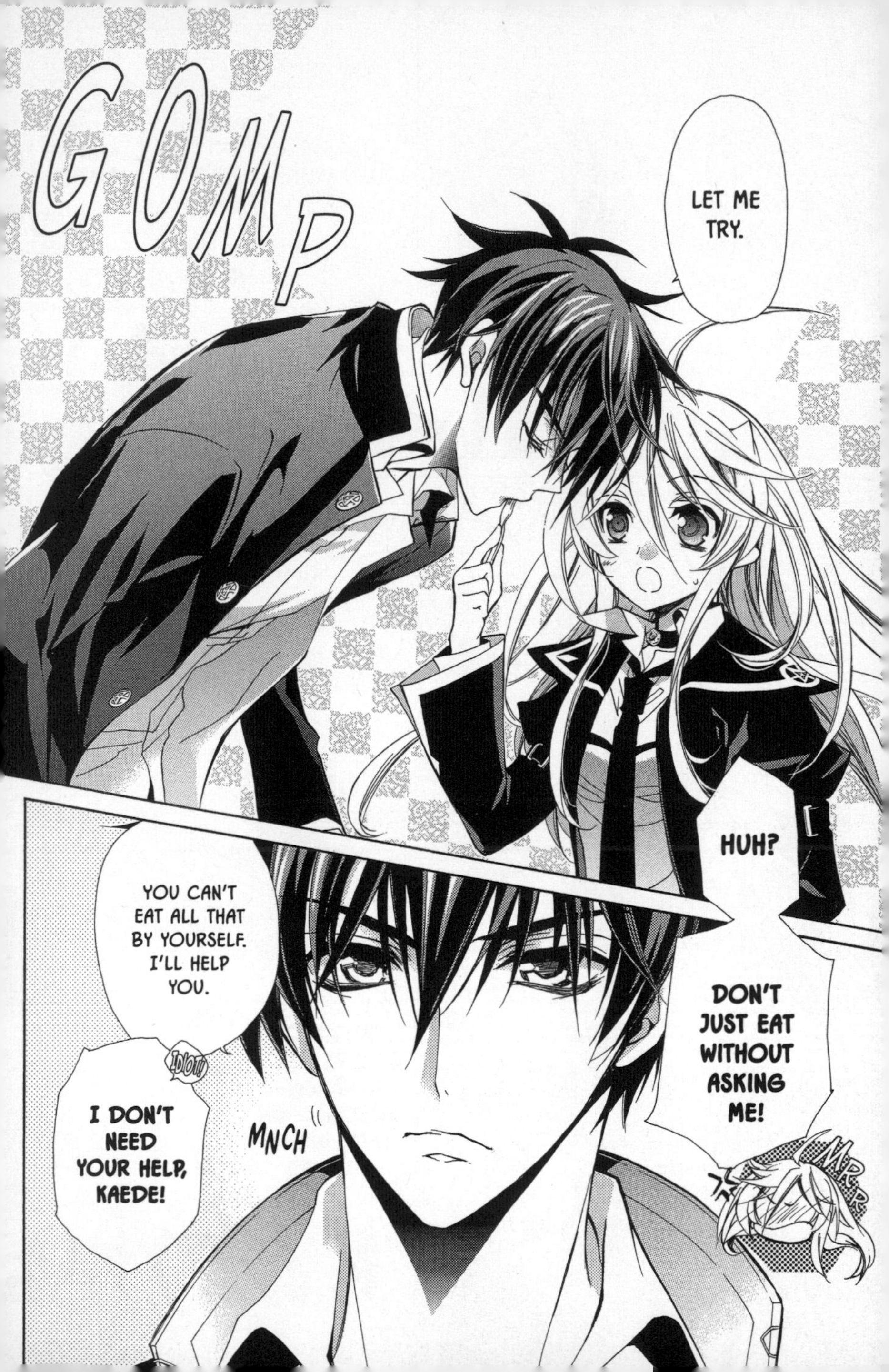
LET ME TRY.
GOMP
HUH?
DON'T JUST EAT WITHOUT ASKING ME!
MRRR
YOU CAN'T EAT ALL THAT BY YOURSELF. I'LL HELP YOU.
MNCH
IDIOT!
I DON'T NEED YOUR HELP, KAEDE!

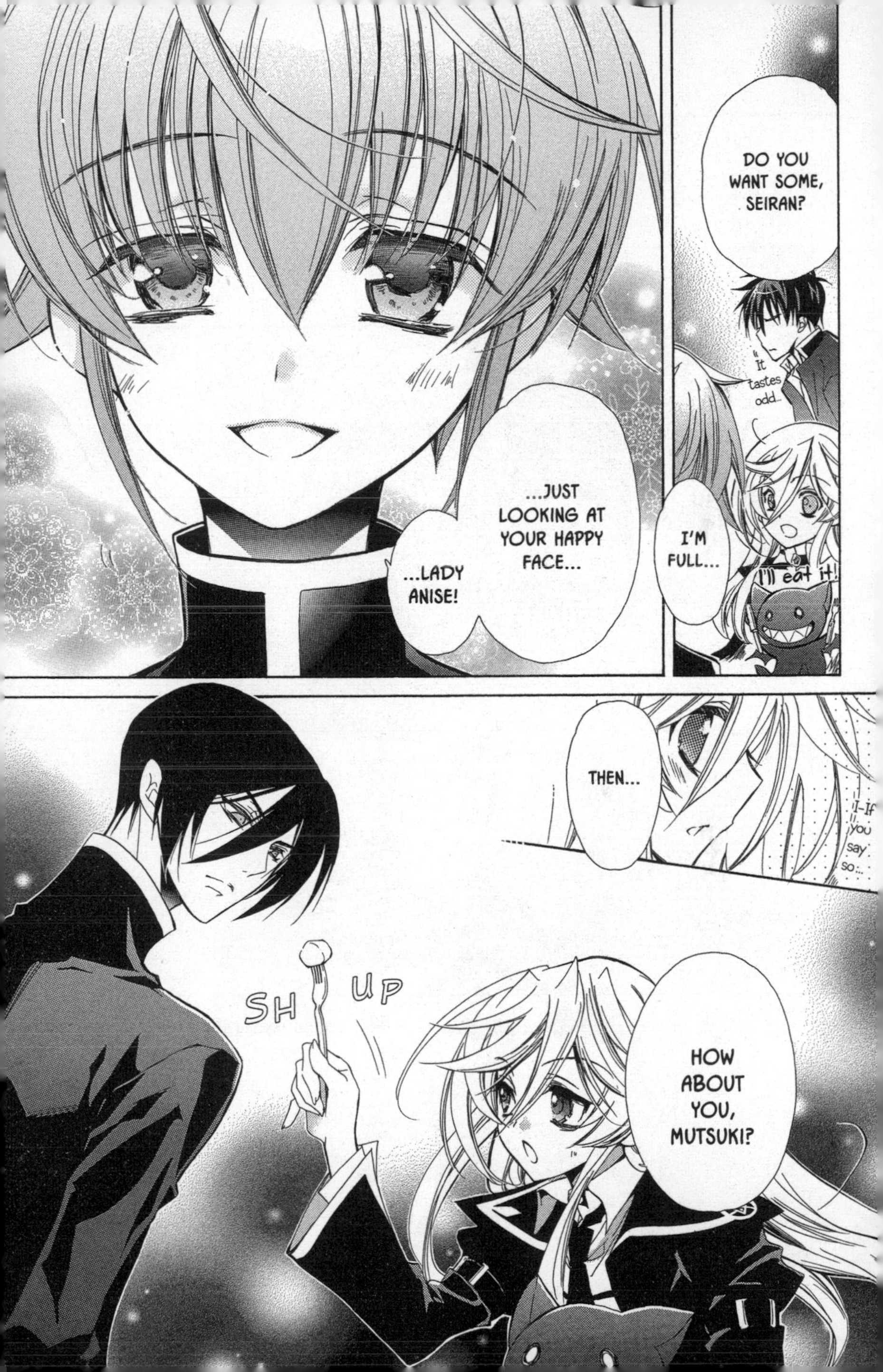
DO YOU WANT SOME, SEIRAN?
It tastes odd...
I'M FULL...
I'll eat it!
...JUST LOOKING AT YOUR HAPPY FACE...
...LADY ANISE!
I-If you say so...
THEN...
HOW ABOUT YOU, MUTSUKI?
SH UP

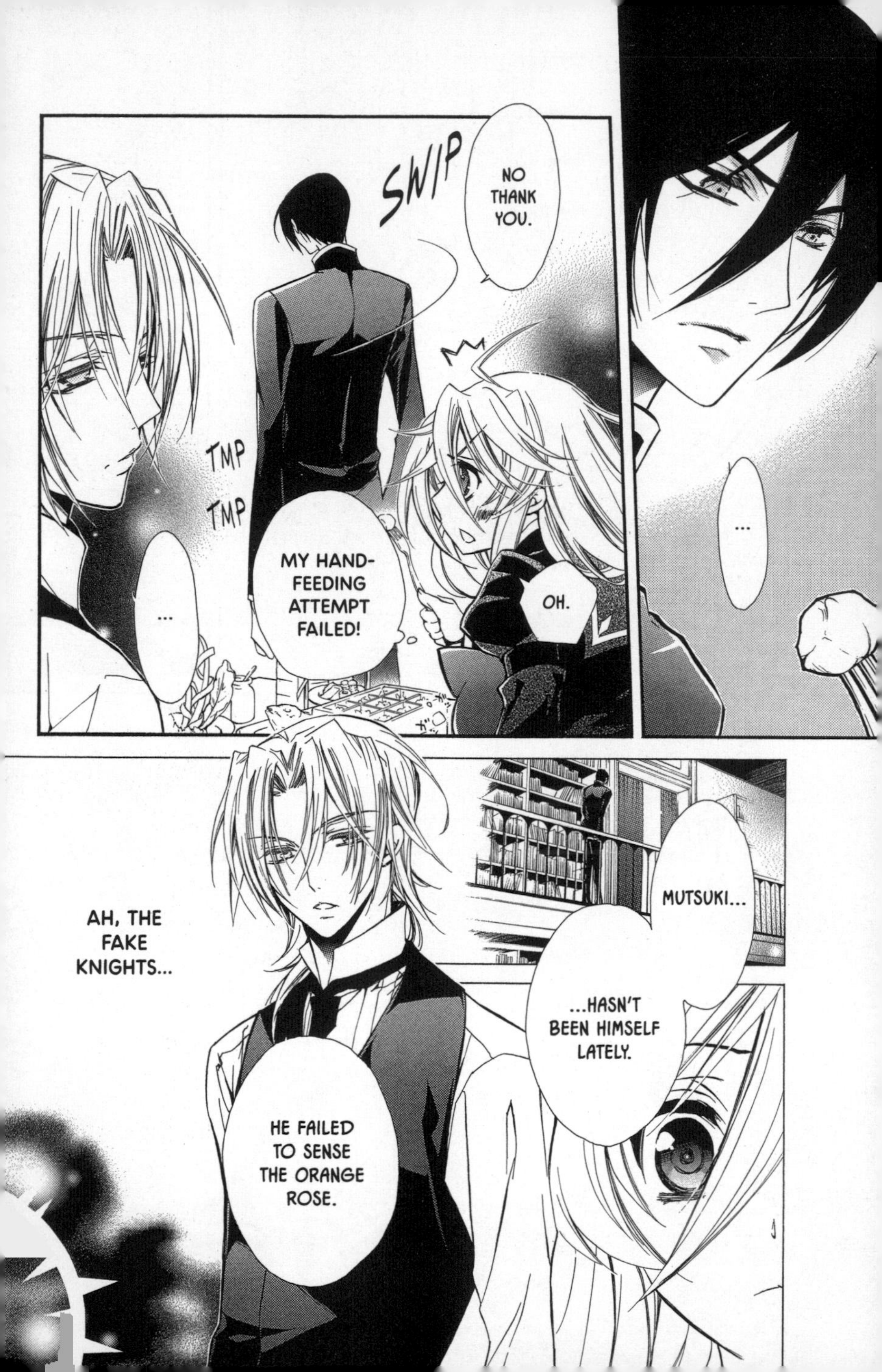
...
NO THANK YOU.
SWIP
OH.
MY HAND-FEEDING ATTEMPT FAILED!
TMP
TMP
...
MUTSUKI...
...HASN'T BEEN HIMSELF LATELY.
AH, THE FAKE KNIGHTS...
HE FAILED TO SENSE THE ORANGE ROSE.

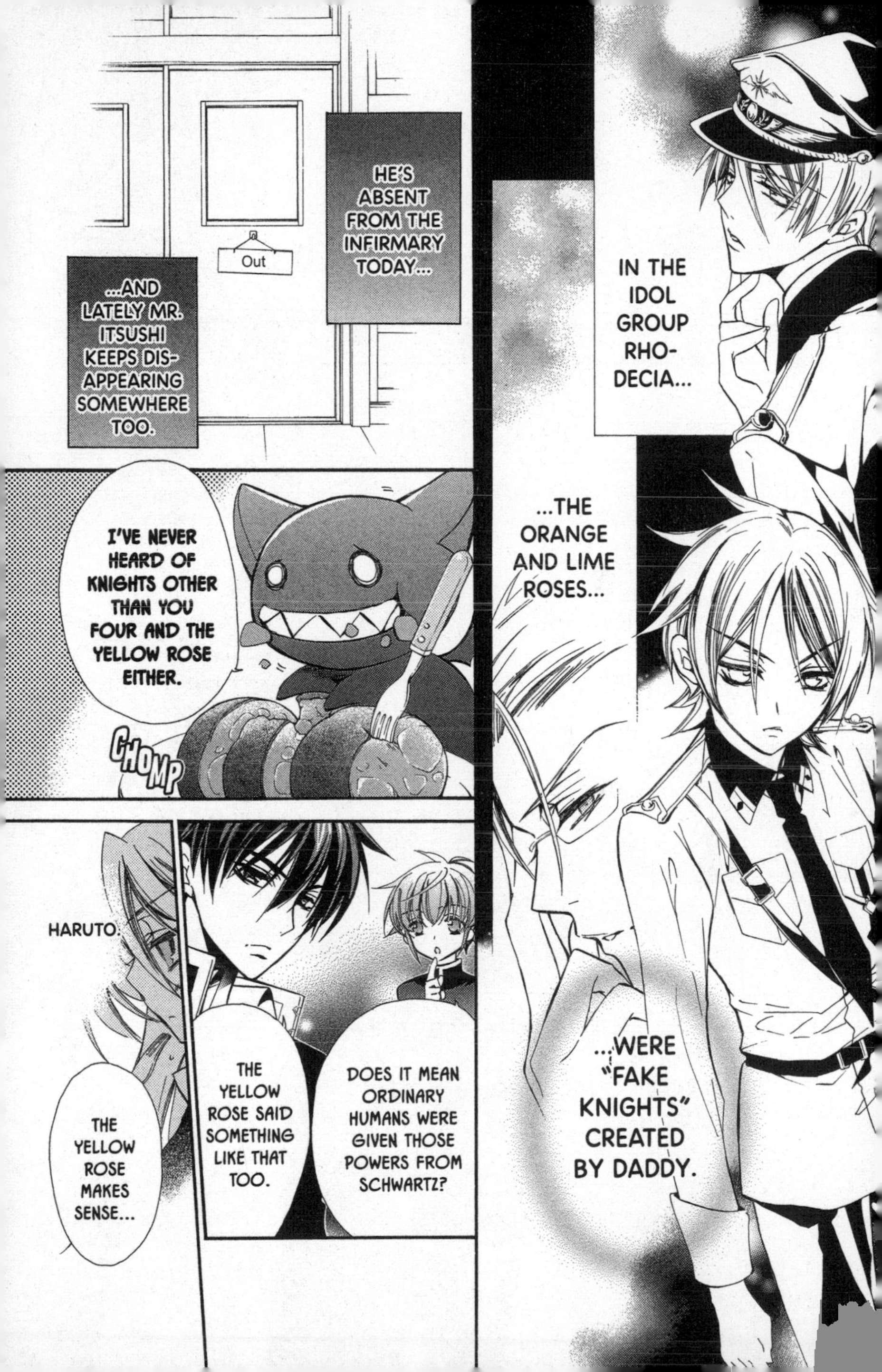
IN THE IDOL GROUP RHODECIA...
...THE ORANGE AND LIME ROSES...
...WERE "FAKE KNIGHTS" CREATED BY DADDY.
HE'S ABSENT FROM THE INFIRMARY TODAY...
Out
...AND LATELY MR. ITSUSHI KEEPS DISAPPEARING SOMEWHERE TOO.
I'VE NEVER HEARD OF KNIGHTS OTHER THAN YOU FOUR AND THE YELLOW ROSE EITHER.
CHOMP
DOES IT MEAN ORDINARY HUMANS WERE GIVEN THOSE POWERS FROM SCHWARTZ?
THE YELLOW ROSE SAID SOMETHING LIKE THAT TOO.
HARUTO.
THE YELLOW ROSE MAKES SENSE...

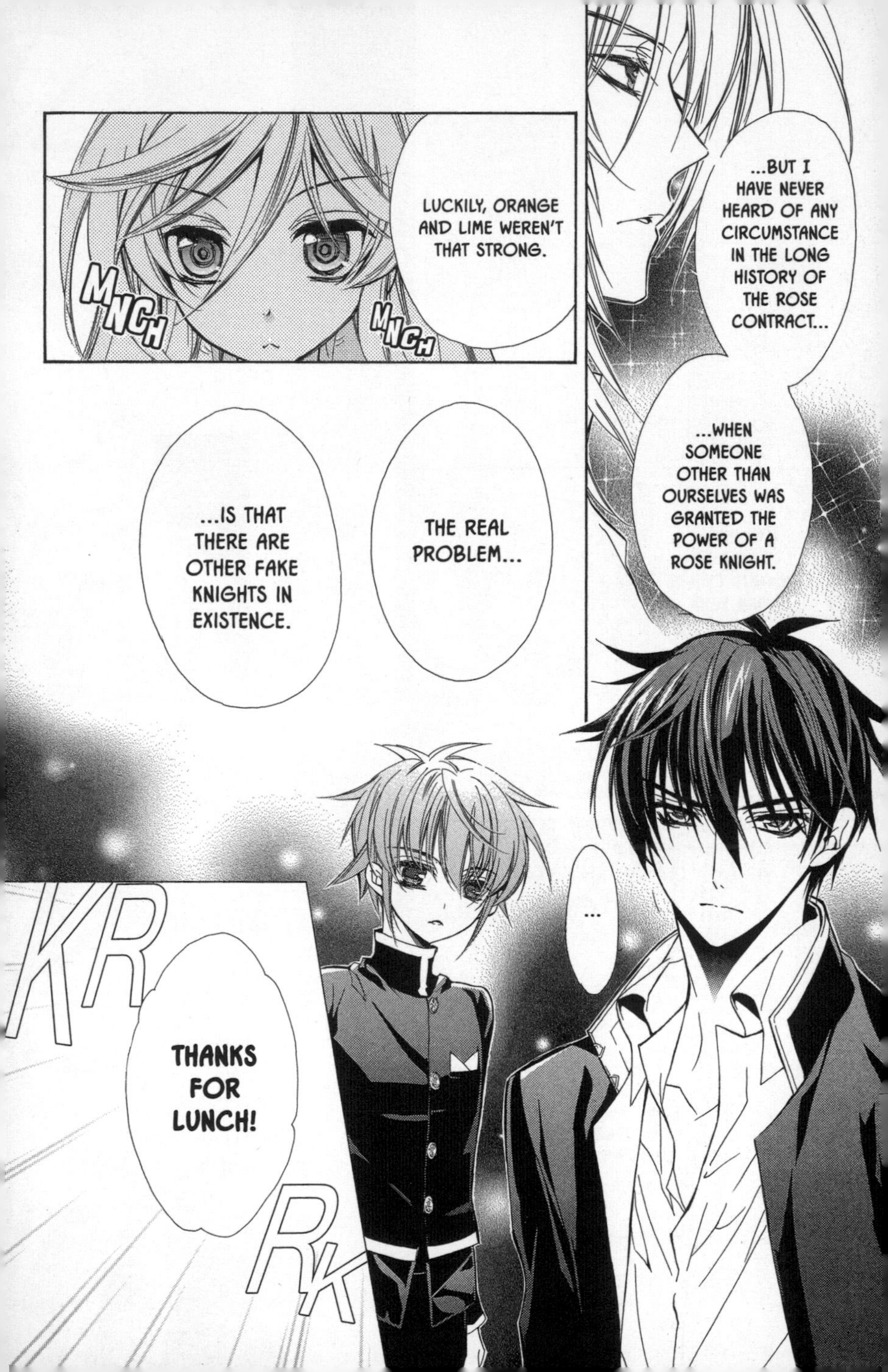
...BUT I HAVE NEVER HEARD OF ANY CIRCUMSTANCE IN THE LONG HISTORY OF THE ROSE CONTRACT...
...WHEN SOMEONE OTHER THAN OURSELVES WAS GRANTED THE POWER OF A ROSE KNIGHT.
LUCKILY, ORANGE AND LIME WEREN'T THAT STRONG.
MNCH
MNCH
THE REAL PROBLEM...
...IS THAT THERE ARE OTHER FAKE KNIGHTS IN EXISTENCE.
...
KR
THANKS FOR LUNCH!
RK

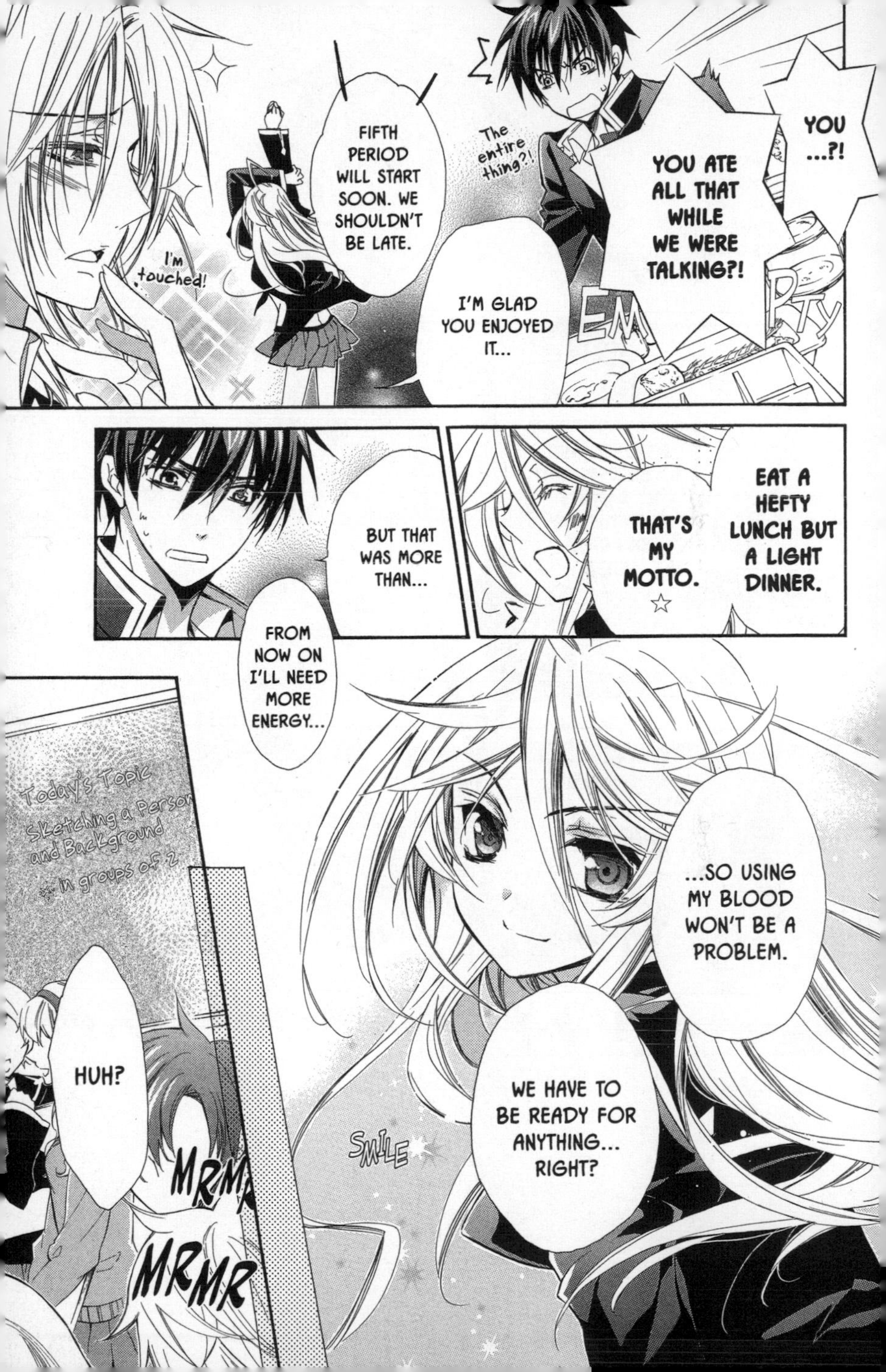
YOU ...?!
YOU ATE ALL THAT WHILE WE WERE TALKING?!
EMPTY
The entire thing?!
I'M GLAD YOU ENJOYED IT...
FIFTH PERIOD WILL START SOON. WE SHOULDN'T BE LATE.
I'm touched!
EAT A HEFTY LUNCH BUT A LIGHT DINNER.
THAT'S MY MOTTO. ☆
BUT THAT WAS MORE THAN...
FROM NOW ON I'LL NEED MORE ENERGY...
...SO USING MY BLOOD WON'T BE A PROBLEM.
WE HAVE TO BE READY FOR ANYTHING... RIGHT?
SMILE
Today's Topic
Sketching a Person and Background
※ in groups of 2
HUH?
MRMR
MRMR

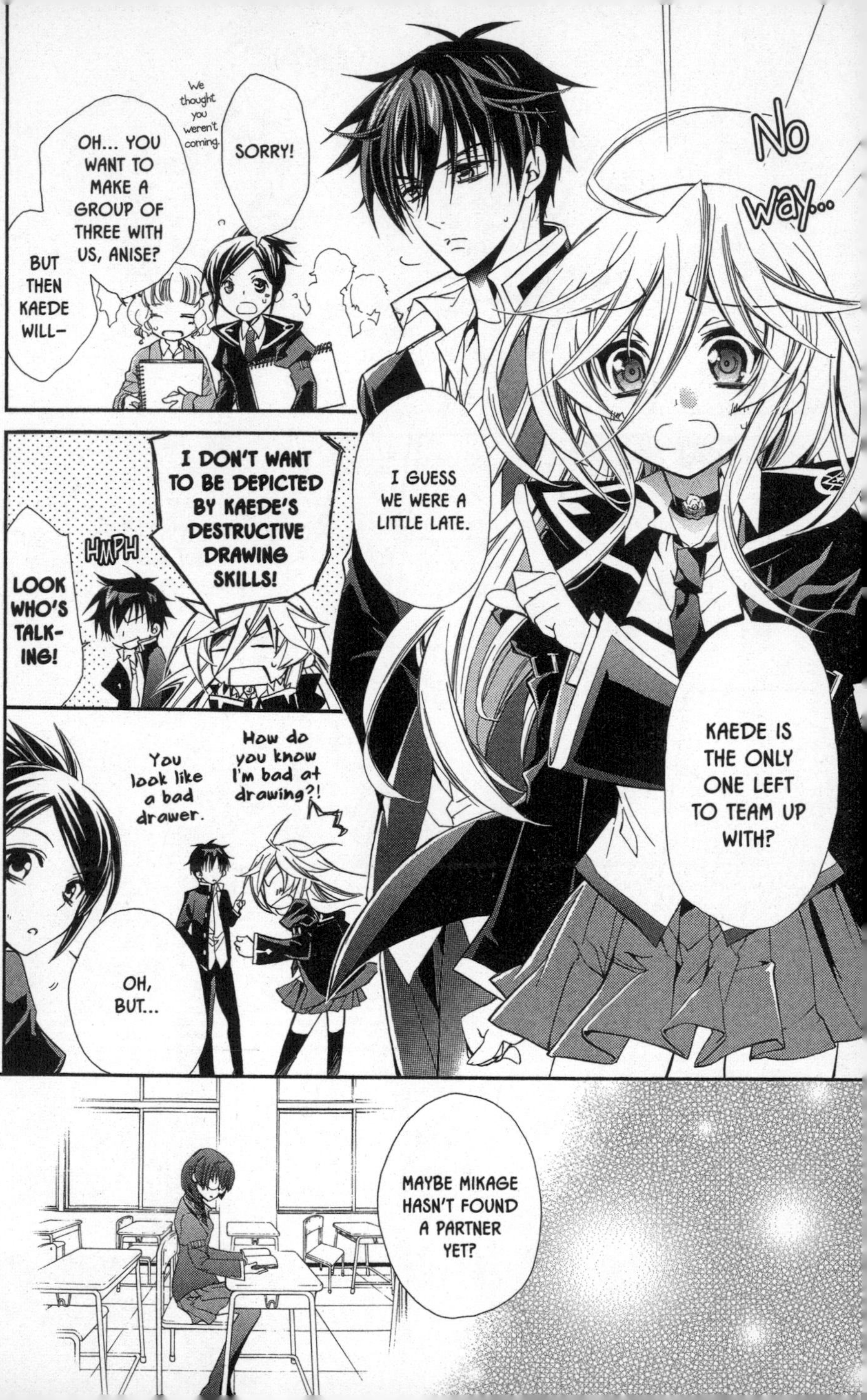
No way...
I GUESS WE WERE A LITTLE LATE.
KAEDE IS THE ONLY ONE LEFT TO TEAM UP WITH?
We thought you weren't coming.
SORRY!
OH... YOU WANT TO MAKE A GROUP OF THREE WITH US, ANISE?
BUT THEN KAEDE WILL–
I DON'T WANT TO BE DEPICTED BY KAEDE'S DESTRUCTIVE DRAWING SKILLS!
HMPH
LOOK WHO'S TALK-ING!
How do you know I'm bad at drawing?!
You look like a bad drawer.
OH, BUT...
MAYBE MIKAGE HASN'T FOUND A PARTNER YET?

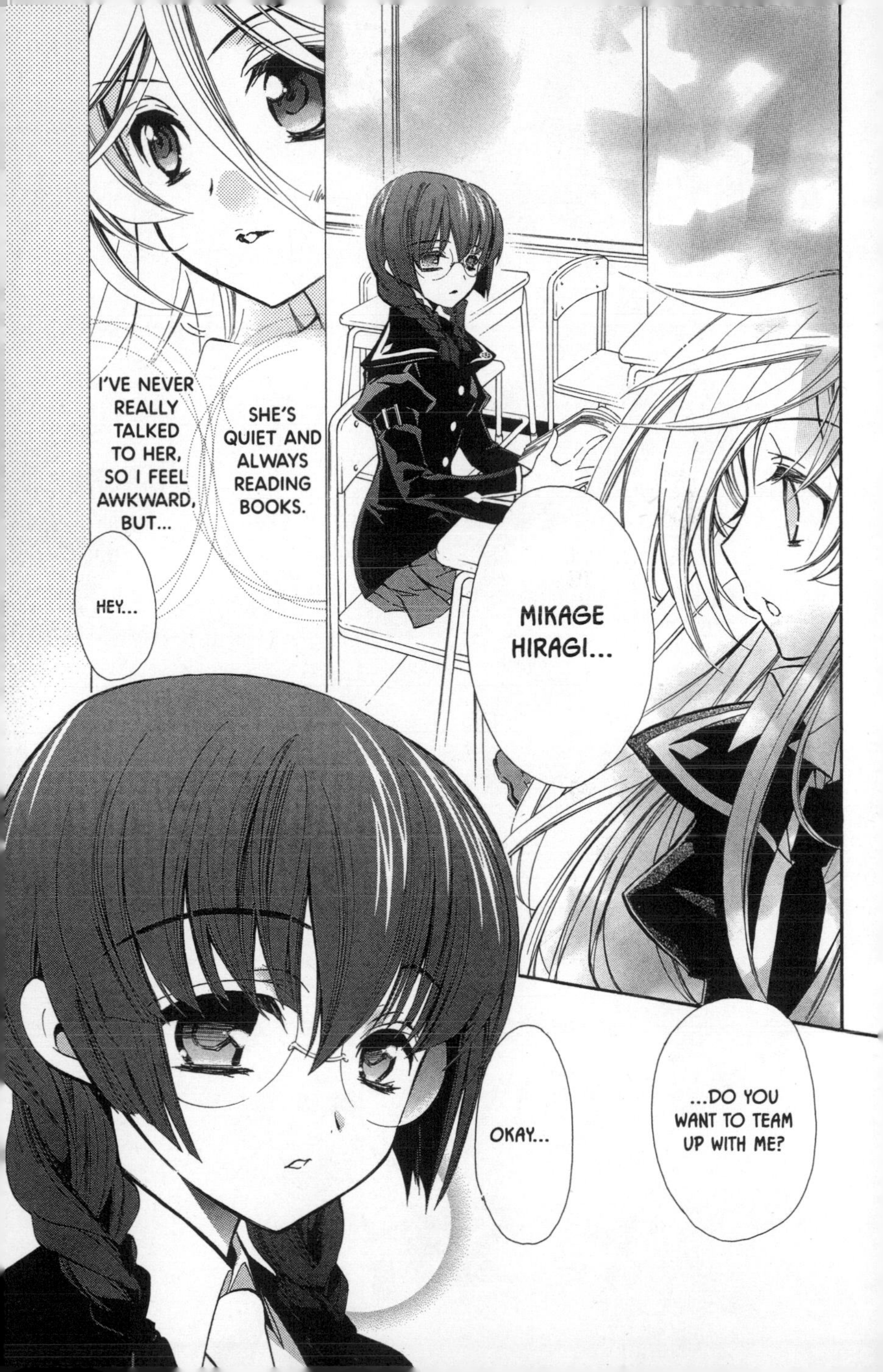
MIKAGE HIRAGI...
SHE'S QUIET AND ALWAYS READING BOOKS.
I'VE NEVER REALLY TALKED TO HER, SO I FEEL AWKWARD, BUT...
HEY...
...DO YOU WANT TO TEAM UP WITH ME?
OKAY...

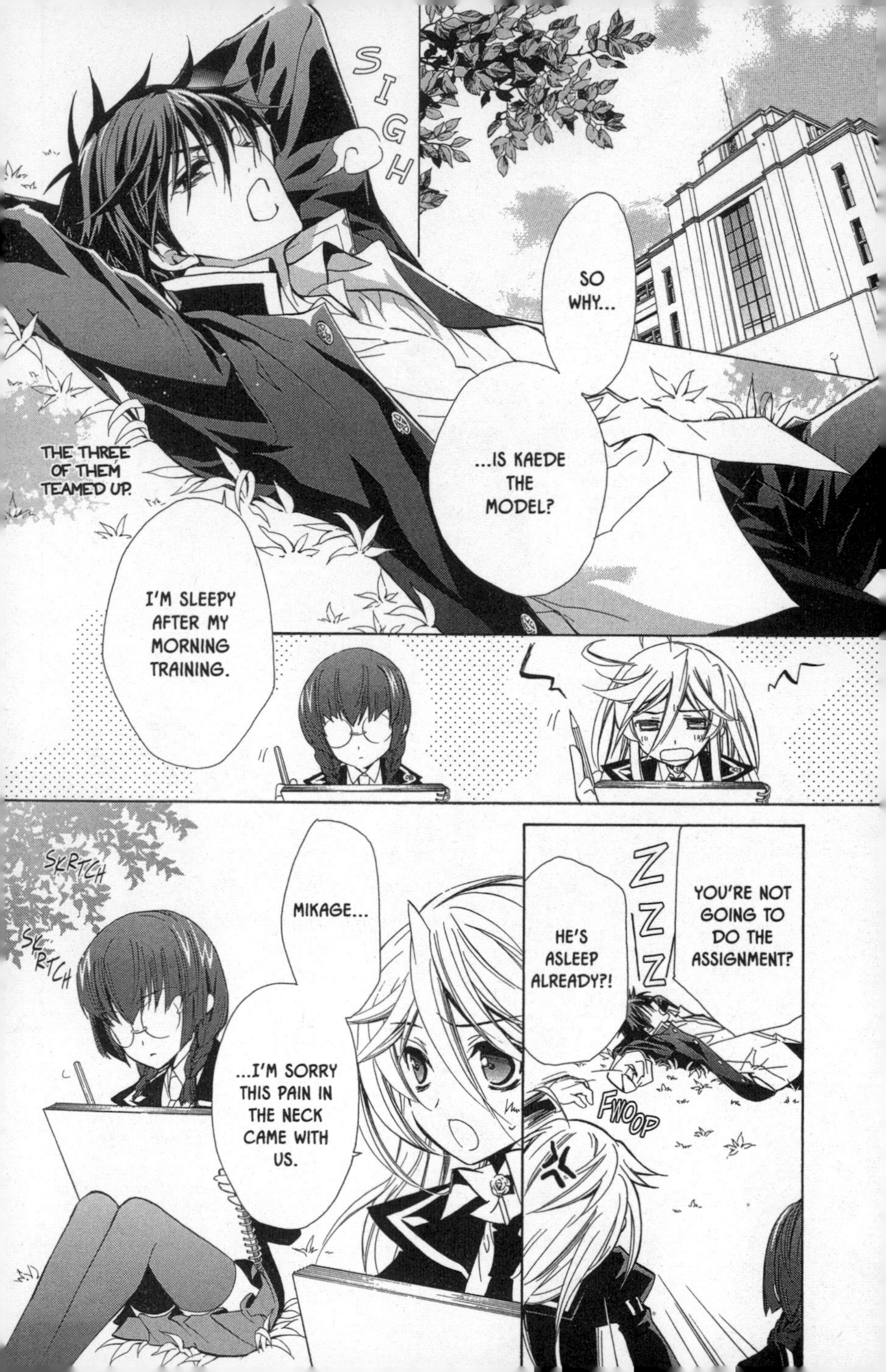
SO WHY...
...IS KAEDE THE MODEL?
SIGH
THE THREE OF THEM TEAMED UP.
I'M SLEEPY AFTER MY MORNING TRAINING.
YOU'RE NOT GOING TO DO THE ASSIGNMENT?
ZZZ
HE'S ASLEEP ALREADY?!
FWOOP
MIKAGE...
...I'M SORRY THIS PAIN IN THE NECK CAME WITH US.
SKRTCH
SKRTCH

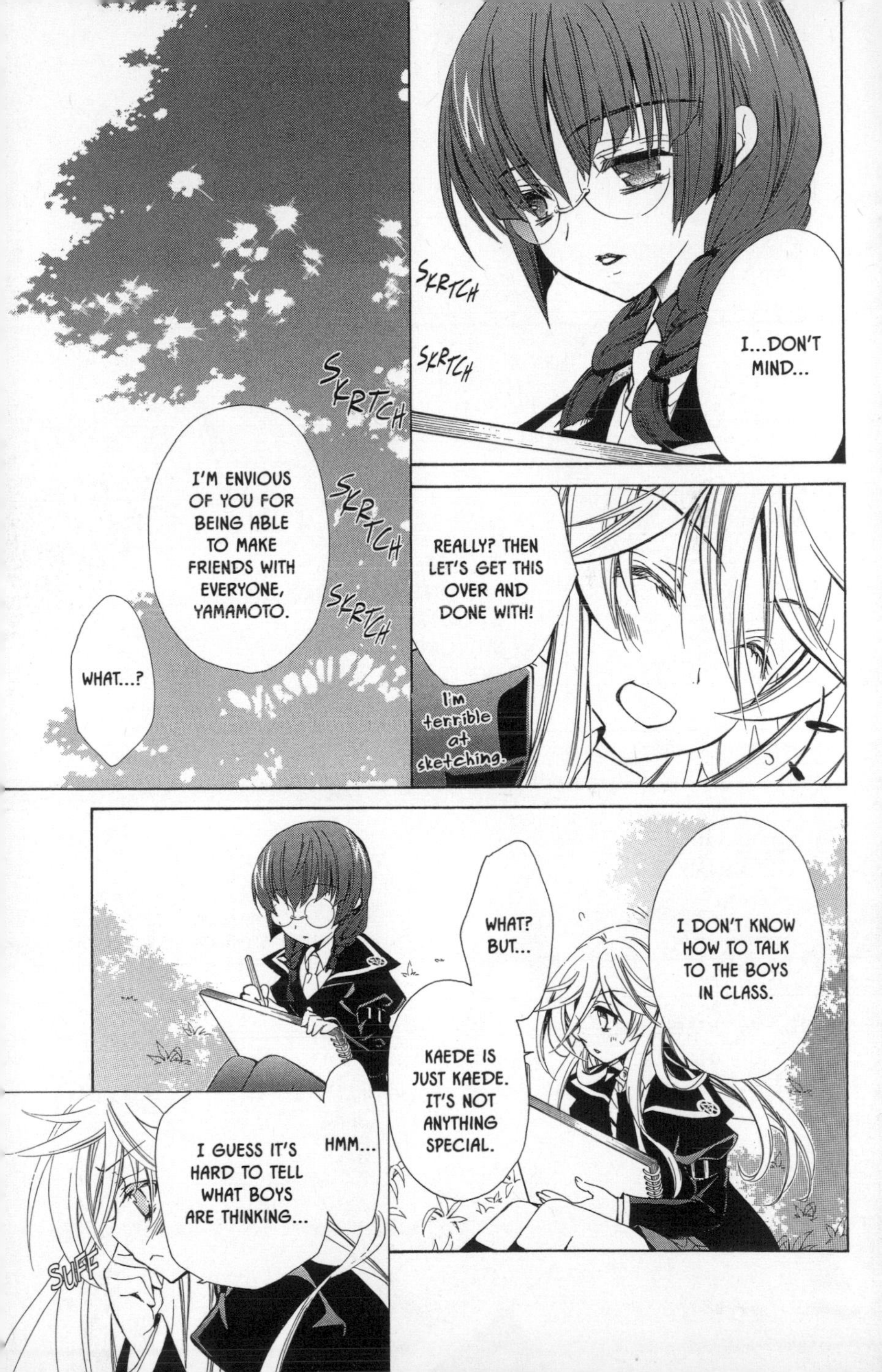
I...DON'T MIND...
SKRTCH
SKRTCH
REALLY? THEN LET'S GET THIS OVER AND DONE WITH!
I'm terrible at sketching.
SKRTCH
SKRTCH
SKRTCH
SKRTCH
I'M ENVIOUS OF YOU FOR BEING ABLE TO MAKE FRIENDS WITH EVERYONE, YAMAMOTO.
WHAT...?
I DON'T KNOW HOW TO TALK TO THE BOYS IN CLASS.
WHAT? BUT...
KAEDE IS JUST KAEDE. IT'S NOT ANYTHING SPECIAL.
HMM...
I GUESS IT'S HARD TO TELL WHAT BOYS ARE THINKING...
SUFF

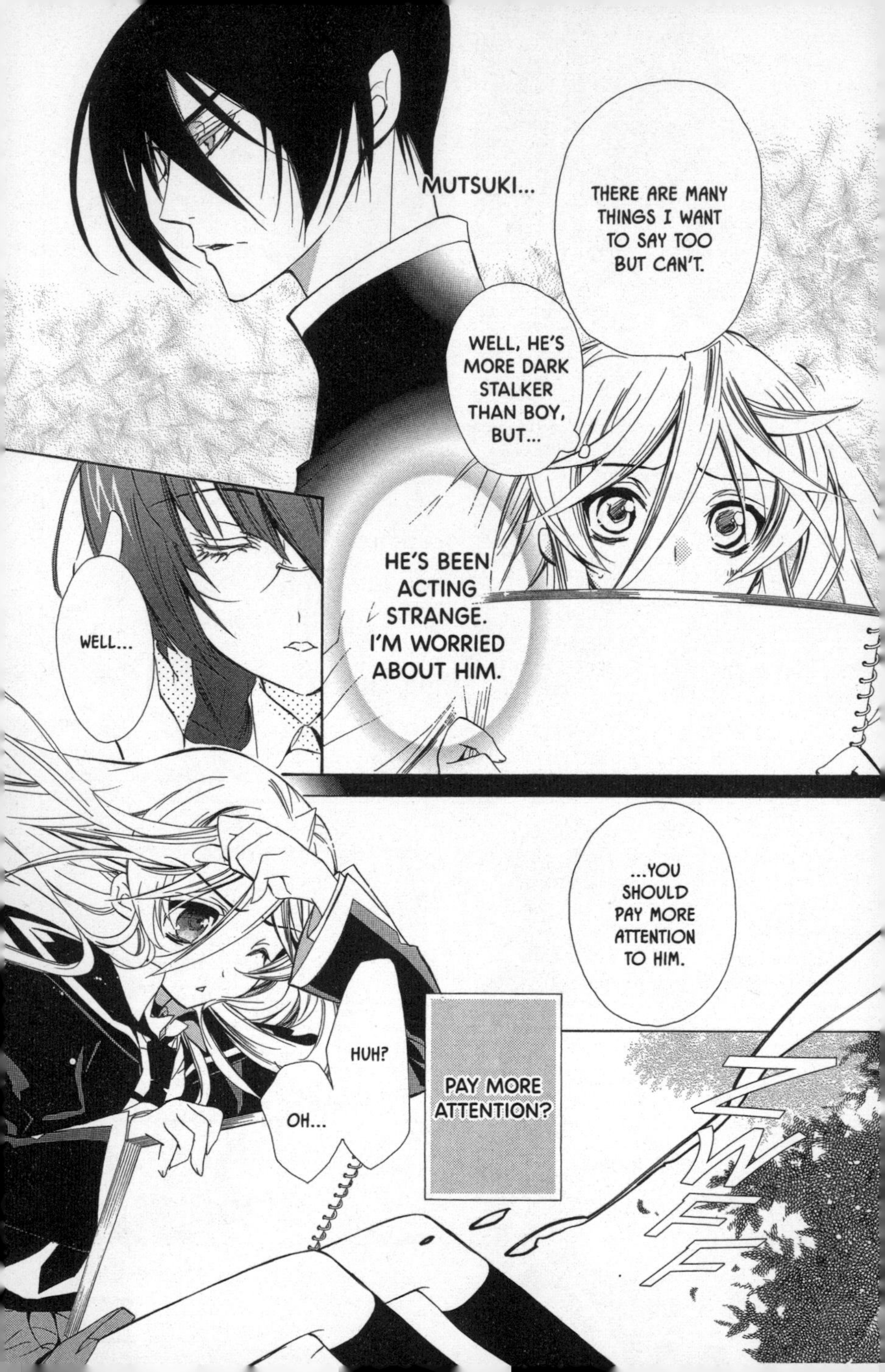
THERE ARE MANY THINGS I WANT TO SAY TOO BUT CAN'T.
MUTSUKI...
WELL, HE'S MORE DARK STALKER THAN BOY, BUT...
HE'S BEEN ACTING STRANGE. I'M WORRIED ABOUT HIM.
WELL...
...YOU SHOULD PAY MORE ATTENTION TO HIM.
ZWFF
PAY MORE ATTENTION?
HUH?
OH...

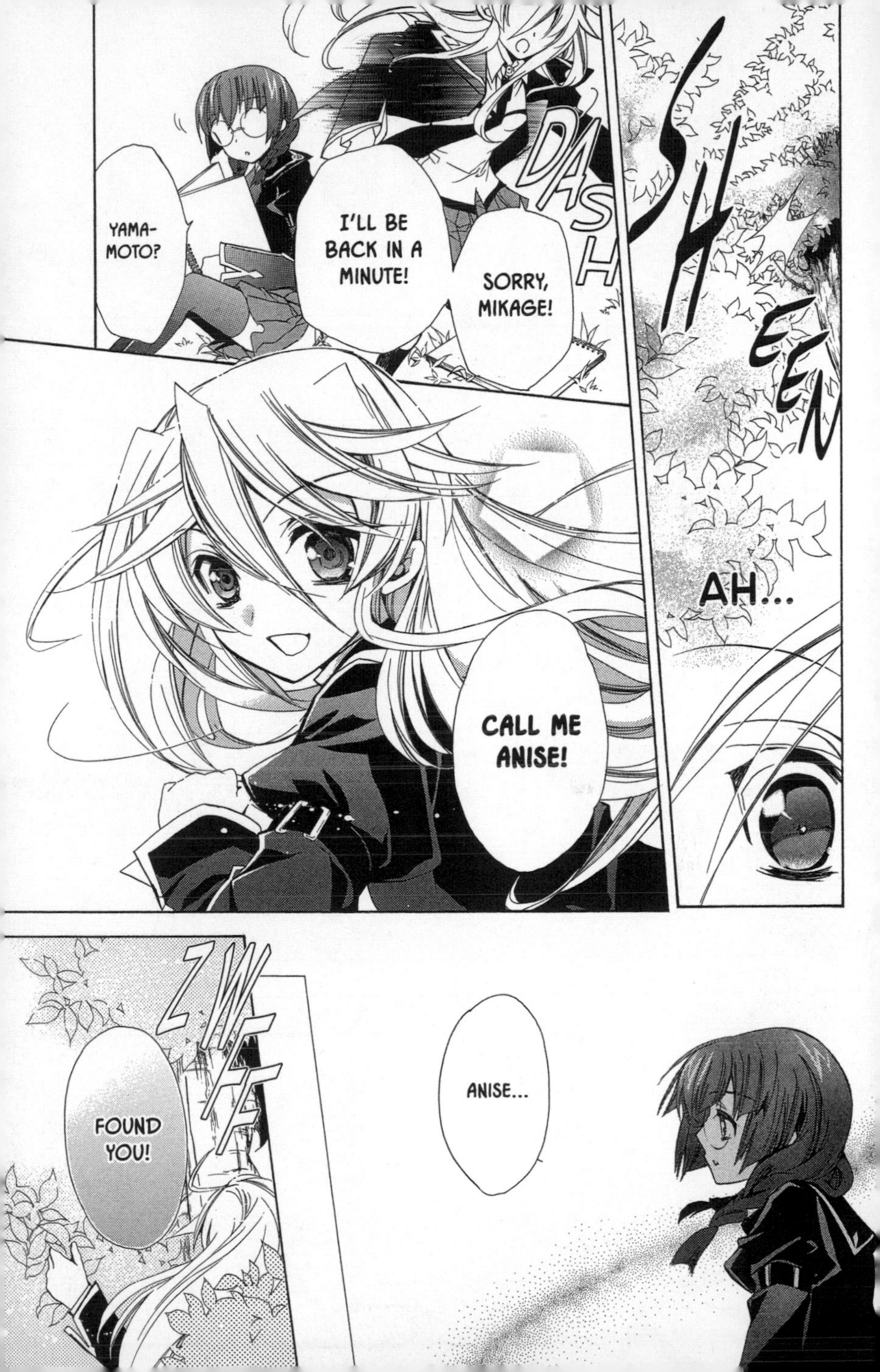
SHEEN
AH...
SORRY, MIKAGE!
DASH
I'LL BE BACK IN A MINUTE!
YAMA-MOTO?
CALL ME ANISE!
ANISE...
ZWIFF
FOUND YOU!

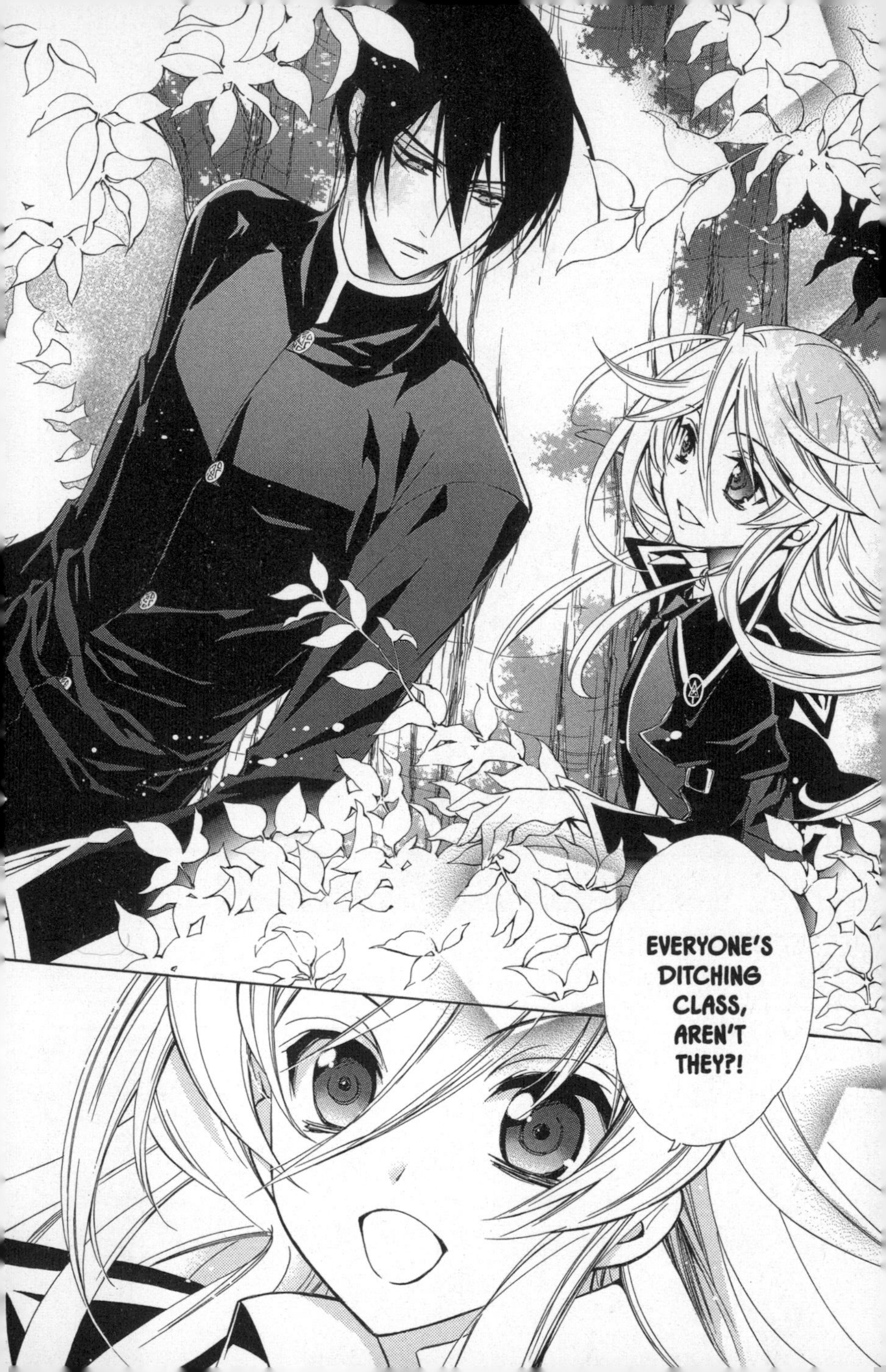
EVERYONE'S DITCHING CLASS, AREN'T THEY?!

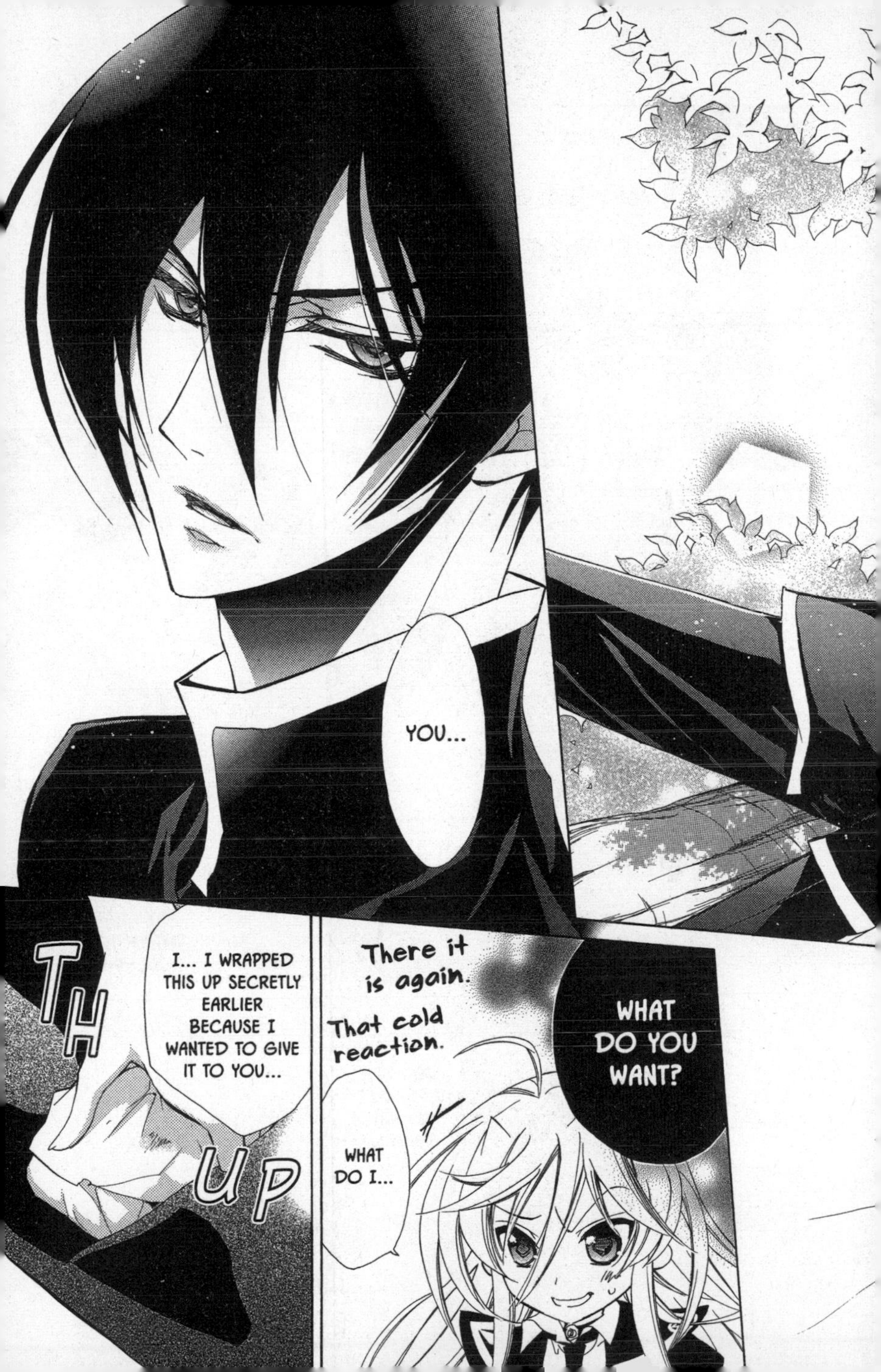
YOU...
WHAT DO YOU WANT?
There it is again.
That cold reaction.
WHAT DO I...
I... I WRAPPED THIS UP SECRETLY EARLIER BECAUSE I WANTED TO GIVE IT TO YOU...
TH
UP

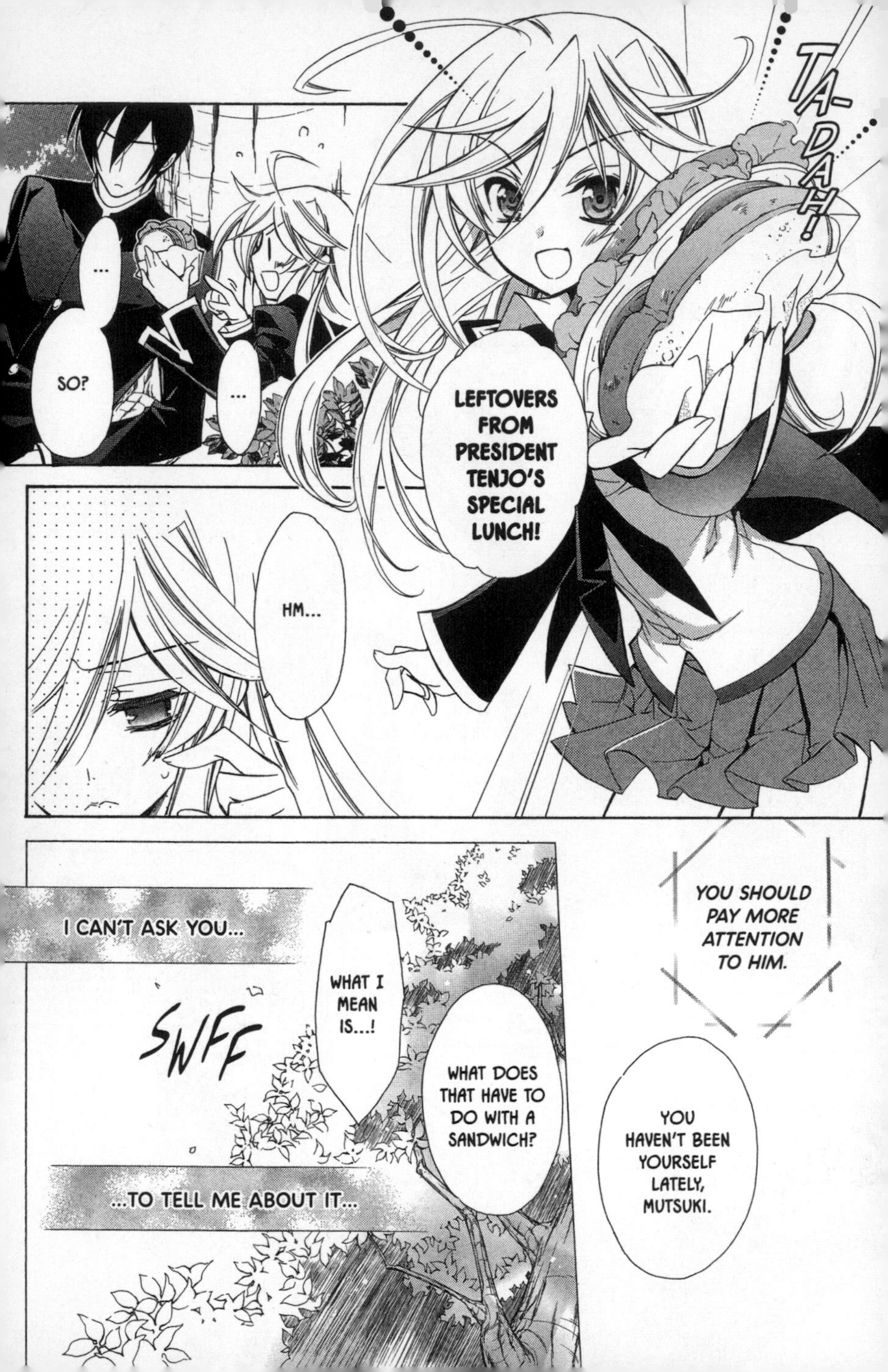
TA-DAH!
LEFTOVERS FROM PRESIDENT TENJO'S SPECIAL LUNCH!
...
...
SO?
HM...
YOU SHOULD PAY MORE ATTENTION TO HIM.
YOU HAVEN'T BEEN YOURSELF LATELY, MUTSUKI.
WHAT DOES THAT HAVE TO DO WITH A SANDWICH?
WHAT I MEAN IS...!
I CAN'T ASK YOU...
SWFF
...TO TELL ME ABOUT IT...

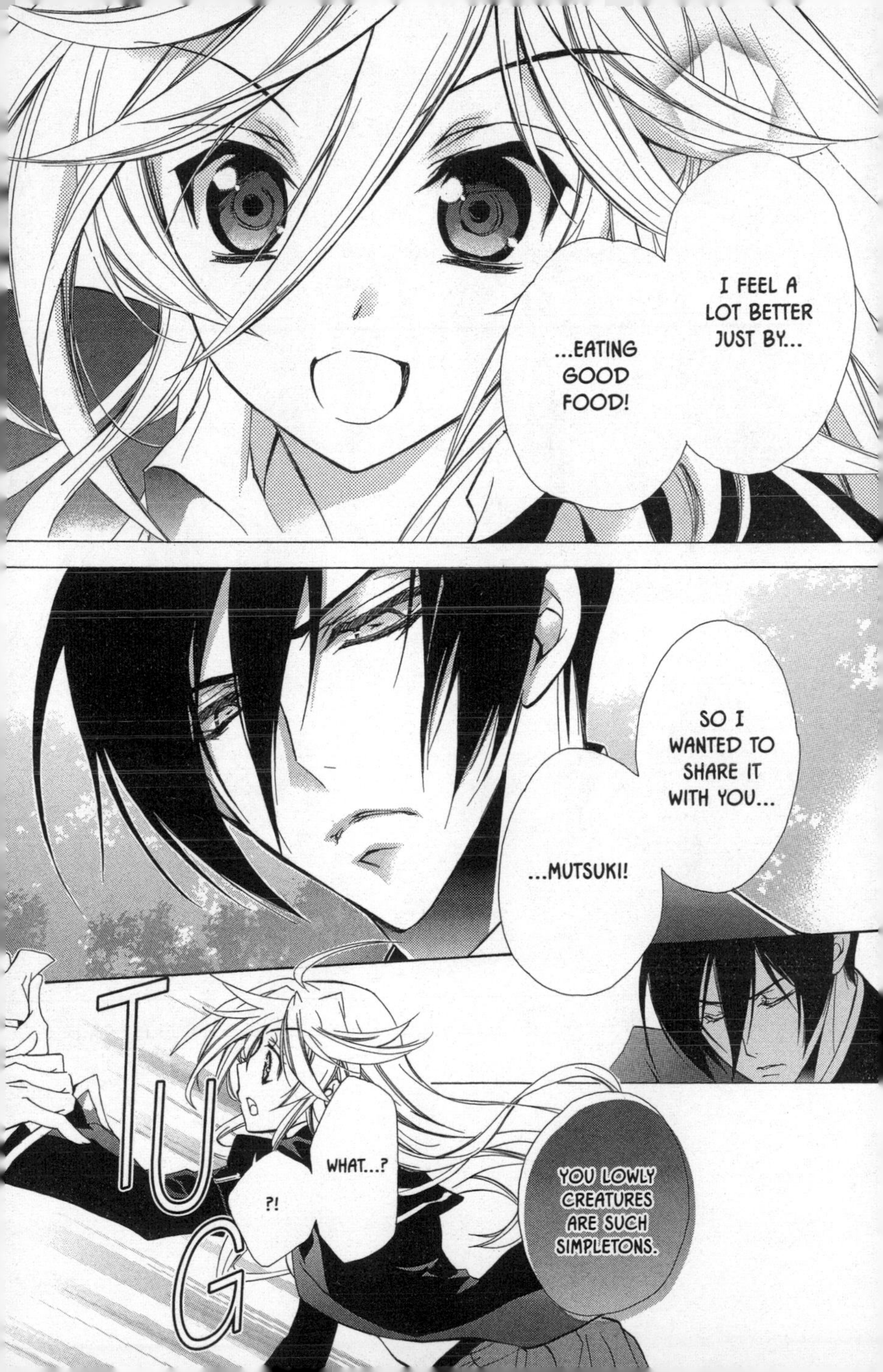
I FEEL A LOT BETTER JUST BY...
...EATING GOOD FOOD!
SO I WANTED TO SHARE IT WITH YOU...
...MUTSUKI!
YOU LOWLY CREATURES ARE SUCH SIMPLETONS.
WHAT...?
?!
TUG

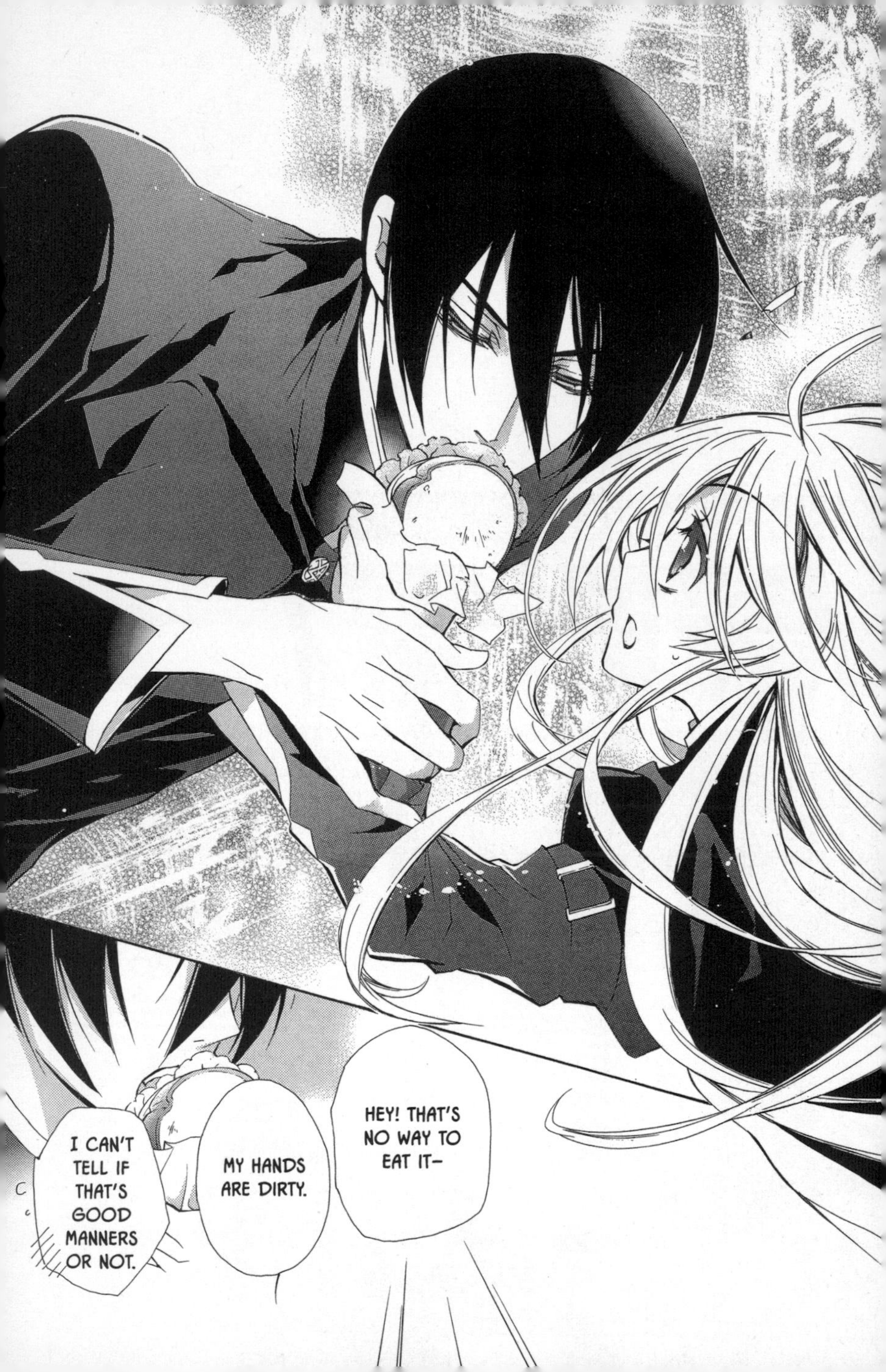
HEY! THAT'S NO WAY TO EAT IT–
MY HANDS ARE DIRTY.
I CAN'T TELL IF THAT'S GOOD MANNERS OR NOT.

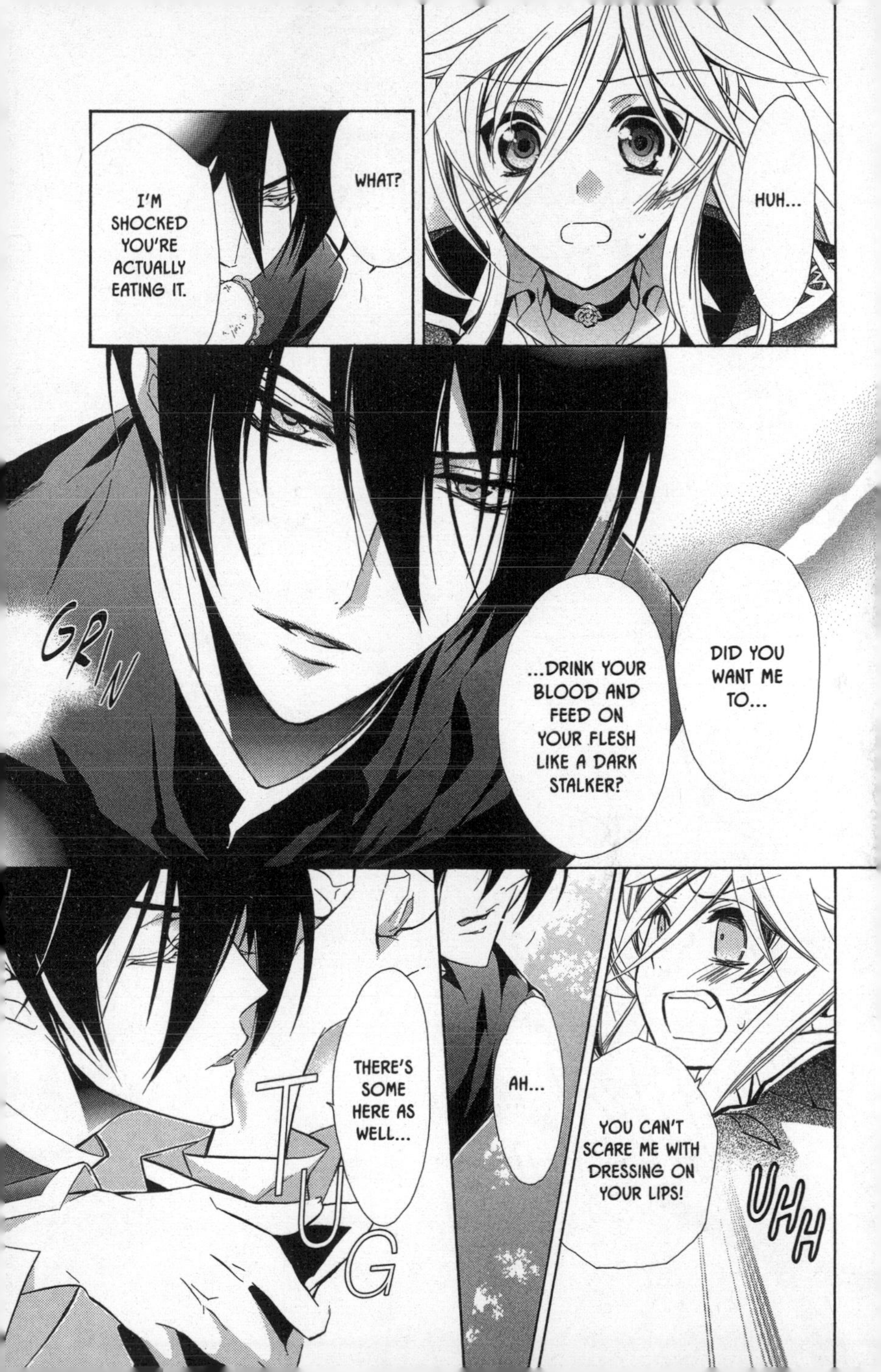
HUH...
WHAT?
I'M SHOCKED YOU'RE ACTUALLY EATING IT.
DID YOU WANT ME TO...
...DRINK YOUR BLOOD AND FEED ON YOUR FLESH LIKE A DARK STALKER?
GRIN
YOU CAN'T SCARE ME WITH DRESSING ON YOUR LIPS!
UHH
AH...
THERE'S SOME HERE AS WELL...
TUG

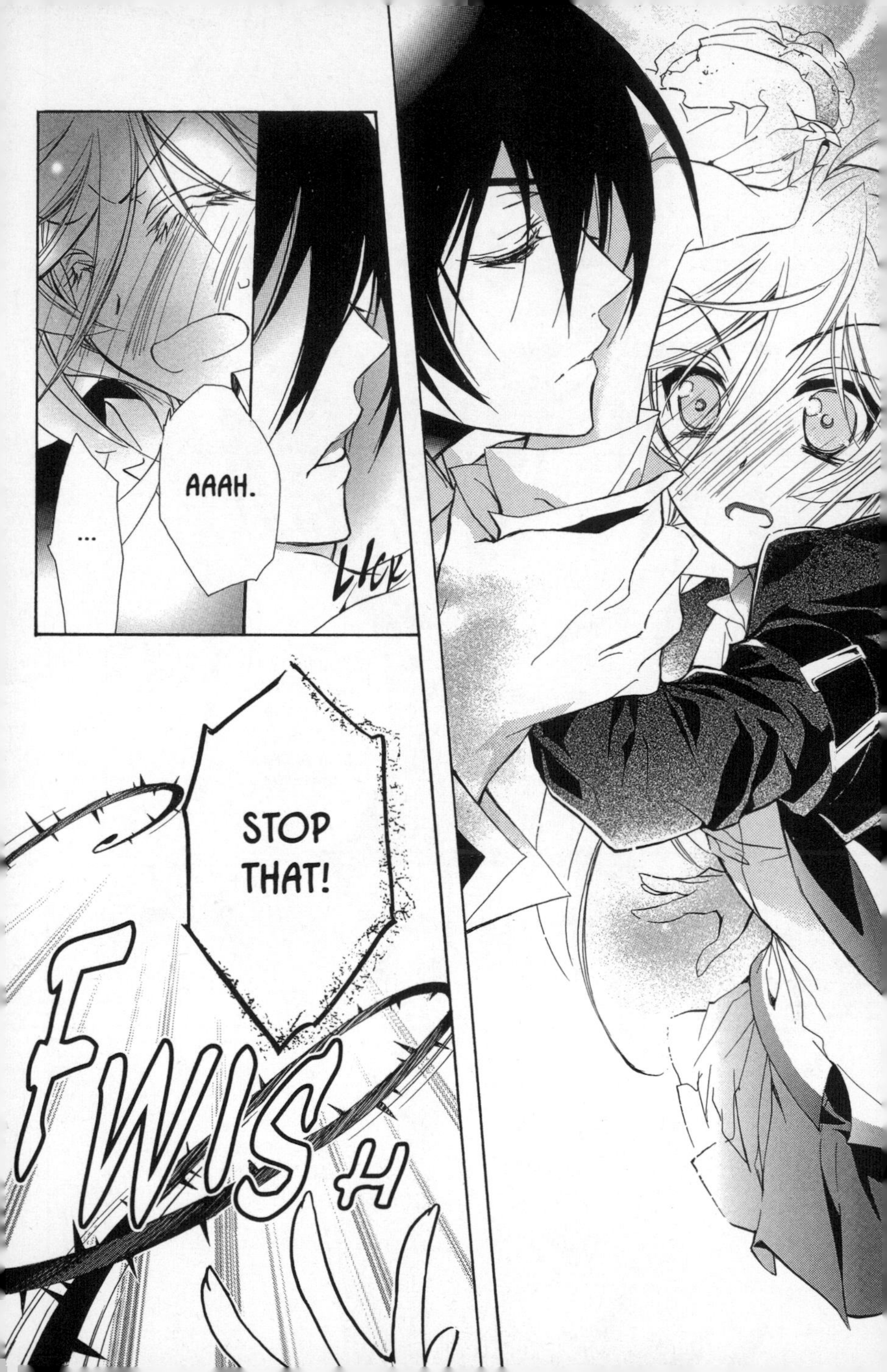
AAAH.
LICK
...
STOP THAT!
FWISH

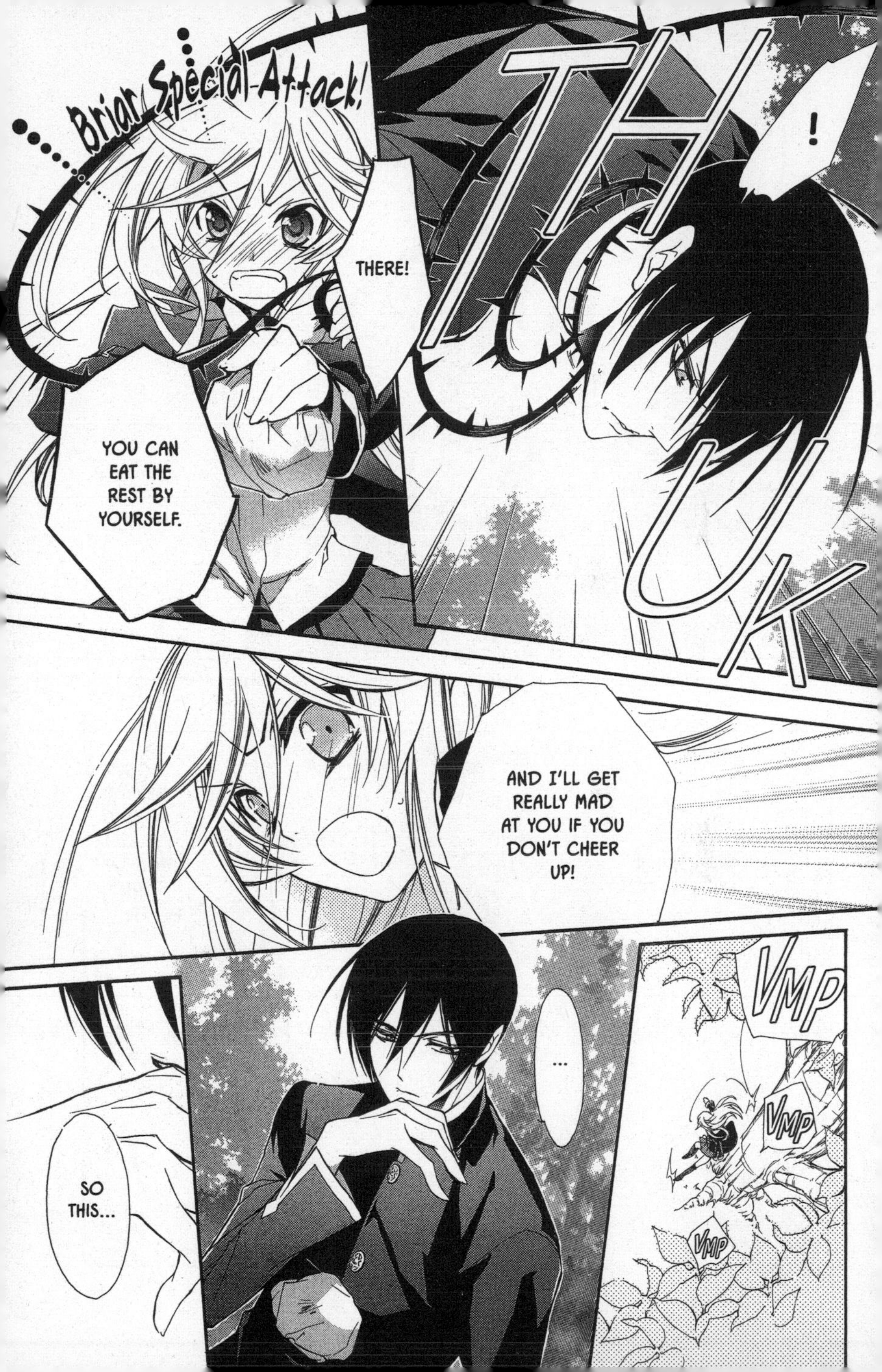
!
THUK
...Briar Special Attack!
THERE!
YOU CAN EAT THE REST BY YOURSELF.
AND I'LL GET REALLY MAD AT YOU IF YOU DON'T CHEER UP!
VMP
VMP
VMP
...
SO THIS...

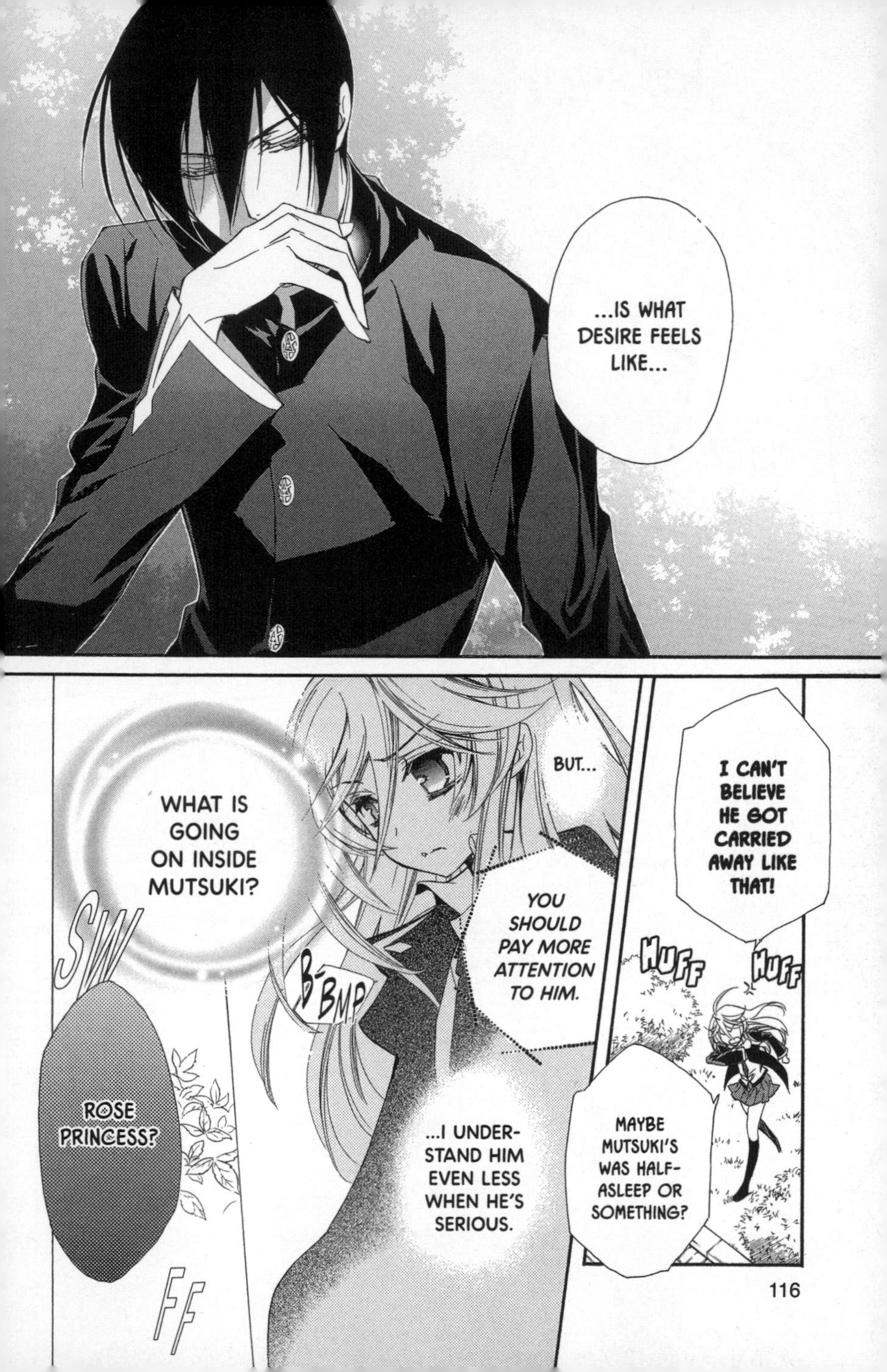
...IS WHAT DESIRE FEELS LIKE...
I CAN'T BELIEVE HE GOT CARRIED AWAY LIKE THAT!
HUFF
HUFF
MAYBE MUTSUKI'S WAS HALF-ASLEEP OR SOMETHING?
BUT...
...I UNDER-STAND HIM EVEN LESS WHEN HE'S SERIOUS.
YOU SHOULD PAY MORE ATTENTION TO HIM.
B-BMP
WHAT IS GOING ON INSIDE MUTSUKI?
SWFF
ROSE PRINCESS?

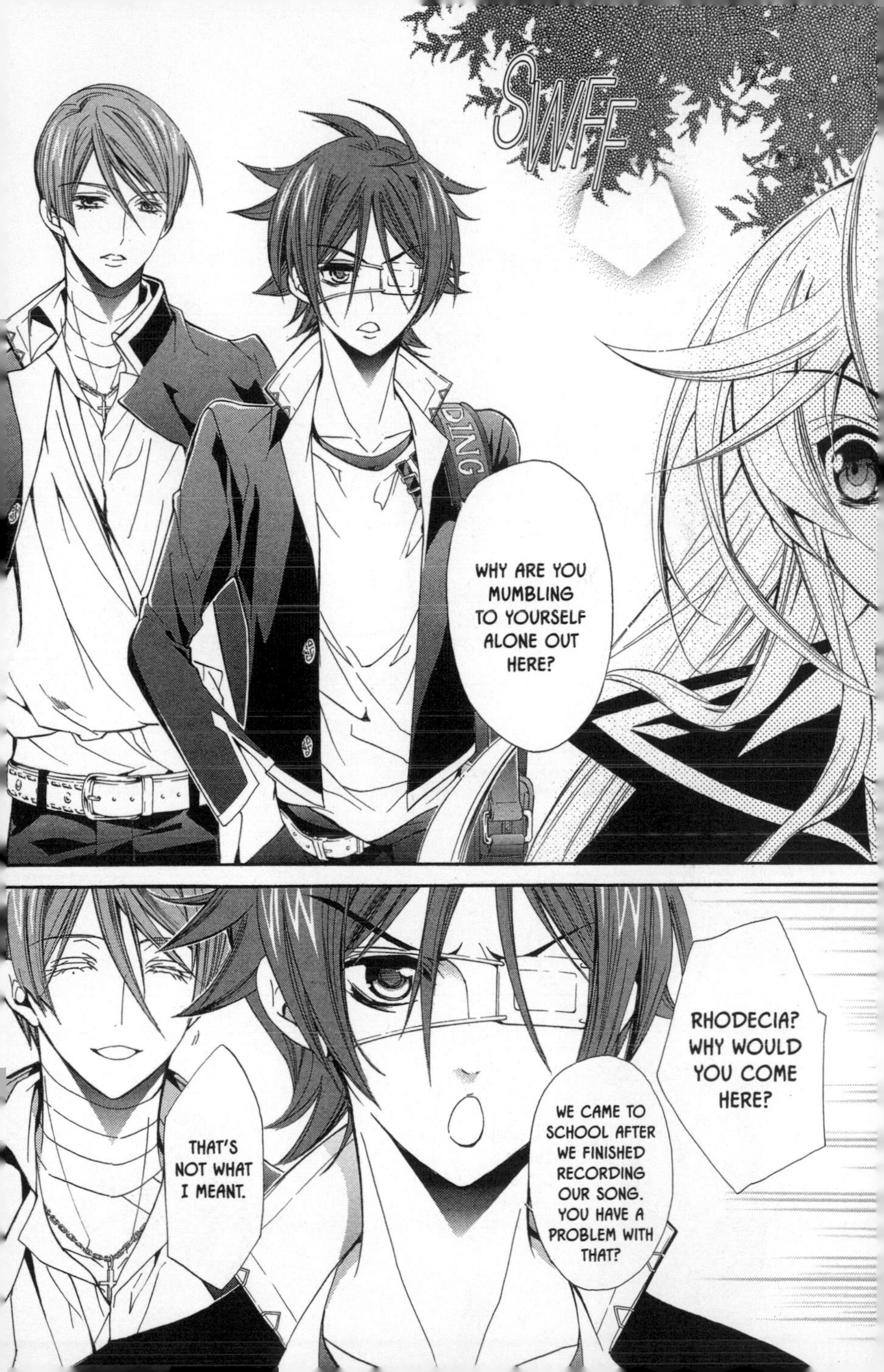
SWFF
WHY ARE YOU MUMBLING TO YOURSELF ALONE OUT HERE?
RHODECIA? WHY WOULD YOU COME HERE?
WE CAME TO SCHOOL AFTER WE FINISHED RECORDING OUR SONG. YOU HAVE A PROBLEM WITH THAT?
THAT'S NOT WHAT I MEANT.

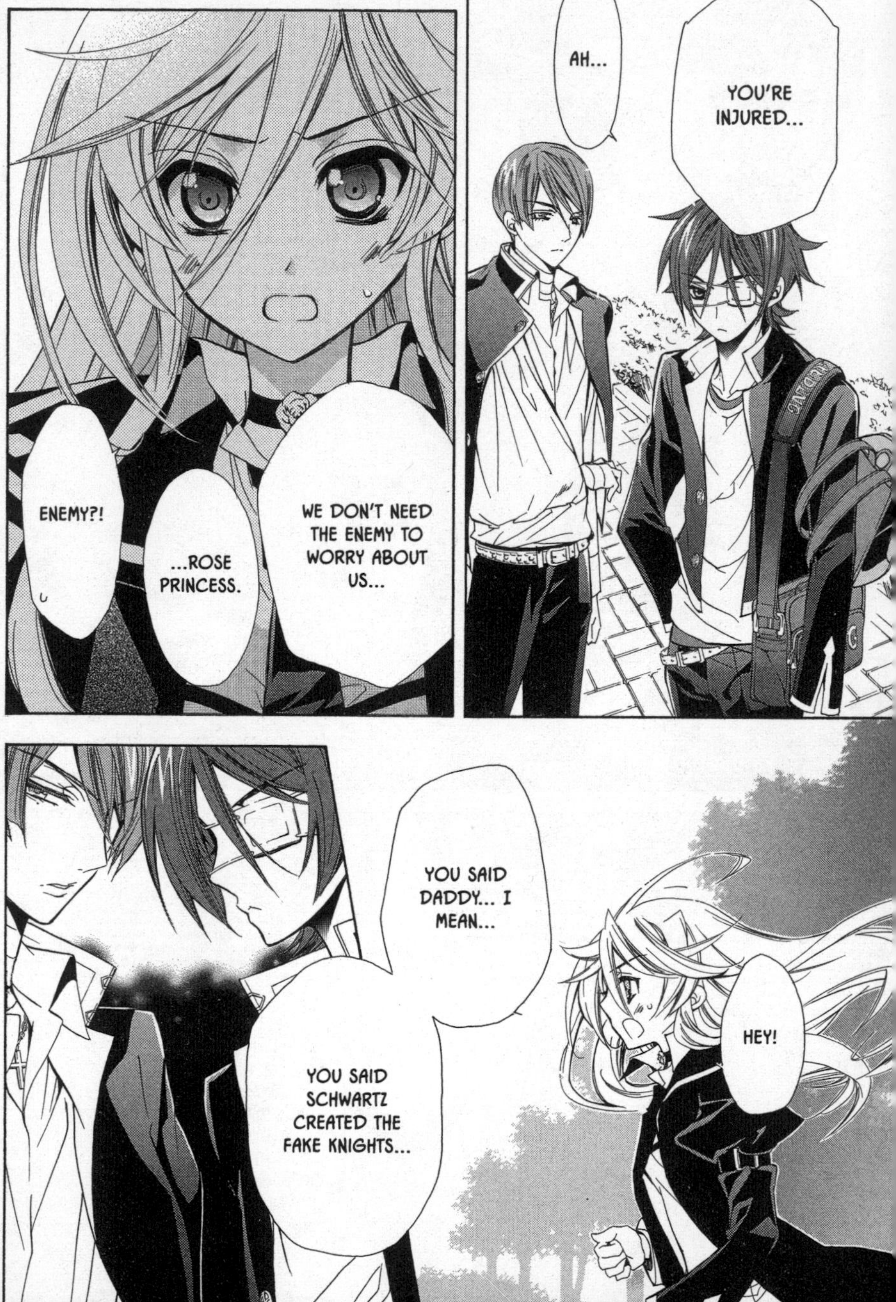
YOU'RE INJURED...
AH...
WE DON'T NEED THE ENEMY TO WORRY ABOUT US...
...ROSE PRINCESS.
ENEMY?!
HEY!
YOU SAID DADDY... I MEAN...
YOU SAID SCHWARTZ CREATED THE FAKE KNIGHTS...

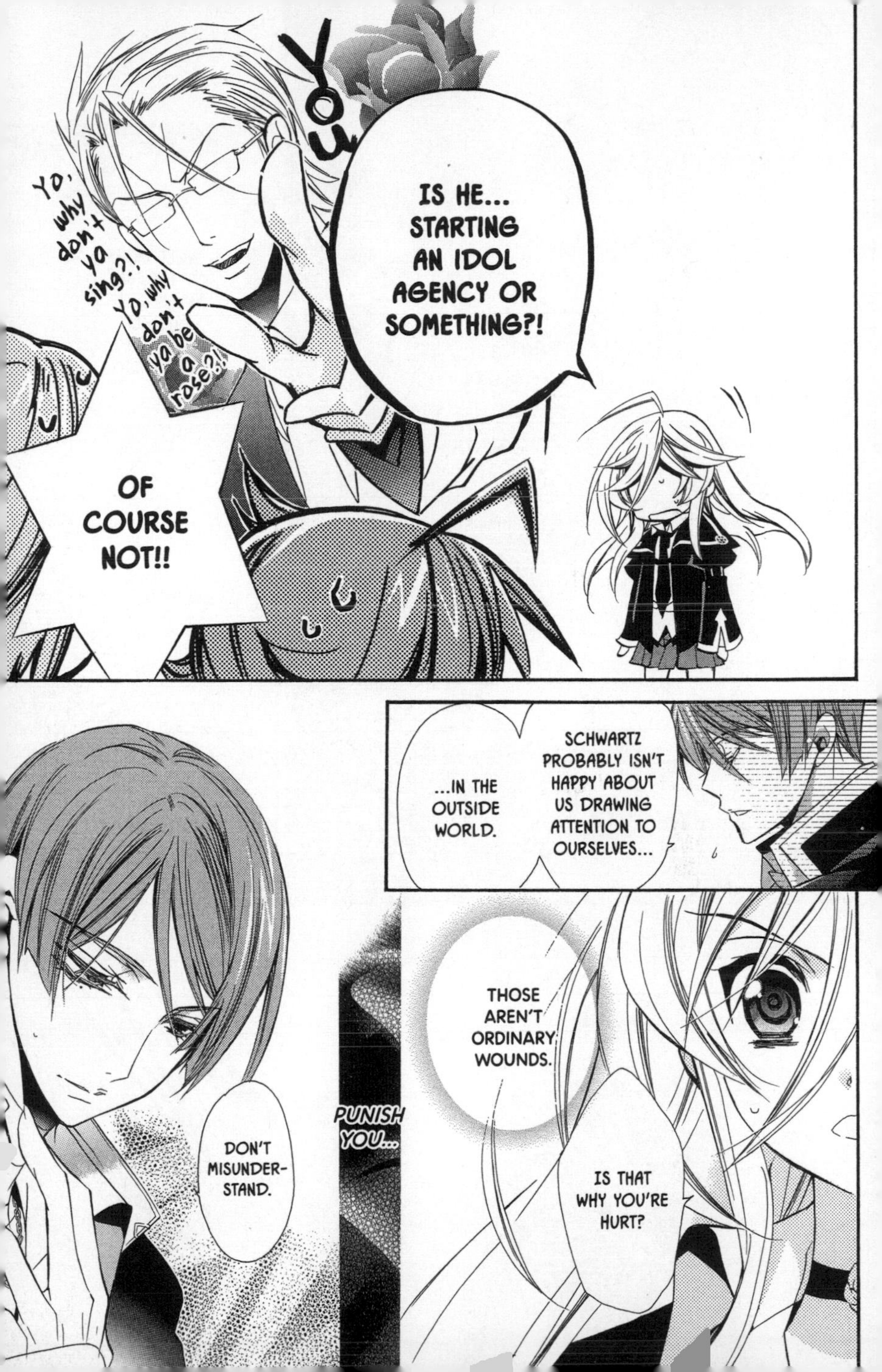
YOU
IS HE... STARTING AN IDOL AGENCY OR SOMETHING?!
Yo, why don't ya sing?!
Yo, why don't ya be a rose?!
OF COURSE NOT!!
SCHWARTZ PROBABLY ISN'T HAPPY ABOUT US DRAWING ATTENTION TO OURSELVES...
...IN THE OUTSIDE WORLD.
THOSE AREN'T ORDINARY WOUNDS.
IS THAT WHY YOU'RE HURT?
PUNISH YOU...
DON'T MISUNDERSTAND.

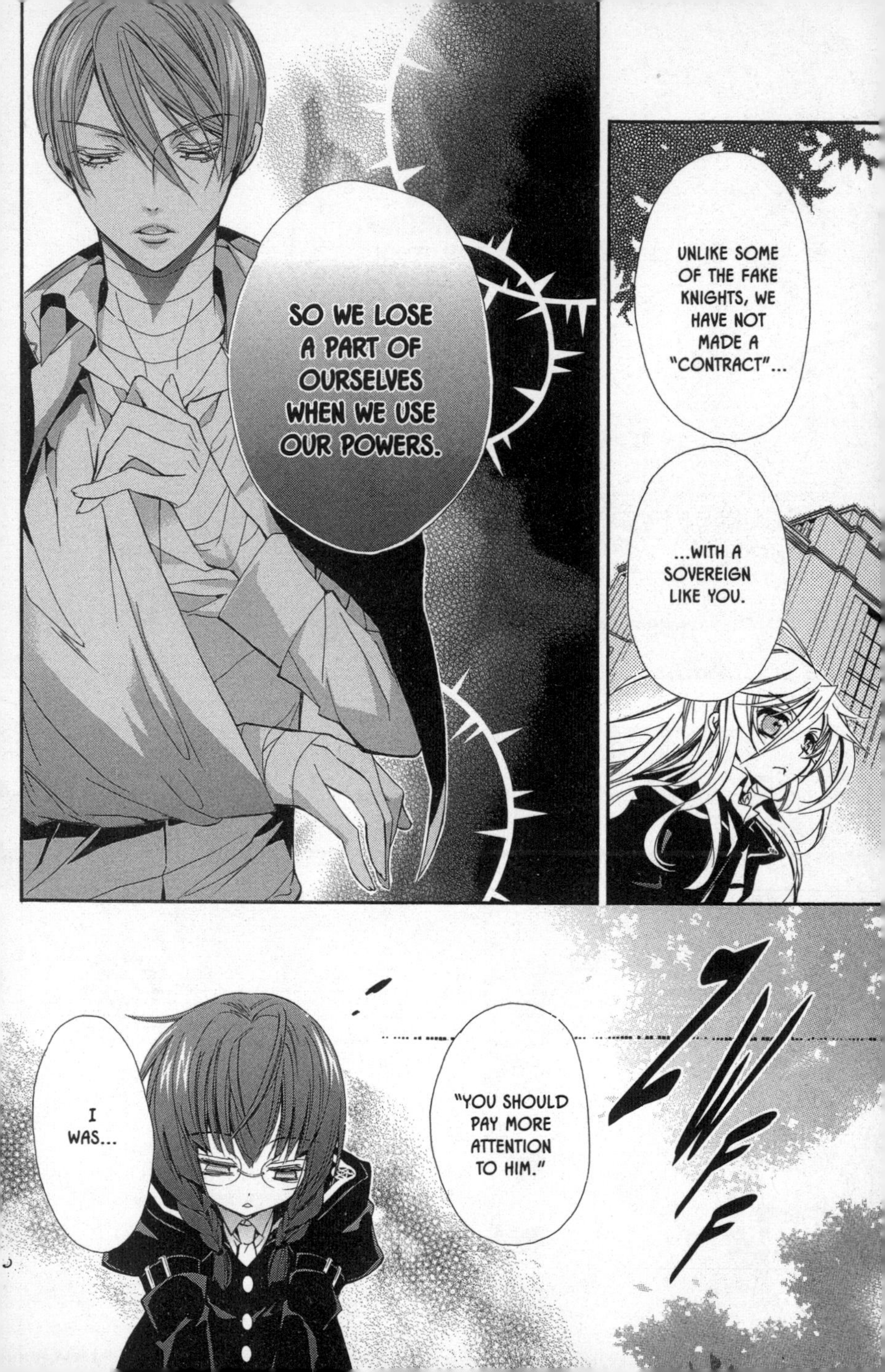
UNLIKE SOME OF THE FAKE KNIGHTS, WE HAVE NOT MADE A "CONTRACT"...
...WITH A SOVEREIGN LIKE YOU.
SO WE LOSE A PART OF OURSELVES WHEN WE USE OUR POWERS.
"YOU SHOULD PAY MORE ATTENTION TO HIM."
I WAS...

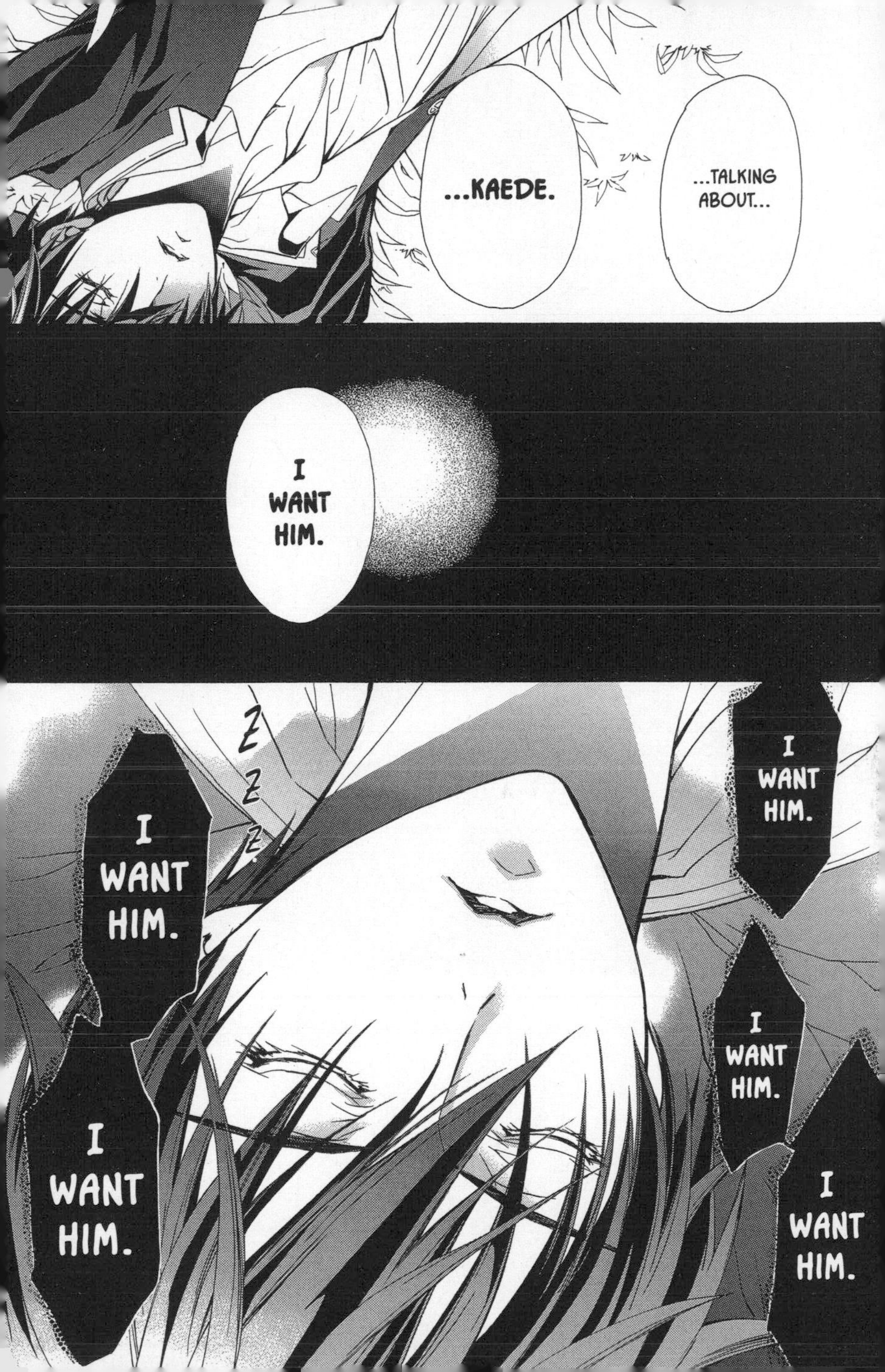
...TALKING ABOUT...
...KAEDE.
I WANT HIM.
I WANT HIM.
I WANT HIM.
I WANT HIM.
I WANT HIM.
I WANT HIM.

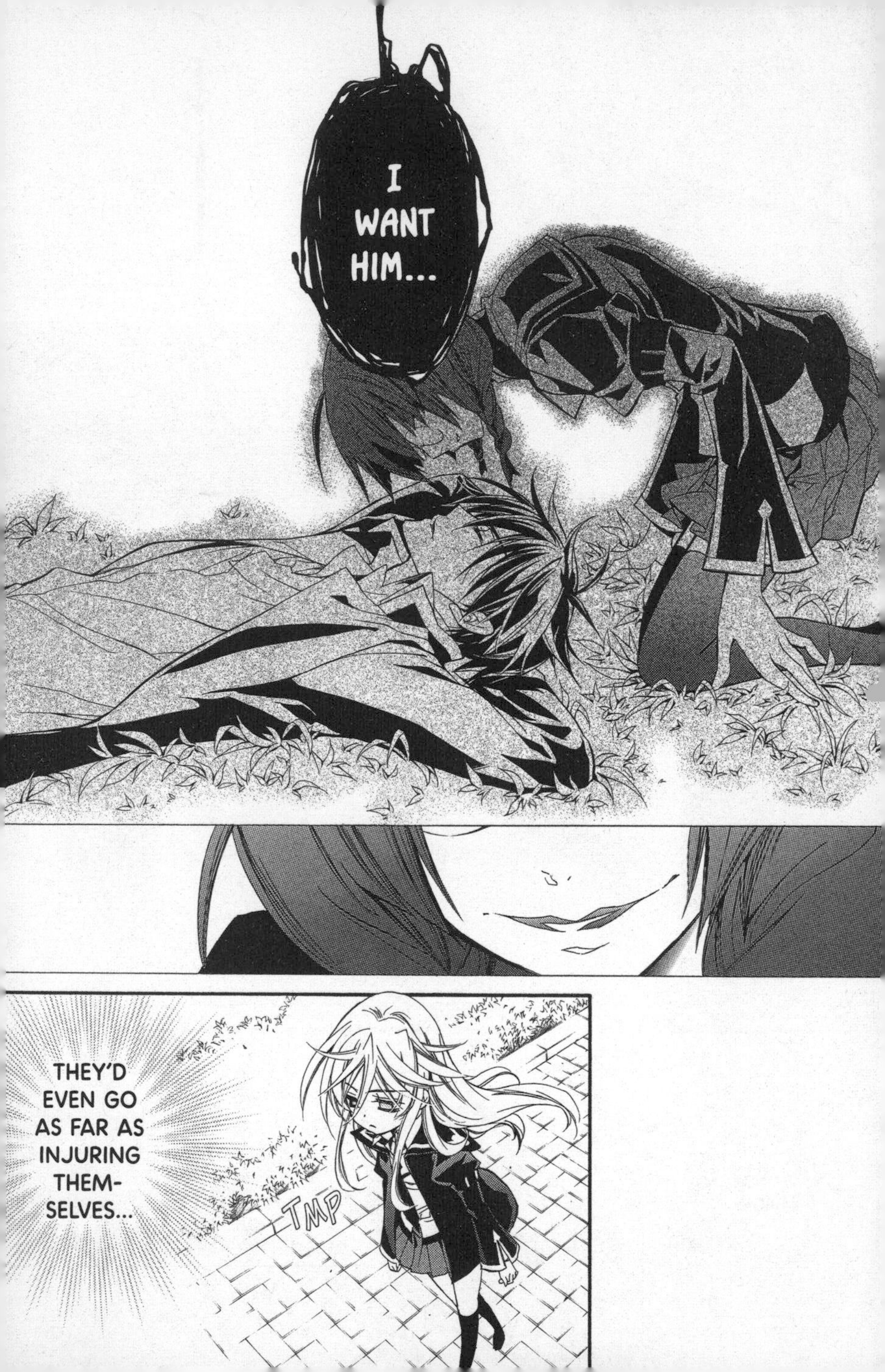
I WANT HIM...
THEY'D EVEN GO AS FAR AS INJURING THEM-SELVES...
TMP

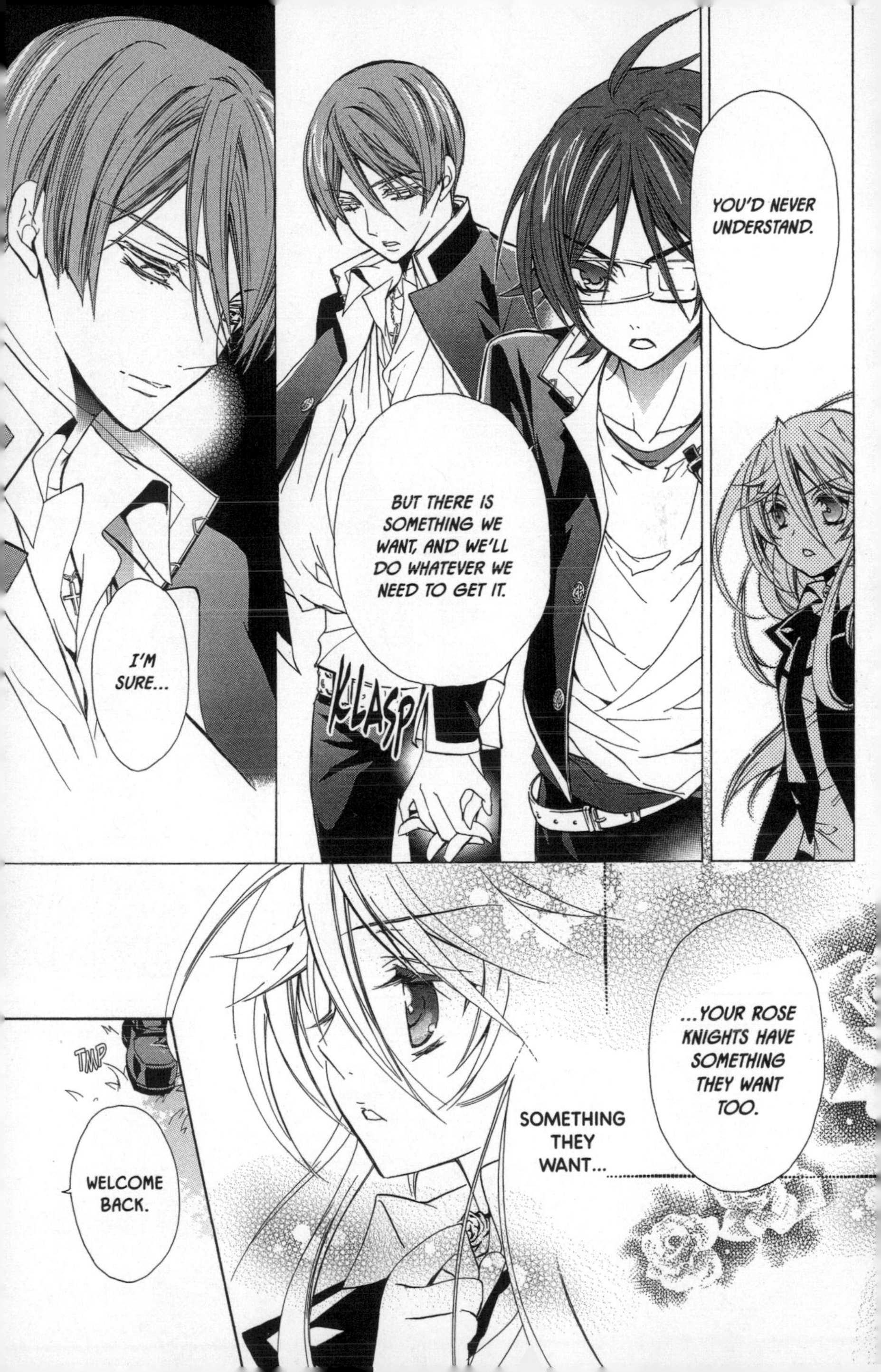
YOU'D NEVER UNDERSTAND.
BUT THERE IS SOMETHING WE WANT, AND WE'LL DO WHATEVER WE NEED TO GET IT.
KLASP!
I'M SURE...
...YOUR ROSE KNIGHTS HAVE SOMETHING THEY WANT TOO.
SOMETHING THEY WANT...
TMP
WELCOME BACK.

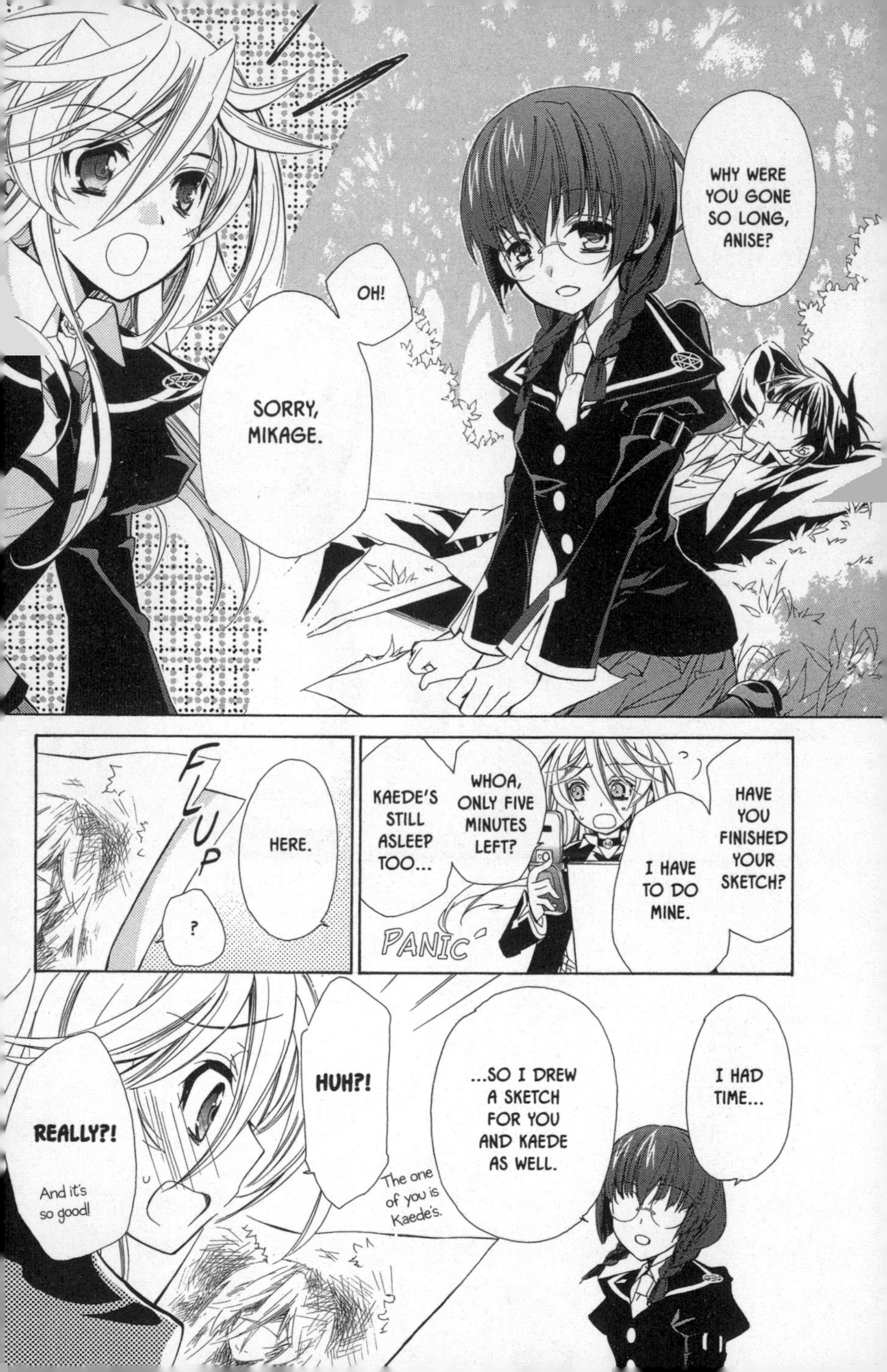
WHY WERE YOU GONE SO LONG, ANISE?
OH!
SORRY, MIKAGE.
HAVE YOU FINISHED YOUR SKETCH?
I HAVE TO DO MINE.
WHOA, ONLY FIVE MINUTES LEFT?
KAEDE'S STILL ASLEEP TOO...
PANIC
FLUP
HERE.
?
I HAD TIME...
...SO I DREW A SKETCH FOR YOU AND KAEDE AS WELL.
The one of you is Kaede's.
HUH?!
REALLY?!
And it's so good!

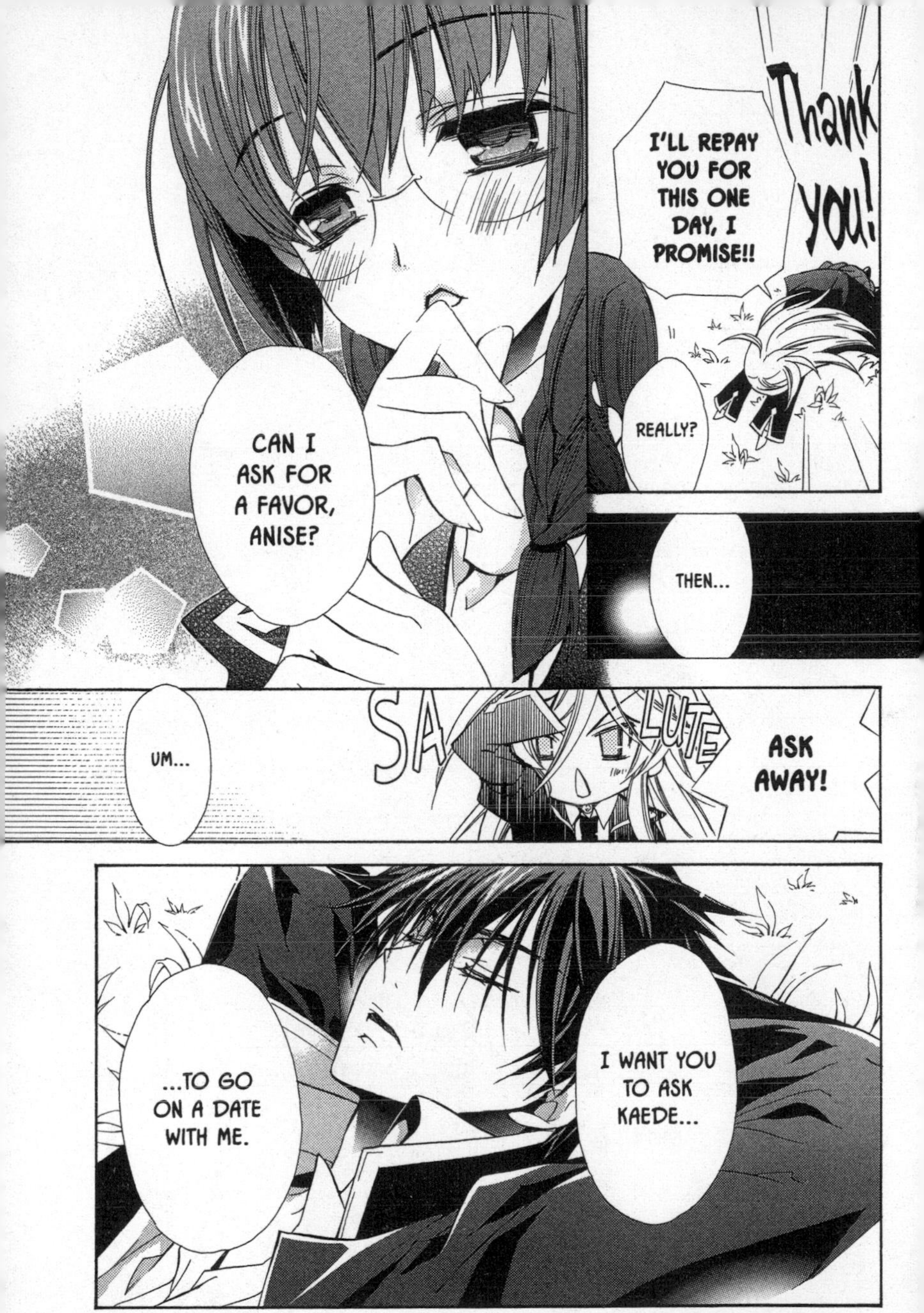
Thank you!
I'LL REPAY YOU FOR THIS ONE DAY, I PROMISE!!
REALLY?
THEN...
CAN I ASK FOR A FAVOR, ANISE?
ASK AWAY!
SALUTE
UM...
I WANT YOU TO ASK KAEDE...
...TO GO ON A DATE WITH ME.

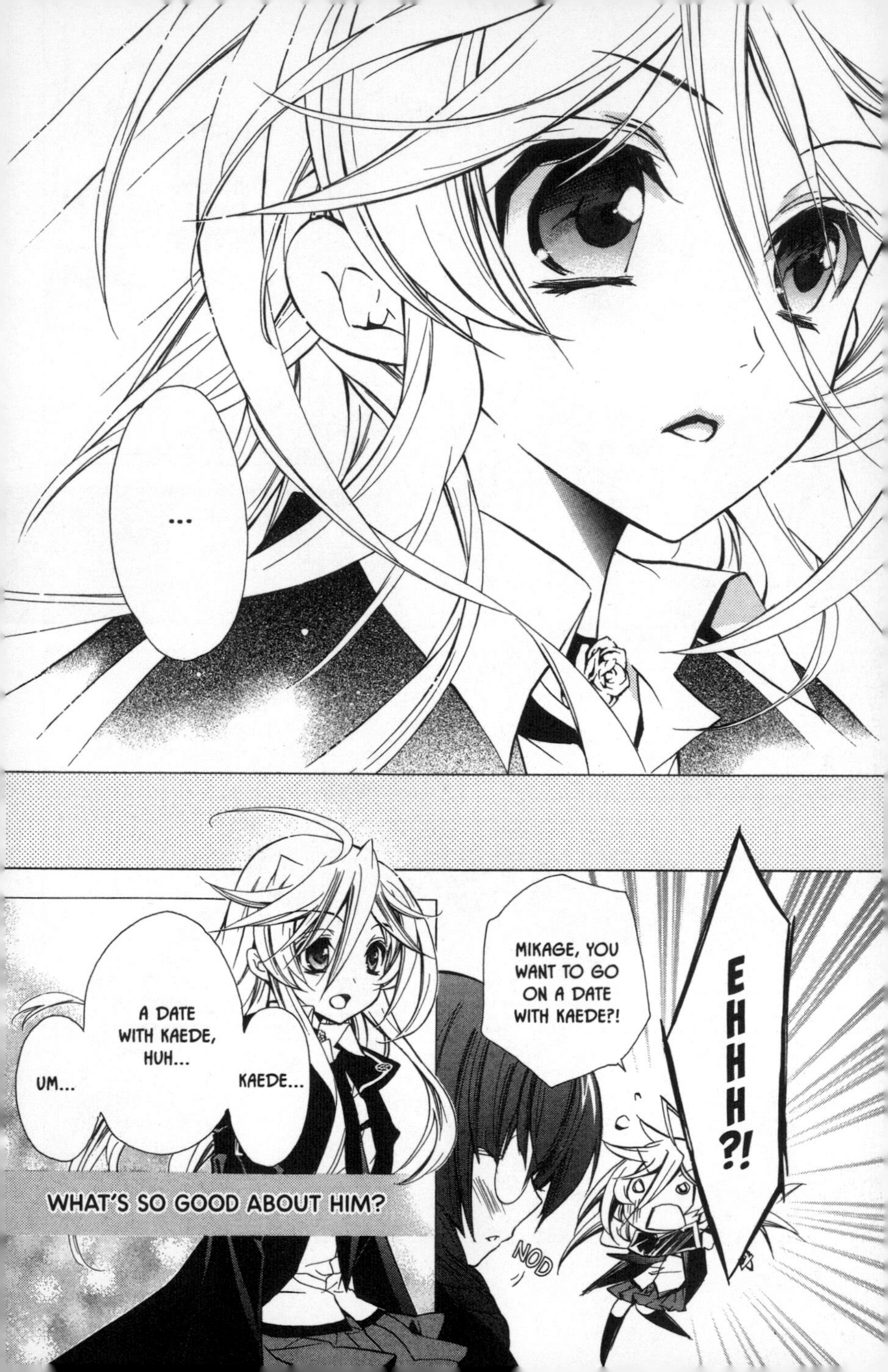
...
EHHH?!
MIKAGE, YOU WANT TO GO ON A DATE WITH KAEDE?!
NOD
A DATE WITH KAEDE, HUH...
KAEDE...
UM...
WHAT'S SO GOOD ABOUT HIM?

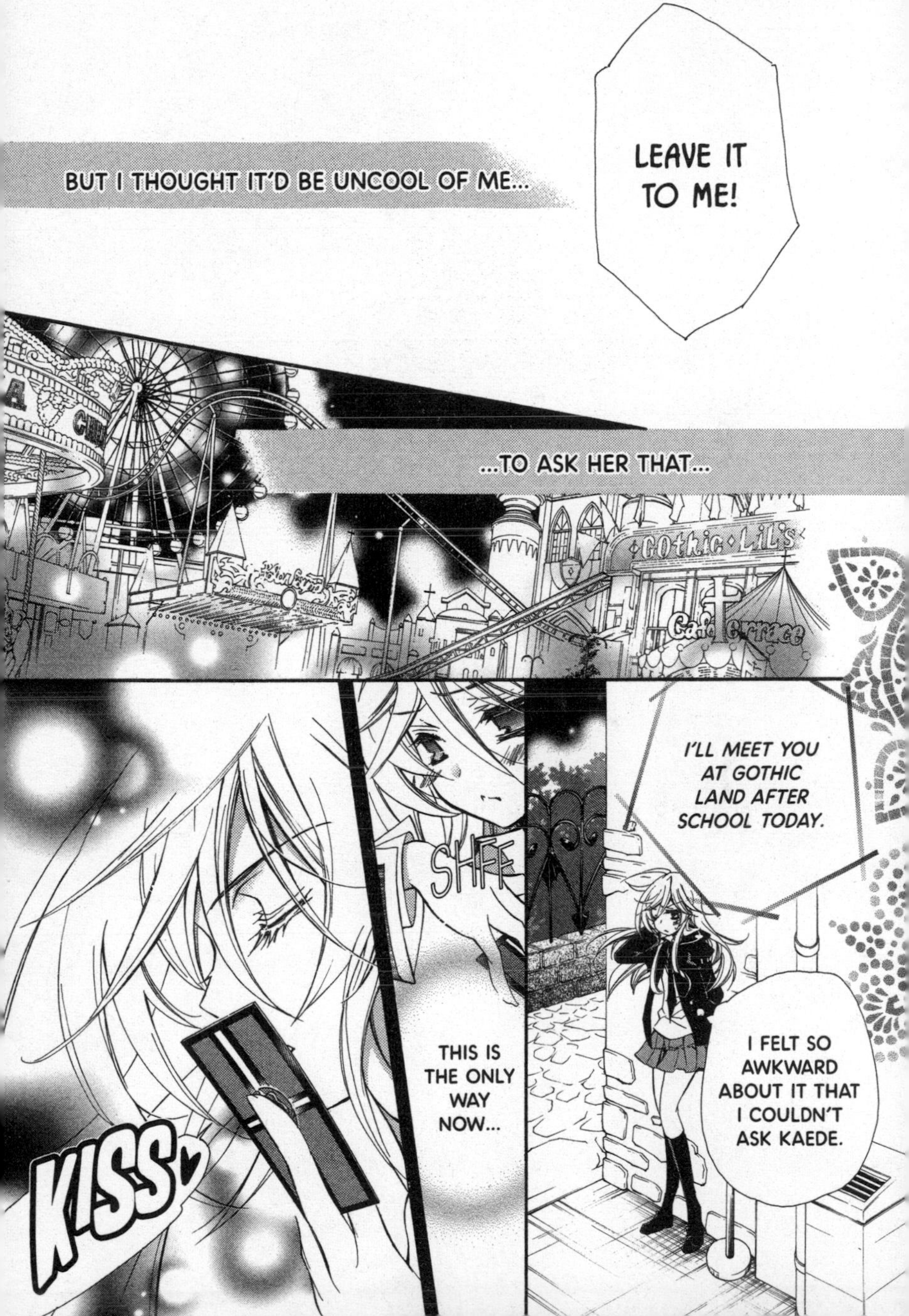
LEAVE IT TO ME!
BUT I THOUGHT IT'D BE UNCOOL OF ME...
...TO ASK HER THAT...
Gothic LiL's
Cafe Terrace
I'LL MEET YOU AT GOTHIC LAND AFTER SCHOOL TODAY.
I FELT SO AWKWARD ABOUT IT THAT I COULDN'T ASK KAEDE.
SHFF
THIS IS THE ONLY WAY NOW...
KISS

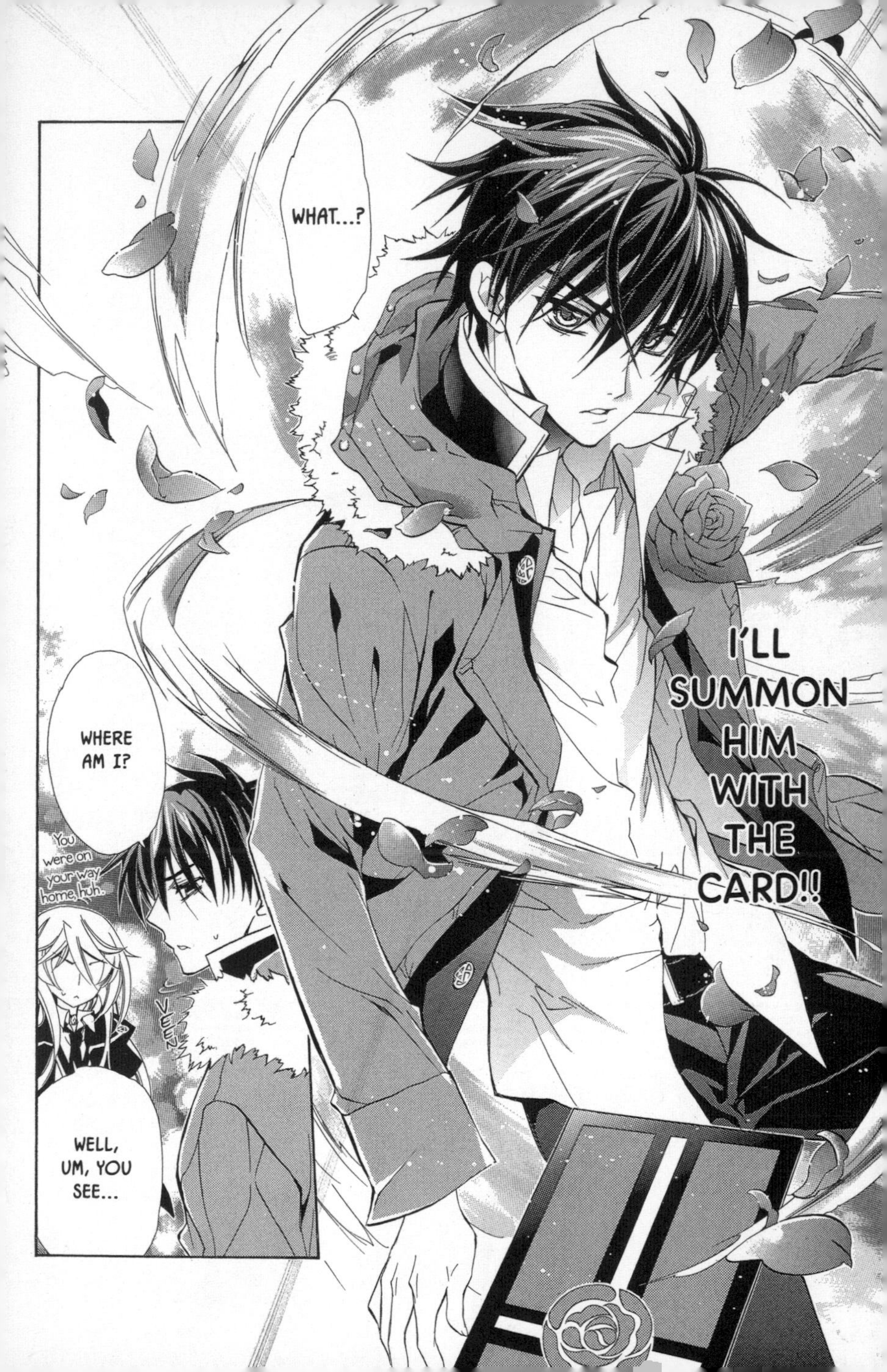

I'LL SUMMON HIM WITH THE CARD!!
WHAT...?
WHERE AM I?
You were on your way home, huh.
VEEN
WELL, UM, YOU SEE...

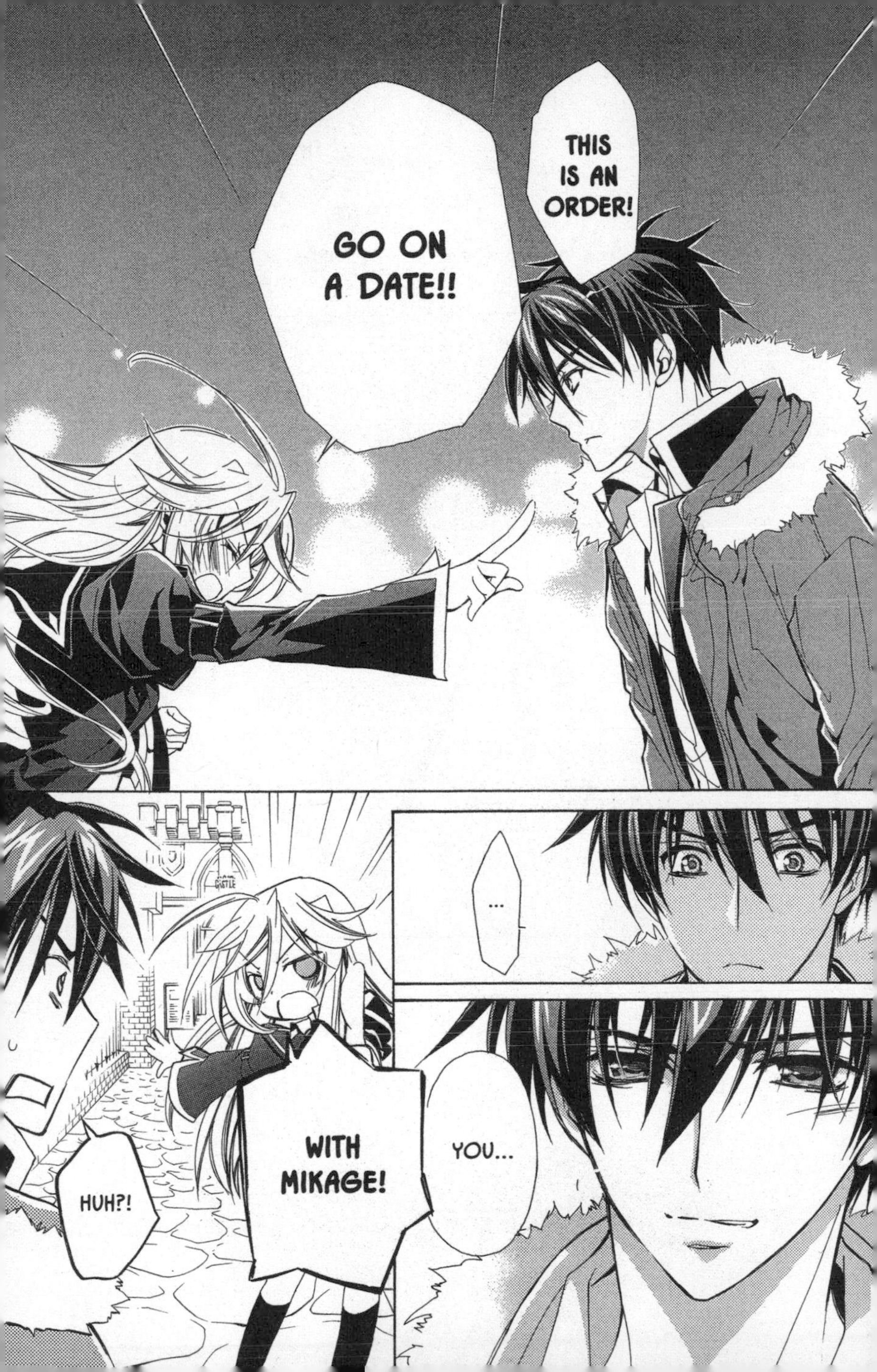
THIS IS AN ORDER!
GO ON A DATE!!
...
YOU...
WITH MIKAGE!
HUH?!

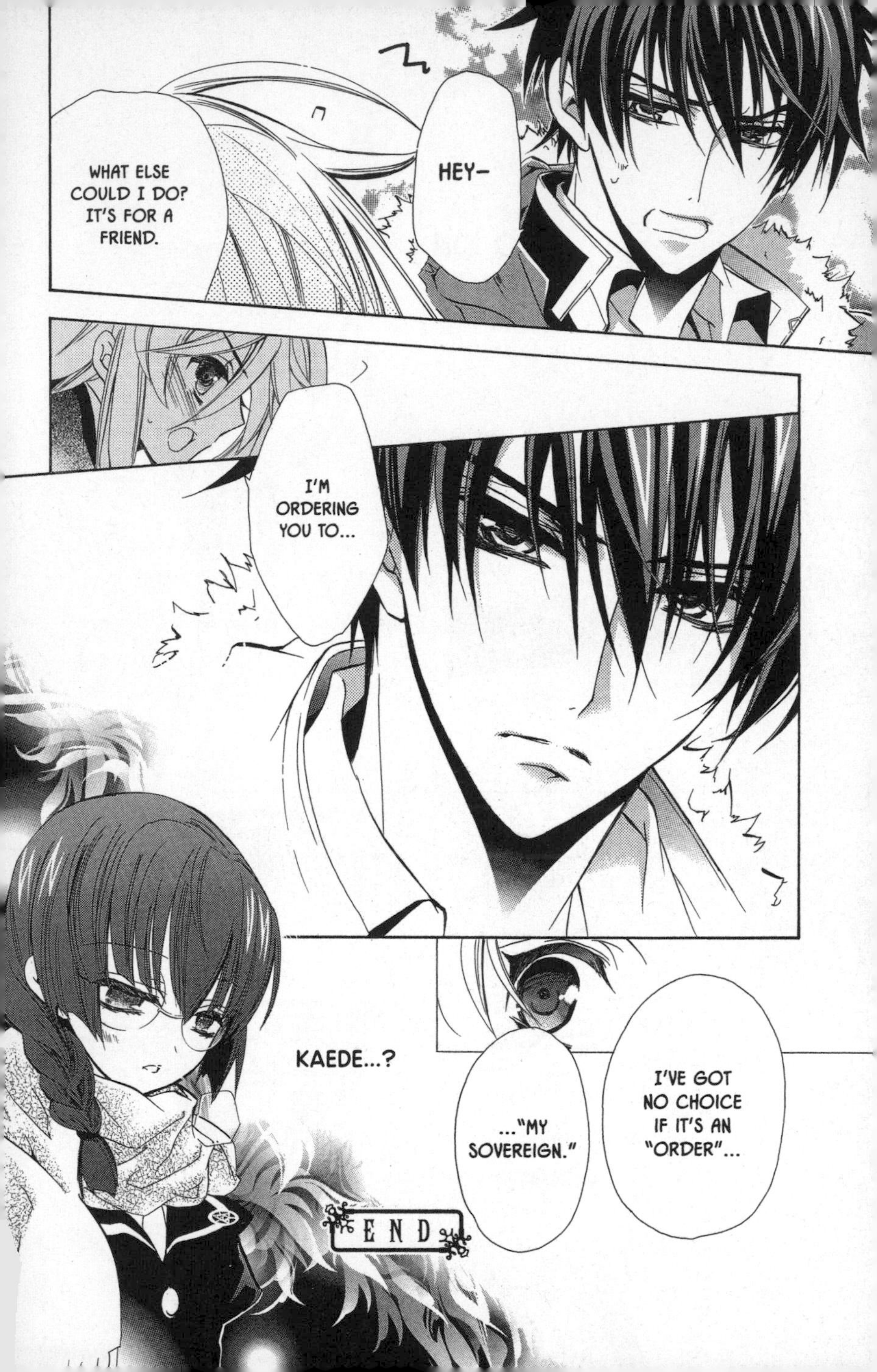
HEY–
WHAT ELSE COULD I DO? IT'S FOR A FRIEND.
I'M ORDERING YOU TO...
I'VE GOT NO CHOICE IF IT'S AN "ORDER"...
..."MY SOVEREIGN."
KAEDE...?
END

Kiss of the Rose
Princess

Kiss of the Rose Princess

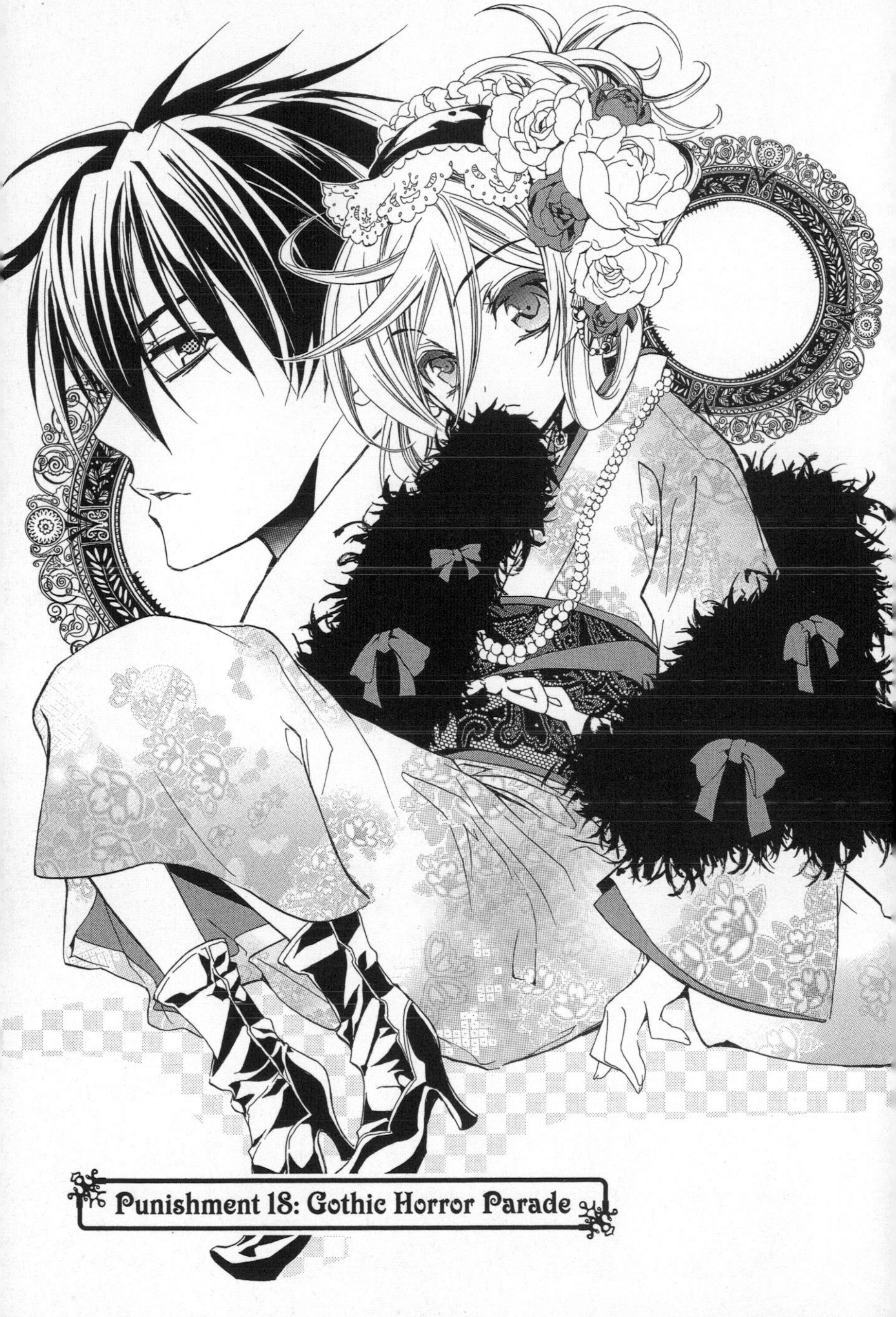

Punishment 18: Gothic Horror Parade

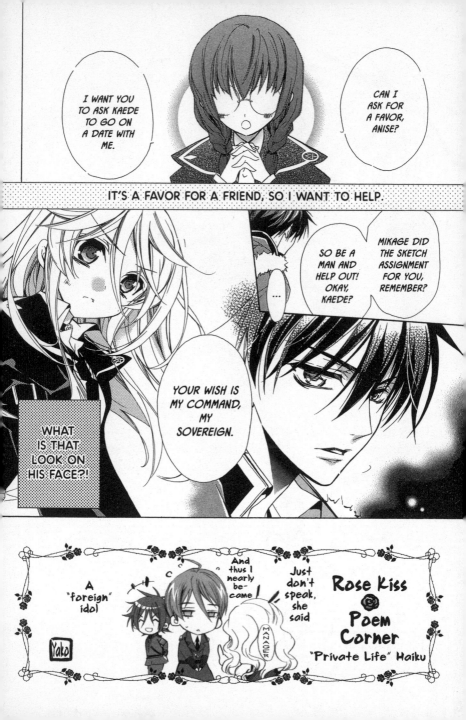

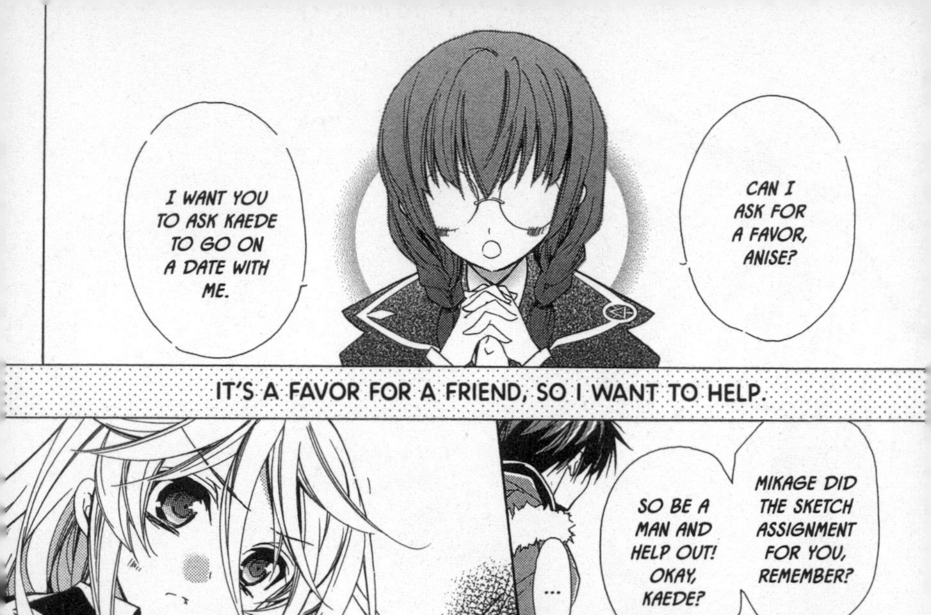
CAN I ASK FOR A FAVOR, ANISE?
I WANT YOU TO ASK KAEDE TO GO ON A DATE WITH ME.
IT'S A FAVOR FOR A FRIEND, SO I WANT TO HELP.
MIKAGE DID THE SKETCH ASSIGNMENT FOR YOU, REMEMBER?
SO BE A MAN AND HELP OUT! OKAY, KAEDE?
...
YOUR WISH IS MY COMMAND, MY SOVEREIGN.
WHAT IS THAT LOOK ON HIS FACE?!

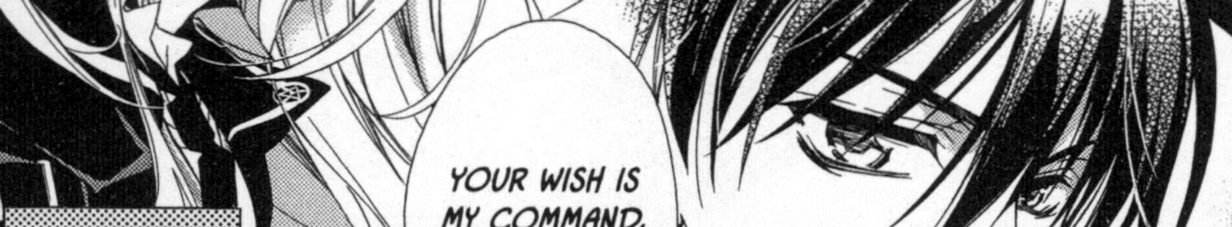
Rose Kiss Poem Corner
"Private Life" Haiku
Just don't speak, she said
And thus I nearly be-came
A "foreign" idol
MANAGER
Yako

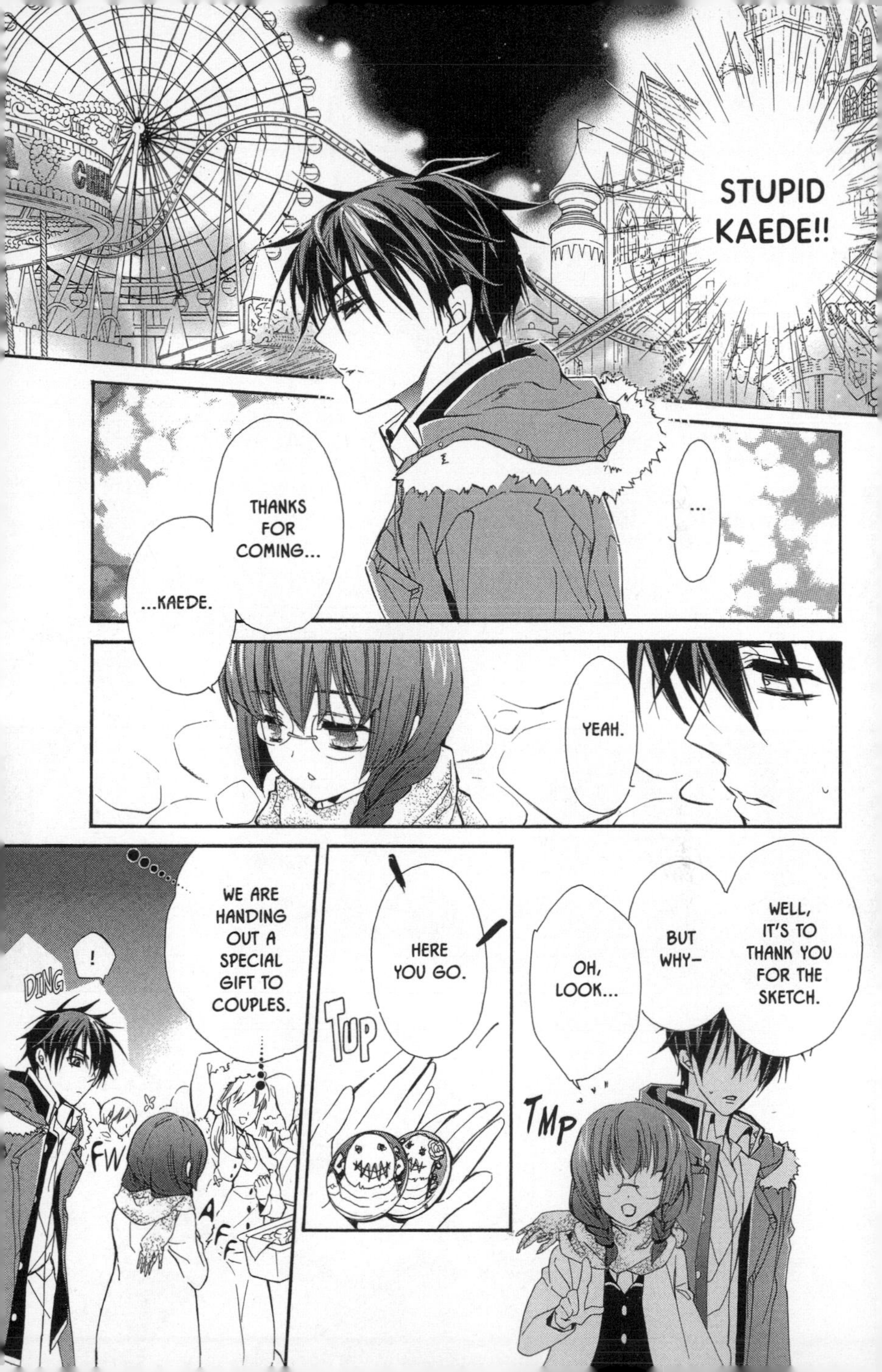
STUPID KAEDE!!
...
THANKS FOR COMING...
...KAEDE.
YEAH.
WELL, IT'S TO THANK YOU FOR THE SKETCH.
BUT WHY–
OH, LOOK...
TMP
HERE YOU GO.
TUP
WE ARE HANDING OUT A SPECIAL GIFT TO COUPLES.
!
DING
FW
AFF

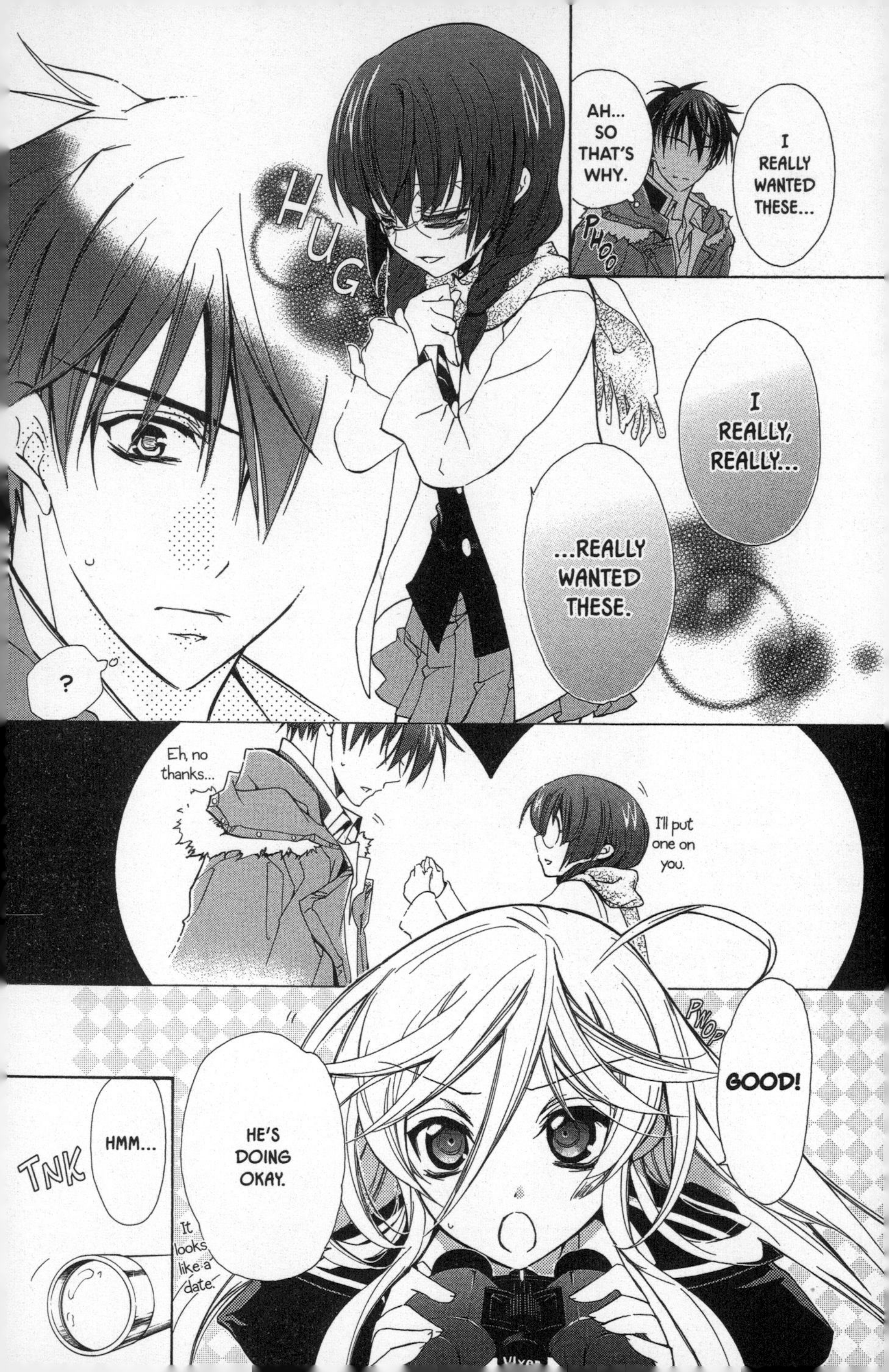
I REALLY WANTED THESE...
AH... SO THAT'S WHY.
PHOO
HUG
I REALLY, REALLY...
...REALLY WANTED THESE.
?
I'll put one on you.
Eh, no thanks...
PWOP
GOOD!
HE'S DOING OKAY.
HMM...
TNK
It looks like a date.

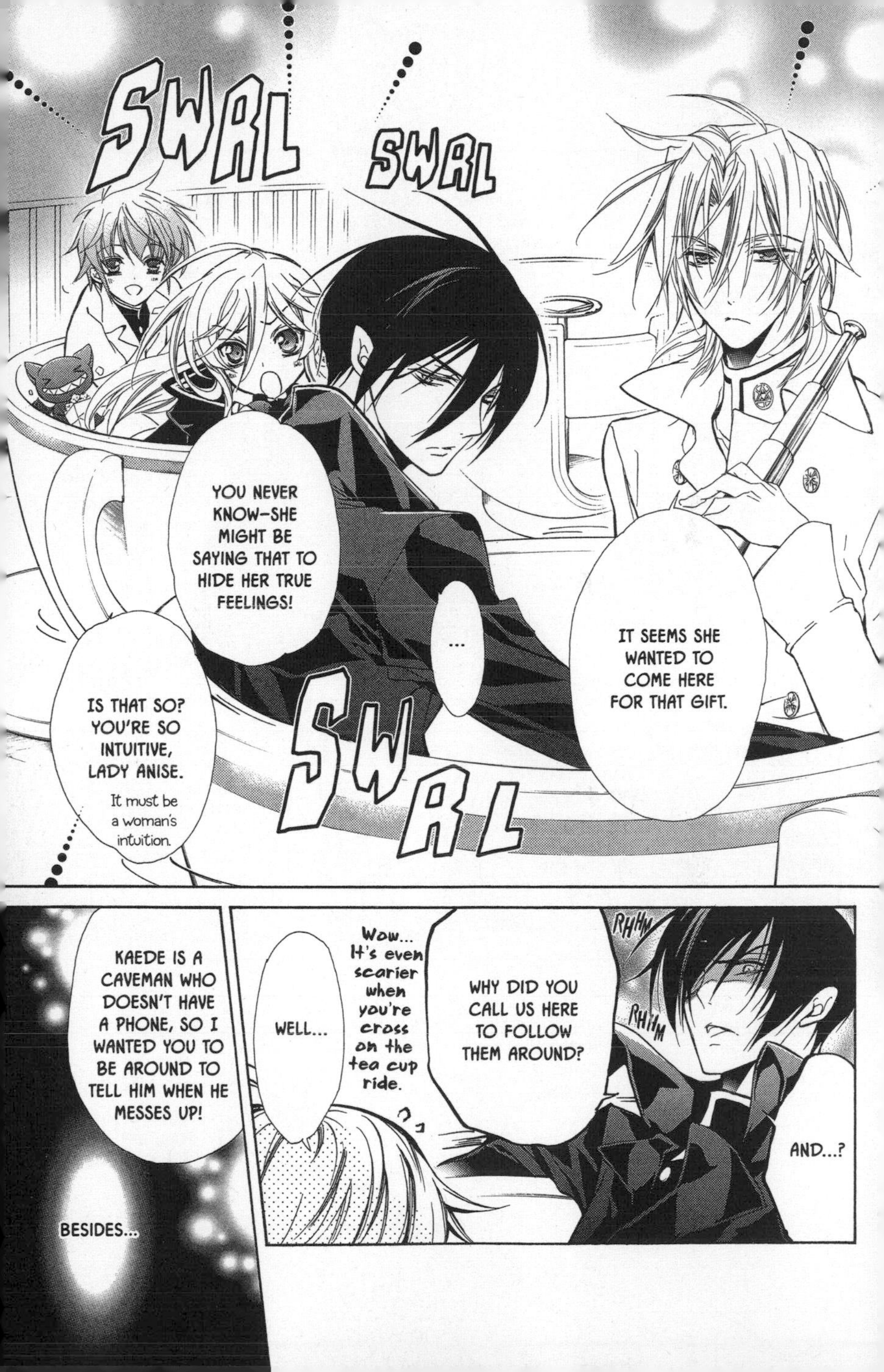
SWRL
SWRL
IT SEEMS SHE WANTED TO COME HERE FOR THAT GIFT.
...
YOU NEVER KNOW—SHE MIGHT BE SAYING THAT TO HIDE HER TRUE FEELINGS!
SWRL
IS THAT SO? YOU'RE SO INTUITIVE, LADY ANISE.
It must be a woman's intuition.
RHHM
RHHM
WHY DID YOU CALL US HERE TO FOLLOW THEM AROUND?
AND...?
Wow... It's even scarier when you're cross on the tea cup ride.
WELL...
KAEDE IS A CAVEMAN WHO DOESN'T HAVE A PHONE, SO I WANTED YOU TO BE AROUND TO TELL HIM WHEN HE MESSES UP!
BESIDES...

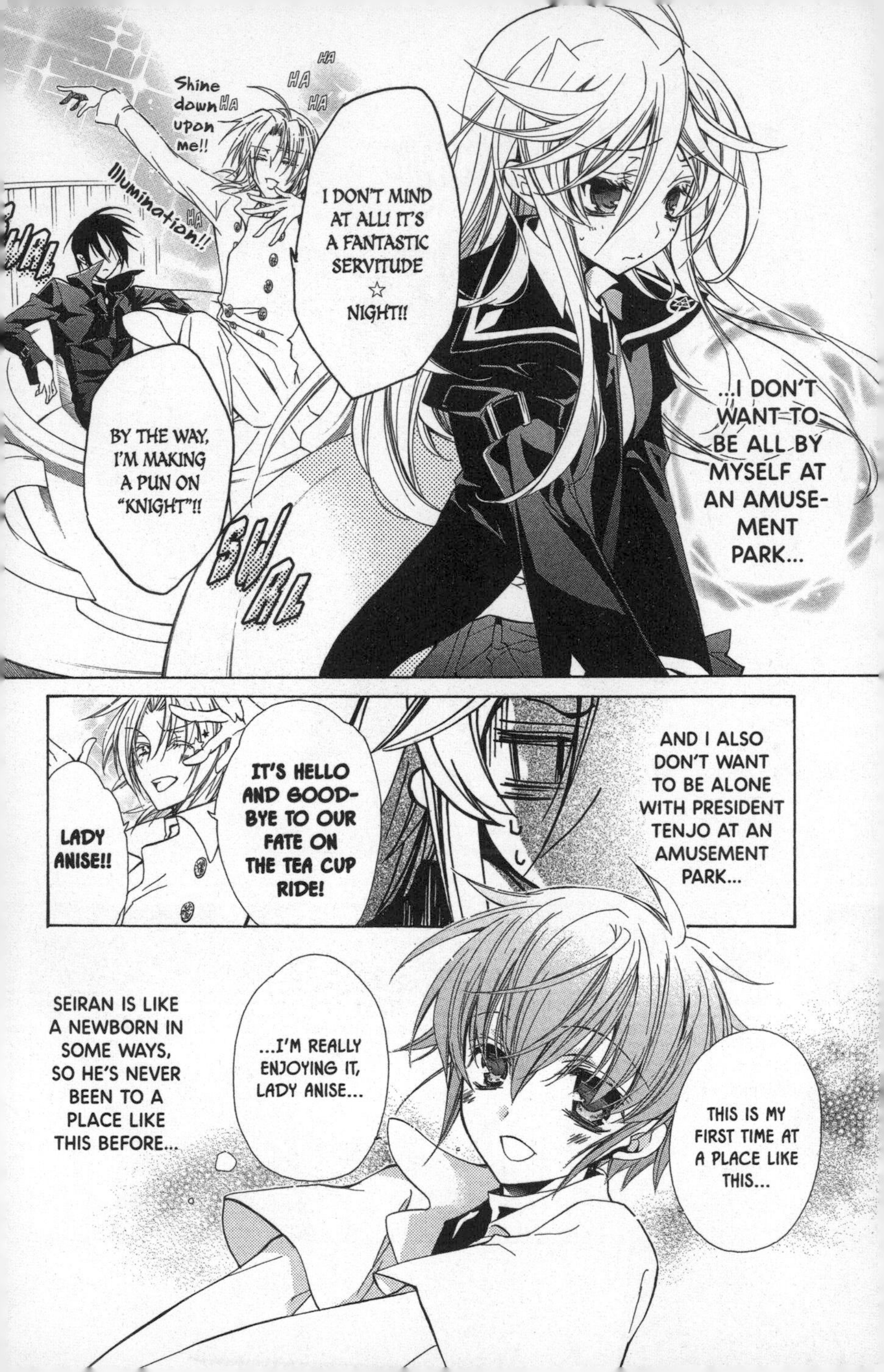
...I DON'T WANT TO BE ALL BY MYSELF AT AN AMUSEMENT PARK...
I DON'T MIND AT ALL! IT'S A FANTASTIC SERVITUDE ☆ NIGHT!!
HA HA HA
Shine down HA upon me!!
Illumination!! HA
BY THE WAY, I'M MAKING A PUN ON "KNIGHT"!!
AND I ALSO DON'T WANT TO BE ALONE WITH PRESIDENT TENJO AT AN AMUSEMENT PARK...
IT'S HELLO AND GOOD-BYE TO OUR FATE ON THE TEA CUP RIDE!
LADY ANISE!!
THIS IS MY FIRST TIME AT A PLACE LIKE THIS...
...I'M REALLY ENJOYING IT, LADY ANISE...
SEIRAN IS LIKE A NEWBORN IN SOME WAYS, SO HE'S NEVER BEEN TO A PLACE LIKE THIS BEFORE...

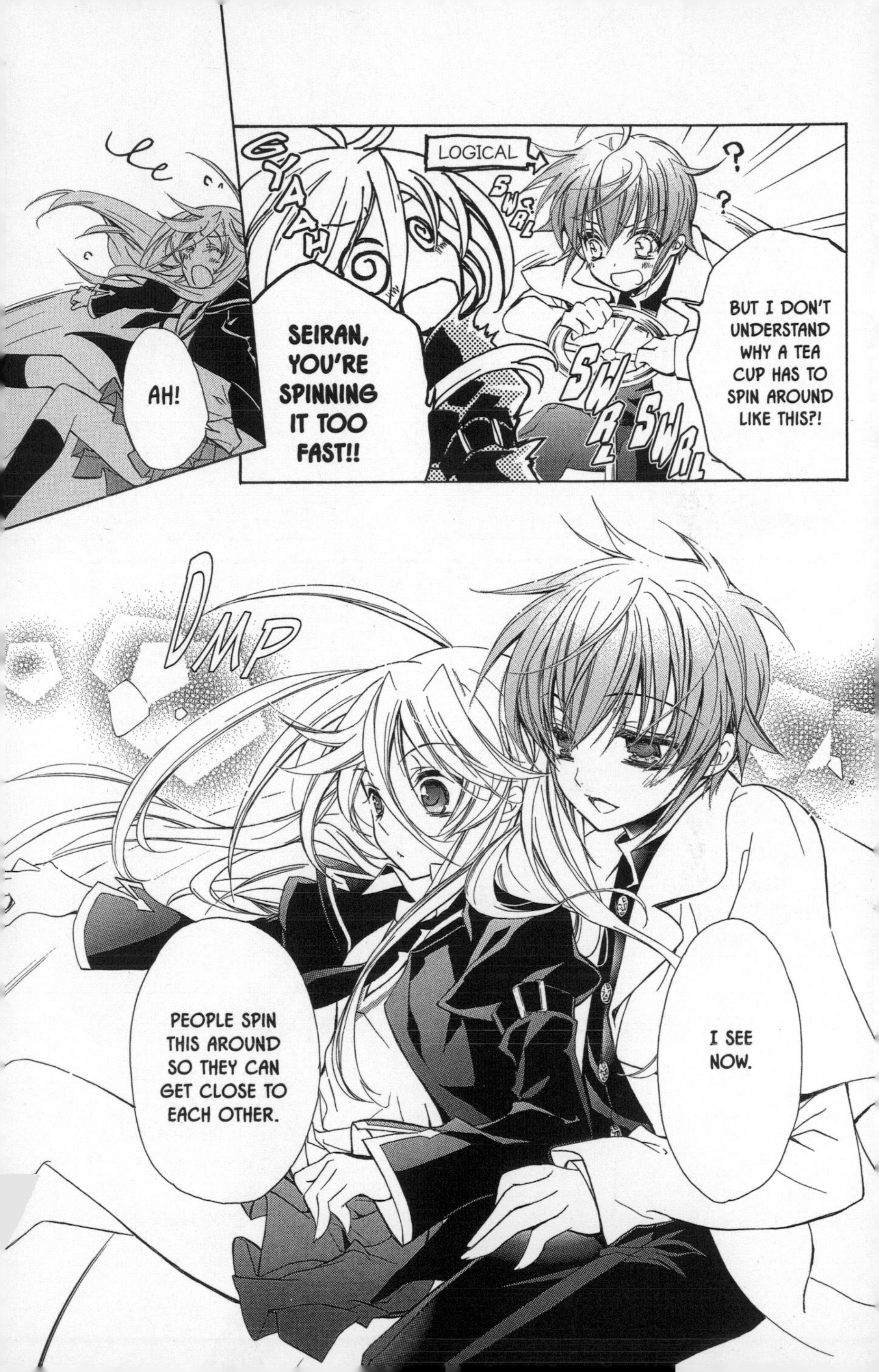
??
BUT I DON'T UNDERSTAND WHY A TEA CUP HAS TO SPIN AROUND LIKE THIS?!
LOGICAL
SWRL
GYAAH
SEIRAN, YOU'RE SPINNING IT TOO FAST!!
SWRL SWRL SWRL
AH!
I SEE NOW.
DMP
PEOPLE SPIN THIS AROUND SO THEY CAN GET CLOSE TO EACH OTHER.

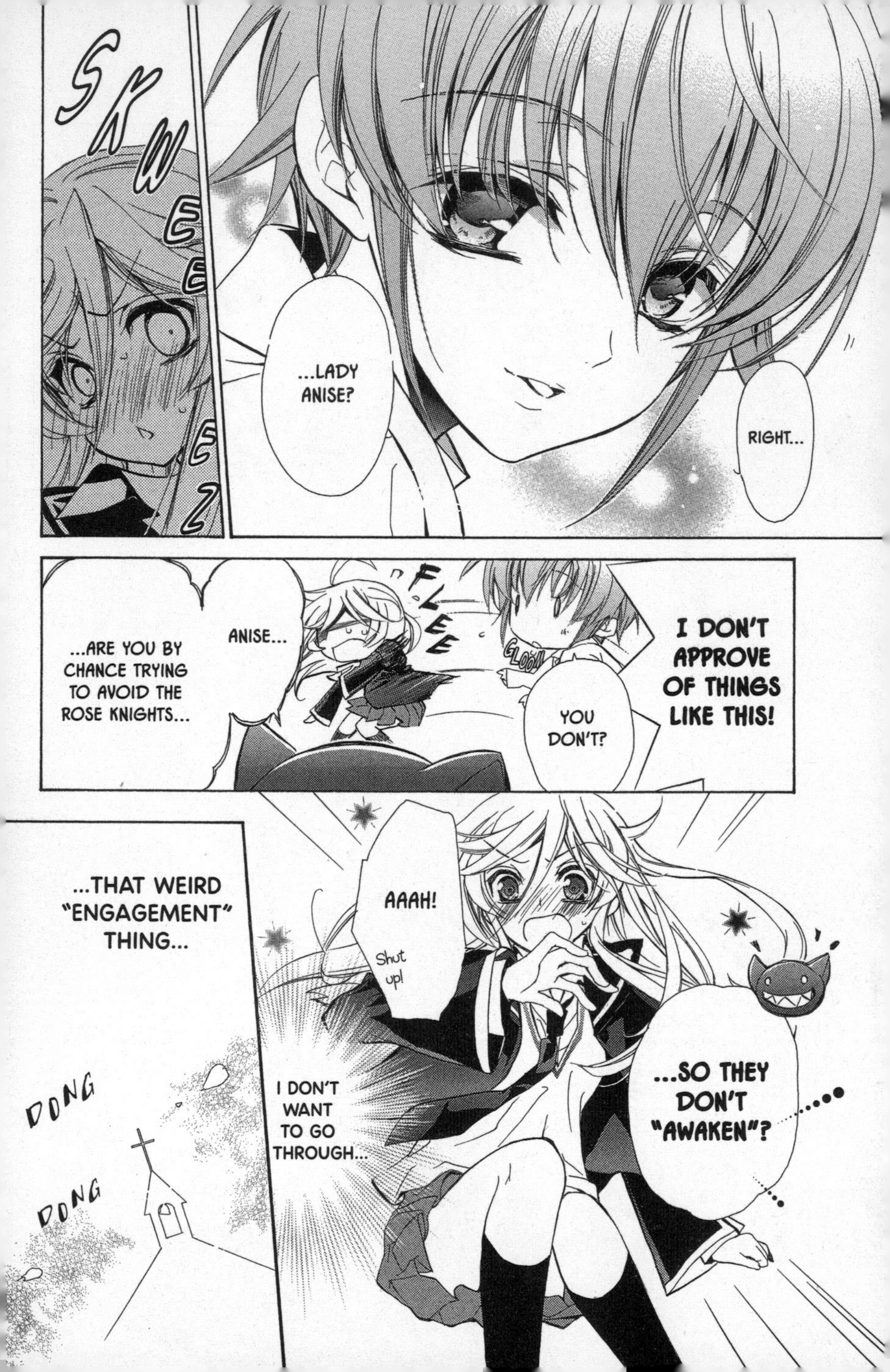
...LADY ANISE?
RIGHT...
SKWEEEZ
I DON'T APPROVE OF THINGS LIKE THIS!
YOU DON'T?
GLOOM
FLEE
ANISE...
...ARE YOU BY CHANCE TRYING TO AVOID THE ROSE KNIGHTS...
...THAT WEIRD "ENGAGEMENT" THING...
...SO THEY DON'T "AWAKEN"?
AAAH!
Shut up!
I DON'T WANT TO GO THROUGH...
DONG
DONG

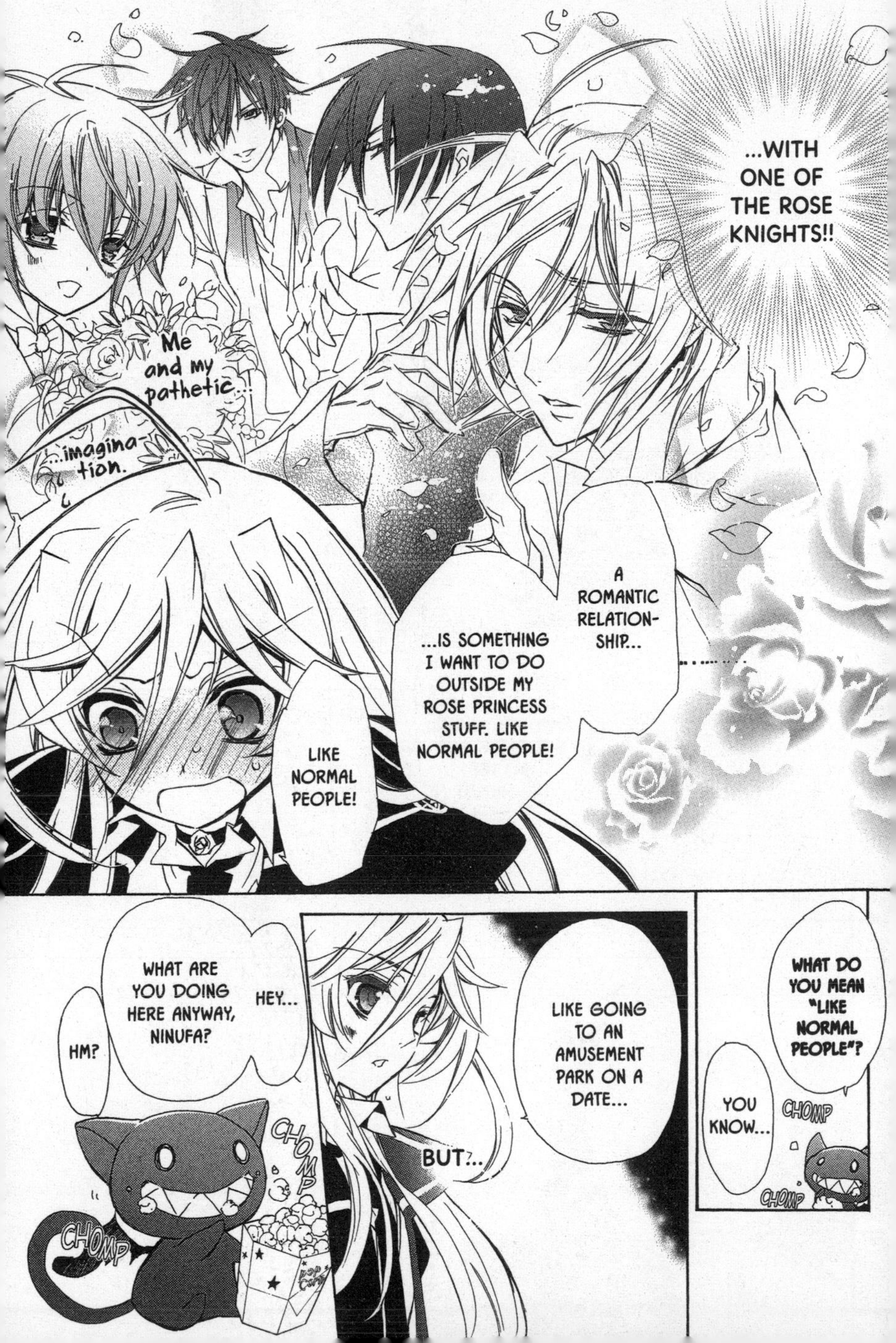
...WITH ONE OF THE ROSE KNIGHTS!!
Me and my pathetic...
...imagina-tion.
A ROMANTIC RELATION-SHIP...
....
...IS SOMETHING I WANT TO DO OUTSIDE MY ROSE PRINCESS STUFF. LIKE NORMAL PEOPLE!
LIKE NORMAL PEOPLE!
WHAT DO YOU MEAN "LIKE NORMAL PEOPLE"?
CHOMP
YOU KNOW...
CHOMP
LIKE GOING TO AN AMUSEMENT PARK ON A DATE...
BUT?...
HEY...
WHAT ARE YOU DOING HERE ANYWAY, NINUFA?
HM?
CHOMP
CHOMP
CHOMP
pop corn

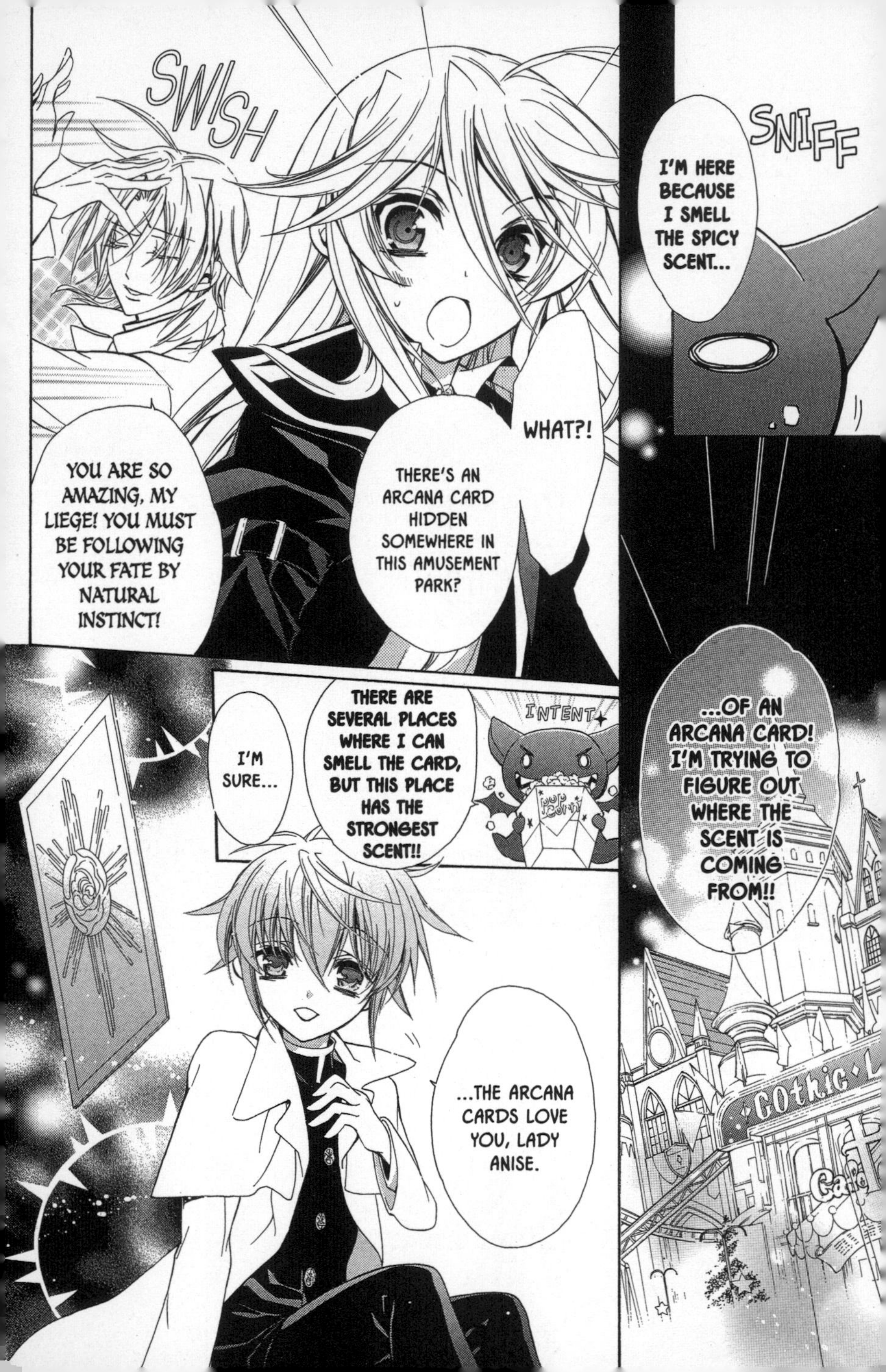
SNIFF
I'M HERE BECAUSE I SMELL THE SPICY SCENT...
...OF AN ARCANA CARD! I'M TRYING TO FIGURE OUT WHERE THE SCENT IS COMING FROM!!
SWISH
WHAT?!
THERE'S AN ARCANA CARD HIDDEN SOMEWHERE IN THIS AMUSEMENT PARK?
YOU ARE SO AMAZING, MY LIEGE! YOU MUST BE FOLLOWING YOUR FATE BY NATURAL INSTINCT!
INTENT
THERE ARE SEVERAL PLACES WHERE I CAN SMELL THE CARD, BUT THIS PLACE HAS THE STRONGEST SCENT!!
I'M SURE...
...THE ARCANA CARDS LOVE YOU, LADY ANISE.

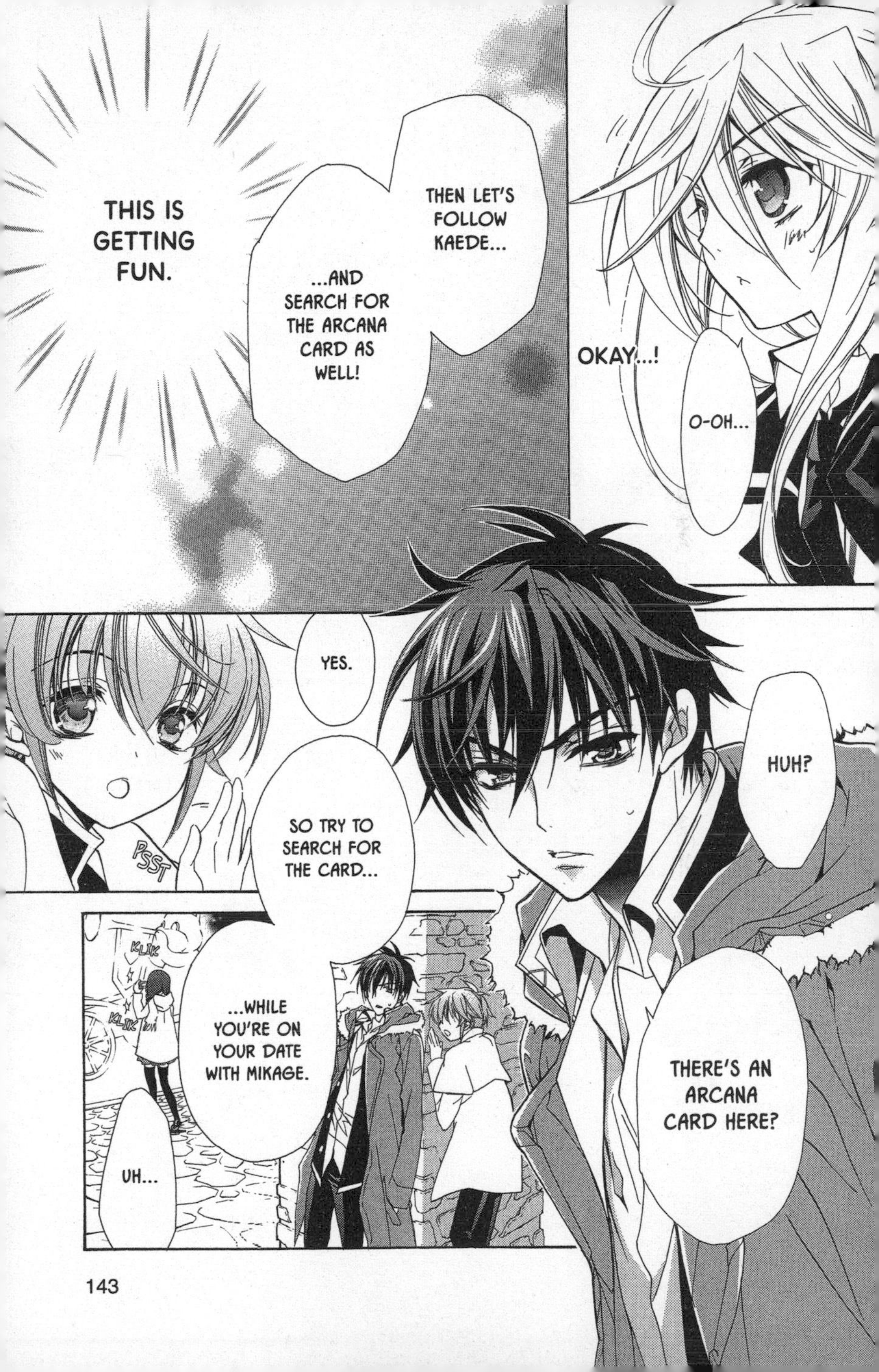
O-OH...
OKAY...!
THEN LET'S FOLLOW KAEDE...
...AND SEARCH FOR THE ARCANA CARD AS WELL!
THIS IS GETTING FUN.
HUH?
THERE'S AN ARCANA CARD HERE?
YES.
PSST
SO TRY TO SEARCH FOR THE CARD...
...WHILE YOU'RE ON YOUR DATE WITH MIKAGE.
UH...
KLIK
KLIK

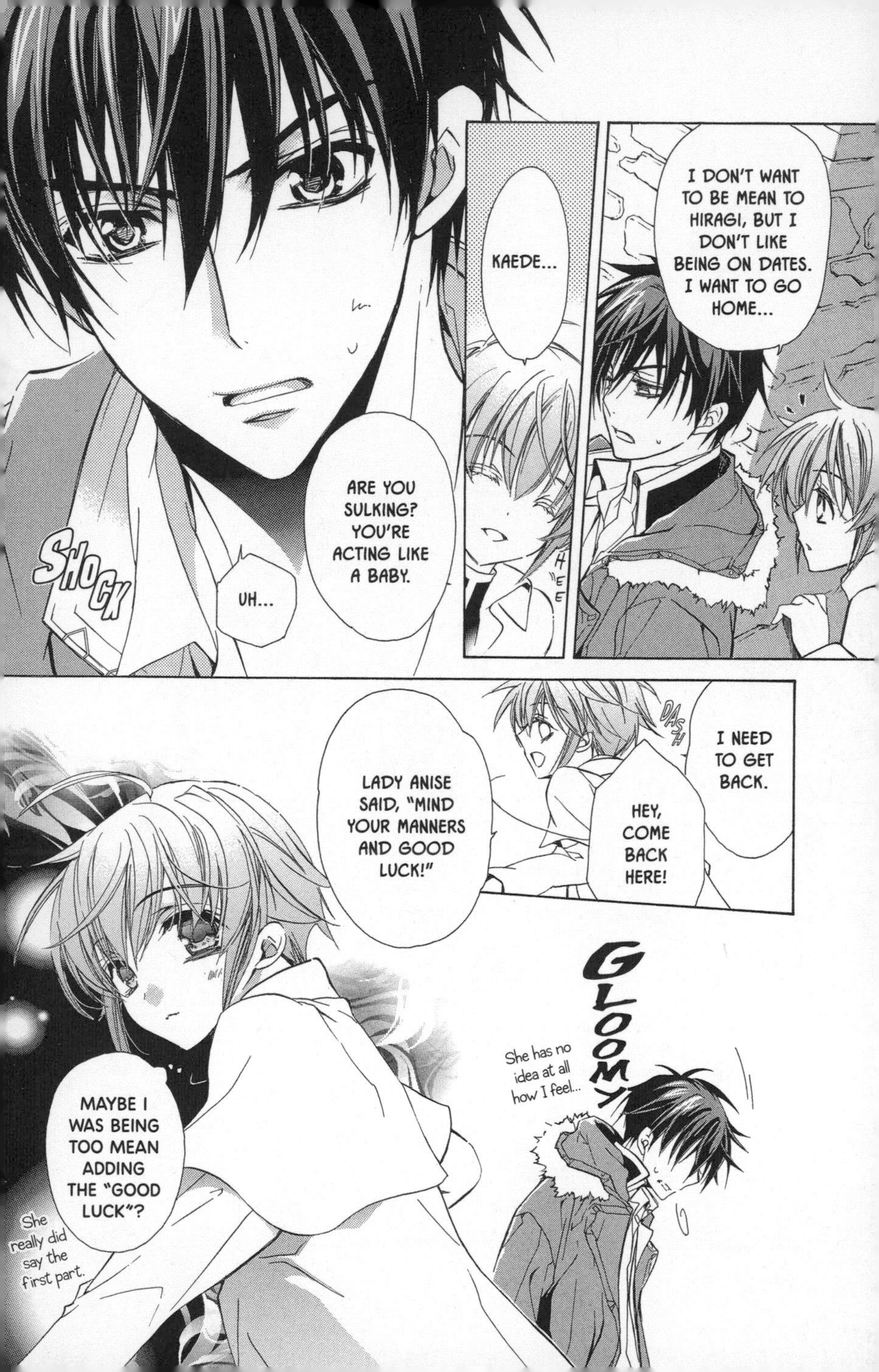
I DON'T WANT TO BE MEAN TO HIRAGI, BUT I DON'T LIKE BEING ON DATES. I WANT TO GO HOME...
KAEDE...
HEE
ARE YOU SULKING? YOU'RE ACTING LIKE A BABY.
UH...
SHOCK
DASH
I NEED TO GET BACK.
HEY, COME BACK HERE!
LADY ANISE SAID, "MIND YOUR MANNERS AND GOOD LUCK!"
GLOOM
She has no idea at all how I feel...
MAYBE I WAS BEING TOO MEAN ADDING THE "GOOD LUCK"?
She really did say the first part.

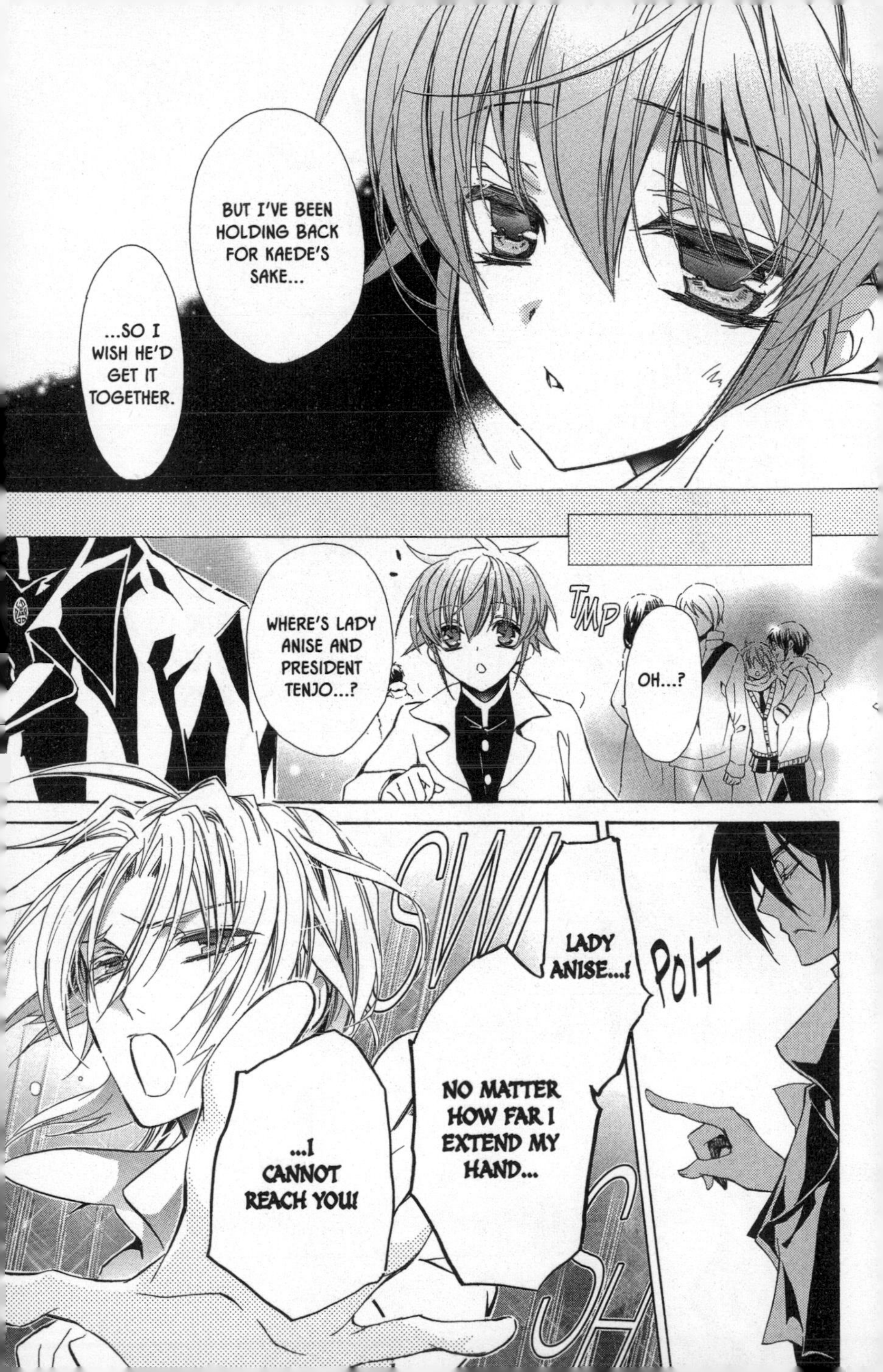
BUT I'VE BEEN HOLDING BACK FOR KAEDE'S SAKE...
...SO I WISH HE'D GET IT TOGETHER.
TMP
OH...?
WHERE'S LADY ANISE AND PRESIDENT TENJO...?
POIT
LADY ANISE...!
NO MATTER HOW FAR I EXTEND MY HAND...
...I CANNOT REACH YOU!

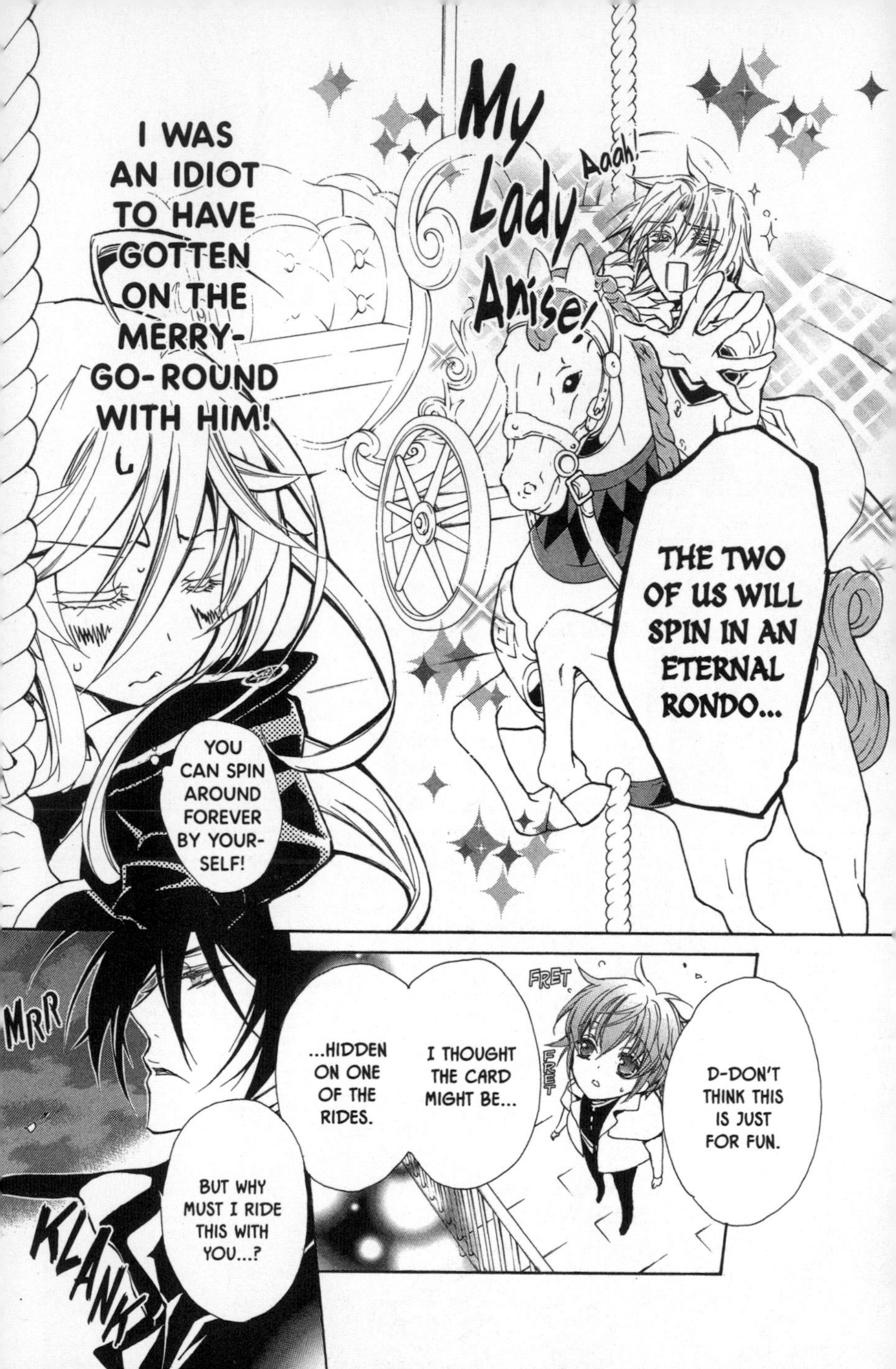
Aaah!
My Lady Anise!
THE TWO OF US WILL SPIN IN AN ETERNAL RONDO...
I WAS AN IDIOT TO HAVE GOTTEN ON THE MERRY-GO-ROUND WITH HIM!
YOU CAN SPIN AROUND FOREVER BY YOUR-SELF!
D-DON'T THINK THIS IS JUST FOR FUN.
FRET
FRET
I THOUGHT THE CARD MIGHT BE...
...HIDDEN ON ONE OF THE RIDES.
BUT WHY MUST I RIDE THIS WITH YOU...?
MRR
KLANK

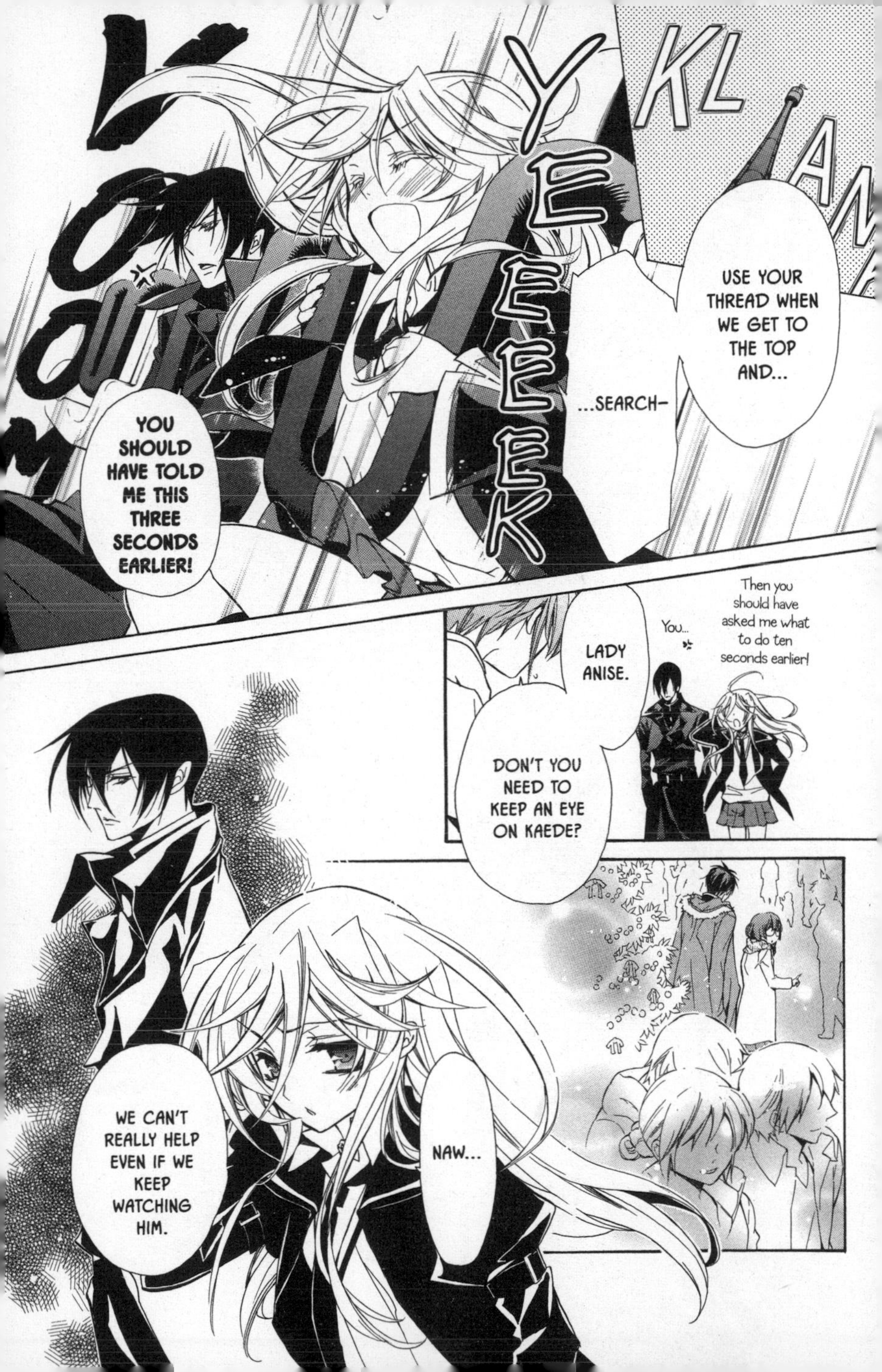
KL
AN
USE YOUR THREAD WHEN WE GET TO THE TOP AND...
...SEARCH–
YEEEEK
YOU SHOULD HAVE TOLD ME THIS THREE SECONDS EARLIER!
Then you should have asked me what to do ten seconds earlier!
You...
LADY ANISE.
DON'T YOU NEED TO KEEP AN EYE ON KAEDE?
NAW...
WE CAN'T REALLY HELP EVEN IF WE KEEP WATCHING HIM.

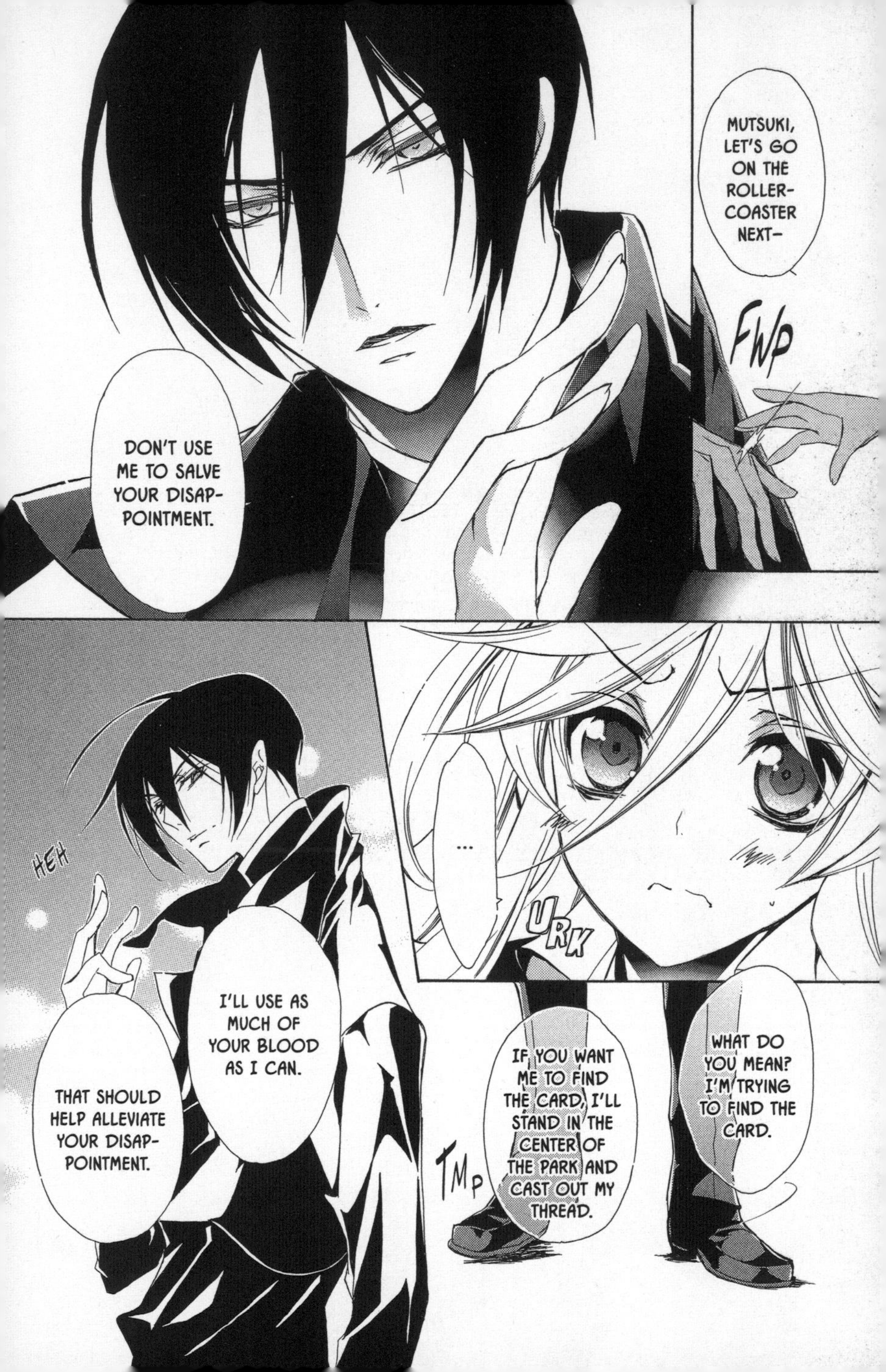
MUTSUKI, LET'S GO ON THE ROLLER-COASTER NEXT—
FWP
DON'T USE ME TO SALVE YOUR DISAP-POINTMENT.
...
URK
WHAT DO YOU MEAN? I'M TRYING TO FIND THE CARD.
IF YOU WANT ME TO FIND THE CARD, I'LL STAND IN THE CENTER OF THE PARK AND CAST OUT MY THREAD.
TMP
HEH
I'LL USE AS MUCH OF YOUR BLOOD AS I CAN.
THAT SHOULD HELP ALLEVIATE YOUR DISAP-POINTMENT.

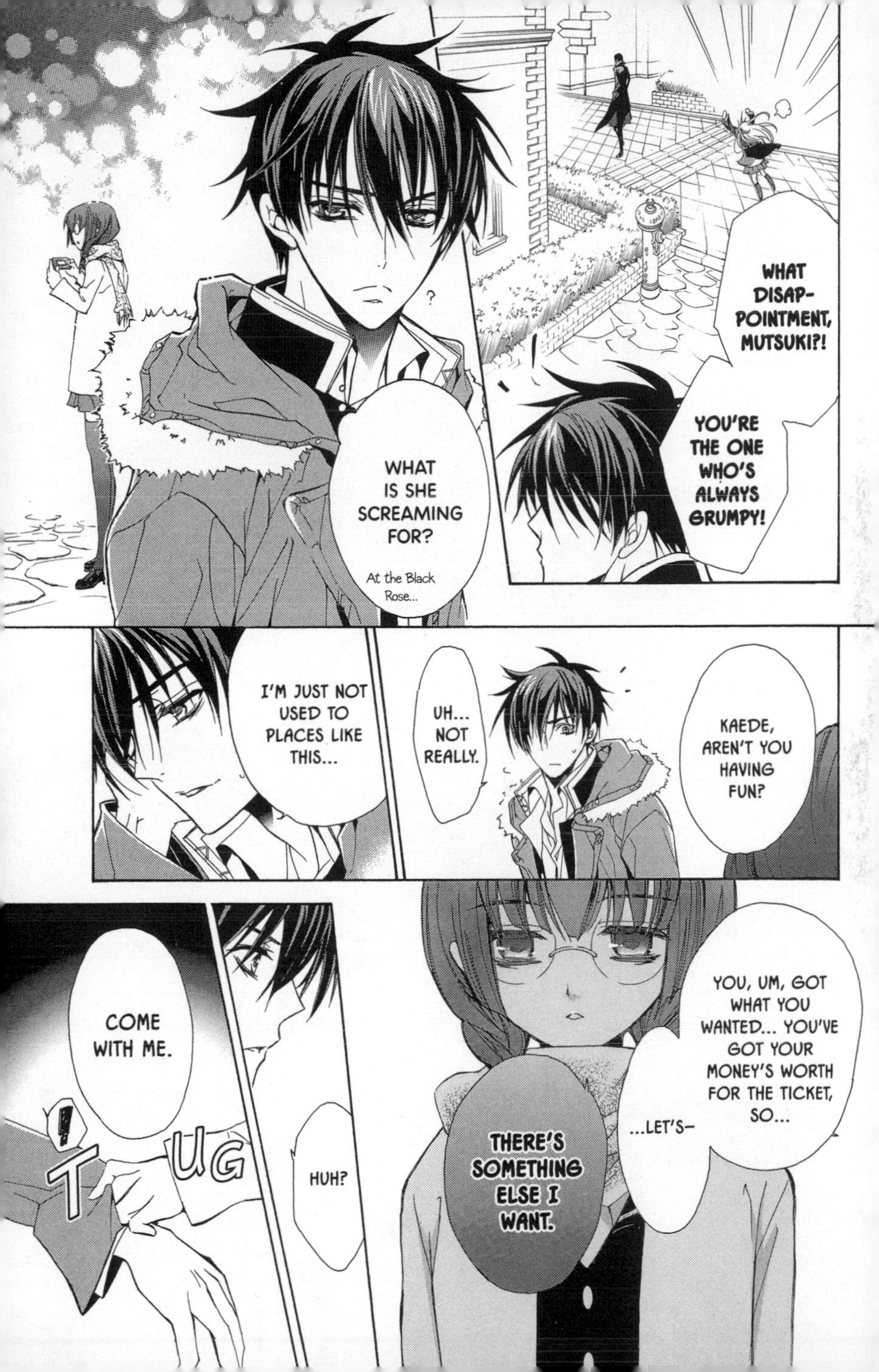
WHAT DISAP-POINTMENT, MUTSUKI?!
YOU'RE THE ONE WHO'S ALWAYS GRUMPY!
?
WHAT IS SHE SCREAMING FOR?
At the Black Rose...
KAEDE, AREN'T YOU HAVING FUN?
UH... NOT REALLY.
I'M JUST NOT USED TO PLACES LIKE THIS...
YOU, UM, GOT WHAT YOU WANTED... YOU'VE GOT YOUR MONEY'S WORTH FOR THE TICKET, SO...
...LET'S–
THERE'S SOMETHING ELSE I WANT.
COME WITH ME.
HUH?
!
TUG

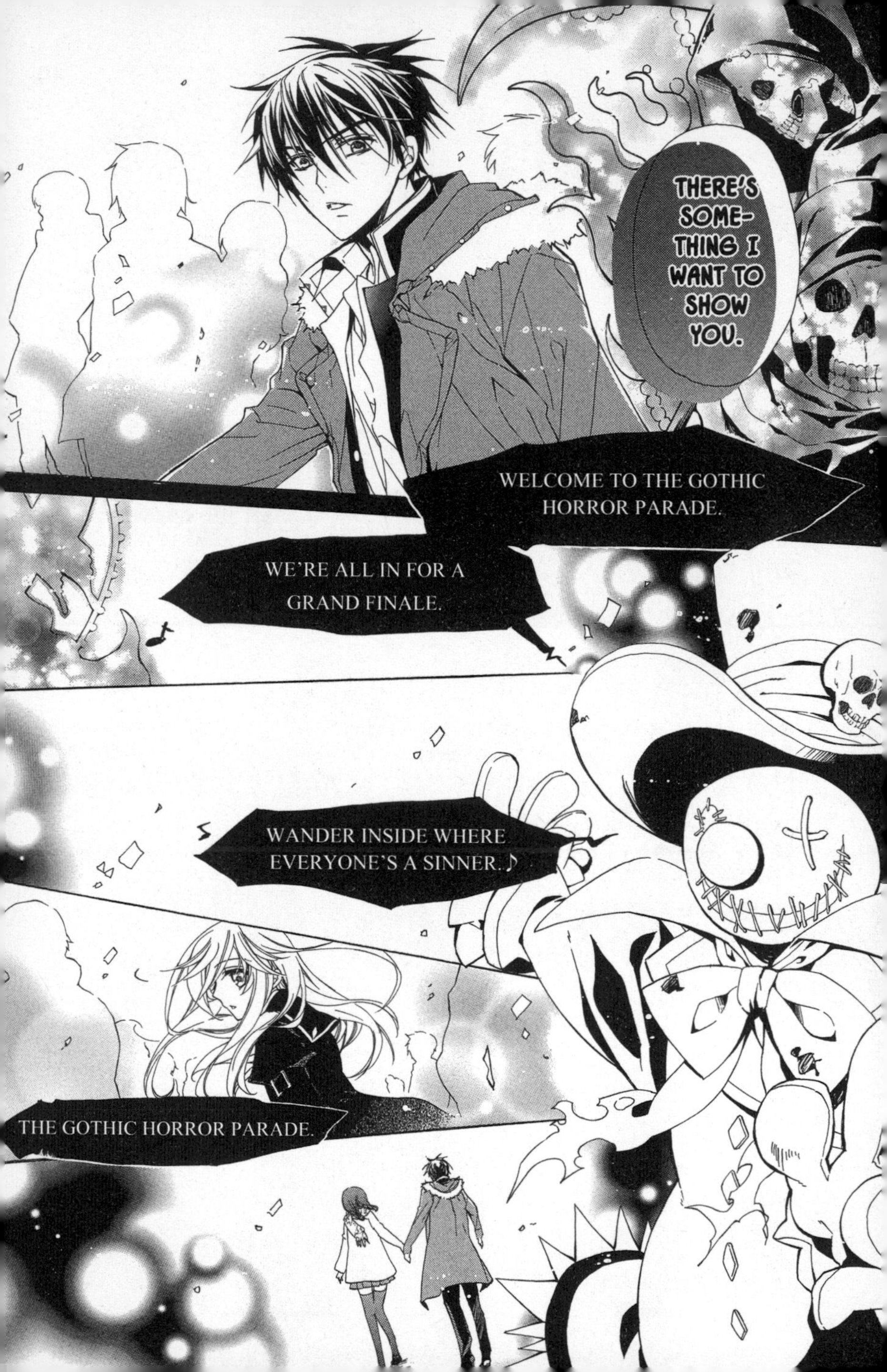
THERE'S SOME- THING I WANT TO SHOW YOU.
WELCOME TO THE GOTHIC HORROR PARADE.
WE'RE ALL IN FOR A GRAND FINALE.
WANDER INSIDE WHERE EVERYONE'S A SINNER.♪
THE GOTHIC HORROR PARADE.

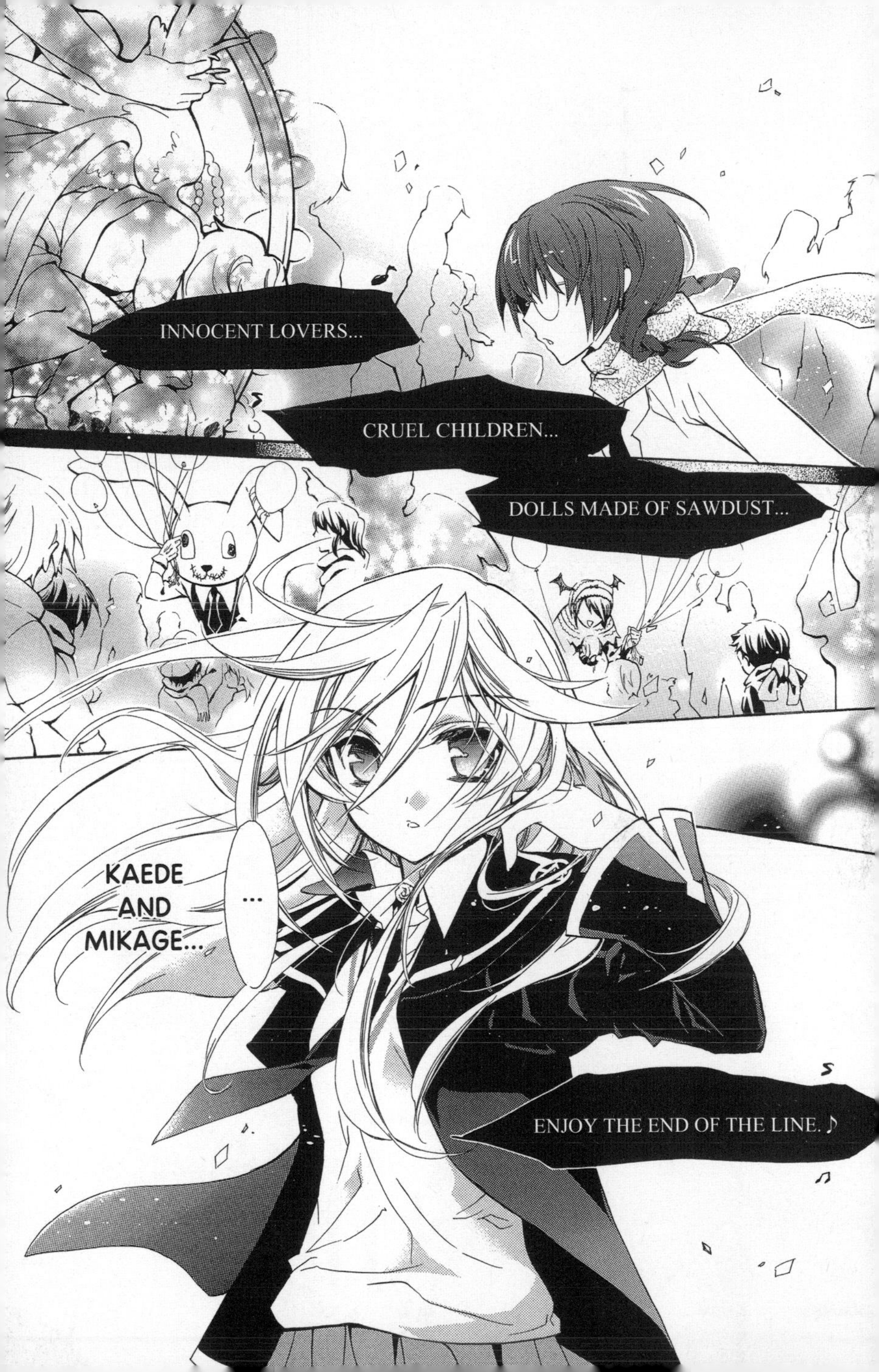
INNOCENT LOVERS...
CRUEL CHILDREN...
DOLLS MADE OF SAWDUST...
...
KAEDE AND MIKAGE...
ENJOY THE END OF THE LINE.♪

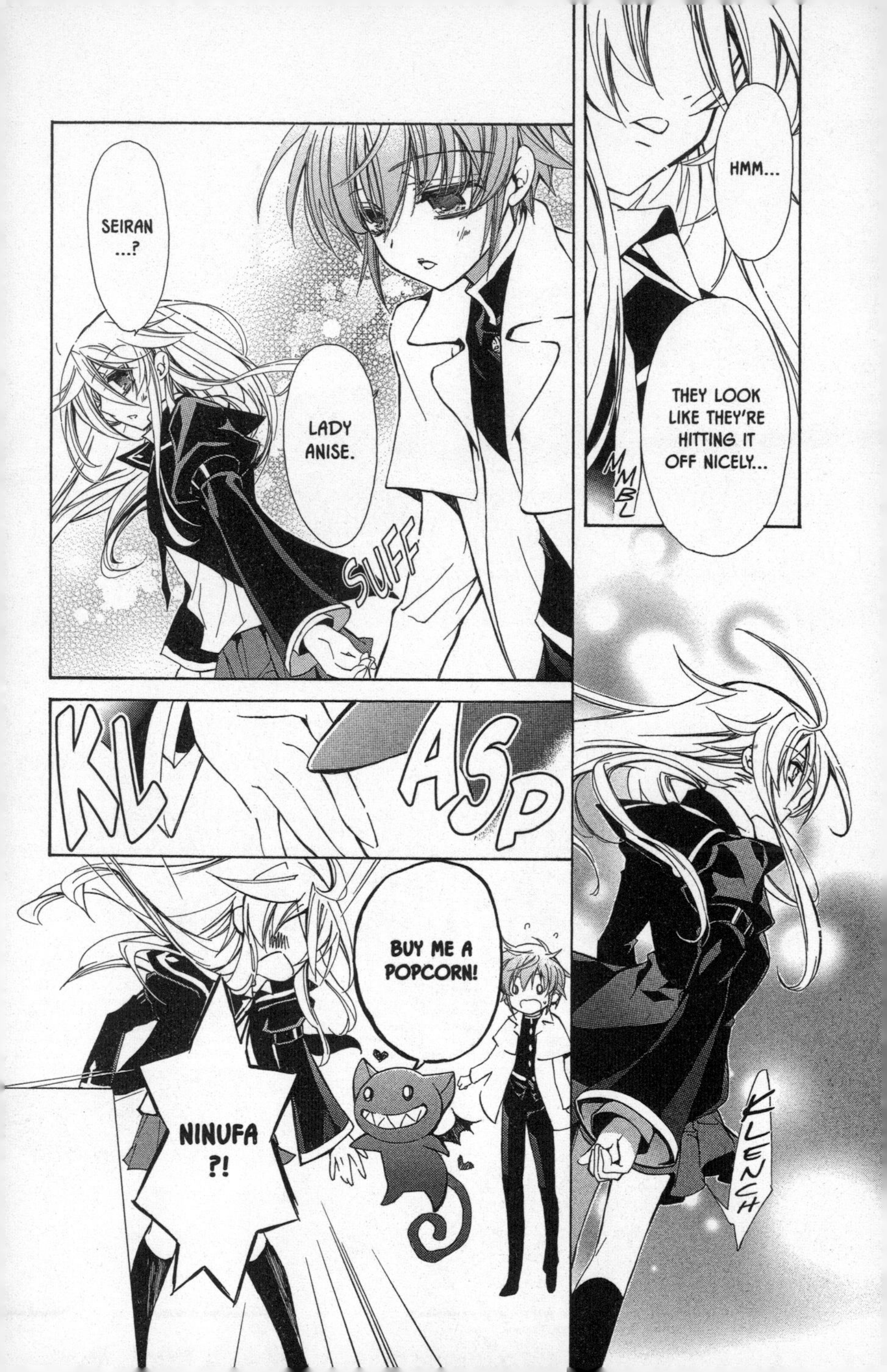
HMM...
THEY LOOK LIKE THEY'RE HITTING IT OFF NICELY...
MMBL
SEIRAN ...?
LADY ANISE.
SUFF
KLENCH
KLASP
BUY ME A POPCORN!
NINUFA ?!

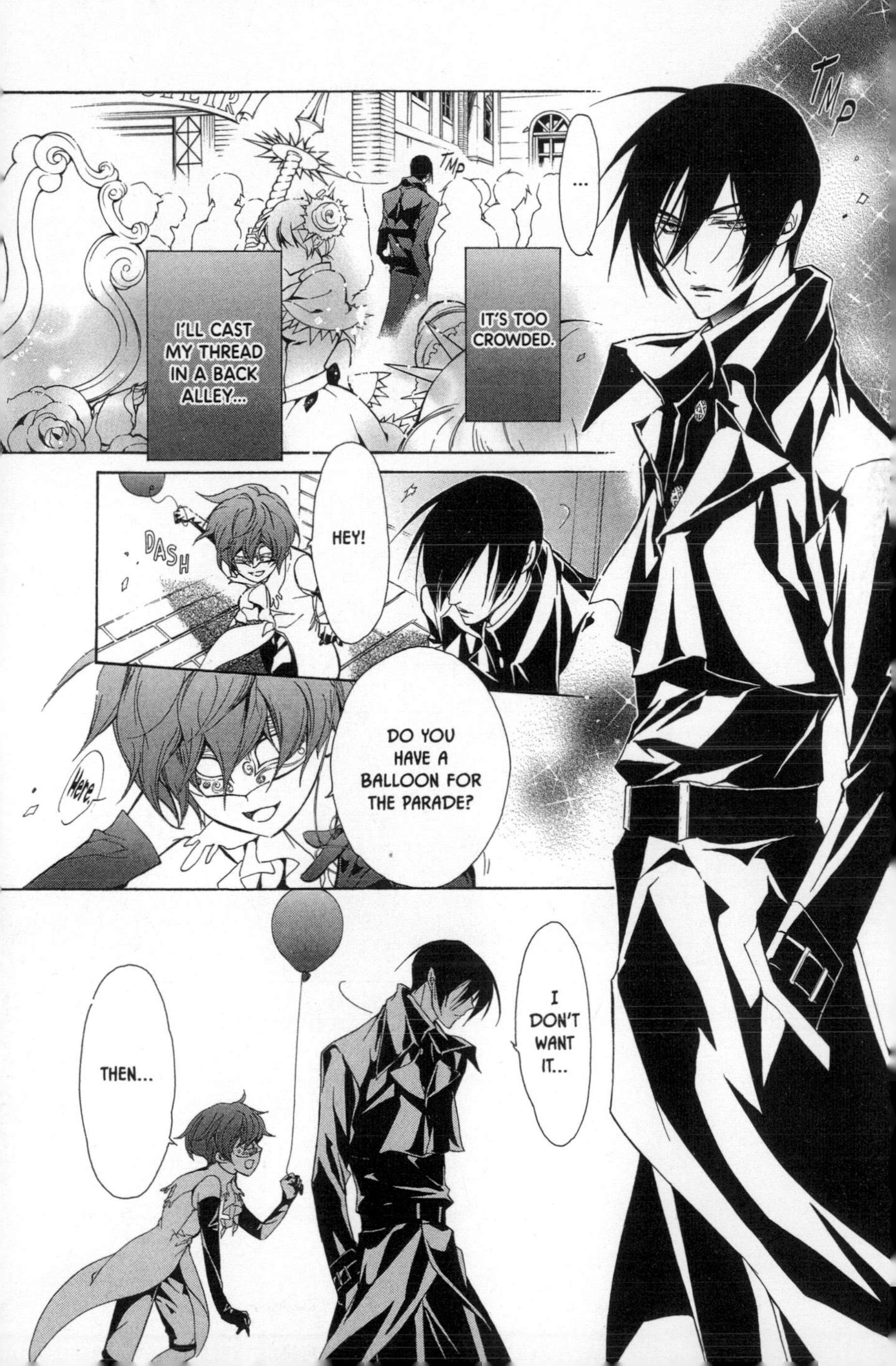
TMP
...
TMP
IT'S TOO CROWDED.
I'LL CAST MY THREAD IN A BACK ALLEY...
HEY!
DASH
DO YOU HAVE A BALLOON FOR THE PARADE?
Here.
I DON'T WANT IT...
THEN...

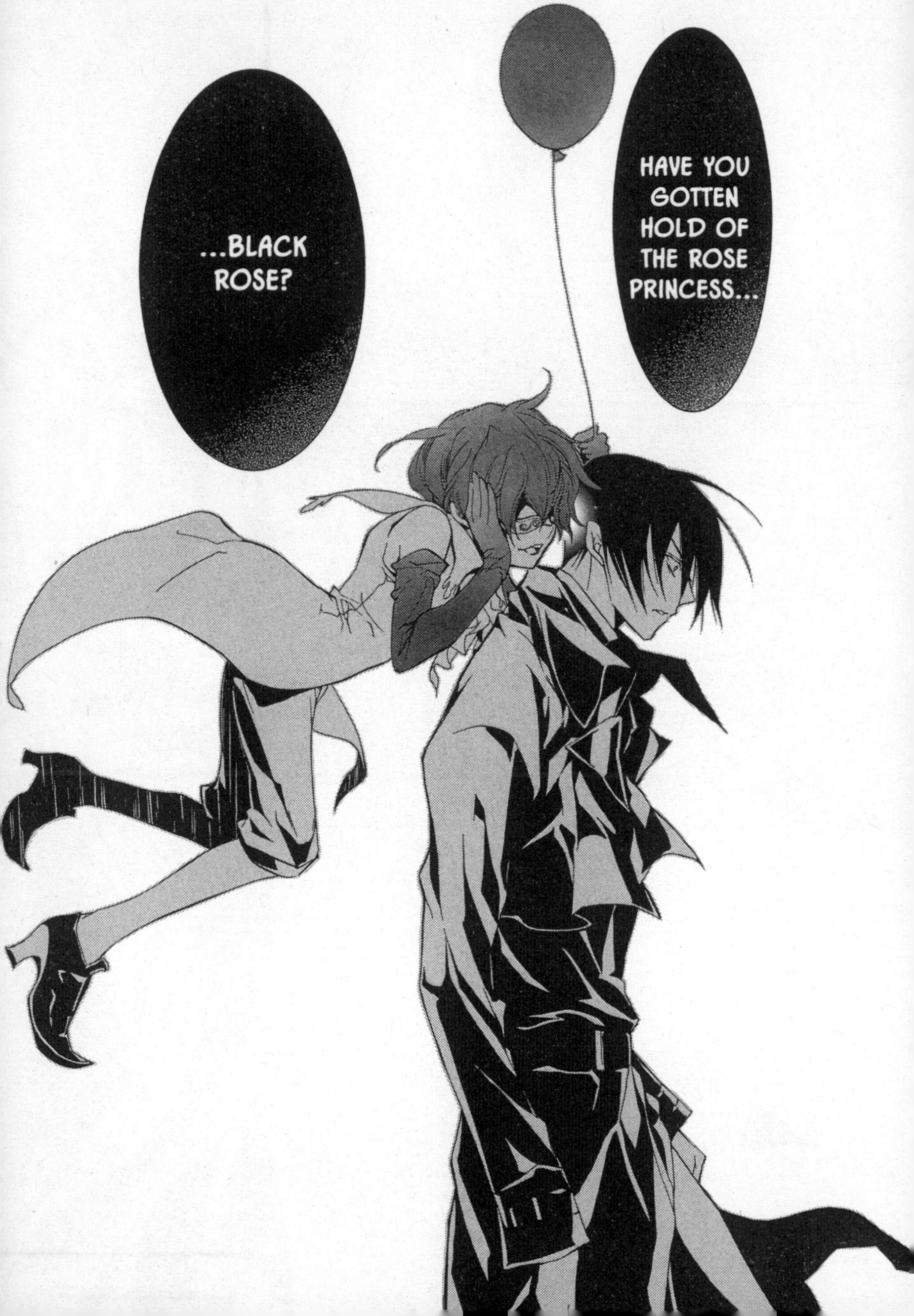
HAVE YOU GOTTEN HOLD OF THE ROSE PRINCESS...
...BLACK ROSE?

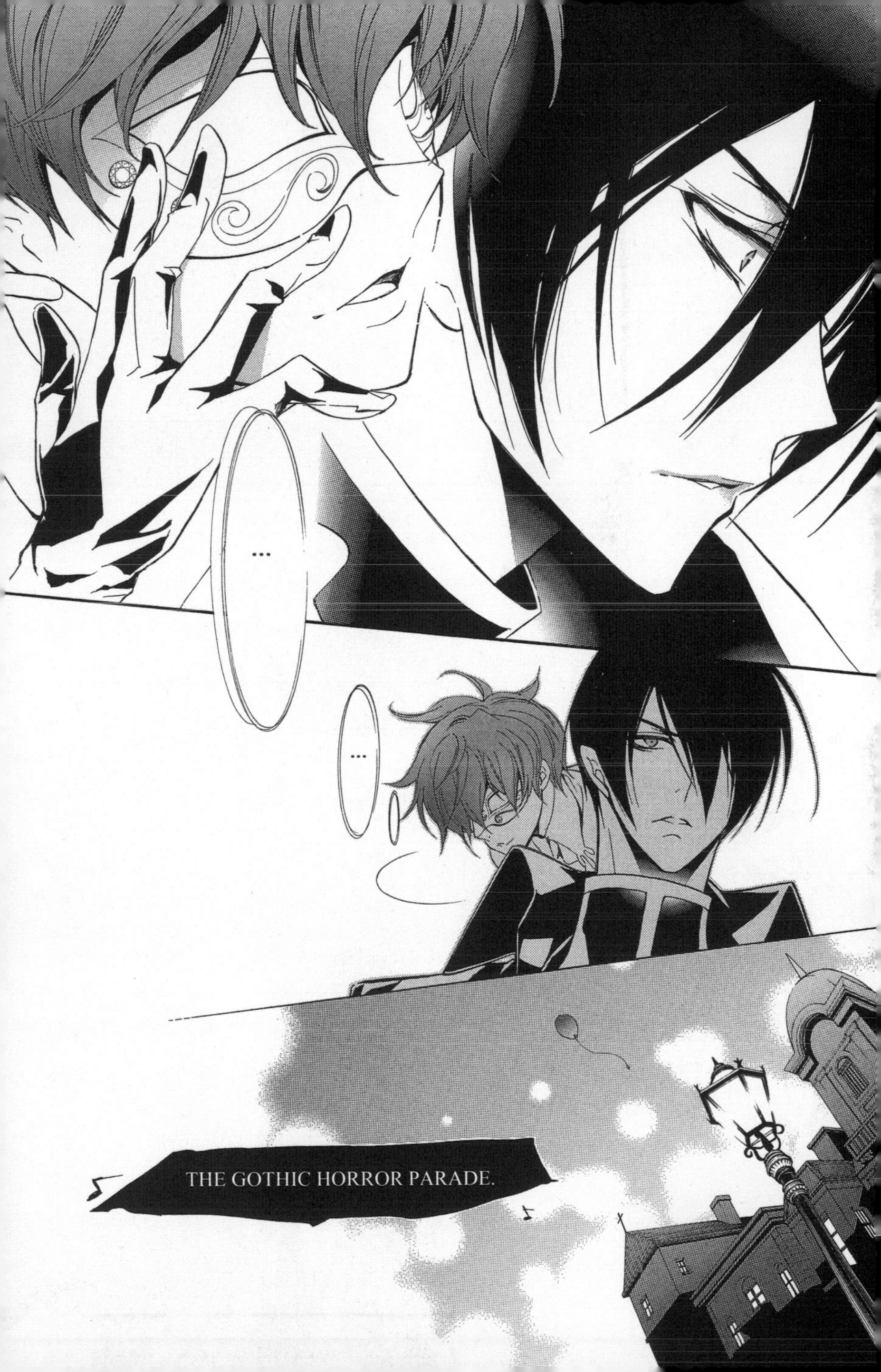
...
...
THE GOTHIC HORROR PARADE.

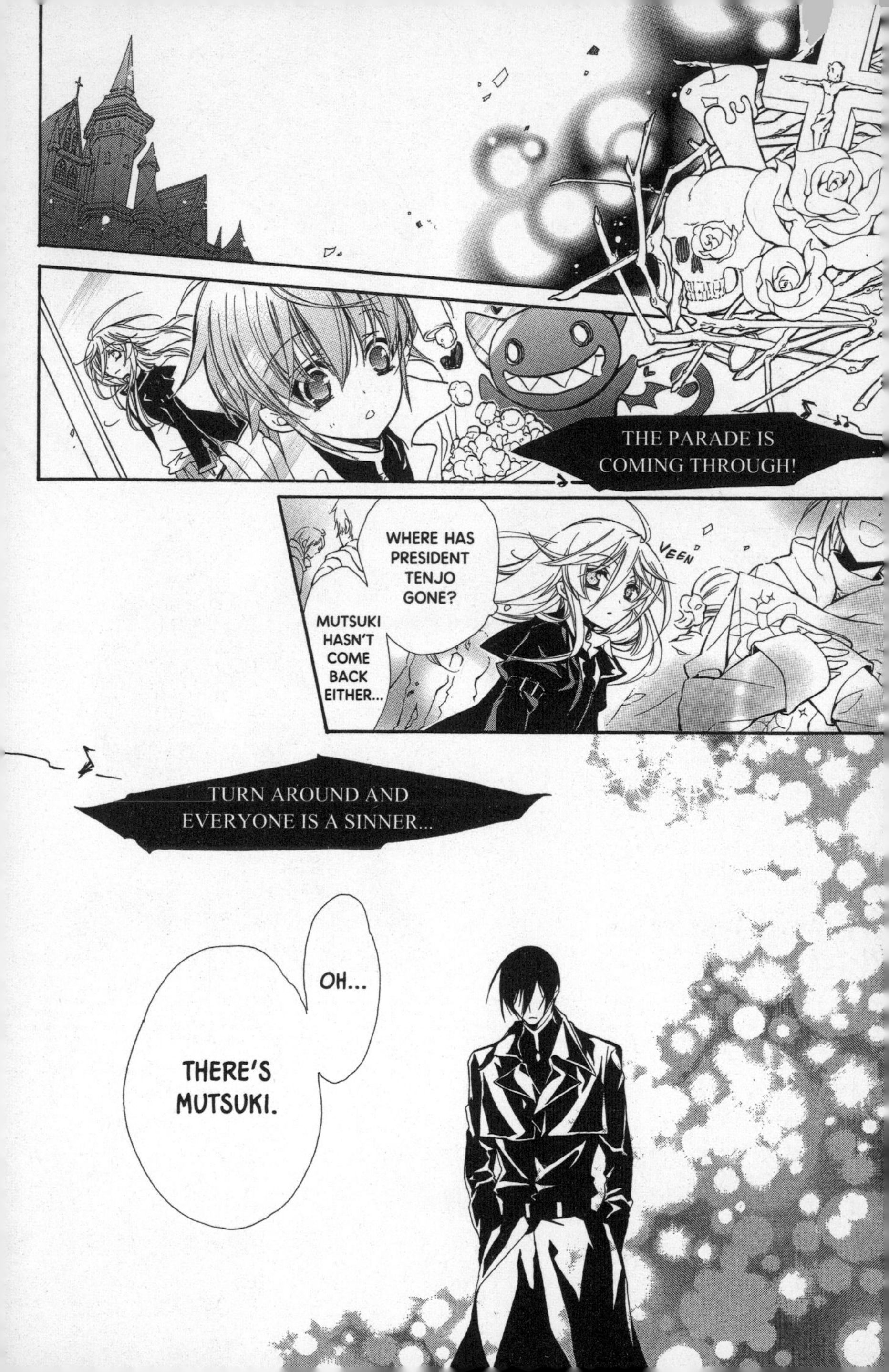
THE PARADE IS COMING THROUGH!
VEEN
WHERE HAS PRESIDENT TENJO GONE?
MUTSUKI HASN'T COME BACK EITHER...
TURN AROUND AND EVERYONE IS A SINNER...
OH...
THERE'S MUTSUKI.

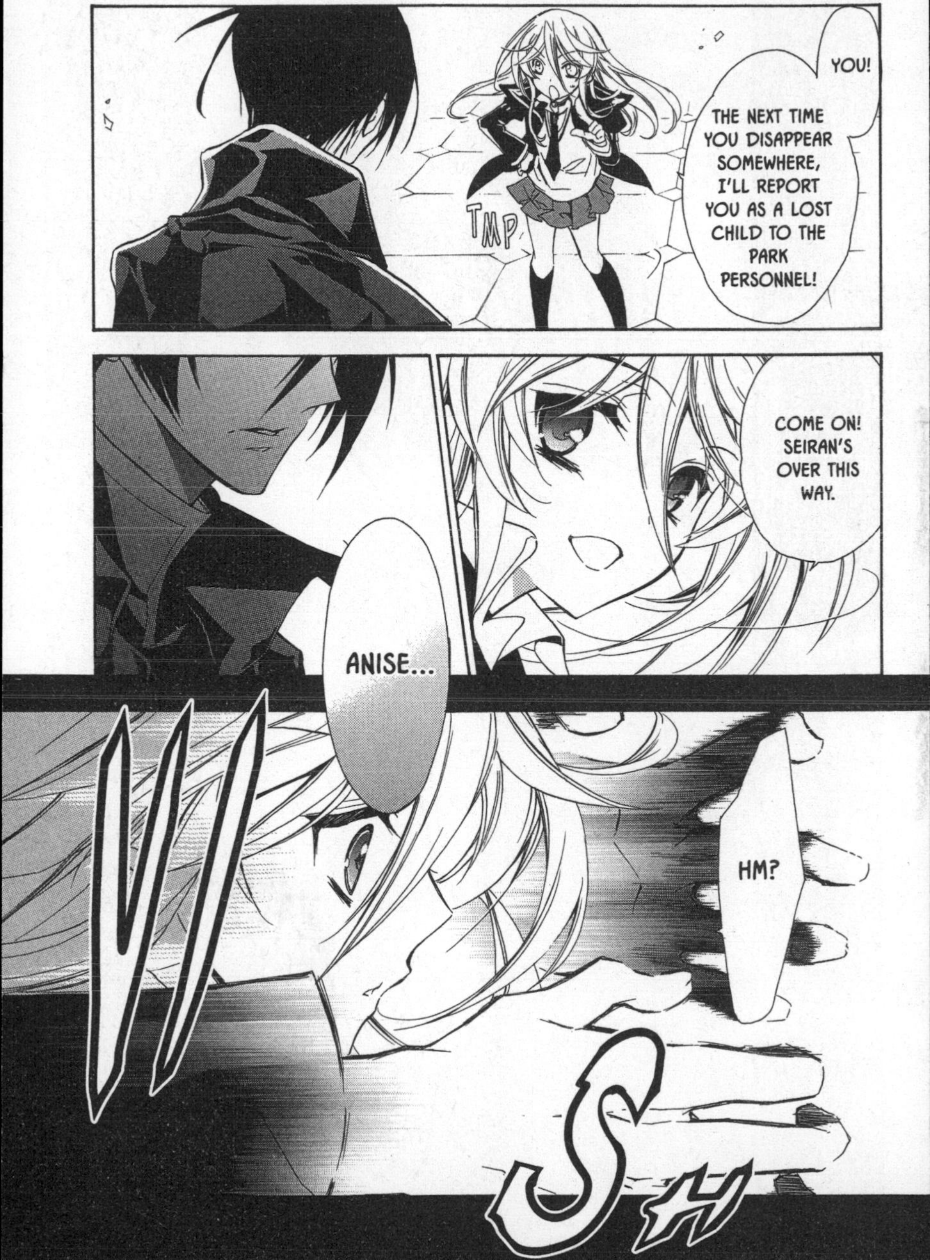
YOU!
THE NEXT TIME YOU DISAPPEAR SOMEWHERE, I'LL REPORT YOU AS A LOST CHILD TO THE PARK PERSONNEL!
TMP
COME ON! SEIRAN'S OVER THIS WAY.
ANISE...
HM?
SH

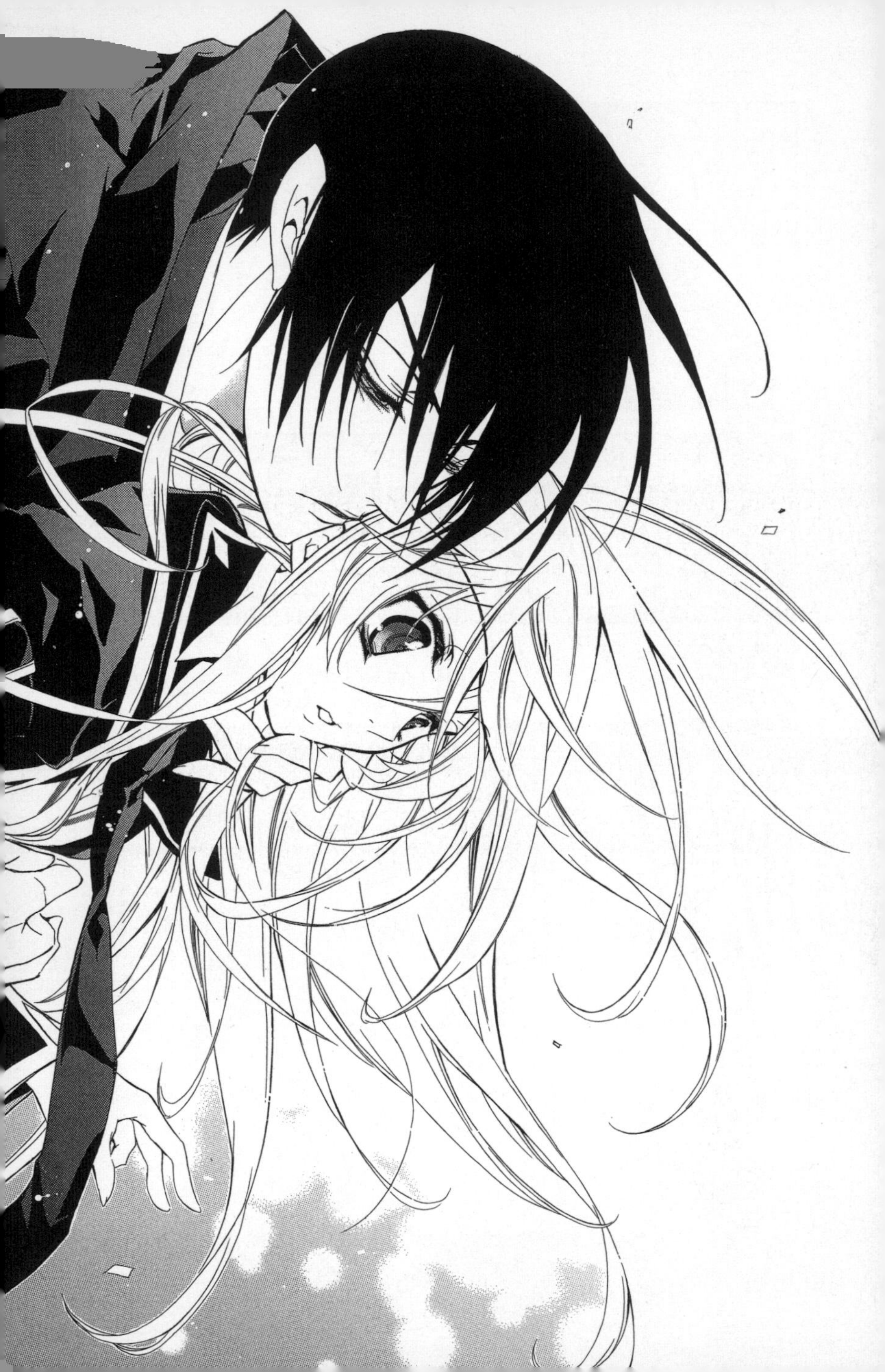

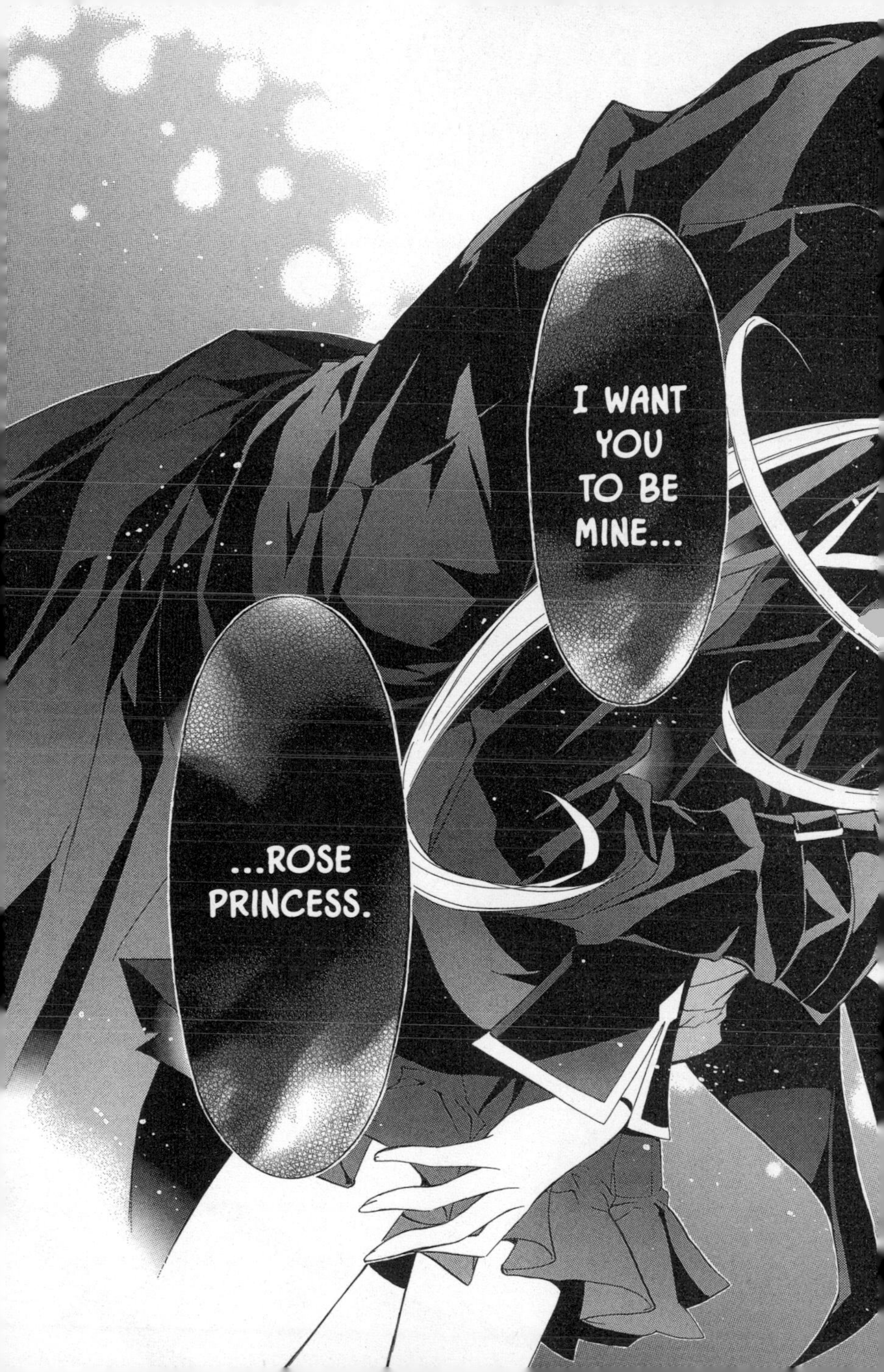
I WANT YOU TO BE MINE...
...ROSE PRINCESS.

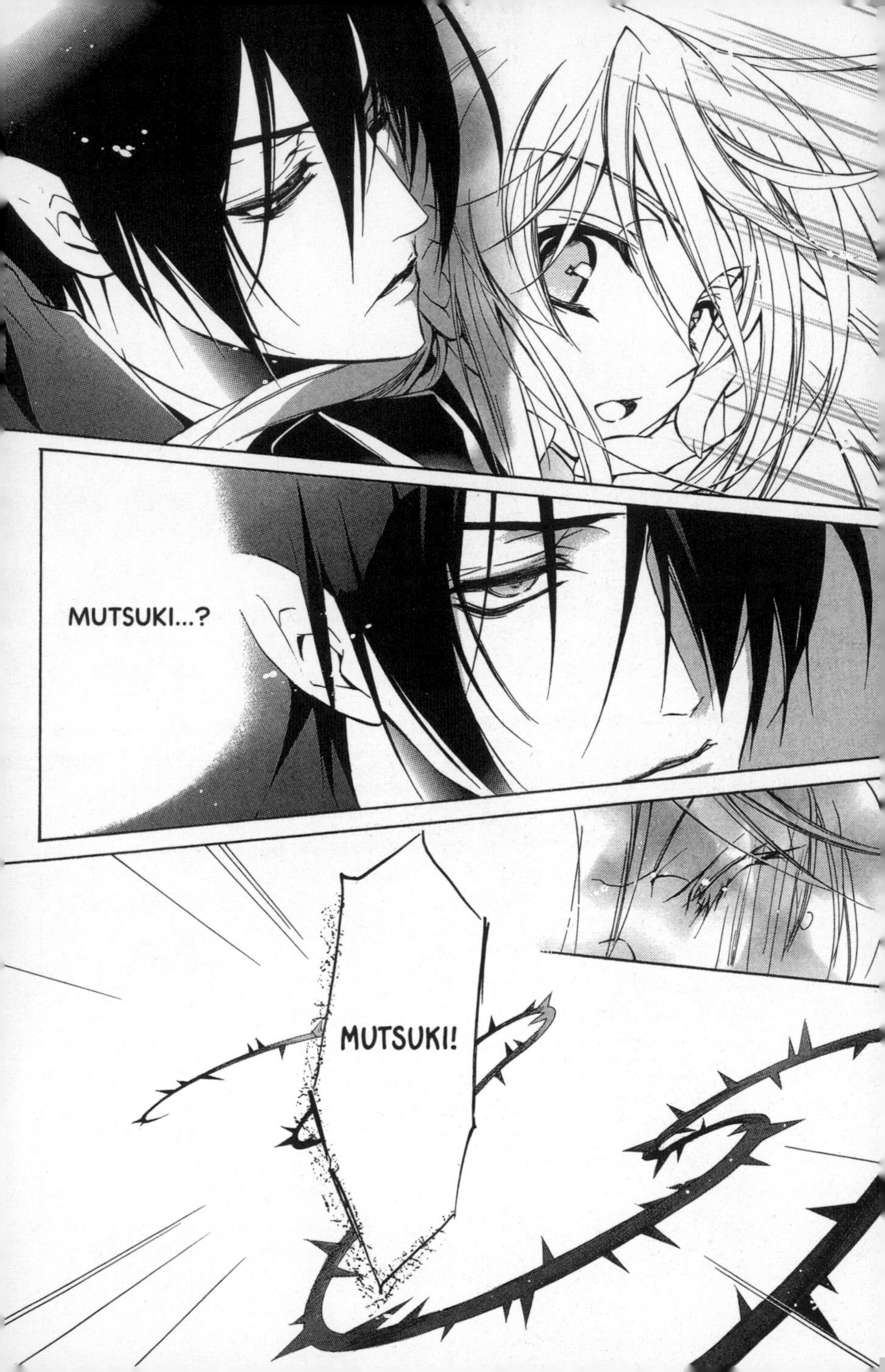
MUTSUKI...?
MUTSUKI!

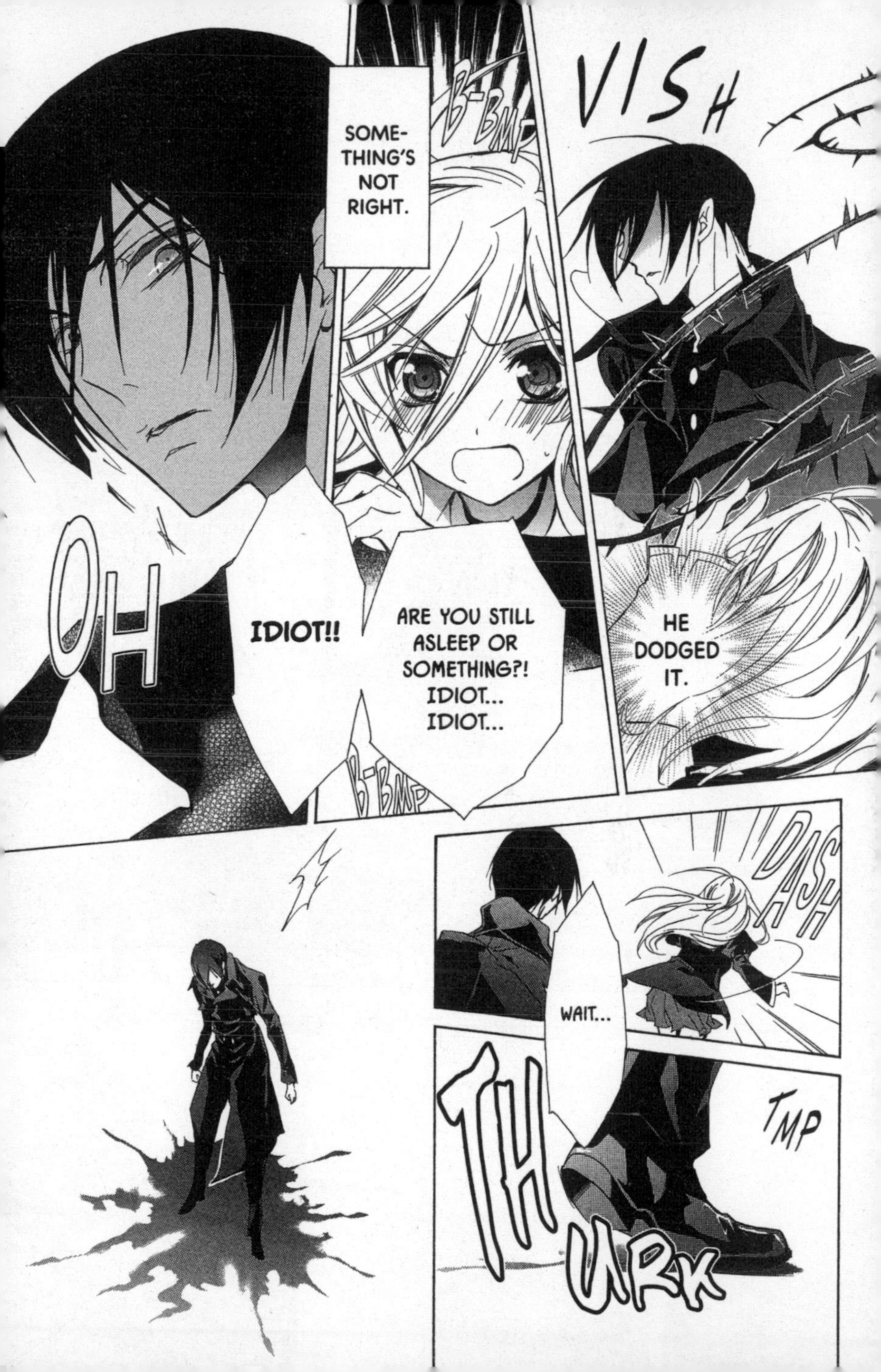
VISH
HE DODGED IT.
B-BMP
SOMETHING'S NOT RIGHT.
ARE YOU STILL ASLEEP OR SOMETHING?! IDIOT... IDIOT...
B-BMP
IDIOT!!
OH
DASH
WAIT...
TMP
TH
URK

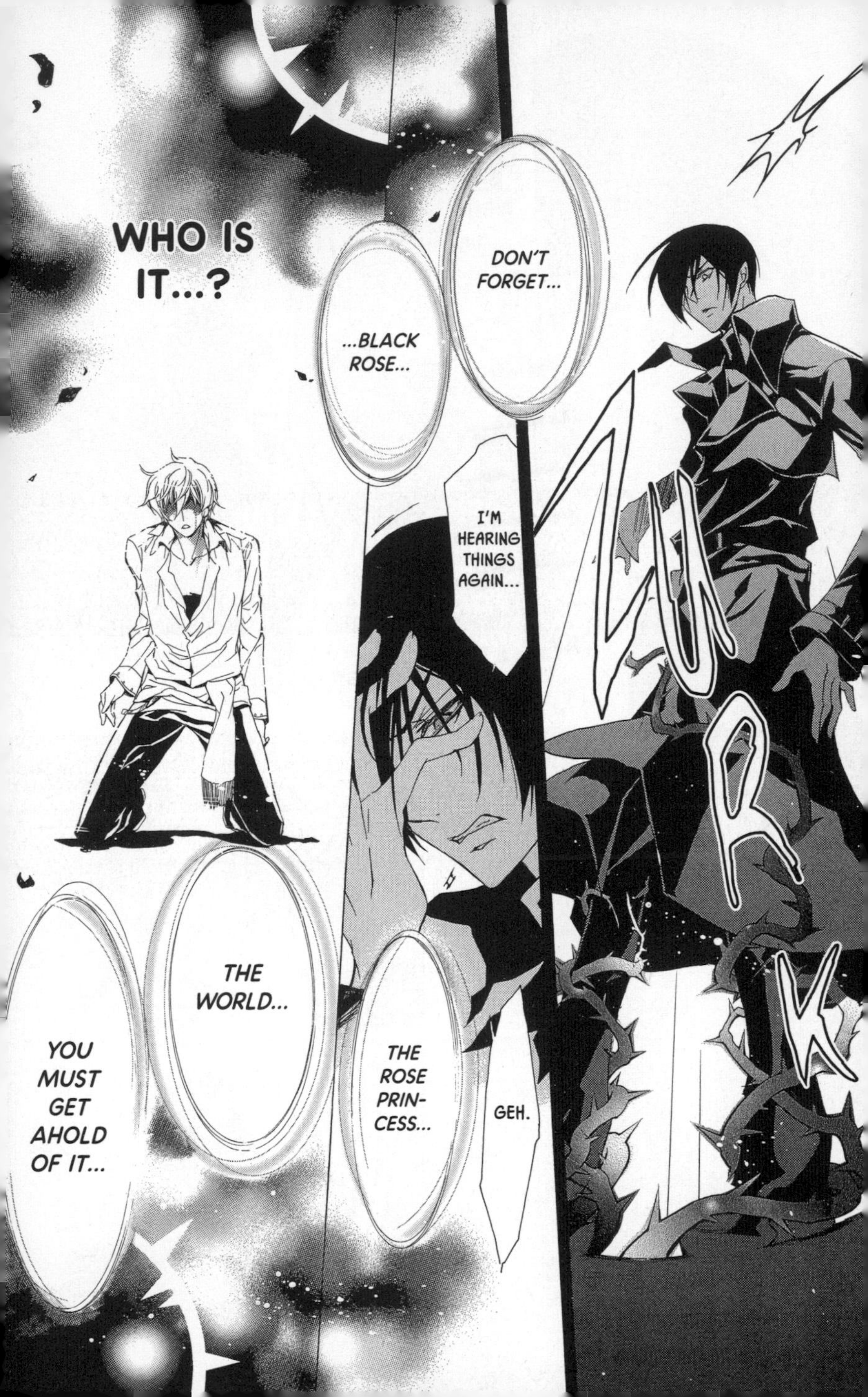
ZURK
DON'T FORGET...
I'M HEARING THINGS AGAIN...
...BLACK ROSE...
THE ROSE PRINCESS...
GEH.
WHO IS IT...?
THE WORLD...
YOU MUST GET AHOLD OF IT...

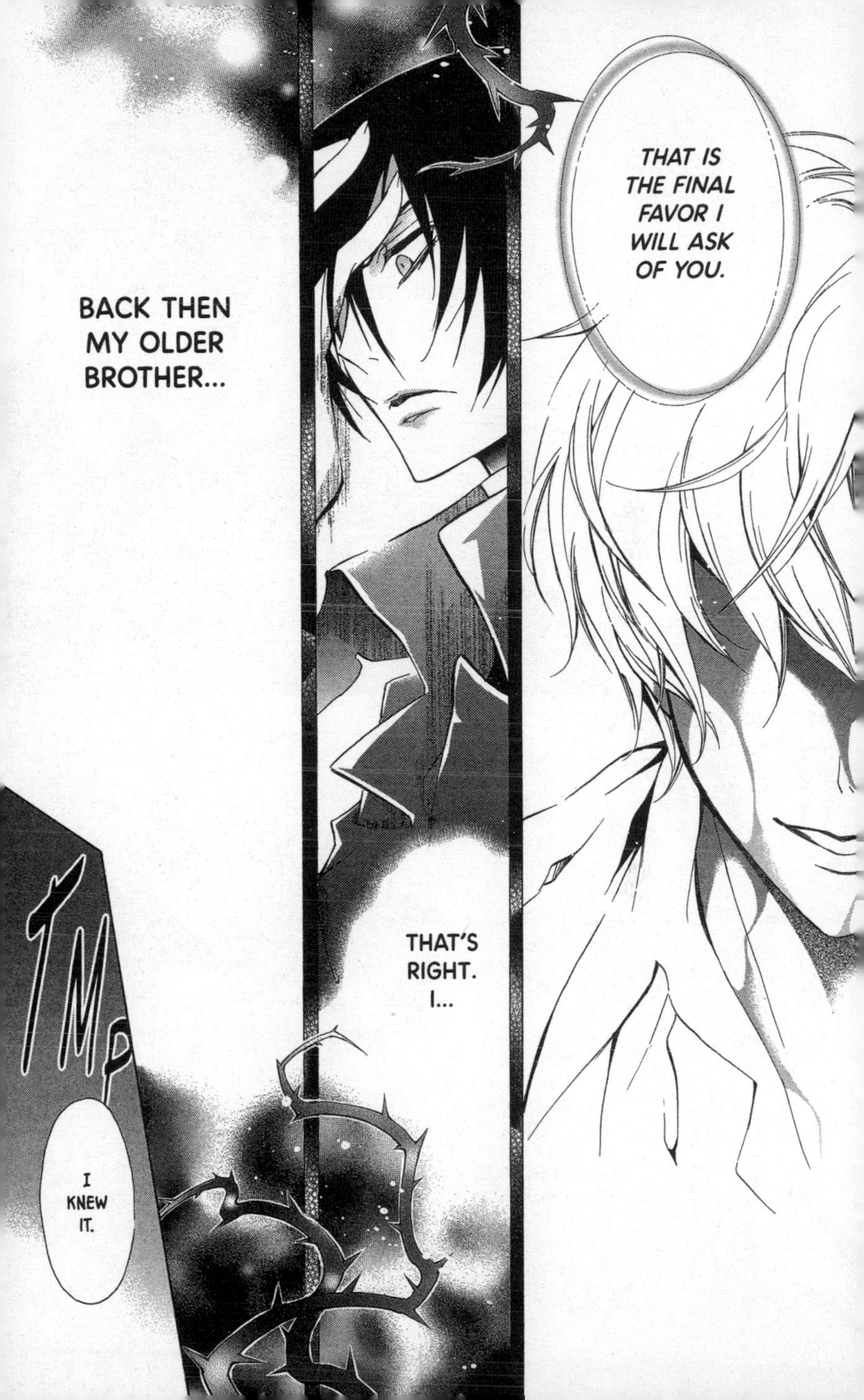
THAT IS THE FINAL FAVOR I WILL ASK OF YOU.
THAT'S RIGHT. I...
BACK THEN MY OLDER BROTHER...
TMP
I KNEW IT.

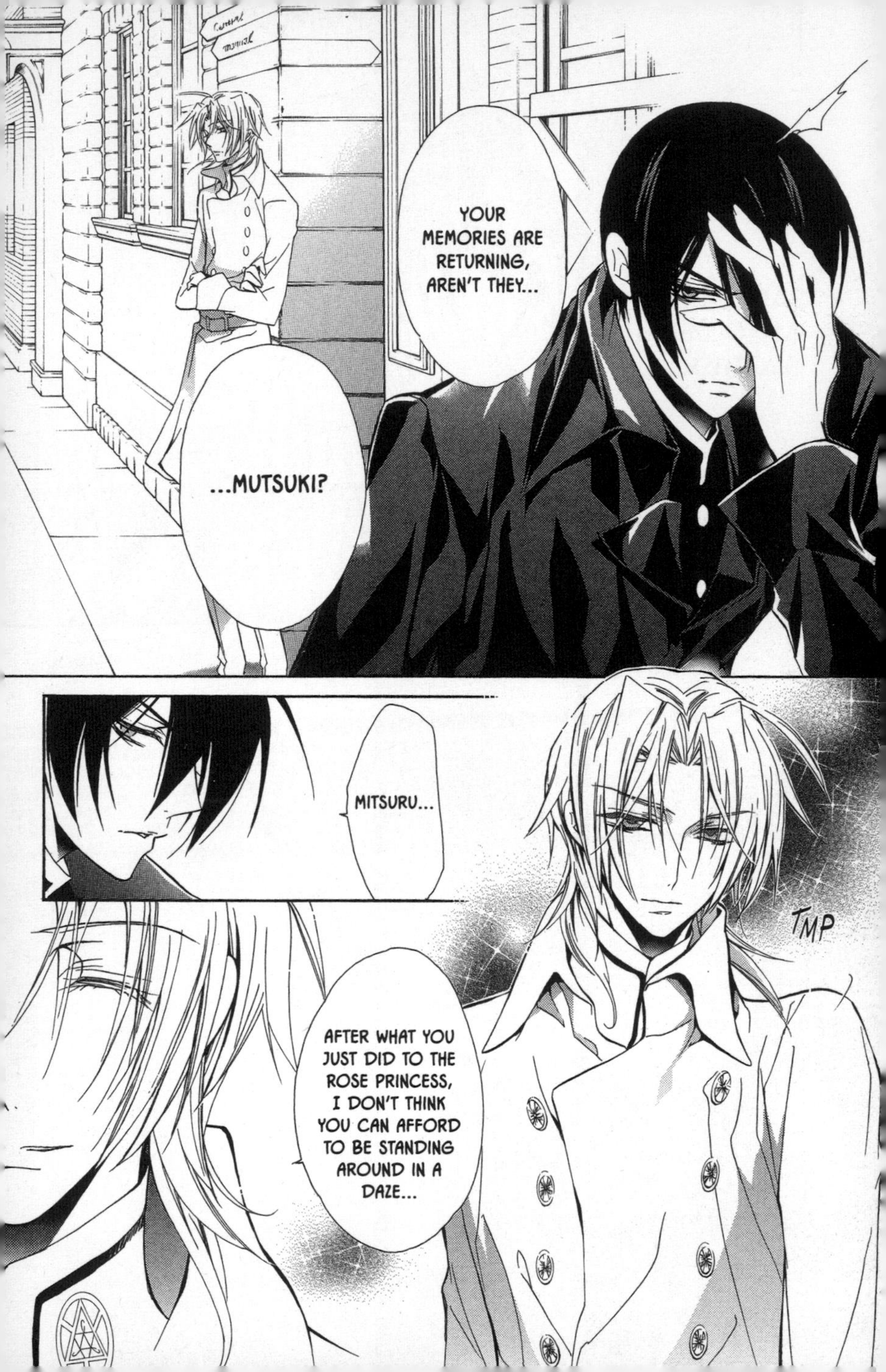
YOUR MEMORIES ARE RETURNING, AREN'T THEY...
...MUTSUKI?
TMP
MITSURU...
AFTER WHAT YOU JUST DID TO THE ROSE PRINCESS, I DON'T THINK YOU CAN AFFORD TO BE STANDING AROUND IN A DAZE...

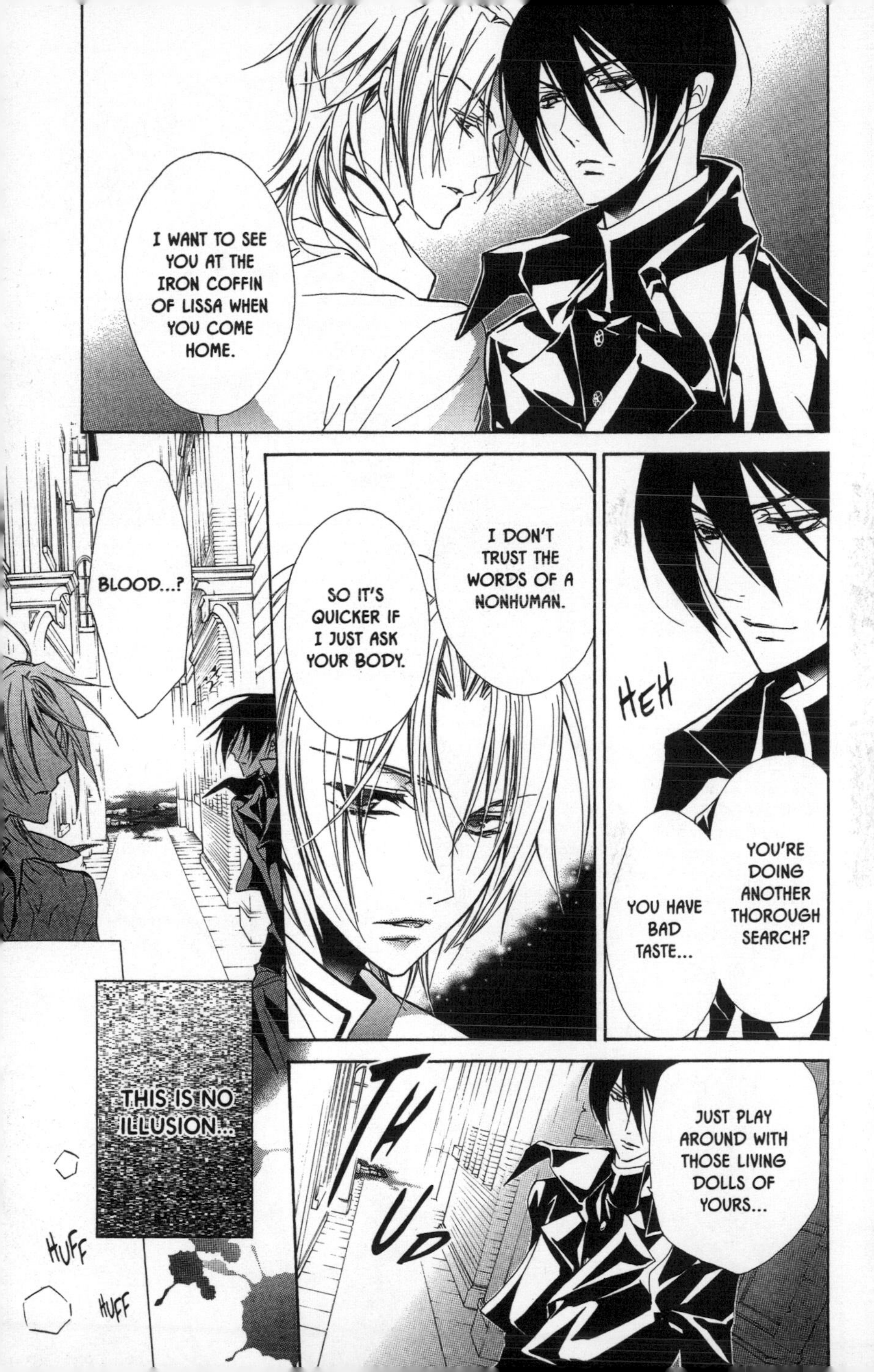
I WANT TO SEE YOU AT THE IRON COFFIN OF LISSA WHEN YOU COME HOME.
HEH
YOU'RE DOING ANOTHER THOROUGH SEARCH?
YOU HAVE BAD TASTE...
I DON'T TRUST THE WORDS OF A NONHUMAN.
SO IT'S QUICKER IF I JUST ASK YOUR BODY.
BLOOD...?
JUST PLAY AROUND WITH THOSE LIVING DOLLS OF YOURS...
THUD
THIS IS NO ILLUSION...
HUFF
HUFF

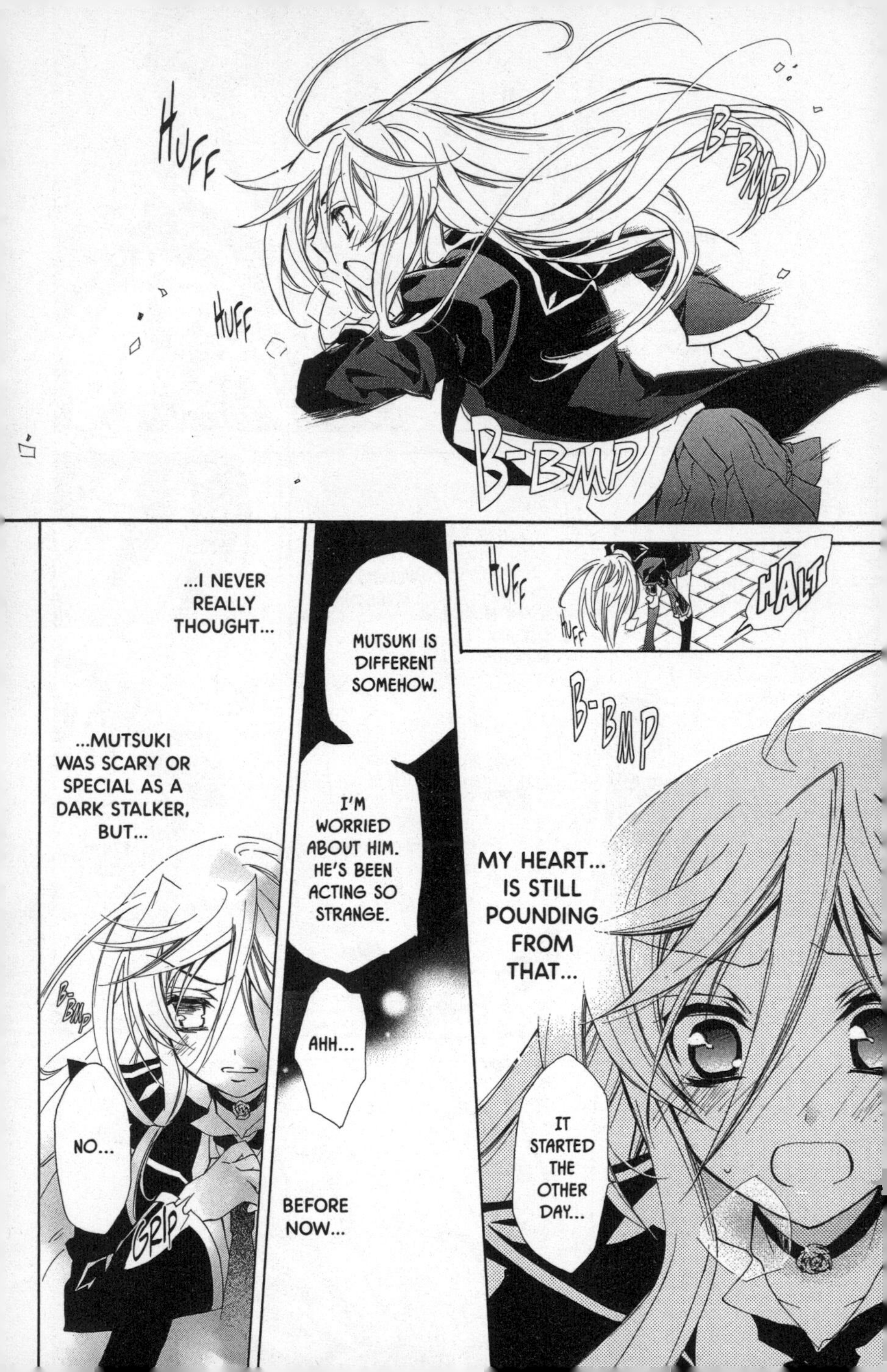
B-BMP
HUFF
HUFF
B-BMP
HALT
HUFF
HUFF
B-BMP
MY HEART... IS STILL POUNDING FROM THAT...
IT STARTED THE OTHER DAY...
MUTSUKI IS DIFFERENT SOMEHOW.
I'M WORRIED ABOUT HIM. HE'S BEEN ACTING SO STRANGE.
AHH...
BEFORE NOW...
...I NEVER REALLY THOUGHT...
...MUTSUKI WAS SCARY OR SPECIAL AS A DARK STALKER, BUT...
B-BMP
NO...
GRIP

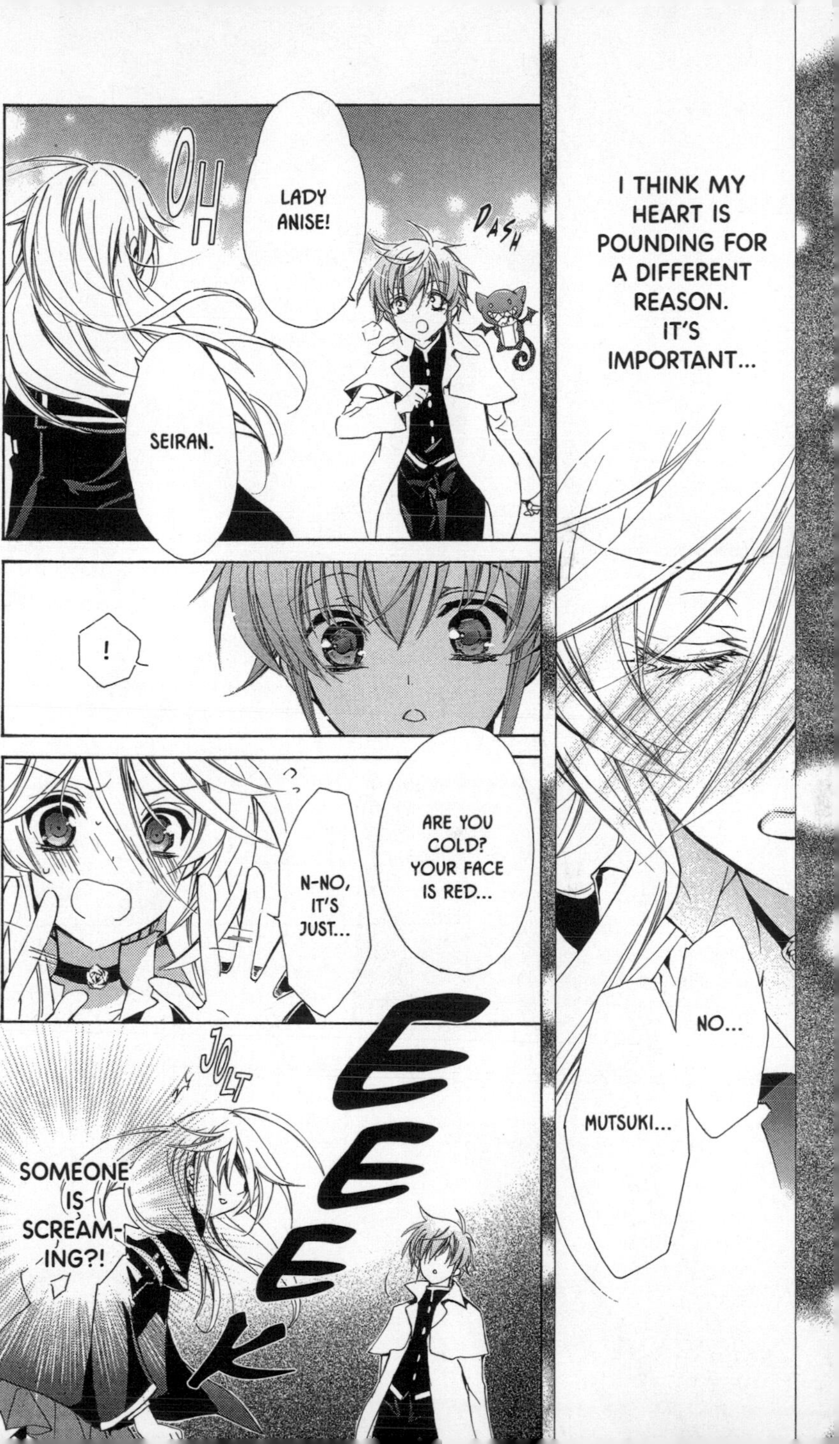
I THINK MY HEART IS POUNDING FOR A DIFFERENT REASON. IT'S IMPORTANT...
NO...
MUTSUKI...
LADY ANISE!
DASH
OH
SEIRAN.
!
ARE YOU COLD? YOUR FACE IS RED...
N-NO, IT'S JUST...
EEEEK
JOLT
SOMEONE IS SCREAM-ING?!

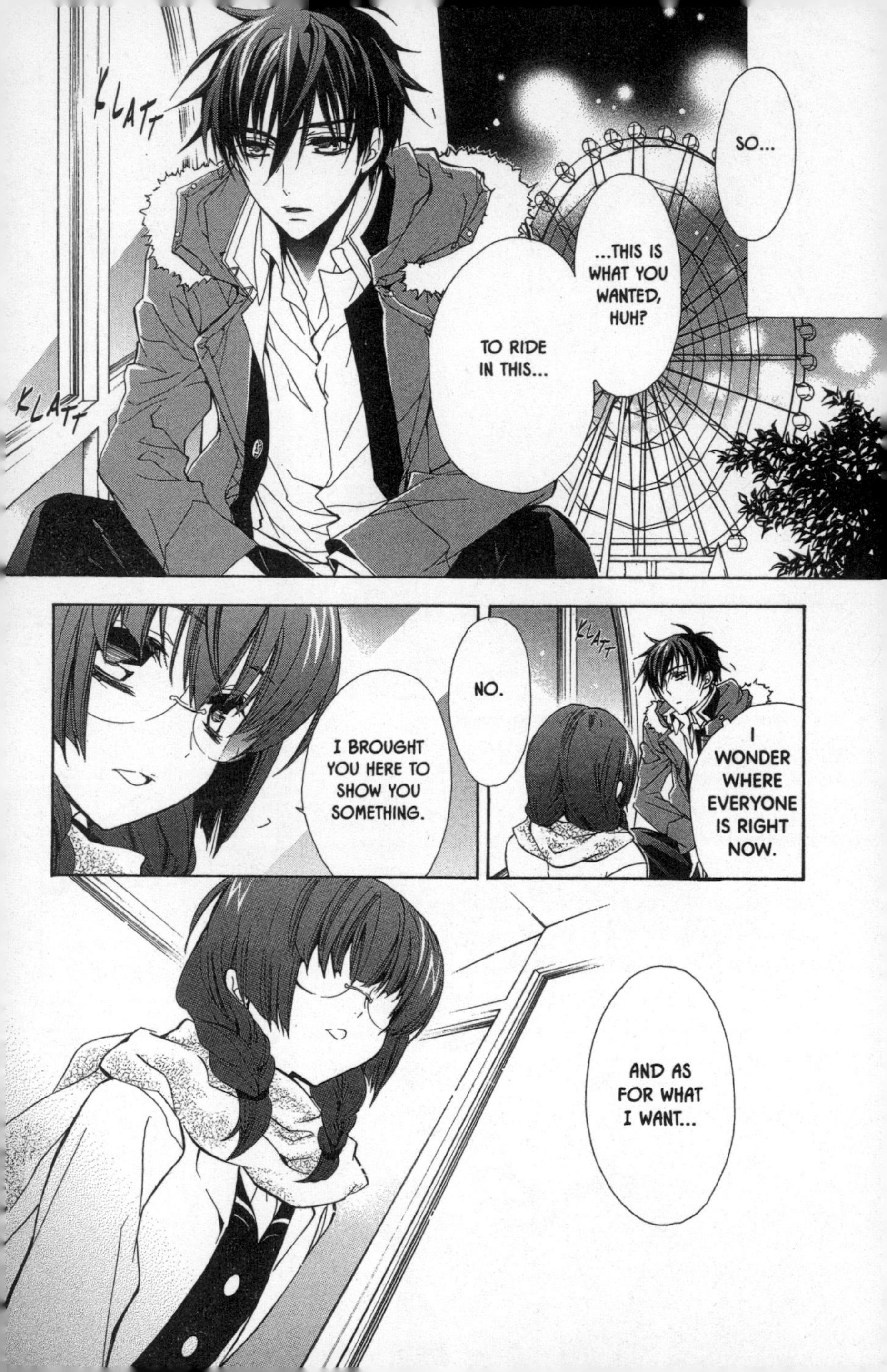
SO...
...THIS IS WHAT YOU WANTED, HUH?
TO RIDE IN THIS...
KLATT
KLATT
I WONDER WHERE EVERYONE IS RIGHT NOW.
KLATT
NO.
I BROUGHT YOU HERE TO SHOW YOU SOMETHING.
AND AS FOR WHAT I WANT...

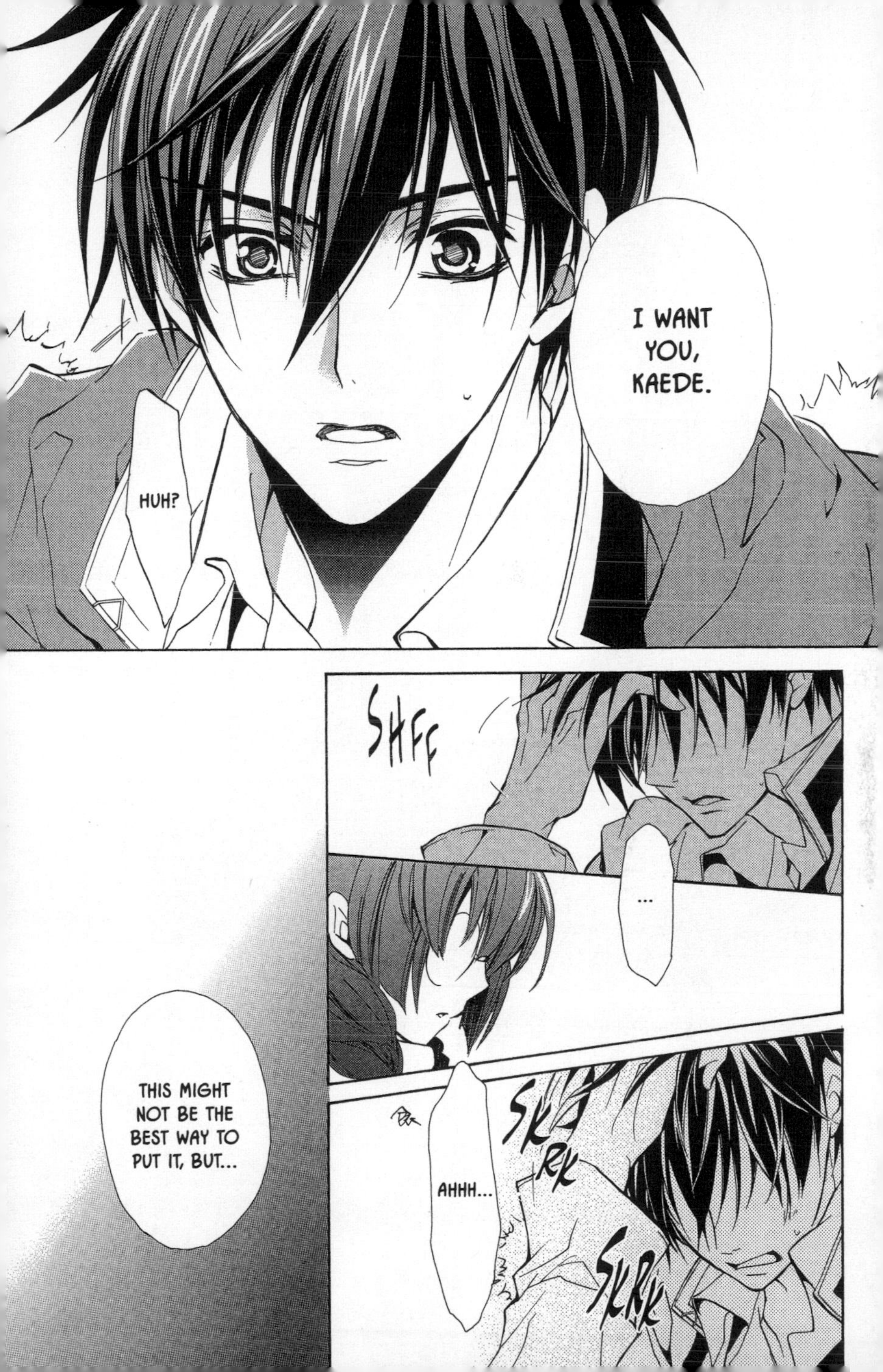
I WANT YOU, KAEDE.
HUH?
SHFF
...
SKRK
AHHH...
SKRK
THIS MIGHT NOT BE THE BEST WAY TO PUT IT, BUT...

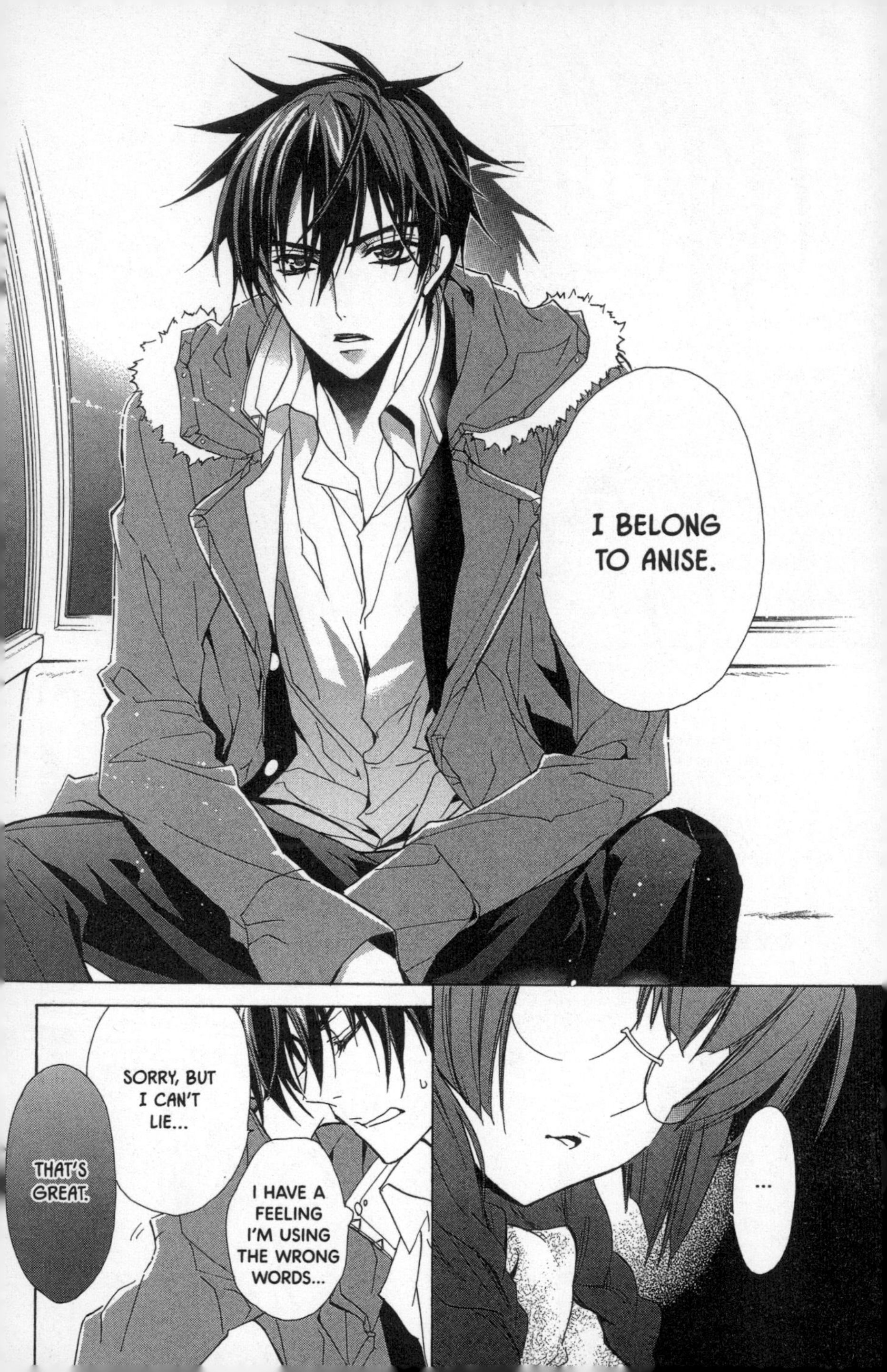
I BELONG TO ANISE.
...
SORRY, BUT I CAN'T LIE...
I HAVE A FEELING I'M USING THE WRONG WORDS...
THAT'S GREAT.

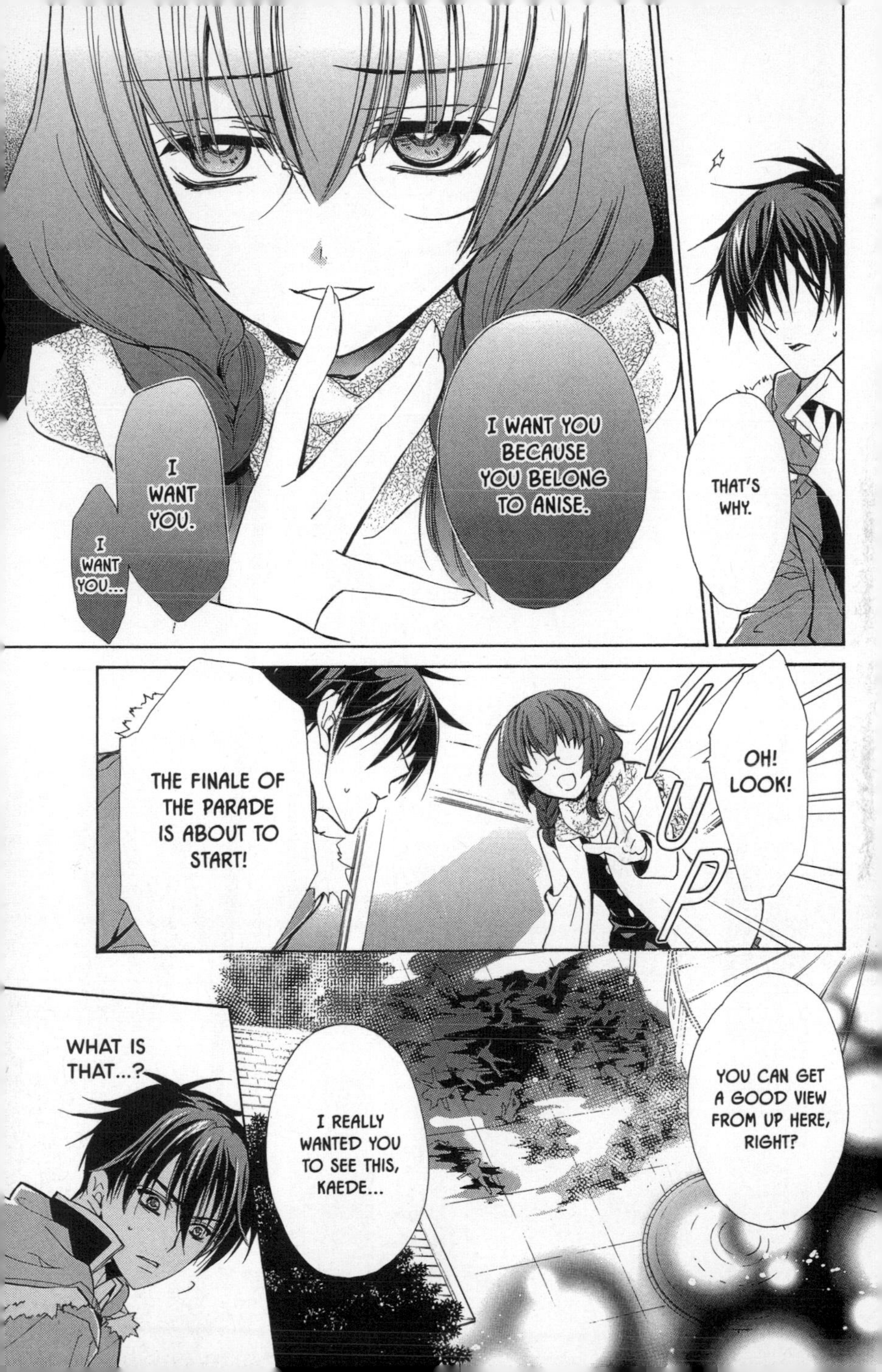
THAT'S WHY.
I WANT YOU BECAUSE YOU BELONG TO ANISE.
I WANT YOU.
I WANT YOU...
OH! LOOK!
VUP
THE FINALE OF THE PARADE IS ABOUT TO START!
YOU CAN GET A GOOD VIEW FROM UP HERE, RIGHT?
I REALLY WANTED YOU TO SEE THIS, KAEDE...
WHAT IS THAT...?

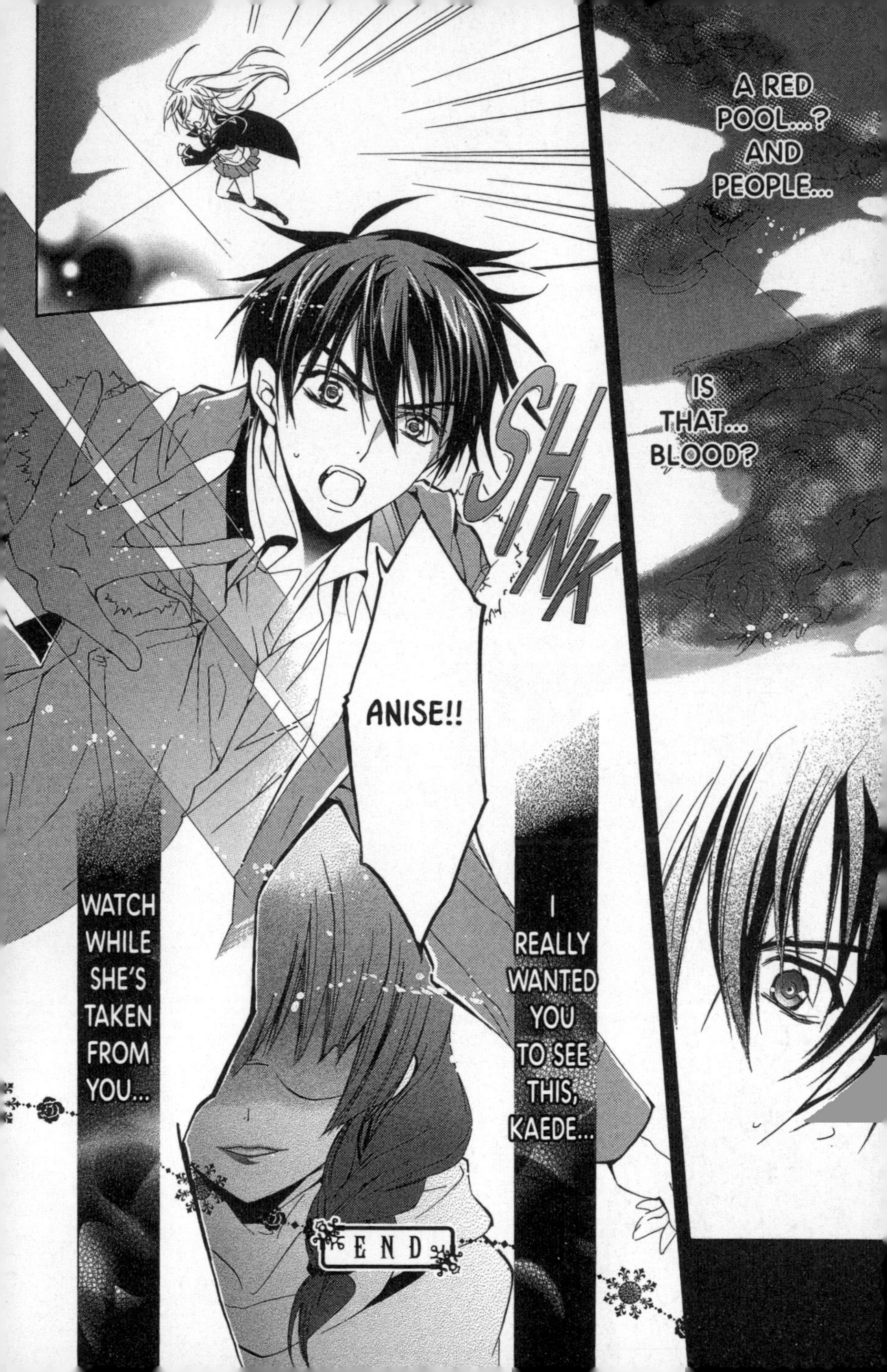
A RED POOL...? AND PEOPLE...
IS THAT... BLOOD?
SHNK
ANISE!!
I REALLY WANTED YOU TO SEE THIS, KAEDE...
WATCH WHILE SHE'S TAKEN FROM YOU...
END

Kiss of the Rose
Princess

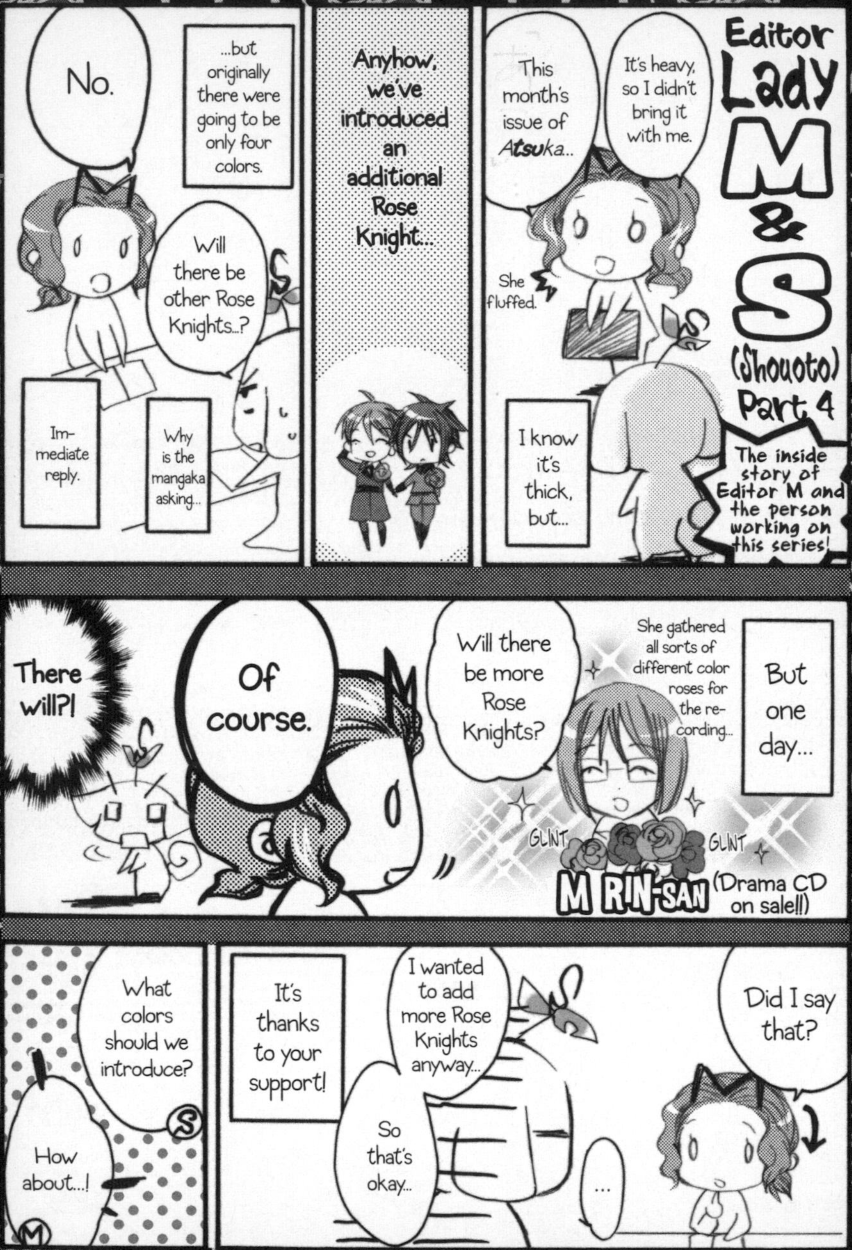
Editor Lady M & S (Shouoto) Part 4
The inside story of Editor M and the person working on this series!
It's heavy, so I didn't bring it with me.
This month's issue of Atsuka...
She fluffed.
I know it's thick, but...
Anyhow, we've introduced an additional Rose Knight...
...but originally there were going to be only four colors.
No.
Will there be other Rose Knights...?
Why is the mangaka asking...
Im-mediate reply.
But one day...
She gathered all sorts of different color roses for the re-cording...
Will there be more Rose Knights?
GLINT
GLINT
M RIN-SAN
(Drama CD on sale!!)
Of course.
There will?!
Did I say that?
I wanted to add more Rose Knights anyway...
It's thanks to your support!
So that's okay...
...
What colors should we introduce?
How about...!

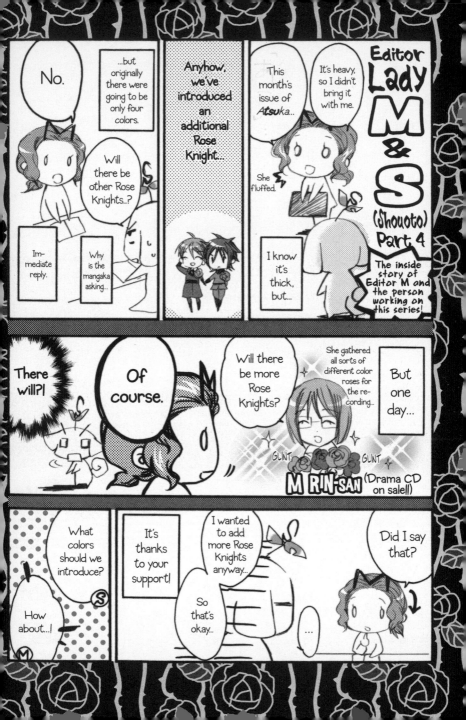

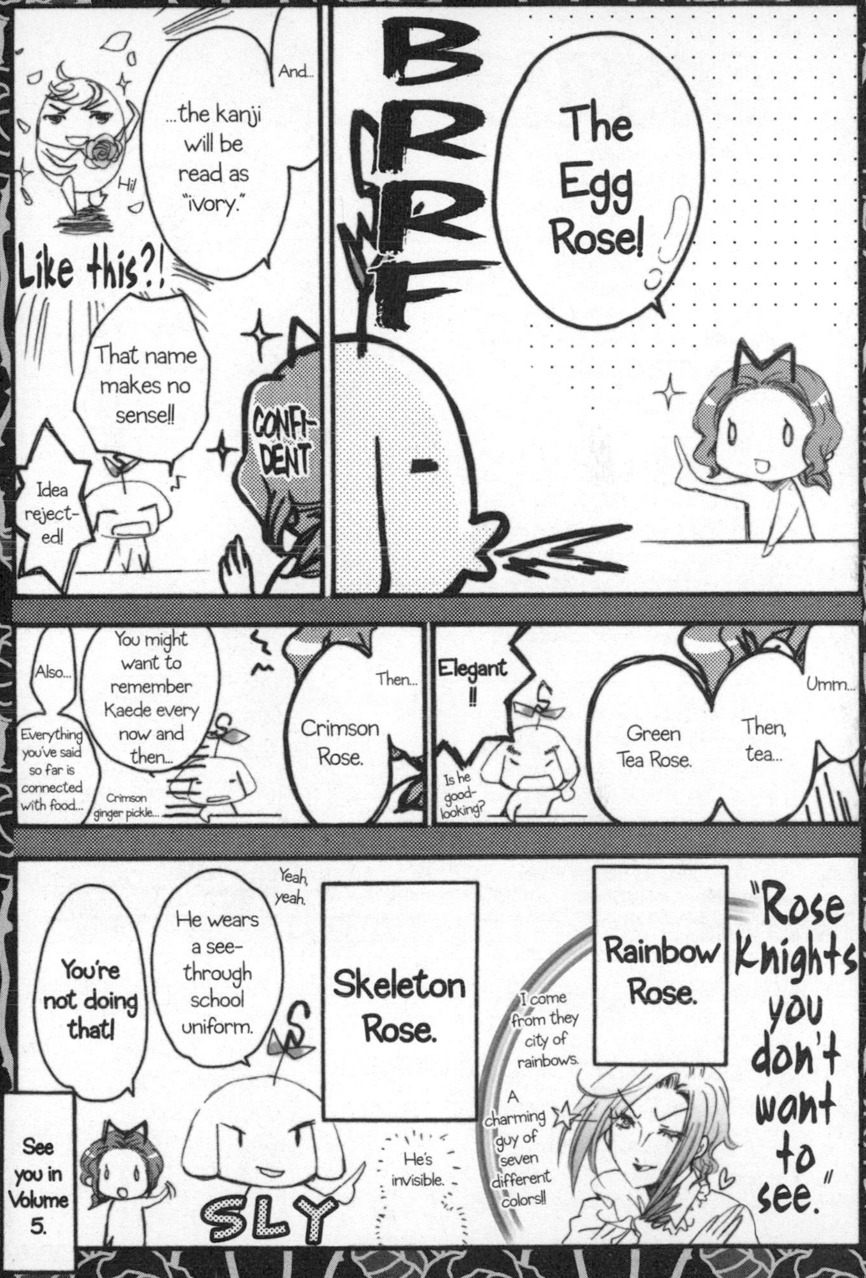
The Egg Rose!
BRRF
And...
...the kanji will be read as "ivory."
CONFI-DENT
Hi!
Like this?!
That name makes no sense!!
Idea reject-ed!
Umm...
Then, tea...
Green Tea Rose.
Elegant!!
Is he good-looking?
Then...
Crimson Rose.
You might want to remember Kaede every now and then...
Also...
Everything you've said so far is connected with food...
Crimson ginger pickle...
"Rose Knights you don't want to see."
Rainbow Rose.
I come from they city of rainbows.
A charming guy of seven different colors!!
Skeleton Rose.
He's invisible.
Yeah, yeah.
He wears a see-through school uniform.
SLY
You're not doing that!
See you in Volume 5.

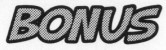

BONUS

■ This is my very first volume four! It's a miracle to have been able to work on Rose-Kiss for this long. It is all thanks to you for purchasing this series...
Thank you very much!!
And we now have all four knights on the cover of a volume. I'm touched... I enjoyed doing the illustration of Orange and Lime for the back cover.

You've probably noticed by now but Rose-Kiss has now entered the "Fake Knight" arc. This is basically an ikemen (good-looking men) comedy. (laugh) I hope you enjoy the serious side of the story as well. There is so much I want to write about. I'll do my best with it.

As for Anise's clothes, I used the ideas from S.N.-san from Hokkaido and H.S.-san from Osaka. (Thank you!) You all have such cute taste. I wish the four knights and Anise could learn from you! (laugh) Maybe I'll ask for clothes for the other characters as well...?

Anyhow, see you soon in Volume 5!
Bye!!

硝音あや Aya Shouoto

Special Thanx: Norie, Nakamura
Maeda, Yoshise, Honma, Rika
Kou, Hiyo, Family
Asuka Editorial Office and...
You!! xxx.

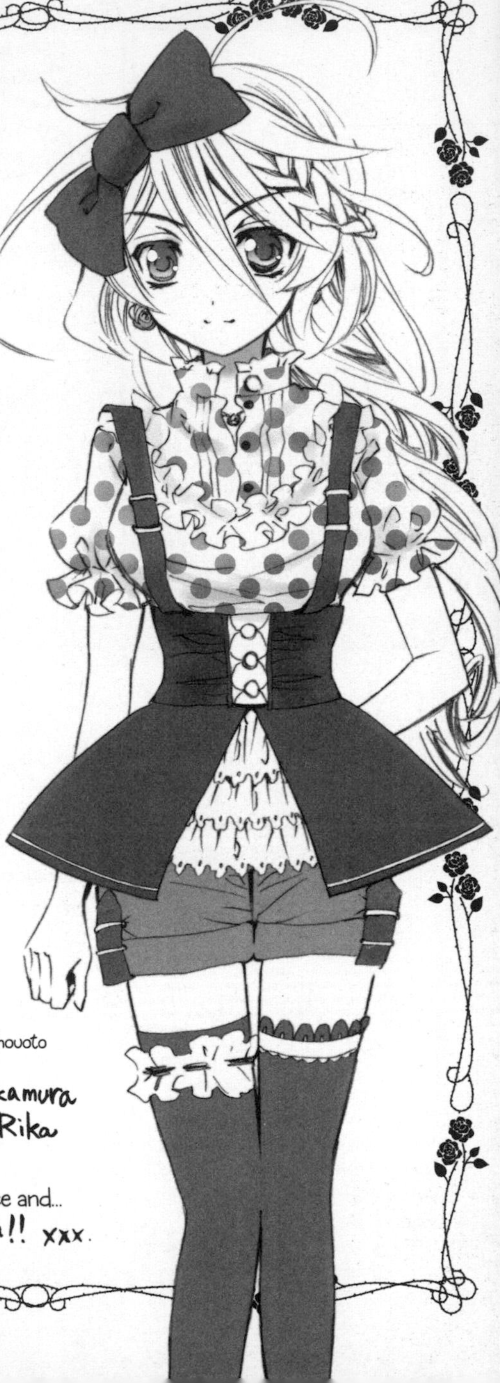

Check out Shojo Beat on social media!

Twitter: @shojobeat
Facebook: OfficialShojoBeat
Tumblr: OfficialShojoBeat

Kiss of the Rose Princess

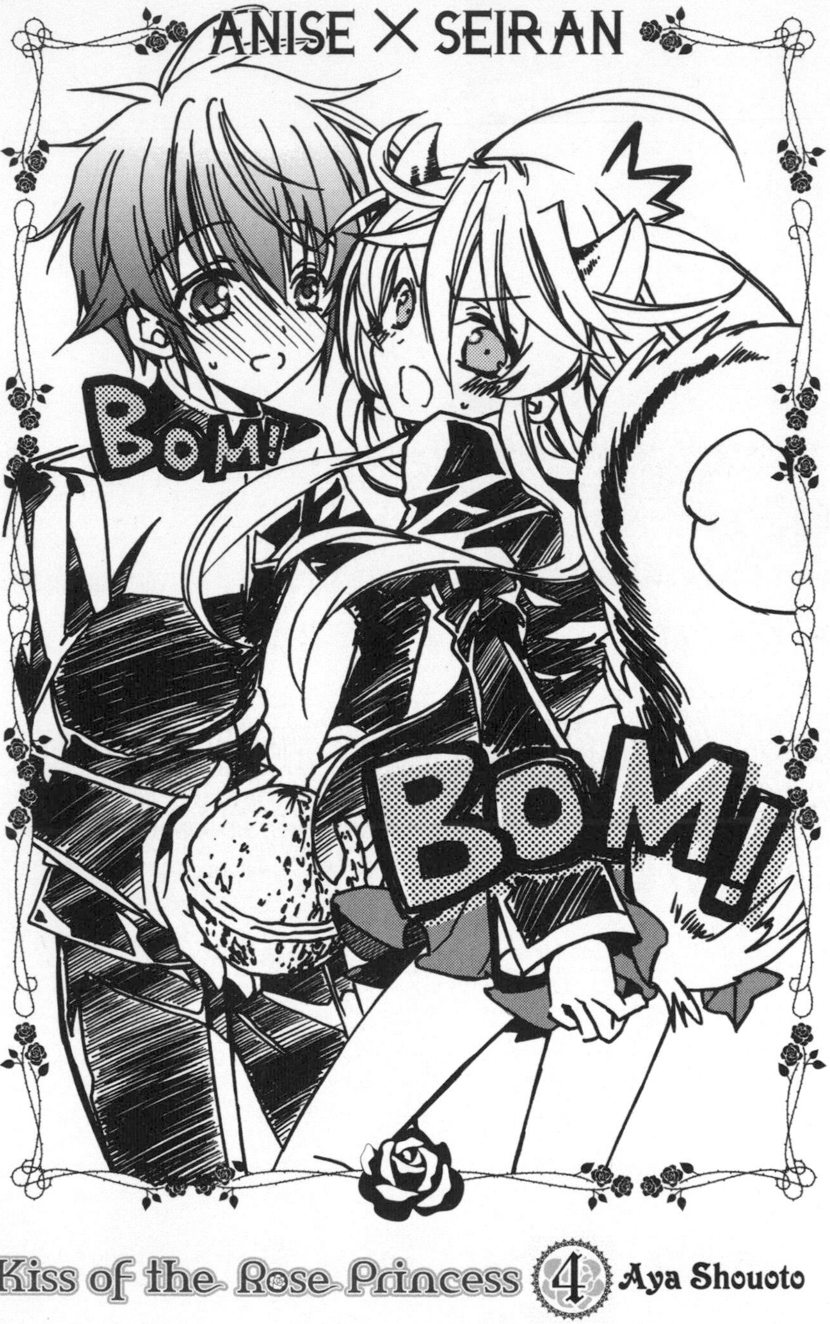
ANISE × SEIRAN
BOM!
BOM!

Kiss of the Rose Princess 4 Aya Shouoto

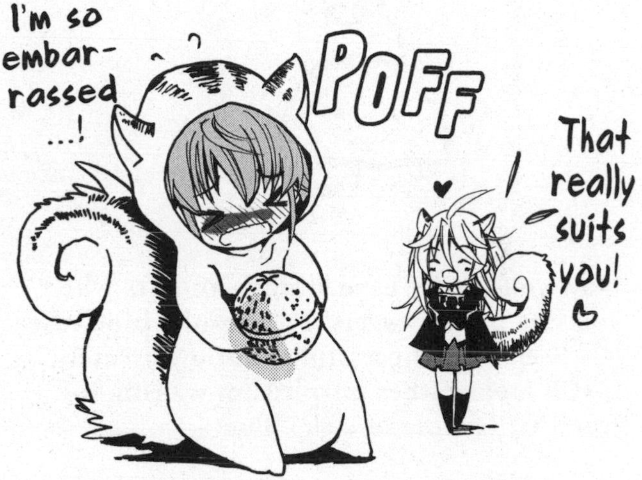
I'm so embar-rassed ...!
POFF
That really suits you!

SQUIRREL OF THE ROSE PRINCESS

AYA SHOUOTO

*There's Japanese wordplay on the word *risu* (squirrel) and *kisu* (kiss).

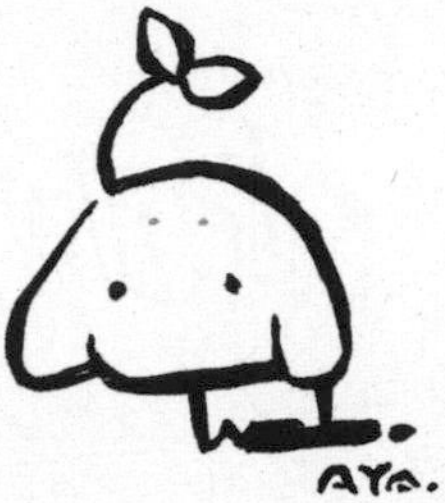
AYA.

Now you finally have all four knights when you line up the covers. I've heard a blue rose has been bred successfully, but unfortunately it still looks rather purple. I'm waiting for a rose that is more of a sky blue.

-Aya Shouoto

Aya Shouoto was born on December 25. Her hobbies include traveling, staying at hotels, sewing and daydreaming. She currently lives in Tokyo and enjoys listening to J-pop anime theme songs while she works.

Kiss of the Rose Princess

Volume 4
Shojo Beat Edition

STORY AND ART BY
AYA SHOUOTO

Translation/Tetsuichiro Miyaki
Touch-up Art & Lettering/Inori Fukuda Trant
Design/Yukiko Whitley
Editor/Nancy Thistlethwaite

KISS OF ROSE PRINCESS Volume 4
© Aya SHOUOTO 2010
Edited by KADOKAWA SHOTEN
First published in Japan in 2010 by KADOKAWA CORPORATION, Tokyo.
English translation rights arranged with KADOKAWA CORPORATION, Tokyo.

Printed in the U.S.A.

Published by VIZ Media, LLC
P.O. Box 77010
San Francisco, CA 94107

10 9 8 7 6 5 4 3 2 1
First printing, May 2015

www.viz.com

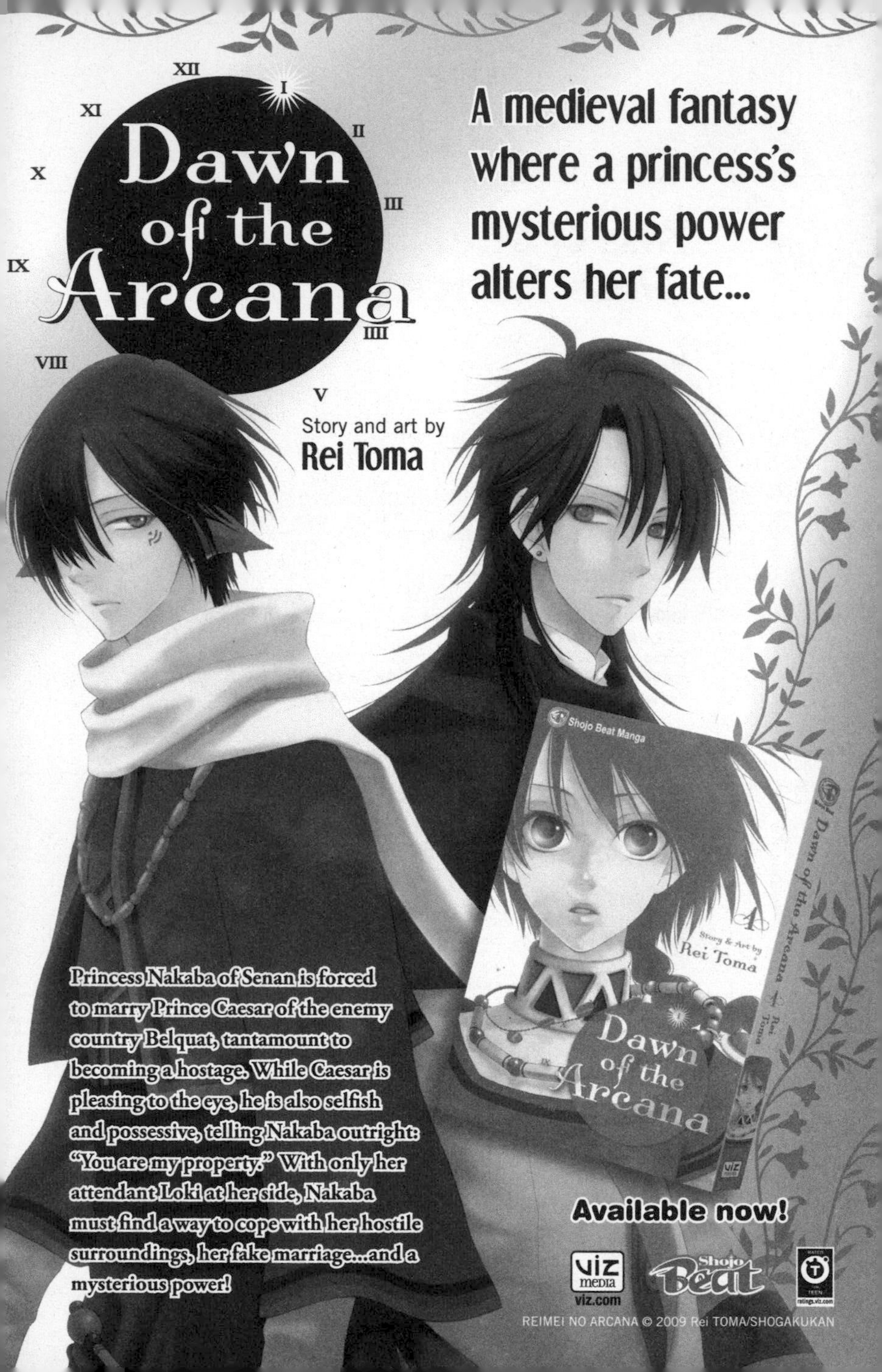
Dawn of the Arcana
A medieval fantasy where a princess's mysterious power alters her fate...
Story and art by
Rei Toma
Shojo Beat Manga
Dawn of the Arcana 1
Story & Art by Rei Toma
Princess Nakaba of Senan is forced to marry Prince Caesar of the enemy country Belquat, tantamount to becoming a hostage. While Caesar is pleasing to the eye, he is also selfish and possessive, telling Nakaba outright: "You are my property." With only her attendant Loki at her side, Nakaba must find a way to cope with her hostile surroundings, her fake marriage...and a mysterious power!
Available now!
viz media
viz.com
Shojo Beat
RATED T TEEN
ratings.viz.com
REIMEI NO ARCANA © 2009 Rei TOMA/SHOGAKUKAN

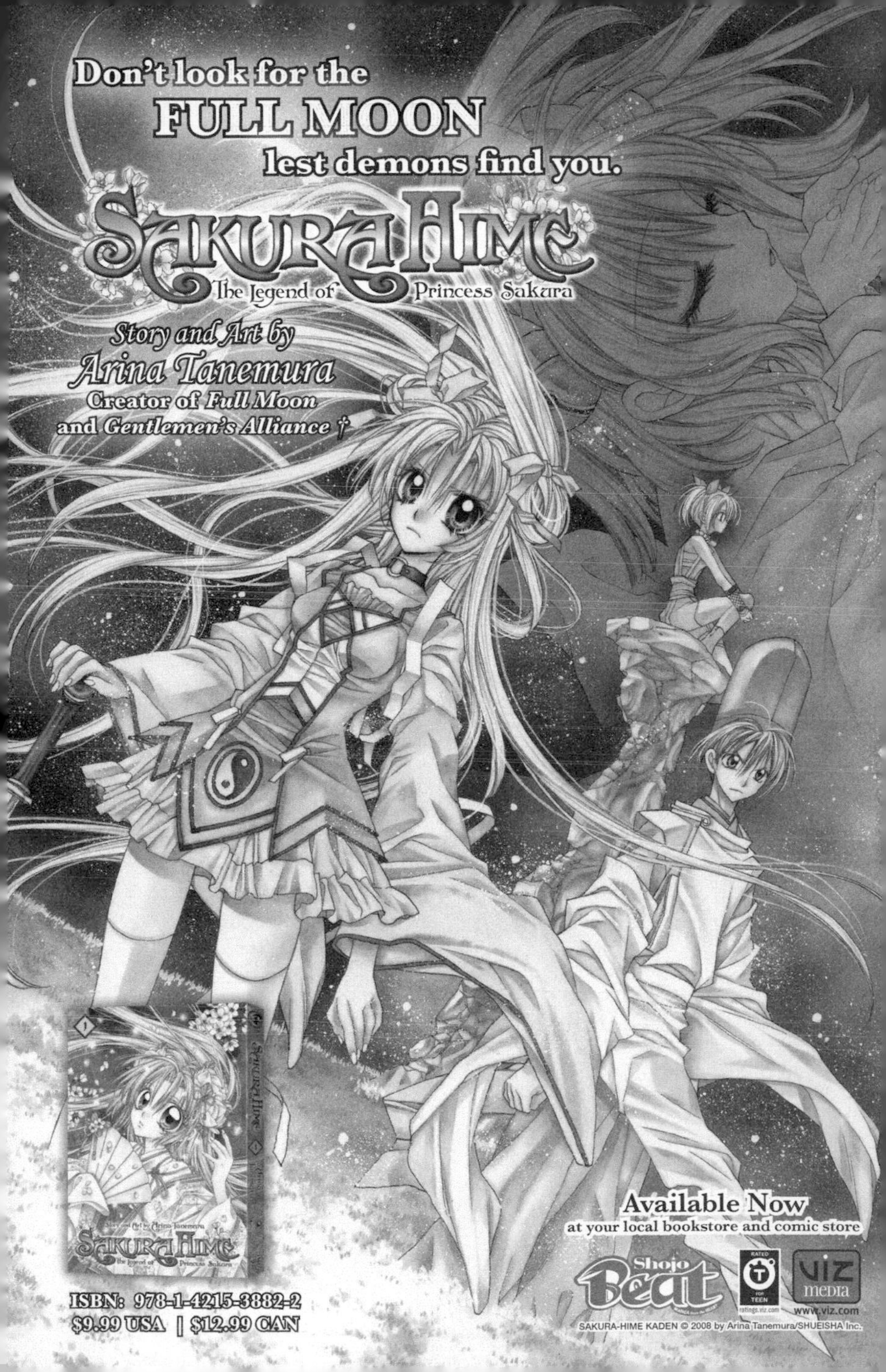
Don't look for the
FULL MOON
lest demons find you.
SAKURA HIME
The Legend of Princess Sakura
Story and Art by
Arina Tanemura
Creator of Full Moon
and Gentlemen's Alliance †
Available Now
at your local bookstore and comic store
ISBN: 978-1-4215-3882-2
$9.99 USA | $12.99 CAN
Shojo Beat
RATED T FOR TEEN
ratings.viz.com
VIZ media
www.viz.com
SAKURA-HIME KADEN © 2008 by Arina Tanemura/SHUEISHA Inc.

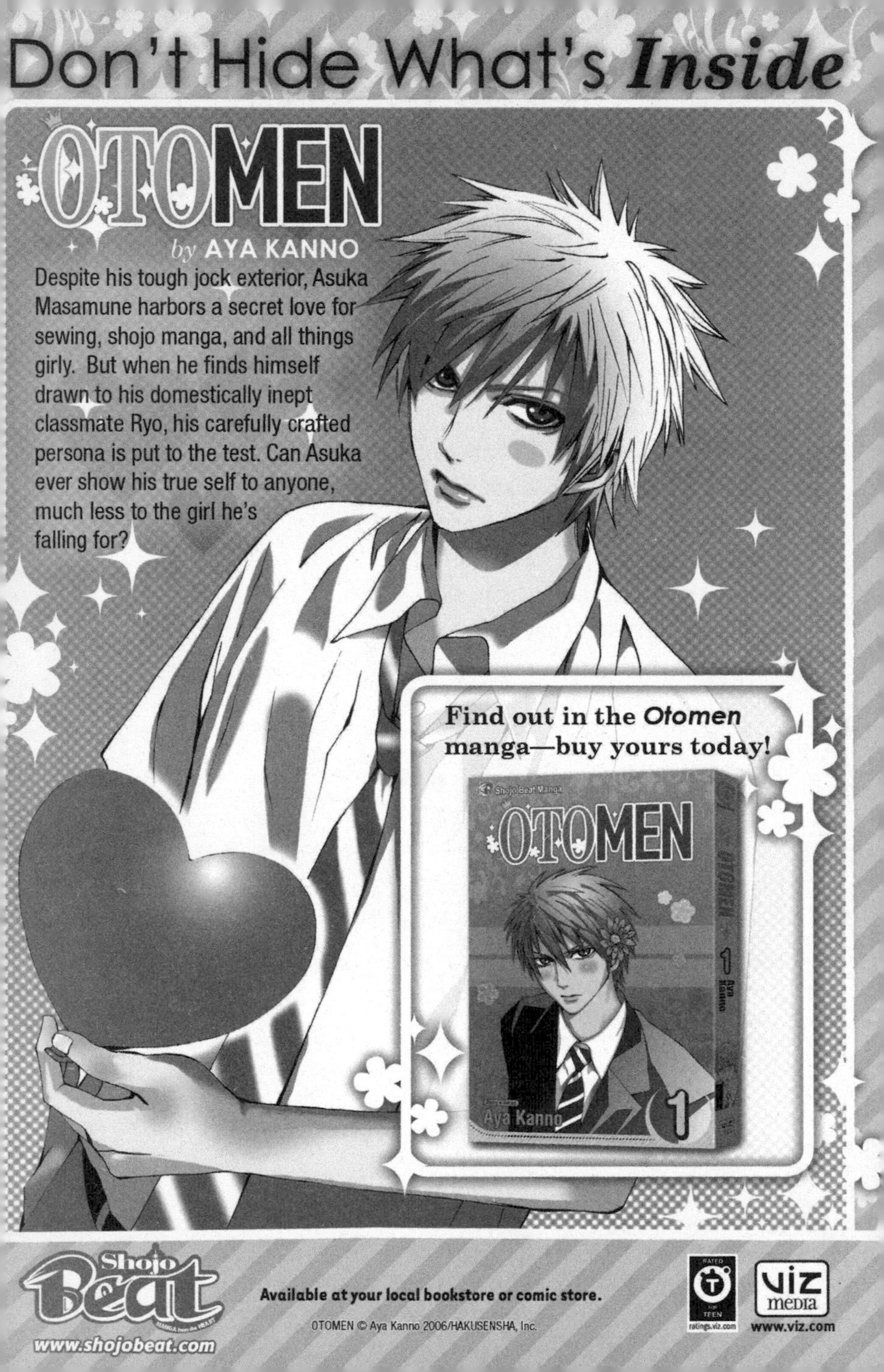
Don't Hide What's Inside
OTOMEN
by AYA KANNO
Despite his tough jock exterior, Asuka Masamune harbors a secret love for sewing, shojo manga, and all things girly. But when he finds himself drawn to his domestically inept classmate Ryo, his carefully crafted persona is put to the test. Can Asuka ever show his true self to anyone, much less to the girl he's falling for?
Find out in the Otomen manga—buy yours today!
Shojo Beat Manga
OTOMEN
1
Aya Kanno
Shojo Beat
www.shojobeat.com
Available at your local bookstore or comic store.
OTOMEN © Aya Kanno 2006/HAKUSENSHA, Inc.
RATED
T
TEEN
ratings.viz.com
viz media
www.viz.com